I0641796

Frontier Taiwan

MODERN CHINESE LITERATURE FROM TAIWAN

Frontier Taiwan

AN ANTHOLOGY OF MODERN CHINESE POETRY

Edited by Michelle Yeh and N.G.D. Malmqvist

COLUMBIA UNIVERSITY PRESS

NEW YORK

Columbia University Press wishes to express its appreciation for assistance given by the Chiang Ching-kuo Foundation for International Scholarly Exchange in the preparation of the translation and in the publication of this series.

Columbia University Press wishes to express its appreciation for assistance given by the Pushkin Fund toward the cost of publishing this book.

Columbia University Press
Publishers Since 1893
New York Chichester, West Sussex

Library of Congress Cataloging-in-Publication Data
Frontier Taiwan : an anthology of modern Chinese poetry / edited by Michelle Yeh and N.G.D. Malmqvist.
    p. cm. — (Modern Chinese literature from Taiwan)
    Includes bibliographical references.
    ISBN 0–231–11846–5 — ISBN 0–231–11847–3 (pbk.)
    1. Chinese poetry—Taiwan—Translations into English. 2. Chinese poetry—20th century. I. Title: Anthology of modern Chinese poetry. II. Yeh, Michelle Mi-Hsi. III. Malmqvist, N. G. D. (Nils Göran David), 1924– IV. Series.
PL2658.E3 F74 2001
895.1'15080951249—dc21   00–024121
⊗

CONTENTS

Preface xiii
Acknowledgments xv
Note on Translation xvii
Map of Taiwan xx

Frontier Taiwan: An Introduction 1

Yang Hua (1906–36) 55

Black Tide (seven selections) / *Heartstrings* (two selections) /
Tawny Cottages / Sad Song of the Female Worker

Yang Chichang (1908–94) 59

Rouge and Lips / The Nun / Burning Cheeks /
Veins and Butterflies / Autumn Sea / Travelogue / Pale Song /
Ruined City / Love Song / Sea of Flowers

Qin Zihao (1912–63) 66

Desert Wind / Remembering / Seashells (I) /
Gallery / Black Narcissus / Hair / Seashells (II)

Ji Xian (1913–   ) 72

City in Flames / To the Maybe Man / Song of Time No. 2 /
My Pagoda-Shaped Plan / Star-Plucking Youth / Dog Howling at the Moon /
Seven and Six / Composition in a Window / My Voice and My Existence /
Painter's Studio / Wine Drinker / Psychoanalysis of Pipe Smoking /
Unfinished Masterpiece / Death of Aphrodite / Type-B Blood /
Before Completion. One / Bird Variations

Chen Xiuxi (1921–91) 83

Grave Sweeping This Year / Love / Taiwan /
My Pen / Maybe It's the Weight of a Poem

Zhan Bing (1921–   ) 87

Affair / May / Planting Rice Sprouts / Liquid Morning /
Seven-Colored Time / Liquid Flows Into the Cup of the Heart

Zhou Mengdie (1921–   ) 92

Caltrops / Diary of a Believer / Mendicant / Prisoner /
Nine Lines / On the Ferry / Twelfth Month /
Sixth Month / Mountain / Polydactylism

Huan Fu (1922–   ) 103

Walking in the Rain / Forest / Carrier Pigeon / Wild Deer / Excuse My
Rudeness / Find an Honorific for Mosquitos / Shadow / Incident

Lin Hengtai (1924–   ) 110

Philosopher / Books / Landscape No. 1 /
Landscape No. 2 / Traces (1–8)

Du Pan Fangge (1927–   ) 116

Rebirth / Paper People / Beyond the Mulberry Tree /
Under the Pomelo Tree / Womb

Luo Fu (1928–   ) 119

Chimney / Death of a Stone Cell (four selections) /
Beyond the Fog / Fish / Gold Dragon Temple /
The Wound of Time / Sharing a Drink with Li He / Because of the Wind /
The Cricket's Song / Metaphysical Game / Mailing a Pair of Shoes /

Beijing Sycamores / Funeral for a Poem /
I Buy an Umbrella Just to Lose It / Silent Pumpkin

Luo Men (1928–   ) 135

The Four Strings of the Violin / Shrapnel—Tron's Missing Leg /
Window / A Wild Horse / Where Light Lives /
Running Away / The Old Man Selling Flower Pots /
The City—Square Existence / Umbrella / Years of Poetry /
Readjustment of Twentieth-Century Space for Existence /
Who Could Purchase the Horizon?

Rongzi (1928–   ) 144

To Morning / No More Blossoms Fly in Our City / A Green Lotus /
Umbrella / When All Living Creatures Go By / The Insect World

Xiang Ming (1928–   ) 149

Dawn at Prosperity Corner / Tumor / Ivy /
The Setting Sun on Manila Bay / Possible / Rolling a Steel Hoop

Yu Guangzhong (1928–   ) 154

When I Am Dead / The Double Bed / Green Bristlegrass /
If a War Is Raging Afar / Nostalgia / When Night Falls /
The Crystal Prison / A Tale on the Hill / Evening /
The Spiderwebs / The Pearl Necklace /
What Is the Rain Saying Through the Night? / The Langlois Bridge

Guan Guan (1929–   ) 164

Cousin Rat / The Ravenous Prince / Long Street /
Talking About the "Emperor Qianlong Tripitaka,
Carved on Knot-Free Unblemished Slow-Cured Blocks
from Prime Pear Trees Felled in Winter"

Shang Qin (1930–   ) 171

The Anthill / The Ladder / The Maple Tree / The Gloves /
A Faun's Afternoon / Giraffe / Overdrawn Footprints / Pigeons /
The Dog / The Mosquito / Electric Lock / Moonlight /
The Cat Who Walks Through the Wall /
Snow / Rooster / Railroad Crossing

Zhang Mo (1931–) 186

A Song with No Melody / I Am a Glass of Unlimited Volume /
Ode to a Shabby Room / Shake the Head, Wag the Tail:
A Seven-storied Pagoda / The Future: Four Versions

Ya Xian (1932–) 190

Umbrella / Shrine of the Village God / Funeral Parlor /
The Mountain God / Babylon / Spring Day /
The Buckwheat Field / Ship Rats / The Beggar /
Red Corn / Salt / Florence / The Monastery /
Abyss / The Catholic Nun / The Colonel /
Diva / Andante cantabile / Courtyard /
Song of the Ordinary / Resurrection Day

Xin Yu (1933–) 211

The Song of the Soil / The Zanzibar Lion / A Leopard /
Seen at the Shunxing Teahouse / The Speech of Stones

Zheng Chouyu (1933–) 217

Life in the Mountains / Mistake / In Dreamland /
Watery Lane / Buddhist Chant / Skylight /
Stopping at a Minor Station / Still Life / Morning /
Afternoon / Pure Clarity / Border Inn /
The Temple Bull / Guests of Snow

Bai Qiu (1937–) 225

Armchair / Sky / Cry / Weight /
Geese / Canary / Vine /
The Square / Silent Gecko

Ye Weilian (1937–) 231

Fugue / Pastiches from Taiwan Countryside (four selections) /
Quest / Traveling in Spring

Lin Ling (1938–) 239

After the Show Is Over / The Man Who Knocked at the Outpost /
Nonmodernist Lyricism / For Lin Ling /
Two or Three Home Repairs in Spring

Xiong Hong (1940–   ) 245

Thinking with Fire / Dark Associations /
I'm Already on My Way to You / Jar / Ripples / Life

Yang Mu (1940–   ) 250

News / Footsteps / Flowing River / In the Midnight Cornfield /
Screen / The Second Renunciation / Floating Fireflies /
Etudes: The Twelve Earthly Branches / Let the Wind Recite /
Zeelandia / Solitude / Forbidden Game (1–4) /
Someone Asks Me About Justice and Righteousness / Frost at Midnight /
For No Reason / The Traveler's Heart: A Variation /
The Proposition of Time / A Tale / Solitude, 1910

Zhang Cuo (1943–   ) 279

Autumn Reminiscence / The Distance of Winter /
Words of a Goose Catcher / In Imitation of the Ancients /
The Secret Garden

Wu Sheng (1994–   ) 285

Rice Straw / Rainy Season / Preface to *Vignettes of My Village* /
The Land / Animal Spirit Tablet / In the Woods of a Foreign Country /
I Won't Discuss It with You / The Worst Thing About Writing Poetry

Li Minyong (1947–   ) 292

Memento of the Deceased / Prisoner of War / Aspiration of Poetry /
Tilting Island / Death Report / Reading Poems on a Late-Night Airliner

Luo Qing (1948–   ) 298

The Invisible Man / Heaven's Revenge / The Avenging Ghost / Once More
Looking out at the Deep Blue Sea After Looking out at the Deep Blue Sea
Many Times Before / Córdoba / I Refuse / Please Just Wink / Quatrain

Su Shaolian (1949–   ) 310

Beast / Peeling a Pear / Photocopier / Mixed Blood / Shadow Burial /
Sleep Deeply, Shore / That Horse Like Moonlight

Jian Zhengzhen (1950–   ) 316

Secret / On the Great Wall / Memory / Reading a Letter

Bai Ling (1951–   ) 321

Childhood Years, Part I: The 1940s / Spring's Brief Visit to Taipei /
Lip Rouge / Kite

Ling Yu (1952–   ) 325

Since You Can't Advance You Can't Retreat Either /
Names Vanished from the Map (five selections) /
The Family of Acrobats / Freeze-Frame in the Midst of War (two selections)

Chen Yizhi (1953–   ) 336

Taiwan Rains / Broken-down Family Tree / Thinking, Worrying (I) / Whale /
An Alzheimer's Kind of Love / Entombed Warrior

Du Ye (1953–   ) 344

Frog / Snowfield / Vermilion Cabinet / A Wish / Universal Love, Not War /
Li Bai / The Tilapia in the Sky

Chen Li (1954–   ) 350

The Lover of the Magician's Wife / The Love Song of Buffet the Clown /
In a City Alarmed by a Series of Earthquakes /
Listening to *Winterreise* on a Spring Night / The River of Shadows /
The Edge of the Island / Microcosmos (ten selections) /
Autumn Song / The War Symphony / Formosa, 1661 /
Dialogue / Butterfly Air / Tunnel /
On the Island / Composition

Yang Ze (1954–   ) 369

Fugue of Violence and Music /
Under a Scorching Sun, a Stifling Noon, I Stared /
This is the Spring of Cynicism /
Rainy Day—Women #12 & 35 /
Clear Day—Women #12 & 35 /
outside is the snow / Nightly Homecoming /
Life Is Not Worth Living / Let Me Be Your DJ

Luo Zhicheng (1955–   ) 378

Father / Darling Letters (five selections) / The Wolf /
The Great Rains of '93 / The Bookstore of My Dreams

Xiang Yang (1955–   ) 385

Train Station / My Cares / Seed / Autumn Words /
Nine to Five / Uniform / Lesser Fullness of Grain / Great Heat /
Waking of Insects / Hoarfrost / Lesser Snow / Great Cold

Jiao Tong (1956–   ) 394

The Story of Her Life / Out of Work / The Demon Platoon Leader /
Reading at Night / Martial Law / Eraser /
The Frequency I Infringe Upon

Xia Yu (1956–   ) 399

Sweet Revenge / Hibernation / Bronze / Poet's Day / Picnic /
The Simple Future Tense / The Hidden Queen and Her Invisible City /
Parable / Children (1, 2) / Yarmidiso Language Family / Excuse /
Afternoon Tea / Memory / Ode on a Thing / Fauves /
Mozart in E-Flat Major / Ensemble Against the Wind /
Dancing with My Back to You / Spring Evening /
The Mercury That We Raised So Carefully / Reading / Postcard /
A Difficult Moral Question / FRICTION. INDESCRIBABLE /
The Ripest Rankest Juiciest Summer Ever /
Written for Others / Playerless Piano

Lin Yu (1957–   ) 420

My Dream Is Taking a Trip / Spring Sings in My Veins / Name Cards /
Numbers / Mr. D / The Idiot / Chair / A Bachelor's Diary

Liu Kexiang (1957–   ) 427

The Lower Reaches / Posthumous Sons / Young Revolutionaries /
Hope / Tropical Rain Forest / Going Home / The Street Performer /
Delta in the Ocean / Showa Grass /
The Central Range of Little Bear Pinocha

Sun Weimin (1959–   ) 435

Delirious / Spring 1985 / The Encounter / Dream / Transfer /
Going to Work / Leaving Work / Motorcycle

Chen Kehua (1961–   ) 441

Clown Spirit / This Life / No Children Are Born in This Instant /
Ballpoint Pen / Bathroom / On TV After Dinner /
Message Board at a Train Station / Butterfly Dream /
Sodomy's Necessity / Still

Walis Nokan (1961–   ) 452

Back to the Tribe! / Atayal (War, 1896–1930)

Lin Yaode (1962–96) 460

The Terminal / Prefatory Poem / The Lie of a Spring I Tightly Wind /
The Concept of "Non" / The Red Chamber

Hong Hong (1964–   ) 466

Zoo City (three selections) / A Drop of Juice Falls /
Woman Translating / No War / Suitcase Lost and Found /
Someone I Loved / Things Free of Me

Xu Huizhi (1966–   ) 476

Corporeal Form / A Flea Attends the Buddha's Sermon /
My Compassionate Buddha / Body in Ruins / A Bowl of Rice /
Soon It Will Be Cold / Purple Hare / The Implorer

Notes on the Contributors 485
Select Bibliography in English 489

PREFACE

On behalf of the editors I wish to express our deep gratitude to the Chiang Ching-kuo Foundation for International Scholarly Exchange, which has been the sole promoter of the Modern Chinese Literature from Taiwan series in which this anthology is included.

The compilation and editing of an anthology is a delicate task involving the selection of the poets to be represented; the choice of poems to be included in the work; the engaging of competent translators; and the editing of the submitted translations. The three members of the editorial board—Michelle Yeh, Xiang Yang, and myself—have been solely responsible for the selection of poets. The poets themselves were asked to suggest which of their poems they wished to see included. The translators were also invited to submit their preferences. The final decisions were made by the editorial board of the anthology. The editing of the translations has been undertaken by Michelle Yeh and myself, in close consultation with the translators. The introduction, biographical notes, notes to the poems, and bibliography were written and compiled by Michelle Yeh, Chief Editor.

The editors gratefully acknowledge the enthusiasm and the fine spirit of cooperation with which the translators have tackled their often very difficult tasks. We also express deep appreciation of the efficient way in which Ms.

Jennifer Crewe, Publisher for the Humanities and Editorial Director of Columbia University Press, has guided the production of this anthology.

The editors find it highly gratifying that two Chinese editions of this book will be published, one in Taiwan in traditional characters and the other, in simplified characters, in the People's Republic of China. The latter contains a preface by Mr. Liu Shahe, poet and literary critic, who has done much to introduce Taiwanese poetry to mainland readers.

It is indeed high time that Taiwanese literature was recognized and better known in the Western world. We sincerely hope that this anthology will be instrumental in promoting and furthering interest in modern Taiwanese poetry.

N.G.D. Malmqvist

ACKNOWLEDGMENTS

A project of this scope and duration would not have been possible without the contributions and support of many people. First of all, I thank all the poets for allowing us to include their wonderful poems in this volume and all the translators, with whom I have enjoyed working throughout. I am equally grateful to Xiang Yang, who has been invaluable in the planning and coordination of the project and in providing much-needed material for the introduction.

To Jennifer Crewe, Editorial Director at Columbia University Press, and David Der-wei Wang, esteemed scholar and dear friend, I express my deepest appreciation for their enthusiastic support of the literature of Taiwan in general, and of this anthology in particular. Leslie Kriesel has done a fabulous job editing the volume; Ellen Yang, my assistant, has been most patient and conscientious; Ch'u Ko graciously provided the painting for the cover; John Balcom and Sophie Volpp read the first draft of the introduction and offered insightful comments. I thank them all.

Thanks also go to the Taipei Economic and Cultural Office in San Francisco and the Information Office in Taiwan for providing the map of Taiwan from *The Republic of China Yearbook of 1999*. Steve Bradbury's translations of Xia Yu's "The Ripest Rankest Juiciest Summer Ever" and "Written for Others" previously appeared in *Fine Madness* and *Poetry International*. Grateful acknowledgment is made to these journals for permission to reprint.

Last but not least, I thank Göran Malmqvist, who invited me to participate in this project in the summer of 1997. It has been a most memorable experience working together, as I have learned so much. Like poetry itself, a friendship formed in poetry never ceases to inspire and to enrich.

Michelle Yeh

NOTE ON TRANSLATION

We use the Pinyin romanization system throughout the anthology, except for a few names in view of previous, more familiar usage. For each poet, the first time the name is introduced in the biographical note, we include the Wade-Giles romanization in parentheses so that readers will recognize it in other publications where the older system is used. Italicized words in the title or text of a poem are in English or French in the original. The date at the end of each poem refers to the year of composition or, when so indicated, the date of first publication.

Michelle Yeh

Frontier Taiwan

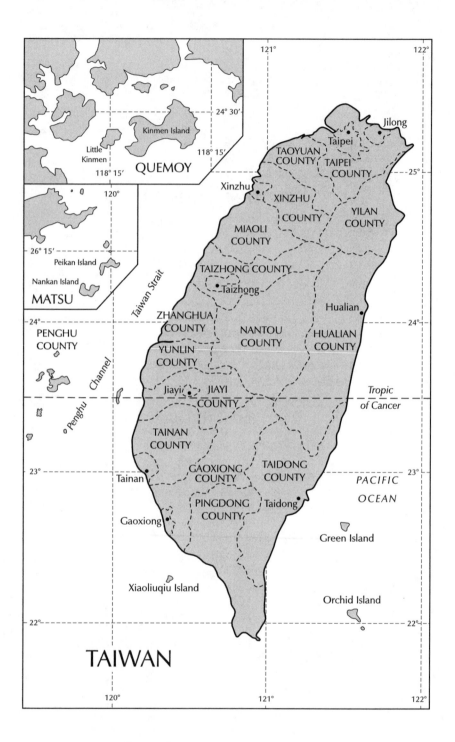

TAIWAN

FRONTIER TAIWAN: AN INTRODUCTION

MICHELLE YEH

PROLOGUE

An island is a paradox; it is simultaneously isolated and open, restricted and free, with the surrounding sea serving sometimes as a protective barrier, other times as a vital passage to other lands and cultures. Situated off the southeast coast of the Asian continent, with Japan and Korea to the north and the Philippines to the south, halfway between Shanghai and Hong Kong, Taiwan not only occupies an important strategic position in the western Pacific region but also is a nexus of diverse linguistic, economic, social, and cultural crosscurrents from Asia and other parts of the world. Over centuries of clashing and converging, these influences have shaped and continue to shape the society on the island. If its small size—only 13,885 square miles, half the size of Ireland but comparable to Switzerland or Holland—has historically been a cause of Taiwan's marginalization, this is compensated for by an openness and an ability to adapt to the new. During the past four centuries, Taiwan has evolved dramatically from a little-known island to an *entrepôt*, an outpost of the Chinese empire, a Japanese colony, and, today, a nation-state with 23 million people and one of the largest economies in the world. Taiwan not only has come to embody an internationally acclaimed economic miracle but also is rightly proud to be a hard-won, mature democracy.

DEFINITION OF MODERN CHINESE POETRY

Equally deserving of worldwide recognition is that some of the best modern Chinese poetry also comes from Taiwan. The history of modern Taiwanese poetry tells the story of how the periphery has transformed itself into the frontier. In the Chinese context, "modern poetry" is more than a chronological designation. Although all modern Chinese poetry was written in the twentieth century, not all twentieth-century poetry written in Chinese is "modern." This term usually describes two things: language and form. Classical Chinese has been the poetic medium for more than three millennia, but modern poetry is written in the vernacular of the twentieth century, which is related to but distinct from the classical language, most notably in vocabulary, idiom, and syntax. Modern poetry does not follow the formal and prosodic conventions prescribed by the classical genre; free verse is the dominant form, although modern poetry freely borrows poetic forms from other cultures, the sonnet being a salient example. The differences in poetic medium, form, and style between classical and modern poetry are so vast that Chinese readers sometimes simply refer to the former as Old Poetry and the latter as New Poetry. Old Poetry continues to be written to this day, but this anthology is devoted exclusively to New Poetry.

MODERN POETRY AS CULTURAL FRONTIER

The first modern Chinese poems appeared in *New Youth* (*Xin qingnian*) in January 1917; they were written by Hu Shi (1891–1962), who also attached a list of "Eight Things" (*bashi*), in essence a manifesto of the burgeoning Literary Revolution:

1. Make sure there is substance.
2. Do not imitate ancients.
3. Observe grammar.
4. Do not groan when you aren't sick.
5. Get rid of clichés and formulaic expressions.
6. Do not use allusions.
7. Do not observe parallelism.
8. Do not avoid colloquial words and expressions. (Hu 1991:145)

Although succinct, "Eight Things" signals an unprecedented, radical departure from the classical tradition. Going beyond language and form, Hu also rejects certain stylistic and aesthetic conventions, such as imitation of earlier masters, use of stock motifs and imagery, and parallelism. Instead, he envisions a new poetry of individuality, originality, and sincerity.

From the very beginning, modern poetry has been in the vanguard of literary experimentation and cultural trends. The earliest modern poems preceded the first piece of modern fiction, Lu Xun's (1881–1936) "Diary of a Madman," by one year, and the iconoclastic thrust of the Literary Revolution laid the foundation for the theory and practice of modern Chinese poetry, a harbinger of the wholesale cultural reform of the May Fourth Movement, which began in 1919.

When modern poetry arose to challenge classical poetry in the early twentieth century, it was not unlike David taking on Goliath. Beginning with Confucius and later consolidated through the institutionalization of Confucianism, poetry had always held a special position in China. First of the three sister arts (along with calligraphy and painting), it was traditionally regarded as the most elevated art and the most prestigious form of writing. To this day, Chinese people still take pride in their glorious heritage of classical poetry and refer to China as a "nation of poets" (*shi de minzu*). Moreover, throughout the history of imperial China, poetry had played an important role in multiple spheres: moral, educational, and political in addition to intellectual and cultural. In other words, although classical poetry was primarily written by and for members of the elite, it occupied a central position in Chinese culture and society.

However, by the beginning of the twentieth century, the role and stature of poetry changed dramatically due to, among other factors, the adoption of a Western-styled education system and the compartmentalization of modern learning, the abolition of the civil service examination system, and the rapid modernization of material culture. Combined, these changes put an end to the moral, educational, social, and political functions that poetry had served for so long and so well, changing once and for all the traditional perception of poetry. The Literary Revolution in 1917 represents the culmination of these historical forces. With modern vernacular Mandarin institutionalized as the national language, New Poetry was linked to and won support from the national project of rebuilding China through modernization. This explains how modern poetry could establish itself as a legitimate form of writing within a relatively short time.

But the task that lay ahead was daunting. Although poetry still retained some of its old prestige as an art form, it no longer played a functional role in other, more "practical" spheres of a society bent on modernization and progress. Insofar as it is unimaginable for us moderns that, before the twentieth century, to become a government official a person had to be a competent poet, modern poetry was marginalized in society, but one among many genres of literature and art (M. Yeh 1991:5–28; M. Yeh 1994:xxiii–lv). The need to validate itself would remain with modern poetry for decades to come.

As a new way of writing, modern poetry is both challenging and challenged. The greatest challenge it faces is the issue of reception in modern China. Not only does modern poetry lack the privileged position that its traditional counterpart occupies, but its newness renders it strange and suspicious to both general readers and intellectuals. Compared with modern fiction, modern poetry represents a more radical paradigm shift vis-à-vis the Chinese tradition. Therefore, the challenge is manifold. First, modern poetry must define itself, which it does through artistic experiments and theoretical investigations on an unprecedented scale. This continuing effort amounts to a fundamental rethinking of the ontology of poetry—its nature and *raison d'être* (M. Yeh 1991:5–28).

Second, given its drastically limited social status and its highly experimental nature, modern poetry is burdened with the constant need to justify its existence to society at large. All too often, an easy justification is that poetry should serve social or political objectives. Depriving poetry of its most fundamental attribute, freedom of expression, such instrumentalism suspects, criticizes, and inhibits any individual exploration in language and form. It also underscores most controversies and debates throughout the history of modern Chinese poetry.

Closely related to the "usefulness" of poetry is the issue of readership. In short, to validate modern poetry, there must exist an audience receptive to the new form of writing. To this day, New Poetry has had mixed results. In a general sense, it has clearly succeeded in establishing itself as *the* representative form of Chinese poetry in the twentieth century and it is likely to remain so in the future. Although Old Poetry continues to be written, it is New Poetry that almost exclusively appears in the media, is the prescribed form of poetry contests, and is canonized in numerous literary anthologies and compendia.

On the other hand, the effort to create a broader, appreciative readership has not been completely successful. Critics, even some poets, have attributed this to obscurantism and solipsism on the part of the poet but have ignored a more fundamental cause: education, the media, and common language use make both general readers and intellectuals far more familiar with, and therefore receptive to, traditional Chinese poetry. Whether in the standardized curricula of mandatory education or, more generally, in the daily use of spoken and written Chinese (which contains a significant percentage of classical Chinese, such as oft-quoted verses and adages), people have far more exposure to traditional poetry than to modern poetry. In fact, the latter was excluded from all levels of formal education in Taiwan until the late 1970s. Even though a few modern poems have since been included in textbooks at the elementary and secondary levels, the selection is invariably limited by traditional, didactic themes (e.g., illustrating Confucian or humanitarian values), not based on originality and artistic merit.

Given these social and cultural conditions, modern poetry finds itself in a strange dilemma.It is simultaneously judged by its critics as too difficult and too easy: too difficult because it is distinctly different from the familiar forms and conventions of classical poetry, yet too easy because presumably it does not require any training in classical literature or technical skills—anyone who speaks modern Chinese can write it. Paradoxically, while some critics tend to disparage modern poetry as "popular," crude, and shallow, others find it elitist and obscure.

To summarize, since its inception in 1917 modern Chinese poetry has grappled with the following issues.

First, a self-proclaimed iconoclast, modern poetry must establish an identity distinct from classical poetry. This involves an overhaul of the concept of poetry. Modern poets seek to redefine its essence and art ("What is poetry?"), its readership ("To whom does poetry speak?"), and its purpose ("Why poetry?") from many new angles. Whereas much literary experimentation is carried out in the name of modernity, reactions often advocate a return to tradition. But modernity and tradition are two sides of the same coin: insofar as no return to tradition can possibly reproduce the letter and spirit of classical Chinese poetry, modernity is often the result of selective, individualistic appropriations of tradition.

Second, modern poetry has to defend itself against the pervasive presence and still powerful influence of classical poetry in modern society and culture. Turning away from the old paradigm, modern poets often find inspiration in other literary traditions. Unfortunately, although perhaps inevitably, the tension between tradition and modernity is often interpreted simplistically as the conflict between the Chinese and the Western, and the identity of modern Chinese poetry gets embroiled in discourses of nationalism or nativism as pitched against cosmopolitanism and westernization. The apparent binary opposition between the local and the global or between the national and the international is a recurrent theme in the history of modern Chinese poetry.

Third, yet another axis of tension divides the individual and the collective. The purpose and intended audience of modern poetry are often simplified and reduced to two opposing camps: the ill-defined "art for art's sake" versus the equally vague "art for life's sake." Both sides associate the former with individualism and the latter with social consciousness. Further, this polarization in the orientation of poetry, grossly generalized as the individual versus society, often translates into a stylistic dichotomy between obscurity and clarity of language or between modernism and realism.

Poetry is the cumulative result as well as a vivid reflection of a confluence of forces within the literary field (the evolution of a particular genre and literary history in general, literary associations and publishing agencies, individual talents) and without (social changes, economic development, and political conditions), which interact with, modify, and shape one another. The history of modern Chinese poetry is, in essence, an ongoing process of artists' negotiation with these forces in the three mutually reinforcing binary oppositions: modernity and tradition, cosmopolitanism and nativism, and the individual and the collective. Although they may be false dichotomies, these themes underscore many debates and controversies revolving around modern poetry, accounting for both its bitter crises and its sustained creativity. They also provide an apt analytical framework within which to understand the uniqueness of modern Chinese poetry from Taiwan.

TAIWAN: FROM PERIPHERY TO FRONTIER

Despite linguistic and historical connections, there are significant differences between the modern poetry of Taiwan and that of post–1949 mainland China. The first and foremost difference has to do with the relationship between poetry and politics. Whereas politics has been the sole determining factor and coercive force in the literary field on the mainland, it has never played a central role in Taiwan. Although modern poetry in the formative period in May Fourth China was diverse and cosmopolitan, the dominance of Communist ideology from the 1940s through the late 1970s reduced it to political slogans in the sanctioned formula of "classical plus folk," leaving little room for free expression of the literary imagination. The situation has only begun to change in the past two decades, during which modern poetry has slowly and painstakingly tried to walk out of the shadow of Maospeak.

Taiwan, in contrast, has always had a more open society and a more cosmopolitan culture. Despite censorship during the Japanese colonial period and under the martial law of the Nationalist regime, a civil society has evolved since the 1950s and reached maturity in the 1990s (Gold 1994). Even under the most repressive circumstances, political control was never complete; poetry still managed to carve out a space of its own outside the official discourse and to take advantage of being on the periphery. If "political poetry"—poetry written to critique a political situation or advance a political ideal—constitutes one category among many in Taiwan, it is simply inapplicable to mainland Chinese poetry written prior to the late 1970s, since all of that poetry is, by definition and in a quite direct way, political.

The second significant difference between Taiwan and mainland China is their cultural makeup. Historically, Taiwan has been exposed to and has assimilated elements of Chinese, European, Japanese, and American cultures, in addition to a rich aboriginal culture. The first modern poetry in Taiwan was written in two languages: Chinese and Japanese. Many poets are fluent in two or more languages, and Chinese, Japanese, and English are the most commonly used languages in Taiwan today. With close to universal literacy (about 93 percent) and mandatory primary and intermediate education, contemporary Taiwan also boasts a level of education that is among the highest in the world. Most poets have college degrees, and quite a few hold M.A.s and Ph.D.s from native or foreign universities. Although there is no correlation between academic qualifications and artistic achievement, the bilingual or multilingual poet moves across national and linguistic boundaries with ease and confidence, tapping into his or her multicultural experience and knowledge, whether it includes the literature, music, art, philosophy, or religion of other lands and traditions, as a boundless resource.

The notion of cultural hybridity is overused and has become a cliché in academic circles these days. To put it simply, what culture in the world is not hybrid, and why should this notion apply only to colonial cultures? One may even say that it is the inherent nature of culture to defy politically imposed boundaries; no matter how closed a society or how stringent external constraints may be, interaction with other cultures and varying degrees of conscious or unconscious fusion cannot be deterred completely. Hybridity, however, is a useful concept for understanding Taiwan because the identity of the island is inseparable from its multicultural history of the past three centuries.

In 1590, on a voyage to China, Japan, and Southeast Asia, a Portuguese vessel crossing the Pacific Ocean caught a glimpse of an island. The lush beauty of the coastal plain made Linschotten, a Dutch navigator aboard, utter in marvel: "*Ilha Formosa!*" This historical serendipity has since been immortalized in the Portuguese name *Formosa*, meaning "beautiful." Geological and archaeological evidence indicates prehistoric human habitation on the island dating back 12,000–15,000 years. The aborigines are Austronesians who spoke a variety of languages, originally as many as twenty-four, of which only nine are extant. They are divided into two broad types based on environment: "mountain aborigines" along the Central Mountain Range, which runs from north to south of the 240-mile-long island, and "plains aborigines," concentrated mainly on the western plains. Today, there are nine major tribes: Atayal, Saisiyat, Bunun, Tsou, Paiwan, Rukai, Puyuma, Ami, and Yami, totaling just under 380,000 in population. Each tribe has a distinct culture rich in music, dance, woodcarving, weaving, basketry, and an oral tradition of myths and folktales. Aboriginal cultures have been an inspiration for modern poets throughout the twentieth century, including both Han Chinese (e.g., Yang Chichang, Zheng Chouyu, Yang Mu, Chen Li) and aborigines (e.g., Mona Neng and Walis Nokan).

Imperial Chinese geographical records often refer to the island as a "barbarous" land, and its modern name, Taiwan, might well be related to the word "savages" (Goddard 1966:xvi). Although for centuries fishermen, pirates, and traders from southeast China had come and gone, significant immigration from the mainland did not begin until the seventeenth century, when the Dutch, having chased out their Portuguese and Spanish competitors, occupied Taiwan from 1624 to 1662. With their headquarters in Fort Zeelandia, near today's Tainan in the southwest, the Dutch colonizers encouraged Chinese immigration to provide labor, especially for sugarcane and rice farming. Poor farmers, mostly from southern Fujian and northern Guangdong Provinces, crossed the ninety-mile-long strait and, through diligence and perseverance, settled down and cultivated the new land. This history is vividly captured by Wu Xinrong (1907–67) in "The Farmer's Song" ("Nongmin zhi ge"). Published in *New Literature of Taiwan* (*Taiwan xin wenxue*) in July 1936, the poem describes how the Chinese settlers brought the seed of fire and urges their descendents to pass on the torch. The last stanza re-invokes the ancestors:

> Ah . . . let us recall the past of our ancestors
> When they first arrived on the land
> With empty hands
> All they had were a skiff and a hoe.
> > (translated by Michelle Yeh)

The theme finds elaborations in Wu Sheng's (1944–) vignettes of rural Taiwan, written in the 1970s, which pay tribute to the continuity of the farmers' tradition:

> Long, long ago
> For generations on this piece of land
> Where no wealth or prosperity grows
> Where no miracles are ever produced
> My ancestors wiped away their sweat
> And brought forth their fated children
> > (translated by John Balcom)

We get a quite different view of the early history of Taiwan in "Formosa, 1661," written by Chen Li (1954–) in 1995 (page 360). Covetous of the sugarcane, banana, and silk abundant on the island, the Dutch traded fifteen bolts of cloth to the aborigines in exchange for land "the size of an ox hide." When the deal was made, the Dutch cut the hide into thin strips, then tied them together to round off a much larger area than the aborigines had ever dreamed was possible. By making the first-person narrator a Dutch missionary sent to Taiwan to proselytize the savages, Chen not only satirizes the greed and cunning of the Europeans but also accentuates the arrogance and hypocrisy of the Christian church in deep complicity with imperialism.

After the Manchus overthrew the Ming dynasty in 1644, Zheng Chenggong (1624–62), also known as Koxinga, led an armed resistance against the new regime for years. After a major setback in Nanjing in 1659, he retreated from the mainland to the Pescadores (Penghu) and looked to Taiwan as a base for restoring the Ming. The decision took into consideration that the island, inhabited by Han Chinese, was prosperous, with "fields and gardens of over ten thousand acres, fertile plains across a thousand miles, taxes reaching tens of thousands, and ship-building and tool-manufacturing" (Chen Zhaoying 1998:36). Warmly supported by the Taiwanese Chinese, Zheng expelled the Dutch in February 1662. The moment before the besieged Dutch surrendered is imbued with much symbolism and ambivalence in Yang Mu's (1940–) "Zeelandia" (page 261), where the gendered roles of the male colonial conqueror and the female conquered island are reversed.

Zheng's plan to restore the Ming was doomed, however, with his untimely death. Under his son, Zheng Jing, and grandson, Zheng Keshuang, the Ming loyalists in Taiwan were defeated by the Qing admiral Shi Lang and surrendered in 1683. Taiwan was annexed to Fujian Province the same year; for the first time in history the island became part of China. In 1875, Imperial Commissioner to Taiwan Shen Baozhen (1820–79) established a prefecture in Taipei, and in 1885 Taiwan became the twenty-second province of the Qing Empire. Under the capable leadership of Shen and succeeding administrators, most notably the first governor of Taiwan, Liu Mingchuan (1836–96), a series of innovative measures were implemented, including building railways, establishing postal service, installing electric streetlights and telegraph lines, and founding modern public schools with an emphasis on Western learning. By the end of Liu's gubernatorial tenure (1885–91), Taiwan had become a prosperous agricultural export province. Compared with the rest of the empire, which had been in decline since mid-century and did not get a reform movement off the ground till 1898, Taiwan was "a generation ahead" (Goddard 1966:xiv) and was even considered the "most advanced province of China," with Taipei as its political, economic, and cultural center (Kuo 1973:237).

Taiwan was also successful in the military arena. In 1840, after the outbreak of the first Opium War on the mainland, the Taiwanese navy, under the command of Yao Ying, defeated the British. In 1884, during the Sino-French War, Liu Mingchuan led Taiwan to victory. But these exceptional feats could not reverse the fate of the island. When China was defeated in 1894–95, Taiwan, along with the Pescadores, was ceded to Japan under the Treaty of Shimonoseki, signed on April 17, 1895, over vehement opposition from mainland reformers. The first twenty years of colonial rule saw a large number of rebellions—from the short-lived Republic of Taiwan under the last Qing governor of Taiwan, Tang Jingsong, in 1895 to the uprising led by Yu Qingfang in 1915—all of which were brutally suppressed. But throughout the Japanese occupation period (1895–1945), native resistance never stopped. According to one study, "from 1895 to 1920 the number of persons arrested for attempts to overthrow the Japanese was never less than 8,200 in any year . . . from 1921 to 1930 the lowest figure for any year was 6,500; and from 1931 to 1940 the number was never below 3,450 in any one year" (Clark 1966:164).

Aiming to use the island as a stepping-stone in its conquest of China and Southeast Asia, Japan tried to make Taiwan a model colony by establishing "benign rule." Restrictive educational, professional, social, and cultural policies were instituted. Rigid political control was imposed on one hand while economic development was promoted effectively on the other. Economic success is indicated by the steady growth of the population, from 2 million in 1895 to 3.5 million in 1920 to 6 million in 1945.

Prosperity, however, came at the expense of the Taiwanese people. Yang Hua (1906–36) depicts the plight of the common people through dramatization in "Sad Song of the Female Worker" ("Nugong beiqu," page 57). In a more general way, he expresses the indignation and anger of all the colonized in *Black Tide (Heichao ji)*, written while he was imprisoned for violating the Japanese "public security law":

> Toyed with.
> Humiliated.
> How many times now?
> Though I cannot well remember,
> Of what use is it to remember well?
>
> (translated by Kirk A. Denton)

Despite its brevity and simplicity, the poem voices a powerful critique of colonialism. The laconic two opening lines, each consisting of a compound word in Chinese, state a simple, irrefutable fact. Economy of language continues into the third line, which raises a question to which the answer is also factual. If the question follows logically from the preceding lines, it is immediately rendered meaningless by the poet's answer in lines 4–5, which poses a rhetorical question. It is futile, even absurd, to demand a tally of the humiliations and sufferings to which the colonized have been subjected, for two reasons: there are simply too many to keep track of, and even if there were a tally, who would care and who could right the wrongs? Behind the plain words, Yang's adroit manipulation of tone and use of juxtaposition reveal the tragedy of Taiwan.

It is meaningful that Yang chooses a female worker to illustrate the suffering of the Taiwanese people, for the traditional view of women as weak and passive provides an apt symbol of the undesirable situation imposed on a colony. It is not surprising, then, that in the 1976 poem, "My Pen" ("Wo de bi"), Chen Xiuxi (1921–91) goes one step further as she turns a woman's face into a metaphor:

> Eyebrows are the colony of the eyebrow pencil
> round lips the territory of the lipstick
> I am happy that my pen
> outlines neither eyebrows nor lips

"colony," "territoriality"
each time I see these words
the sorrow of having been colonized rises in me again
count tonight's sighs
caressing my veins
surging blood moves my pen
on paper moistened by tears
it fills the page:
I am Chinese
I am Chinese
We all are Chinese

(translated by Wendy Larson)

The power of the poem derives from the originality of the metaphors comparing cosmetics to a colonizing agent and a woman's face to a colony. Contrast is the key device. The first-person narrator rejects the "feminine" pen and picks up a writing pen, with which she asserts repeatedly her Chinese identity. More subtle is the contrast in the color images. There is a similarity between the black eyebrow pencil and the black ink of the pen, as well as between the lipstick—literally "mouth red" in Chinese—and the blood that pushes the pen across the page. In each case, the poet's active stance replaces a passive one and her independence replaces submission. Coming from a woman, the poem is particularly meaningful, since it also implies defiance of traditional gender roles, in which a woman is expected to beautify herself to please men.

Japanese colonization of Taiwan for economic and political interests took on a harsher form toward the end of the Pacific War, when approximately 200,000 Taiwanese men were conscripted, under the name of "volunteers," to serve in the Japanese military in Southeast Asia. Huan Fu (1922–) was among those who were sent to Java, and "Carrier Pigeon" ("Xin'ge," page 105), written in 1964, is a moving rendition of that experience. Although it is tempting to read the poem autobiographically, the text yields another reading that may perhaps be more rewarding. This alternative reading hinges on the ambivalence with which death is described throughout the poem. The first-person narrator claims that he "did not die"; nevertheless, his death "was hidden in a forest corner" on an island in Southeast Asia, and he forgot to bring it back. The seeming contradiction and the wording ("buried") suggest that the soldier narrator is indeed dead; the repeated disclaimer only reinforces the opposite.

The poem follows the journey of the soldier at two levels: physical/real and psychological/symbolic. Like the narrator, the poem begins with the arrival on a pristine tropical island, passes through the battle scenes, and ends with the "dark dense jungle." The only glimpse of hope on this journey to the "heart of darkness," where the narrator is buried, is his indomitable spirit. It is as if the soldier's longing for homeland is so intense that even in death he refuses to rest. In Chinese, "carrier pigeon" contains the word *xin*, which means "message" as well as "faithfulness" or "being true (to one's words)." Evoking the image of a carrier pigeon, the soldier-narrator vows to return home, if only in spirit, to fulfill a promise to the loved ones he left behind.

Although tragic for all concerned, the war experience was different for Taiwan than for the mainland, and we see representations from both perspectives in the work of Taiwanese poets. While Taiwan was forced to contribute to Japan's offensive forces, China was defending itself against Japan. While Taiwan was under Japanese "benign rule," the worst war atrocities imaginable were inflicted on the land and people of mainland China. "Memento of the Deceased" ("Yiwu") by Li Minyong (1947–) (page 293), for example, portrays the sorrow of a Taiwanese soldier's widow; using four metaphors in a row, the poem compares the soldier's handkerchief to a court sentence, a corrosive acid, a landslide, and a seal, all of which put an irreversible end to her youth and happiness. In contrast, Bai Ling's (1951–) "Childhood Years, Part I: The 1940s" ("Tongnian," page 322) remembers the war from a child's point of view: bomb explosions are like cotton candy, bomb pits like popcorn, and tanks and airplanes like toys. The mother scavenging for food in the field screams when she spots a human arm, but the child narrator naively thinks it belongs to a broken doll. The understatement, through a temporal and perceptual distancing, helps bring the horror of war to the fore.

Still another perspective is presented in Jiao Tong's (1956–) "The Demon Platoon Leader" ("Mogui fenduizhang"), written in 1993:

> Yamaguchi Shintaro held the rank of second-class private and was assigned to the 124th Infantry Company. He was a fierce fighter, distinguished for the blazing intensity of his performance in battle. Everyone honored him with the title "Demon Platoon Leader," and he received an imperial medal of honor.

> The Demon Platoon Leader survived a hundred battles. He was only wounded once, on the Siberian Front, when seven regiments lost a whole regiment's worth of fighting strength to syphilis. Thank heaven for penicillin: he escaped from the jaws of death and was sent to the Chinese battlefield.

> From the time the Imperial Army landed at Hangzhou Cove until it took Nanjing, our intrepid platoon leader won the highest favor with bold exploits of raping four women each day.

> The Demon Platoon Leader was a man of exceptional endowments. Each centiliter of his sperm contained 25,999 fero-

cious spermatozoa, with a volume per ejaculation of 20 milliliters. Each month he could produce seventeen gallons of highly corrosive sperm fluid. When the moon was full, his third testicle would appear, and his metal-hard penis would lengthen by 13 centimeters.

Patriotism smoldered in the heart of the Demon Platoon Leader: before each act of intercourse, he stood at attention and sang the national anthem.

(translated by Denis Mair)

Of all the war crimes, the satire focuses on those committed against women by Japanese soldiers. That a whole regiment was lost to syphilis suggests how pervasive rape was. That the private is honored with medals indicates that rape was in fact encouraged and rewarded by military commanders. Drawing a parallel between valor on the battlefield and sexual exploits, the poem not only critiques the violence of both war and rape but, more poignantly, debunks two popular myths that still cause much injustice and suffering: the equation of masculinity with sexual aggression and the use of patriotism and nationalism to justify inhumanities perpetuated by one racial or ethnic group against another. The entire poem is cast in the pseudo-language of historiography from a positively Japanese point of view. The hyperbole with which it describes—in fact pays tribute to—the platoon leader's superhuman endowment renders the atrocity more chilling and disgusting.

During the colonial period, Taiwanese people were not only barred from the political arena but also discriminated against in the educational system. The colonial government provided basic education but offered few opportunities for advanced learning. The cream of the crop was allowed to go into medicine and often received training in Japan. Between 1915 and 1922, the number of Taiwanese students in Japan increased dramatically, from just over 300 to more than 2,400 (Peng 1991:4).

Ironically, when these youths went to Japan, they formed organizations and launched publications that mounted explicit or implicit resistance against colonization and asserted a Taiwanese identity. The first journal in Taiwanese history, *Taiwanese Youth* (*Taiwan qingnian*), was founded by overseas students in Tokyo in June 1920 and moved back home two years later under the name *Taiwan*. The first literary magazine published in Taiwan, *Literature and Art* (*Wenyi*), was founded in 1924. *Formosa* was also founded by overseas Taiwanese students, including Wu Yongfu (1913–), Zhang Wenhuan (1909–78), Su Weixiung, Wang Baiyuan (1901–65), Wu Kunhuang (1909–), Weng Nao (1906–40?), and others in Tokyo in July 1933. In Taipei, writers founded *The Vanguard* (*Xianfa budui*)— later renamed *The First Line* (*Diyi xian*)—in January 1935. Other magazines in the 1920s and '30s include: *Everyone* (*Renren*), *Modern Life* (*Xiandai shenghuo*), *Morning Bell* (*Xiaozhong*), *The Equator* (*Chidao*), and *Southern Tune* (*Nanyin*). The newspaper *Taiwanese People's Journal* (*Taiwan minbao*) was founded in April 1923; originally published in Japan twice a month, it gradually evolved into a Chinese daily published in Taiwan beginning in July 1927. Despite Japanese censorship, these and other publications provided a fertile ground for literary and cultural development in Taiwan (Chen Shaoting 1977).

One development that was to have a profound impact on Taiwanese culture was the vernacular movement initiated by Huang Chengcong and Huang Chaoqin in early 1923. Enlightenment and modernization were clearly their objectives, and they looked to the mainland as their model. As Huang Chengcong reasoned, "If our compatriots understand the vernacular, we can purchase new modern books, newspapers, and magazines from China to enlighten our stagnant society" (Li 1979:14). In more detail, Huang Chaoqin explained that classical Chinese was an impediment to modernization due to its extreme difficulty and inaccessibility to common people, who did not have the leisure or ability to study it. Citing the recent success of the vernacular movement on the mainland, where it had even won the support of such great classical scholars as Zhang Binglin (1869–1936) and Liang Qichao (1873–1929), Huang criticized Taiwan as conservative and backward and offered practical advice not unlike that of Huang Chengcong: "Those gentlemen who wish to study the vernacular can consult the Shanghai Commerce Press" (Li 1979:32). There is no doubt that the vernacular movement paved the way for modern poetry in Taiwan; it was the first effort toward a native literature in Taiwan and a precursor to the Native Literature Movement of the 1970s and poetry written in Hokkien, which has gained much currency since the 1980s.

At the time when both Huangs wrote from Japan, a young man from Taiwan named Zhang Qingrong (1902–55) was studying at Beijing Normal College. Inspired by the Literary Revolution that had swept the mainland a few years earlier, he published "A Letter to the Youth of Taiwan" ("Zhi Taiwan qingnian de yi feng xin"), under the penname Zhang Wojun ("my army"), in *Taiwanese People's Journal* on April 21, 1924. In the letter, he attacked classical poetry as decorative and dead, and those who wrote it as slaves to archaic poetic conventions. After returning to Taiwan in October of the same year, Zhang wrote another critique titled "The Terrible Literary Scene in Taiwan" ("Zaogao de Taiwan wenxuejie"), which triggered a debate between the old school of poets and the new. Like the New Poetry Movement in China led by Hu Shi, the call for modern poetry in Taiwan embodied iconoclasm, aspirations to modernity, and a new orientation of poetry. As editor of the *Taiwanese People's Journal* from 1924 to 1926, Zhang introduced both the theory and creative work of modern poetry from the mainland. He also published, in Taipei in December 1925, the first book of modern Chinese poetry in Taiwanese history. Titled *Love in a Chaotic City* (*Luandu zhi lian*), the collection records Zhang's romantic relationship while living in Beijing.

There is another line of development in the history of modern poetry in

Taiwan. The earliest modern poems published in Taiwan were in fact written in Japanese. Authored by Zhui Feng ("chasing the wind"), the pen name of Xie Chunmu (1902–67), the sequence of four poems under the title "Imitations of Poetry" ("Shi de mofang") was written in 1923 and published in *Taiwan* on April 10, 1924, slightly earlier than Zhang Wojun's work.

By the time modern poetry appeared, Taiwan had been ruled by Japan for thirty years. Modern Japanese poetry began to emerge in the late nineteenth century. The first collection of modern poetry in translation appeared in 1882 and free verse flourished from 1912 to 1922; the latter is best represented by Kotaro Takamura (1883–1956), author of the 1914 *Itinerary*, and Sakutaro Hagiwara (1886–1942), whose *Howling at the Moon* was published in 1917. There are many parallels between modern Chinese and modern Japanese poetry. Both had been undergoing a transition from tradition to modernity since the late nineteenth century, and by the 1920s both had taken free verse as a vital new form. (It should be noted, however, that a significant difference is that while modern Chinese poetry rejects all traditional forms, modern Japanese poetry continues to use some: while it is common for a modern Japanese poem to be written as a tanka or haiku, a modern Chinese poem in the form of a "quatrain" [*jueju*] or "regulated verse" [*lushi*] simply does not exist.) Both were greatly inspired by Western poetry, first through translation but increasingly in the original as the poets acquired foreign languages. More specifically, it is interesting to note that in both cases the introduction of Western poetry began with romanticism, followed by symbolism, naturalism, and various strands of high modernism. Further, many of the pioneers in both China and Japan had firsthand experience with the West. Hu Shi studied at Cornell and Columbia Universities in the 1910s; Takamura studied sculpture in America, France, and England from 1906 to 1910. Xu Zhimo (1897–1931) and Wen Yiduo (1899–1946), leaders of the Crescent School, attended graduate school in the United States in the 1920s, and Junzaburo Nishiwaki (1894–1982), the most important Japanese surrealist, studied English literature at Oxford and published his first book of poetry, *Spectrum*, in English in 1925.

From the beginning, then, modern poetry in Taiwan has drawn on two traditions: mainland Chinese and Japanese. These should be seen not as diametrically opposed but as complementary and mutually reinforcing because they were often inspired by the same sources. For example, Yang Hua's petit poems were influenced by those of Bing Xin (1900–99) on the mainland, but the immense popularity of the miniature form in China in the 1920s was itself the result of multicultural influences, including at least ancient Greek epigrams, Rabindranath Tagore's (1861–1941) short lyrics, Japanese haiku, and classical Chinese poetry. While many pioneers of modern poetry on the mainland, such as Lu Xun, Guo Moruo (1892–1978), and Mu Mutian (1900–71), studied in Japan, the same can be said of many Taiwanese poets, who had extensive

interaction with Japanese poets in Japan as well as in Taiwan during the co-
lonial period.

Another example of the complex genealogy of modern poetry in Taiwan is
the appearance of surrealism. Although there were cursory references in *Xian-
dai* (or *Les Contemporains*), a modernist journal published in Shanghai from
1932 to 1935, the first serious introduction to and experiment in surrealism in
modern Chinese poetry was carried out by *Le Moulin* Poetry Society (Fongche
shishe), founded by four Taiwanese and three Japanese poets in 1933 (Ye Di
1996). Consciously veering away from the more popular trend of realism, which
emphasized the writer as a spokesperson for the oppressed common people, *Le
Moulin* poets developed a "pale-skinned aesthetic" ("Sea of Flowers" ["Hua zhi
hai"], page 65). Emphasizing the senses as the gateway to reality, these poets
created a world filled with superimposed, often synaesthetic, images and subtle
moods. Nature, in contrast to the city, is immanently sensual, and there is
perfect correspondence between the poet and nature. Although they sought
harmony and unity between the flesh and the spirit, *Le Moulin* poets were
besieged by ambivalence, confusion, and frustration—in short, a sense of de-
feat—which is reflected in their work. Women figure prominently as a para-
doxical symbolic representation of ultimate sensuality and ultimate spirituality.

A good example is Yang Chichang's (1908–94) "The Nun" ("Nigu"). Written
in December 1934, the poem depicts the sexual awakening of a young Buddhist
nun named Duanduan (page 60). At the beginning of the poem, the open
window suggests a bridge to the outside world, the world of the senses neces-
sarily blocked off from the sacred shrine of Buddhist deities. The contrast in
color images is used effectively to intimate the conflict between the nun's sexual
awakening and her religious belief: the white of Duanduan's arms and breasts
versus the red and green of the statues in the prayer hall. Interestingly, the poet
reverses the traditional symbolism of the colors: white is associated with the
body and sexual desire rather than with spirituality, whereas red and green are
associated with Buddhism instead of the mundane world of "red dust." Thus,
contrary to Buddhist teachings, the poet implicitly approves carnal desire by
elevating it to a higher status.

The tension between sexual desire and religious belief reaches climax in the
last part of the poem. There are sexual overtones in Duanduan's vision of the Bud-
dhist statues coming alive: Weituo's sword is clearly phallic, and even the image
of the Arhat who literally "mounts" the tiger is sexually suggestive. Yet the fact
that Duanduan faints when the statues come alive suggests a profound sense of
shame and guilt on her part. At the end of the poem, as she comes to in the
morning and begins her daily routine of sutra chanting, Duanduan calls out to
her mother. By evoking a secular tie that has supposedly been severed upon
her "renouncing the world" and joining the Buddhist order, the poet not only
intimates Duanduan's regret and inability to repress sexual desire but also im-
plicitly questions the unnaturalness of religious celibacy. To the extent that

Duanduan sacrifices her virginity to the gods in a symbolic sense, her relationship to them is not any purer or less "illusory" than physical attachments between humans. Finally, sarcasm underscores the poem in the nun's name, Duanduan, as the character "duan" connotes propriety and conformity to conventions.

Their contemporaries regarded *Le Moulin* poets as "decadent," "aesthetist," and "ugly" (Liu 2000), but this attitude reduces literature to sociology and art to a vehicle of moral teaching. The fact is that the teaching that poetry does is most effective and lasting when it seems least like teaching. The critique of traditional religion that we have seen in Yang's "The Nun" is subtle but powerful. Another fine example of reflection on tradition is Li Zhangrui's (?–1951) "This Family" ("Zhe yijia"), published in 1936:

> The color of bricks passed down from generations
> Chokes on the early autumn sunset
> Memory lies dead beneath the pomelo tree in the yard
> The tradition of this family is piled on with
> The green fatigue of branches and twigs. Soon
> A new couplet will be pasted on the door, but
> A wordless burden penetrates sleep . . . .
> No words are needed for blood to coagulate
>
> —What's buried beneath the pomelo . . .
> The maiden in a long gown   even
> Her bright forehead dims
> (That thing—don't you know it?)
> Quickly uttered words, unknown to her ancestors
> Spread on her rouged lips
>
> (translated by Michelle Yeh)

The image of the pomelo tree symbolizes family lineage, but "fatigue" has taken over and it is headed toward oblivion ("memory is dead") and death (as suggested by the images of "choking" and "sleep"). It is an old Chinese custom to paste a couplet, written in calligraphy on red paper, on the door to usher in the lunar New Year. In the poem, however, the custom continues but brings no renewal. By juxtaposing written words and "wordless burden," the poet suggests a separation of form and substance. "Burden" is further associated with "blood" in the next line, since both have no use for words. Why such pessimism? The answer is revealed in the second stanza, in which the poet chooses the image of a young woman to drive home the theme of rupture or discontinuity. Although the same blood flows in the family, words have caused a break in the lineage. There are a number of contrasts between the first and second stanzas:

between the old house and the young woman, the faded bricks of the building and her bright red mouth, the "wordless burden" and her "quickly uttered words." The maiden's dimming forehead and the vague reference to "that thing" hint at the possibility that she is lovesick. When she opens her mouth, probably coyly to refute someone's speculation, the words that she speaks belong to another language than that of her ancestors. If we interpret the family metaphorically, the poem, at one level at least, expresses the sadness of colonial Taiwan.

Although both Chinese and Japanese were taught at public schools for the Taiwanese before 1937, programs of Japanization, known as *Kōminka*, were vigorously promoted by the colonial government and included adopting Japanese-style names, speaking Japanese at home, converting to Shintoism, and adopting Japanese customs and lifestyle in general. Those who conformed were rewarded with social prestige (e.g., a plaque) and material privileges (e.g., more food supplies) (Chou 1996). In April 1937, three months before Japan launched a full-fledged invasion of China, Chinese was banned at school and in the media, and only Japanese—referred to as the "national language" (*kokugo* in Japanese)—was allowed in public. Thus, Taiwanese youths who grew up in the last eight years of colonial rule received little education in Chinese, although typically they spoke Hokkien or Hakka—the language of another major subethnic group on the island at home.

In Japanese-occupied Taiwan, as in other colonies, writers had to face the painful dilemma that their resistance against colonial rule had to be carried out in the colonizer's language. In the 1935 poem "Thought," Wu Xinrong refers to his generation as "poets with no language." Comparing the situation of the Taiwanese poet to that of Tagore, the Nobel laureate from India who wrote much of his work in English, Wu asks: "What do they [his writings] really bring for the Indians?" That such introspection and self-questioning were prevalent among Taiwanese poets can be seen in the fact that many did write in Chinese. The spirit of independence also lies behind the various efforts to promote a literature written in Hokkien from the mid-1920s to 1945. From 1930 to 1933 Huang Shihui advocated "homeland literature" (*xiangtu wenxue*) and triggered a debate on whether Chinese or Taiwanese (Hokkien) should be the medium for Taiwanese literature (Yang 1996). In practice, much of the literature in the 1920s, '30s, and '40s was a mix of Chinese and Hokkien. These early experiments were to inspire later poets who began to write poetry in Hokkien in the 1970s, such as Lin Zongyuan (1935–), Xiang Yang (1955–), Huang Jinlian (1947–), Huang Shugen (1946–), and Lin Yongmin (1955–) (Zheng 1990). They also paved the way for the eventual appearance and recognition of Hakka poetry in the 1990s.

When the island was returned to China in 1945 under the Cairo Agreement, the cultural difference between mainland China and Taiwan, especially in terms of linguistic background and practices, was significant. Ironically, although Taiwan had always identified with China as the motherland throughout the Japanese colonial period, the mother with whom she was finally reunited after fifty years was more or less a stranger whose language she could hardly comprehend. In April 1946 the Committee on Popularization of the National Language (Guoyu puji weiyuanhui) was formed, and branches were set up in every county in Taiwan within two years. More than two hundred new journals and newspapers mushroomed, many in both Chinese and Japanese (Ye Shitao 1990:145). Bilingual publications did not last long, however. On October 24, 1946, on the eve of the first anniversary of the retrocession of Taiwan to China, Japanese was banned in the media, which marked the next step in the Guomindang's "resinicization" or decolonization effort. Some of the titles of the essays in the last Japanese edition of *China Daily* (*Zhonghua ribao*) suggest that although not without a touch of uncertainty, Taiwanese writers supported the new policy as a positive step toward unifying the people: "What Will Happen to Taiwan?" (Long Yingzong), "Goodbye, Japanese Edition" (Chen Huiyu), "Wait Till the Day of Fluent Chinese" (Chen Shengsheng), "Lift the Spirit and Learn the National Language" (Sun Linmao) (Ying 1985:13).

Granted, Japanese did not disappear completely after 1946; for a while Japanese books were still published. Efforts to bridge the two linguistic groups also continued: Japanese works by Taiwanese writers were translated and published in newspapers and magazines such as *Everyone*, edited by Yang Kui (1905–85), and seminars for writers were organized, notably by Ge Lei, editor of *Bridge* (*Qiao*), the literary supplement of *New Life Daily* (*Xinsheng bao*) (Peng 1995). However, the ban on Japanese in the media deprived most Taiwanese of access to new information, which deepened their distrust of the government (Ye Shitao 1990:146).

Inflation, devaluation of the old currency, food shortages, unemployment, corruption of the Nationalist government under the administration of Chen Yi—these and other factors contributed to the escalating tension in the days following retrocession. The brewing discontent of the Taiwanese people exploded in the February 28 Incident in 1947, during which the Nationalist army was sent in from the mainland to suppress local uprisings. In the process, thousands of innocent Taiwanese, including many members of the elite, were killed and more arrested and incarcerated; many new immigrants from the mainland were also killed by the Taiwanese.

The "2–28 Incident" had severe long-term consequences (Lai, Myers & Wei 1991). It aggravated the already difficult transition from Japanese colonialism to Nationalist rule. The fragile trust that had been established between the Nationalist government and the Taiwanese people—especially the intellectuals— after the war was largely destroyed. Subsequently, the regime stepped up its control and, as the civil war on the mainland worsened and retreat to Taiwan seemed imminent, tightened its grip even more, ushering in the era of White Terror in the 1950s and 1960s. The official discourse can be characterized as one of nationalism, anticommunism, and conservatism (Winckler 1994; Lee 1996).

After 1949 Hokkien was forbidden in public, severely restricted in the media, and stigmatized socially. Certain aspects of Taiwanese culture were regarded as remnants of Japanese colonialism and were categorically dismissed. Taiwanese literature from the Japanese colonial period was also banned, along with much pre-1949 modern Chinese literature written by "leftist" writers, i.e., those who lived under the Communist regime after 1949. When two million refugees came from the mainland in 1949, disoriented and stressed, they merged into a society that had just gone through a traumatic event, discussion of which was to remain a political taboo until 1987. The disenfranchisement of the Taiwanese people, along with their unspeakable anger and resentment toward the ruling GMD, would drive a wedge between the Taiwanese and the recent mainland émigrés for decades to come, with profound social, political, and cultural ramifications.

The intensely complicated modern history of Taiwan thus presents an unusual case of postcolonial culture. While many other modern countries in Asia, Latin America, and Africa that achieved independence had to—or still have to—wrestle with the issue of using the colonizer's language, postwar Taiwan's situation was reversed. Taiwanese writers in 1949 were caught between two languages yet could hardly identify with either: Japanese, the former colonizer's language that they were no longer allowed to speak, and Chinese, the language that was rightfully their mother tongue but that they could not speak. In short, Taiwanese writers were faced with the unique quandary of having no language of their own. This condition of "cultural aphasia" exerted a far-reaching impact on the development of modern Chinese poetry in Taiwan.

First of all, the generation of Taiwanese writers who were in their twenties when the war ended were handicapped linguistically: they were unable to continue to write and publish either in Japanese, which was banned, or in Chinese, of which they had yet to achieve full command. Some simply gave up for this reason, although a few would continue to write in Japanese for the drawer or publish their work in Japan. Most of those who persisted would need fully ten years to acquire enough proficiency in Chinese to write and publish in that language. While the second group constitutes "the translingual generation" (*kuayue yuyan de yidai*), a term coined by Lin Hengtai (1924–) in 1967, the first group may well be called "the silenced generation."

Second, the lacuna thus created on the poetry scene in the postwar period was filled mainly by poets who had recently sought refuge in Taiwan. Although a few Taiwanese poets made a smooth transition from Japanese to Chinese, such as Wu Yingtao (1916–71), Lin Hengtai, Jin Lian (1928–), and Zhang Yanxun (1925–), most of the poets active in the 1950s, including Ji Xian (previously under the pen name Luyishi, 1913–), Qin Zihao (1912–63), Zhong Dingwen (pen name Fan Cao, 1914–), Li Sha (1925–), Ge Xianning (1908–61),

Yang Huan (1930–54), and Yu Guangzhong (1928–), had previously published on the mainland and a few had established a substantial reputation there. With their credentials, some of them were able to obtain editorial positions in state-run newspapers and magazines, become teachers of workshops and correspondence courses sponsored by the Nationalist government, and in general play an active role on the literary scene.

This state of affairs is evident in publications and other related activities. The first poetry journal published in postwar Taiwan was *New Poetry Weekly* (*Xinshi zhoukan*); founded in November 1951, it was edited by Ji Xian (issues 1–26) and Qin Zihao (from issue 27 onward). Qin was also the editor of the *Blue Star Weekly* (*Lanxing zhoukan*), a supplement to *Public Opinion Daily* (*Gonglun bao*), founded in June 1954; after the first 110 issues he was succeeded by Yu Guangzhong. In addition, Qin served as the poetry teacher at the Chinese Literature and Art Correspondence School in the 1950s and 1960s. When *Today's New Poetry* (*Jinri xinshi*) was founded in 1957, its deputy directors were Zhong Lei (1920–) and Ji Xian, and the chief editor was Shangguan Yu (1924–). Also founded in 1957 was the *Literary Star* (*Wenxing*), whose poetry section was edited by Yu Guangzhong.

Books of modern poetry published between 1949 and 1955 were almost all authored by new émigrés; besides some of the poets mentioned above, others include Jin Jun (1910–), Mo Ren (1920–), Wang Yan (1920–66), Deng Yuping (1925–85), Chu Qing (1926–), Fang Si (1925–), Sha Mu (1928–86), Rongzi (1928–), Xia Jing (1925–), and Zheng Chouyu (1933–). Conspicuous exceptions to the list are Wu Yingtao, Lin Hengtai, and Ye Di (1931–), three poets who made a smooth transition from Japanese to Chinese (Zhang Mo 1992:3–9).

Finally, all the poetry societies formed in the 1950s, including the Modernist School, Blue Star, and Epoch, were dominated by émigré poets. Although the journals and poetry societies by no means excluded Taiwanese poets, the émigrés' linguistic skills clearly provided a valuable form of cultural capital, which put them in an advantageous position.

POETRY IN THE WILD

Faced with the threat of military attack from the mainland, the Nationalist government adopted a hard anticommunist line in the 1950s and 1960s, backed by military assistance and economic aid from the United States. While control of the media and censorship served as deterrents to politically incorrect literature and art, there were attractive incentives for those writers and artists who actively supported the official cultural policy. As early as October 1949, the literary supplement of *New Life Daily* initiated discussions on "combat literature and art." On December 16, 1949, the inaugural issue of the literary supplement of the *National Daily* (*Minzu bao*), the former incarnation of the *United Daily* (*Lianhe bao*), announced: "The current responsibility of all workers of literature and art—to engage in combat to fight back the enemies" (Ying 1985:29).

Two important incentives were publication and prizes. In March 1950 the Committee of Prizes in Chinese Literature and Art (Zhonghua wenyi jiangjin weiyuanhui) was formed. Twice a year, usually on May 5 and November 12 (the latter being the anniversary of Dr. Sun Yat-sen's birthday), the committee gave out lucrative prizes in various genres, including poetry and song lyrics. It also offered generous honoraria on a regular basis for selected works, which were published in the official press. By the time the committee was dissolved in July 1957, more than a thousand writers had received prizes and honoraria from it. The criterion for selection states that the work must "use many literary and artistic techniques to raise nationalist consciousness and convey the meaning of anticommunism and countering-the-Soviets" (Ge & Shangguan 1965:81–82). The honorarium for a selected poem was NT$100–200, and the first prize for a long poem was NT$1,000. Considering that the average income of a state employee was a little over NT$100 a month, those rewards were extremely attractive. The titles of the song lyrics that won the top prizes in May 1950 indicate the successful implementation of the cultural policy: "Anticommunist March" (Zhao Youpei), "Anticommunist and Counter-the-Soviets Song" (Zhang Ganlin), and "Protect My Taiwan" (Sun Ling). Many other organizations of a similar nature were formed, such as the Chinese Youth Writing Association (August 1953) and the Chinese Women's Writing Association (May 1955). Needless to say, the poetry written under this cultural policy was formulaic, nationalistic, and sentimental. It was an obstacle that modern poetry would have to overcome in order to grow and excel.

Besides the official discourse, another formidable challenge to modern poetry in postwar Taiwan was its low status vis-à-vis classical poetry. Classical poetry had a long history in Taiwan, starting before Zheng Chenggong. The first noted poet, Shen Wenguang, came to Taiwan in 1649, and the first classical Chinese poetry club, East Chanting Society (Dongyin she), was founded in 1685. When Taiwan was ceded to Japan in 1895, it is estimated that there were more than two hundred poetry clubs on the island (Chen Zhaoying 1998:8). Although the colonial government promoted Japanization and suppressed Chinese culture, classical Chinese poetry was preserved because of its prestige in traditional Japanese culture. Thus it was written not only by Taiwanese poets but also by Japanese elites in Taiwan. This is evident in the fact that when the colonial government banned Chinese in 1937, the only exception was the "Chinese Poetry Column" (Hanshi lan) in the newspapers.

The tradition of classical Chinese poetry in Taiwan, in short, was transferred from the mainland and remained unbroken despite Japanese colonialism. Although by the 1920s the composition of classical poetry had become a polite social function more than a serious literary endeavor, it continued to be held in high regard. In "The Terrible Literary Scene in Taiwan," Zhang Wojun mounted an attack on those who wrote classical poetry to advance their worldly fame and curry favor with the ruling regime. He was worried that even young people were engaged in this frivolous activity:

> They write poetry because it is an easy way to gain fame (but what kind of fame is that?) and takes no effort (actually poetry is not as easy as they think). From time to time, His Honor the Governor invites them to tea and asks them to compose poetry; from time to time, poetry clubs, too, invite them to drink wine and compose poetry. Their names are printed in newspapers and they are often bestowed with gifts. Therefore, never mind life or death, they keep on making a fuss about writing poetry (actually they are just fooling around).
>
> (Zhang 1979:65)

Despite the relative success of modern poetry as a new form of writing since the 1920s, it could not compete with classical poetry in social status. As late as the early 1950s, the disparity between the two genres was still significant. In the editorial in the second issue of *Modern Poetry Quarterly* (*Xiandaishi jikan*), Ji Xian laments: "There is no need to conceal the fact that New Poetry is looked down on by most people" (August 20, 1953). This and other comments show that those who wrote classical poetry tended to belong to the cultural establishment:

> In view of the huge gathering that Old Poetry organized on Poet's Day, some [fellow modern poets] become nervous, worrying that New Poetry might get trampled on and die an early death. Actually this concern is unnecessary. . . . Old Poetry is in the court, New Poetry is in the wild. Those of us who write New Poetry have neither power nor connections. Further, we are hard-pressed financially; we use our own money to publish poetry journals and can barely afford it.
>
> (*Modern Poetry Quarterly* no. 15 [Aug. 1956]:80)

Even on college campuses Old Poetry enjoyed more popularity. At the Gaoxiong Medical School, for instance, students were encouraged to write classical poetry, which was published in the student magazine. Modern poetry was not to be seen in the school publication until 1963, and a modern poetry society was founded in 1964 (*Amoeba* 1985:327). Modern poetry first entered the standardized national curricula in Taiwan in 1968, when two poems were included in a middle school textbook of Chinese literature (Xu 1990:115).

Classical poetry has always enjoyed prestige in Chinese literature and culture, but the political climate in postwar Taiwan reinforced its emblematic stature. For the Nationalist Party, to uphold the classical Chinese tradition was part of the justification for its claim to be the only legitimate government of China. A parallel case can be made of the state's preservation and promotion of the Peking opera, elevated to the status of "national drama" (guoju), as another "quintessential symbol of Chinese history and culture" (Guy 1996:2). There was no contradiction between giving literary prizes to anticommunist poetry in the modern form and granting a higher status to classical poetry. All evidence indicates that in the first decade or two of postwar Taiwan, the legitimacy crisis of modern poetry was far from over. Thus, to establish an identity, modern poetry had first to distinguish itself from classical poetry and second to find resources for publication and other related activities.

The standard history of modern poetry in Taiwan usually refers to the three major poetry societies as constituting the three legs of a tripod: the Modernist School, founded by Ji Xian in 1956 (preceded by *Modern Poetry Quarterly*, founded in 1953); the Blue Star, founded by Qin Zihao, Zhong Dingwen, Xia Jing, and others in 1954; and the Epoch, founded by Zhang Mo (1931–), Luo Fu (1928–), and Ya Xian (1932–) in 1954. In my view, the first played a leading role and deserves closer attention. More than any other journal or society, *Modern Poetry Quarterly* and the Modernist School brought about significant changes in the ecology of the poetry scene—through creative work, theoretical discourse, and related activities—and exerted a profound influence on contemporary and later poets.

According to Ji Xian, classical poetry was "in the court" and modern poetry was "in the wild." If classical poetry was a hobby in which the elites dabbled at leisure, modern poetry was a calling, requiring the poet's wholehearted dedication. Thus, Ji Xian advised young poets: "First of all, adopt a serious attitude toward writing and do some research on what constitutes New Poetry. . . . Don't pick up your pen hastily, and don't rush to publish your work!" (*Modern Poetry Quarterly* no. 3 [Aug. 1953]). An important function of *Modern Poetry Quarterly* and other privately funded poetry journals in the 1950s was to assert the independence of poetic art from other pursuits. In view of the disparity in social status between Old and New Poetry, modern poets emphasized that the only criteria applicable to poetry were those intrinsic and unique to the art form. Poetry was personified as God of Poetry (Shishen) (e.g., Peng Bangzhen's [1919–] "Definition of Poetry" ["Shi de dingyi"]). While equality and justice did not always exist in society, poets upheld these ideals in their work:

> In the world of poetry, all are equal. Whoever has talent can freely enter
> and stay with no strings attached. All that the great God of Poetry cares

about is whether a poem is good or bad. Whatever your social status is, whether you are rich and powerful, or poor and lowly . . . he really doesn't care. If your poetic talent is truly great, even if you are a peddler or servant, you will be treated like a guest of honor in his palace . . . on the other hand, if your poetic talent is mediocre and poor, even if you are an important official, you cannot receive his kindness.

(*Modern Poetry Quarterly* no. 15:81)

Emulating the Literary Revolution of 1917, Ji Xian declared a second revolution whose goal was to further modern poetry. Responding to the still frequent use of rhyme and regular form at the time, he made a sharp distinction between "poetry" and "song," rejecting the latter as a remnant of antiquated tradition. Also implicit in his discourse is the dissociation of modern poetry from state-endorsed, politically oriented verse, which closely resembled anticommunist songs. Once freed from the conventions of song, poetry is no longer bound by a predetermined form but is free to develop its own; the content determines the form, not the other way around. This idea opened up a wide vista for literary experimentation, including Lin Hengtai's concrete poetry and Jin Lian's "ciné-poèms."

The rise of prose poetry in the 1950s was therefore no accident. Although it was first introduced and experimented with by Lu Xun and Liu Bannong (1891–1934) in China in the 1920s, the genre was insignificant and virtually disappeared from the mainland after the 1930s. Among possible causes are the influence of the Crescent Poets, who advocated the "architecture" of form, and the outbreak of the Sino-Japanese War, which gave birth to a "literature of resistance" that included the heavily rhymed "street-corner poetry" and "poetry for recitation." The first major writer of prose poetry in modern Chinese history, Shang Qin (1930–), appeared in Taiwan in the 1950s. Influenced by French surrealism, Shang Qin celebrates the world of authenticity, innocence, and mystery, which lies just beyond the mundane world ruled by hypocrisy and conventional norms (M. Yeh 1996). His prose poetry from the 1950s and '60s has served as a model for later Taiwanese poets, most notably Su Shaolian (1949–) and Du Ye (1953–). This minor tradition of prose poetry in Taiwan constitutes yet another significant difference from mainland China (M. Yeh 2000).

Ji Xian and the Modernist School sought to instill in the younger generation a "professional" attitude—a spiritual identification with poetry that excluded all extrinsic concerns and motivations. The young Zheng Chouyu likens "the poet's profession" to running an inn in a vast desert that provides a haven for lonely travelers. He sings of the poet's genealogy in "Life in the Mountains" ("Shan ju"):

Displayed above is the poet's family tree.
Oh, the blood relation of wisdom needs extension.
So I carve transparent names deeply in the whole sky
And sing. Here alone and undaunted I can be high-sounding.
(translated by Shiu-Pang Almberg)

The high respect and seriousness accorded to poetry as art and the space pro-
vided for free expression by *Modern Poetry Quarterly* and other journals in the
1950s made possible a new generation of poets in postwar Taiwan. Many of
them were students, quite a few were servicemen, but with rare exceptions all
were outside the cultural establishment and came from the middle or lower-
middle economic strata. Although not explicitly defiant of authority, they cele-
brated individuality, even eccentricity.

Individuality was essential to asserting the independence of poetry from the
formulaic genre endorsed by the establishment on the one hand, and from the
superior-positioned classical style on the other. A third aspect of the social-
cultural milieu to which modern poetry reacted in the 1950s and 1960s was
popular culture, which modern poets saw as dominated by philistines and con-
sisting of commercialized art. Xiu Tao's (1934–) "The Newly Castrated" ("Xin
yan zhe"), published in *Modern Poetry Quarterly* in 1957, presents a succinct
but poignant picture:

When she told me the price for that Debussy
I became a castrated man
Helpless
I walked away
Though she still pressed me with her disdainful eyes
And drew *WM* on the glass counter with her breasts
(translated by Michelle Yeh)

The first-person narrator cannot even afford an album—probably a pirated
copy!—of classical music. When art runs up against the dollar sign, it has no
choice but surrender. As a metaphor, castration vividly captures the sense of
defeat and frustration that he experiences, but it goes further. The saleslady is
a perfect embodiment of society's values, which equate manhood with earning
power and money with success. The last two lines drive home the point, as
from behind the counter the saleslady seems to taunt the narrator with her
explicit sexuality as he walks away. The English letters "WM" pictographically
evoke her breasts; they are also the first letters of "woman" and "man." Thus,
the poem makes a sarcastic comment on society from the viewpoint of an
economically disadvantaged poet.

All of the above explains the recurrence of the image of the poet as solitary wanderer, rebel, eccentric, or even madman. Running through the work of the 1950s is the opposition between the singular "I" and the plural "They," based on vast differences in lifestyle and values. Understandably, many modern poets satirize conformity and empathize with those on the periphery, whether the poor and downtrodden or the faceless individual whose daily struggle and triumph define what is human. It is also in this context that we can understand the widespread interest in surrealism and other forms of the avant garde, which linked poetry and visual arts in a fruitful alliance in the 1950s and '60s. The radical approach to writing poetry parallels the fearless rebellion poets mounted against all conventions—social as well as literary. In their best work, poets such as Ya Xian, Shang Qin, Luo Fu, Lin Hengtai, and many others molded a language uniquely fit for their probe into the human condition, and their work has exerted a long-lasting influence on subsequent generations of poets.

The journals that nurtured many poets were all independently funded. *Modern Poetry Quarterly*, for example, was financed almost entirely by Ji Xian himself. Although subscriptions increased from five hundred in 1953 to two thousand by 1956, the journal was still hard-pressed to make ends meet. In the editor's postscript to issue 21 in 1958, Ji Xian could not help crying out: "Poverty is our Achilles' heel! . . . This issue came out late for the simple reason that I didn't have money to buy paper and pay for the printing costs. . . . As to why this issue was finally published, it's because I sold a ring of much sentimental value and a big bag of expensive books. I also pawned some winter clothes. In addition, a friend generously donated a few hundred dollars." Similarly, the three editors of the *Epoch Poetry Quarterly* took turns going to the pawnshop in order to keep their journal going.

Therefore, it is not surprising that when negotiating with the dominant discourse, the modern poetry movement in the '50s and '60s adopted a completely different tactic from its way of dealing with classical poetry. Confrontation or explicit defiance would not only carry serious political risks but also do little to help advance modern poetry. Given the fact that all cultural resources were in the hands of the establishment, many modern poets chose to participate in the anticommunist discourse and use the cultural capital they thus obtained to sustain their own poetry journals. In doing so, they transformed the literary field gradually. Ji Xian, for instance, repeatedly won awards from the Committee of Prizes in Chinese Literature and Art, in 1950, 1952, 1953, and 1954. In its inaugural issue *Epoch Poetry Quarterly* advocated the "new model of national poetry" and it devoted the fourth issue (October 1955) to "combat poetry." One of the editors, Ya Xian, received a second prize for long poems from the committee in 1956; he also won in a competition sponsored by the Department of Defense in July 1957. Other poets who were successful include Zheng Chouyu and Ye Shan (later known as Yang Mu).

But by the mid-1950s, modern poetry had made such headway that the Chinese Literature and Art Association and the Chinese Youth Writing Association, both official organs, joined private poetry societies in sponsoring poetry competitions. In 1955 Qin Zihao was one of the referees for a poetry competition sponsored by the Chinese Literature and Art Association. Among those who received the prizes (of NT$100 each) were Bai Qiu (1937–), Chui Heiming (1929–), Lin Ling (1938–), Sun Jiajun (1927–), Xu Kuang, and Peng Jie (1919–). Some of these young poets went on to enjoy long careers.

It is fair to say that the strategies modern poets used were highly successful. By redefining the nature of poetry and the image of the poet, modern poetry clearly distinguished itself from classical poetry. By participating in the official discourse of anticommunism, it was able to appropriate some of the cultural capital offered by the establishment and channel it into privately run poetry journals to develop the burgeoning field of modern poetry. Thus, despite the dominance of the official discourse, modern poetry was able to carve out a space for poets to pursue their art as individuals, relatively free from political intervention. This new space is best expressed as first, an ontologization of poetry (as a pure, spiritual pursuit); second, a self-awareness of the poet's inferior status and resulting compassion for the disadvantaged in society; and, finally, a radical individualism vis-à-vis the world represented by the establishment and popular culture. The introduction of this new conception of poetry changed the existing literary field and in turn generated new symbolic and cultural capital, which further solidified its position. By the mid-1960s, a mature modern poetry scene was firmly in place. Although classical poetry remained aloof, it no longer posed a major threat in terms of cultural resources.

By 1965, a number of active poets, such as Fang Si, Lin Ling, Ye Weilian (1937–), and Ye Shan, had left Taiwan to study abroad. Ya Xian had stopped writing poetry completely and begun what would be a long and illustrious career as an editor and journalist. In February 1964, *Modern Poetry Quarterly* folded after forty-five issues published over more than a decade. The founder and spiritual leader of the Blue Star Poetry Society, Qin Zihao, died of cancer in 1963. Except for an annual collection in 1964, the *Blue Star Poetry Page* (founded in 1959) ceased publication in June 1965 after seventy-three issues; it was not till 1971 that the next "annual" collection appeared. From 1961 to 1963 the *Epoch Poetry Journal* only published one issue per year. Although Grape Orchard Poetry Society (Putaoyuan shishe) was formed in 1962, it did not play a significant role on the poetry scene mainly due to the quality of the work published in its journal. In short, 1964–65 seems to mark a low point in modern poetry in Taiwan.

On March 8, 1964, five poets—Zhan Bing (1921–), Lin Hengtai, Huan Fu, Jin Lian, and Gu Bei (1938–)—gathered at Zhan Bing's home in Zhuolan to discuss starting a poetry society. They were inspired by the founding of *Taiwanese Literature and Art* (*Taiwan wenyi*), made possible through the persistent and skillful negotiation of Wu Zhuoliu, but at the same time they were frustrated that poetry would receive little attention in that new journal. So they decided to start a poetry journal of their own. Lin came up with the name that received unanimous support. They would call the new poetry society and journal "Li" ("Bamboo Hat") (Chen Qianwu 1989:382). "Crown" was the name of a popular literary monthly founded in February 1954; the contrast between the aristocratic associations of the crown and the rural connotations of the bamboo hat is obvious. With eight more poets joining the group, a bimonthly journal was launched in mid-June 1964; it has continued publication, almost always on time, ever since.

In its early days, from 1964 through the 1970s, *Bamboo Hat Poetry Journal* quite consciously carried on the modern poetry movement of the preceding decade. The letter of invitation undersigned by the founding members states:

> Although the poetry scene is somewhat lively, many poetry journals have not reached a satisfactory level. First, the selection of creative work is affected by personal connections; the sacred criterion of selection based on the work, not on the author, is yet to be established. Second, flattery and name-calling have taken the place of proper criticism and hampered progress on the poetry scene. In view of these weaknesses, we have decided to come forward resolutely to organize a serious, high-quality poetry journal in order to address the corruption on the poetry scene.
>
> (Zhao 1989:393)

As indicated by the essays and poems published therein, *Bamboo Hat* saw itself as a successor of Ji Xian and the Modernist School. The inaugural issue stated that postwar modern poetry had gone beyond the May Fourth tradition and rightly reflected the spirit of the time. In the second issue, Bai Qiu wrote an overview of the Taiwanese poetry scene, which begins: "The 'seed of fire' was brought over by Ji Xian. He was then joined by Zhong Dingwen and Qin Zihao. This is how the furnace was lit up" (1964:10). Priding themselves on being solitary rebels and members of the avant garde, many modern poets were less enthusiastic about Qin Zihao and the Blue Star Poetry Society's more conservative approach to poetry and were highly critical of Yu Guangzhong, whose traditionally flavored *Associations of the Lotus (Lian de lianxiang)* was published in 1964. Yu was regarded as retrograde for writing poetry in regular form that was reminiscent of mainland poetry of the 1920s and 1930s. (After 1964, however, Yu underwent a dramatic transformation into a "modernist.") Bamboo Hat emphasized pure poetry (i.e., poetry as an art devoted to experiments in language), criticized sentimental poetry (as opposed to "intellect," the foundation of modern poetry), and dissociated itself from popular culture (e.g., Chinese musicals, popular songs, American rock-and-roll). All of these were consistent with the modernist aesthetics of the 1950s and '60s.

No doubt, this resonance was partly due to personal ties between *Bamboo Hat* and *Modern Poetry Quarterly*. Lin Hengtai was closely associated with *Modern Poetry Quarterly* from its beginning. Bai Qiu began his career in the same journal. Huang Hesheng (1938–) was a former student of Ji Xian at Chenggong High School and contributed frequently to *Modern Poetry Quarterly*. Other contributors included Wu Yingtao and Jin Lian, who were now members of Bamboo Hat. Lin Zongyuan even served as the president of *Modern Poetry Quarterly* in 1959 before he joined the Bamboo Hat Poetry Society.

In terms of creativity, Lin Hengtai published some of his best work in *Bamboo Hat*, including reprinting the pair of poems titled "Scenery" (issue 4). These poems inspired an imitation by Rui Cun (pen name of Wu Yingtao) under the same title in the following issue. Others such as Lin Zongyuan, Jin Lian, and Bai Qiu also published bold experimental poems. Finally, in the area of translation, the manifestos of American imagism, French surrealism, Italian futurism, and German *Neue Sachlichkeit*, among others, were published in *Bamboo Hat*, although the journal did not necessarily endorse those positions.

Bamboo Hat made several important contributions to modern poetry in Taiwan. First, it provided extensive introductions to Japanese as well as Western poetry and poetics. Translation of foreign work was a salient feature of the journal, as indicated by the call for contributions, which lists the following categories:

1. Poetry of originality
2. Translation and introduction of modern poetry of foreign countries
3. Translation and introduction of the manifestos and basic theories of all poetic schools of foreign countries
4. Insightful poetic theory
5. Profound, fair-minded, sincere reviews of books of poetry
6. Correspondence with foreign poetry circles
7. Study and introduction of major foreign poets

Of the seven categories, four had to do with the introduction of non-Chinese poetry. The cosmopolitan breadth of the journal not only resonates with *Modern Poetry Quarterly* and others in the 1950s but also harks back to the very beginning of Taiwanese poetry in the 1920s and 1930s. Understandably, the facility in Japanese of many Bamboo Hat members allowed them to translate a wide range of Japanese writings, or writings in other languages via Japanese. Further, they were able to interact with contemporary Japanese poets directly. Their translations and personal exchanges broadened the scope of the poetry scene and enriched modern poetry in Taiwan.

Second, unlike the other poetry journals, *Bamboo Hat* also focused on literary history and criticism. Despite Ji Xian's lament in the early 1950s that there was no literary criticism in Taiwan, the situation did not seem to have improved much by the mid-1960s. *Bamboo Hat* repeatedly criticized the virtual absence of literary criticism; critics and scholars either blindly praised or blindly denigrated a work based on its superficial elements or place of origin. To combat such "corruption" of the poetry scene, *Bamboo Hat* devoted much space to practical criticism. Regularly featured columns provided literary history ("Shadow under the Bamboo Hat") and "group critique," where specific poems were selected for comments by a group, sometimes even several groups, of poets.

Finally, in contrast to the other poetry societies active in the postwar period, Bamboo Hat consisted (and still consists) almost exclusively of native Taiwanese poets. As indicated by the "group critique," it had a well-organized network all over the island. Although other poetry journals never excluded anyone based on geographic location, in both number and connectedness Bamboo Hat clearly stood out. With a shared linguistic and cultural background, the poets had a perspective on the early history of modern Taiwanese poetry that was not available under the Nationalist regime. In 1967 Lin Hengtai coined the by now classic term, "translingual generation," to describe those Taiwanese poets who wrote poetry in Japanese before they switched to Chinese. Equally important, Huan Fu traced the origins of Taiwanese poetry to both Japanese and May Fourth influences and established the notion of the "twin balls of roots" in 1980. The fact that none of the members was a mainland émigré was not made an issue until the 1980s (and then it became a highly politicized issue). In its original context, Huan Fu did not see the "twin balls of roots" as separate or conflicting but emphasized their "fusion" (*ronghe*). As Bai Qiu said in a seminar organized by the journal in 1982, "I think at the beginning Bamboo Hat did not try to raise nativist consciousness. [Members] wrote poetry based on their existential circumstances" (Bai Qiu 1989:260).

THE IDENTITY OF TAIWANESE POETRY

One of the topics that received much discussion in *Bamboo Hat* was the difficulty of reading modern poetry. This had been the main cause of much criticism, especially from outside poetry circles, throughout the 1950s and 1960s. Lin Hengtai rightly attributed the situation to the lack of qualified literary criticism and the common misunderstanding of the "methodology" and "critical nature" of modern poetry (*Bamboo Hat* no. 4). Although poets such as Wu Yingtao expressed concern that the obscure language of modern poetry seriously limited its readership and even caused its isolation from general readers, most poets in *Bamboo Hat* defended poetry as an experiment with language, no matter how radical. Bai Qiu, for instance, quoted Valéry as saying that "A poem would rather be read a thousand times by someone who understands it than be read by a thousand readers who don't" (*Bamboo Hat* no. 37).

But obscurity eventually led to the biggest debate on poetry in postwar Taiwan, triggered by a series of essays written in 1972 by John Kwan Terry (Guan Jieming, 1939–), a professor of Chinese descent who taught in the English Department at Singapore National University. Terry's criticism of modern poetry in Taiwan for having lost its Chinese identity in blindly imitating the West touched off an explosion of responses, the majority in agreement. Most notable are a special issue of the *Dragon Race Poetry Journal (Longzu shikan)* and a series of essays by Tang Wenbiao (1936–85), a poet and Ph.D. in mathematics from the University of Illinois-Urbana, in 1973. Although there are significant differences among the various views expressed, these essays reintroduced the binary oppositions that have been a constant undercurrent throughout the history of modern Chinese poetry: tradition and modernity, China and the West, nativism and cosmopolitanism. In his preface to the special issue of *Dragon Race*, the editor, Gao Shangqin (pen name of Gao Xinjiang, 1944–), summarized the debate this way: "To give an overview of the special issue on poetry criticism, we note in it a general tendency that readers and authors both demand an identity of modern poetry. In terms of time, they expect it to be connected properly with tradition; in terms of space, they expect it to correspond truthfully to reality" (Gao 1978:166).

The target of the debate is "modernist" poetry, which was identified with Ji Xian's Modernist School and reached an extreme with the Epoch Poetry Society, which had advocated surrealism from the late 1950s on. According to critics, such poetry lacked both Chineseness and social consciousness. Although Terry admitted, "The fate of Chinese literature is inextricably related to Western literature" (1978:139), he nevertheless rejected postwar modern poetry as a product of "cultural colonialism" (142) by the United States and Japan. Tang derided modernist writers as "cultural compradors" (1978:56). Accusing modern poetry of being formalistic, decadent, escapist, and nihilistic, they advocated realism over modernism and a return to the Chinese tradition over slavish imitation of the West. The debate in Taiwan preceded the comparable controversy over Misty Poetry in post-Mao China by nearly a decade; in both cases the obscurity of language that characterized "modernist" poetry was seen as a sign of decadent individualism, attributed to corruption by Western ideas.

It is beyond the scope of this essay to go into the critics' partial understanding or misunderstanding of both Western and Taiwanese modernism (M. Yeh 1998), but some glaring fallacies in their argument are worth pointing out. First of all, it is perfectly valid to criticize a poem for its lack of artistic merit. Proper criteria for judging poetry are, in fact, what modern poets, from *Modern Poetry Quar-*

terly to *Bamboo Hat*, tried to establish from the 1950s onward. However, to focus on some of the worst poems (whether by different poets or in one poet's *oeuvre*) in support of an argument gives an unbalanced view and does not do justice to modern poetry as a whole. Besides, while it is true that of all the poems written during this period, only a tiny percentage is outstanding, this can be said of poetry in any period, place, or style. Modernism claims no exclusive right to bad poems!

Further, although it is valid for critics to wish to broaden the base of readership for modern poetry, they only see the surface of the problem (i.e., most readers have problems understanding modern poetry) but not its root, which has to do with the paradigm shift resulting from the emergence of modern poetry in the 1910s and the concomitant need to educate the reading public.

A third fallacy of the criticism of modern poetry is that it equates subject matter with poetic style. To say that realism is better suited for expressing concerns of contemporary society than modernism represents a gross misunderstanding of the necessarily mediated nature of poetry. The social critique that underlies some of the best work from the 1950s and 1960s is completely ignored.

Finally, it is natural and healthy to revitalize the poetry scene periodically. When a movement peaks, it inevitably goes downhill. By the end of the 1960s, modern poetry had shown signs of lack of creativity and sincerity. The introduction of new ideas and new directions in the debate provided a much-needed impetus for the next phase of development. However, many critics fell into cultural purism or essentialism when they predicated their arguments on a rigid dichotomy of China versus the West, the native versus the foreign. In doing so, they denied the fact that "China" always already included and was inseparable from "the West." Ironically, when Terry called modern poetry "neither a donkey nor a horse" and when Tang disparagingly referred to it as a "hodgepodge" of the East and the West, they overlooked what is probably the most important source and strength of Taiwan's identity. The "real China" that they identified with inevitably repressed the transcultural, hybrid subjectivity of Taiwan.

The dual focus of the debate—Chinese tradition and contemporary social reality—reveals an acute identity crisis that is more national than literary. In the early 1970s, Taiwan suffered a series of setbacks in the international arena. In 1970–71, the dispute between China and Japan concerning the territorial rights over Diaoyutai (or Senkaku) Islets, a cluster of fishing islands in the East China Sea, led to widespread demonstrations against Japanese imperialism both in Taiwan and abroad. In the United States, the Protecting Diaoyutai Movement, abbreviated as "Bao Diao," owed much of its momentum and organization to graduate students who had come from Taiwan. Also in 1971, Taiwan, the seat of the Republic of China, withdrew from the United Nations under mounting pressure from the international community in support of the People's

Republic of China as the legitimate representative of China on the Security Council. This was followed a few months later by Richard Nixon's historic visit to the PRC and signing of the Shanghai Communiqué in February 1972, which paved the way for the resumption of diplomatic relations between the two powers after more than two decades. In the same year, Taiwan also terminated diplomatic relations with Japan, with which it had had close ties since 1895. The quick succession of setbacks invalidated the Guomindang's claim as the sole legitimate government of China, and the betrayal of former allies left people in Taiwan feeling isolated and bitter. The debate on modern poetry in the early 1970s can be seen as the eruption of the most recent identity crisis in Chinese history. The effort to raise nationalist consciousness in society through poetry served a political purpose more than a literary one.

But the tide could not be stemmed. The appeal to nationalism and social consciousness carried such self-evident moral authority and political urgency that the "modernist" poets under attack could hardly defend themselves; some changed their style decidedly while others simply remained silent. The rhetoric of nationalism and social realism is couched in two tropes derived from the world of plants and the human body. The former concentrates on the plant's growth, blossoming, fruit bearing, and, most important, rootedness. A literature that has lost its distinct national identity is compared to a plant that is uprooted and is bound to wither and die. Hence, the trope of plants evokes the idea of root-seeking and thus is an implicit critique of the metaphor that Ji Xian used in 1956 in his controversial manifesto of the Modernist School: "We believe that New Poetry is the result of horizontal transplantation, not vertical inheritance" (*Modern Poetry Quarterly* no. 13).

It is ironic that Ji Xian's metaphor of transplantation also denotes an organic process: once transplanted, the seedling adapts to the new environment, takes root, and grows and flourishes. However, the organic nature of literary and cultural transplantation was peremptorily ignored or denied by critics who insisted on dichotomizing modernism and Chineseness. Instead of seeing Western (or other) influences as an "organic" part of modern Chinese poetry, they only emphasized unrootedness. Modern poetry in postwar Taiwan was seen as having "lost the earth where its roots are planted" (Gao 1978:167), and it was but a short step from the word "transplantation" (*yizhi* in Chinese) to "colonization" (*zhimin*). A few years later, Lin Hengtai would employ a related metaphor to defend modernist poetry. Using the hybridization of fruit and vegetables as an analogy, he said: "To refuse influence is to refuse growth" (*Bamboo Hat* no. 100 [Dec. 1980]). Pointing out the fallacy of insisting on irreconcilable differences between modernism and nativism, Lin advised a more tolerant and open-minded approach to poetry.

The root-seeking trend was adumbrated by the founding of the Dragon Race Poetry Club in 1971. The name invokes the myth that Chinese people descended from the dragon, an ancient symbol of imperial strength and male power (the dragon being the archetype of Yang energy in the cosmology based on the *Book of Changes*). The famous manifesto of the Dragon Race Poetry Club, written by Chen Fangming (1947–) and Shi Shanji (1945–), reads: "We strike our own gong, beat our own drum, and dance with our own dragon" (Chen Fangming 1983:200). The images refer to a national cultural activity: the traditional dragon dance in celebration of the lunar New Year. Some of the other poetry clubs that emerged in the wake of the debate came up with names that were equally explicit about their identification with the traditional and the local, such as Grass Root (Caogen), Great Earth (Dadi), and Green Earth (Ludi).

The other trope widely used in the debate is the human body. Parallel to the contrast between rootedness and rootlessness is the dichotomy between health and sickness, life and death. Just as a plant cannot survive long when severed from its roots, so a man cannot be healthy and strong when he is separated from his cultural roots and social reality. Words often used to describe modern poetry include "pathological" (*bingtai*), "deformed" (*jixing*), "anemic" (*pinxie*), "handicapped" (*canfei*), and "dead" (*siwang*). Weakness and illness are further linked to human sexuality, including impotence and masturbation, which appeared in the writings of such critics as Chen Yingzhen (1937–), Yu Tiancong (1935–), and Tang Wenbiao.

Finally, sexuality relates to gender, and here we see the intersection of nationalism and sexism, of cultural politics and gender politics. Critics often attribute such qualities as strength, independence, and dignity to the male, while their opposites—weakness, dependence, and submissiveness—are associated with the female. The reification of gender is pervasive in the debate. Critics identify modern poetry either with male impotency and castration or with the female. To the extent that the male stands for subjectivity, the female has none. To the extent that those critics desired a strong cultural identity for Taiwan, they unconsciously subscribed to, and thus reinforced, traditional gender stereotypes.

Written in October 1975, Su Shaolian's "Mixed Blood" ("Hunxieer") represents a thoughtful reflection on the issue of identity, which underscored the debate three years earlier (page 312). Like his surrealist predecessor Shang Qin, Su creates a flowing narrative that presents a situation of everyday life in a matter-of-fact tone: one morning the poet goes to the local police station to look at the household registry and spots his own name in it. Also like Shang Qin, Su punctures the smooth textual fabric with tantalizing details which, by creating a disjuncture in meaning, achieve the effect of defamiliarization and mystery. Through these devices, the poet suggests that there is a deeper reality lying just beyond the threshold of what we normally accept.

In the poem, the poet has two names: "my name" and "another name"; the latter is "Su Shaolian," but "my name" is never revealed. Further, the names that huddle in the registry are described as "*zu*," meaning "race" or "ethnicity." Not only are the names like a people, but they are of "unknown skin color." Contrary to conventions, we are told that "Su Shaolian" is not the poet's real name, that it is only a substanceless being that attaches itself to "my name, my nationality, my heritage, my linage." The poem suggests that names are arbitrary labels, not reliable indicators of personal identity. Further, although the poet acknowledges the tie, established through time, between a man's name and his familial, cultural, and national origin, what is kept unrevealed throughout the poem is his "real name," which cannot be identified by any of these common indexes. The "self" remains more elusive and intangible, thus perhaps truer and freer, than can be defined by any conventional markers (even the most basic marker, skin color, is rejected by the poet). Written in the mid-1970s, "Mixed Blood" inadvertently foresaw the growing importance and contentiousness of the issue of identity in the following decades.

With its call for return to cultural roots and local reality, the debate on modern poetry in the early 1970s was a precursor of the large-scale Native Literature Movement from 1977 to 1979, which advocated native consciousness in literary representations (Wang 1980). The same axes of tension ran through the movement, although poetry played a negligible role. As the political opposition movement grew in Taiwan, the demand for a Taiwanese identity in contradistinction to a Chinese identity began to be expressed openly, culminating in demonstrations known as the Formosa Incident (Meilidao shijian) in Gaoxiong at the end of 1979. Whereas in the early 1970s native consciousness meant unequivocally Chinese consciousness, a split into the "China complex" and the "Taiwan complex" took place as the decade drew to a close. The double foci of the earlier debate on modern poetry—Chineseness and contemporary social reality—were gradually replaced by a single focus on Taiwanese reality in the 1980s. A poetry oriented toward rediscovering and re-presenting the history of Taiwan was clearly on the ascent.

Nativist poetics found a powerful expression in "political poetry." According to Li Qin'an, the term was coined in 1983, when a few literary journals, such as *Taiwan Literature and Art* and the poetry journal *A Gathering in the Sunshine* (*Yangguang xiaoji*), started new sections called "political poetry" (Wu 1984:77). Also in 1983, the poetry anthology published by the nativist Avant-Garde Press included a group of poems dealing with political topics that had thitherto been taboo; they ranged from the February 28 Incident of 1947 to the Formosa Incident of December 1979 and the politically motivated murders of the Lin family in 1980. Although veiled expressions of protest could be found before the 1980s (e.g., Wu Sheng's "Animal Spirit Tablet," page 288), taking advantage of the liberalizing trend under President Chiang Ching-kuo, many poets tried to rediscover Taiwan's history that had been either suppressed or distorted by the Nationalist regime. Going beyond one-dimensional, sentimental social grievance, some of the political poetry in the 1980s succeeded in supporting idealism with art. Liu Kexiang's (1957–) "Posthumous Sons" ("Yifuzi"), written in 1983, is a fine example:

1890 . . .

1915, posthumous son, Remember-China Chen,
Who liked to speak in Chinese, died in the fighting at Tapani

1951, posthumous son, Establish-Taiwan Chen,
Who liked to speak in Taiwanese, took his own life on a small
    island

1980, posthumous son, Unity Chen,
Who liked to speak in English, succumbed to illness in a foreign
    land

2010, posthumous son . . .

                              (translated by Andrea Lingenfelter)

The poem provides a sweeping perspective on Taiwanese history. Language, like history, religion, or lifestyle, is a defining aspect of cultural identity. Through shared language, a community takes on a shared identity, or at least is in a better position to imagine one. In Liu's poem, the linguistic transition, first from Chinese to Taiwanese, then from Taiwanese to English, suggests the complexity and elusiveness of Taiwan's identity and its ongoing quest. The use of the posthumous son as the central metaphor points directly to Taiwan's sufferings as a result of various political conflicts in the twentieth century. "Tapani" in line 3 refers to the largest uprising of Taiwanese people during the Japanese occupation period. Led by Yu Qingfang and known as the Xilai Convent Incident, it involved such places as Tapani, Daqiuyuan, and Hejuezai, all near the city of Tainan, in July–August 1915. The uprising was brutally suppressed by the Japanese ruler, who executed not only Yu and his followers but also many residents of Tapani. According to the official Chinese account, "more than 10,000 local Taiwanese lost their lives" (*The Republic of China Yearbook of 1999* 1999:72).

That one of the martyrs in the anticolonial uprising bears the name "Nianzhong" ("Remember-China") conjures up a family history of loyalty to China and resistance against Japan. A posthumous son, Nianzhong followed in his father's footsteps, identified with China as his motherland (as suggested by the fact that he loved to speak Chinese rather than the colonizer's language), and took part in the local uprising. Also like his father, he died for a patriotic cause. The irony, as the poem continues, is that if the first posthumous son died for China, shortly after 1945 China changed from the past object of loyalty to the present target of resistance. In the second stanza, the year 1951 is probably associated with two major historical events: the February 28 Incident of 1947 and the White Terror under the GMD beginning in the 1950s. In the repressive atmosphere of postwar Taiwan, as I have mentioned, Hokkien (or Taiwanese) was forbidden in public and stigmatized. Those who voiced criticisms of the regime and articulated a native Taiwanese consciousness suffered political persecution, such as being sent to the infamous Green Island (Lüdao), an offshore islet for imprisoning political dissidents. Could it be that the posthumous son Litai ("Establish-Taiwan") was a political prisoner and committed suicide because he could not endure the bleak conditions there?

If the above tragedies suggest Taiwan's thwarted quest for cultural identity, the poem takes a sharp turn in the fourth stanza. By 1980 opposition to the Nationalist government could no longer be successfully contained and the popular demand for democratization no longer dismissed. Soon after Chiang Kai-shek passed away in 1975, opposition was organized under the name *Dangwai*, meaning "outside the [Nationalist] Party," and in 1978 the League of Dangwai Election Campaigns was launched, posing a serious challenge to the ruling party at local elections. Although the 1979 Formosa Incident was suppressed and led to the arrests and indictments of many leading dissidents, the trials were made public in the media and the opposition views articulated there won widespread sympathy. A positive outcome of the incident was that the government was pressured into holding free elections at the national level at the end of 1980, which further consolidated the opposition and heightened nativist consciousness. Pluralization and democratization, once started, could not be reversed.

In light of the historical circumstances, the fourth stanza strikes a sarcastic note, implicitly criticizing those who have moved permanently to foreign countries. The motivation behind immigration is intimated by the name *Heyi*, which means "Unity." It alludes to the heated contention between those for Taiwan's eventual unification with China and those for Taiwan's independence. The fact that the posthumous son lives in an English-speaking country, most likely the United States or Canada, suggests that he belongs to the former camp. Further, that he likes to speak English and lives for the rest of his life away from Taiwan makes a wry comment on the loss of native identity, whether Chinese or Taiwanese.

It is important to note that the poem is written in a pseudo-historiographical style. As in an official chronicle, the language is formal, terse, and unembellished. When we look more closely, however, the poem reveals meticulous art. Parallelism is the major device used, as seen in the parallel dates (1915/1951, 1890/1980), places (China/Taiwan, Taiwan/U.S.), languages (Chinese/Japanese, Chinese/Taiwanese, Chinese/English), and names. Perfect parallelism underscores contrasts as well as similarities among the various phases of Taiwanese history. The open ending intimates the uncertainty of the future, as Taiwan continues its quest for cultural identity.

The exposés and contemplations of repressed history in the early 1980s signaled the emergence of what Jiao Tong calls an "oppositional poetics" (*fandui shixue*) (Ye Zhenfu 1996:470). Political poetry represented an attempt to give voice to the disenfranchised and the oppressed, and it inspired a wide range of perspectives from the margins of the society that eventually went beyond politics in a narrow sense. These new voices addressed such topics as the plight of the aborigines, the devastation of the environment, the degraded living conditions of GMD veterans, child prostitution, and gender inequality. The tendency continued into the 1990s, encompassing an ever-broadening scope of concerns (e.g., discrimination against homosexuals). The change of the official name for the aborigines from "mountain people" (*shandiren*) to "indigenous residents" (*yuanzhumin*) in 1984 is an apt emblem of this collective consciousness. In his own way Mona Neng (1956–) recalls what has been forgotten and retrieves what was lost:

> From "raw barbarians" to "mountain compatriots"
> Our name
> Was gradually forgotten in a corner of the History of Taiwan
> To stop wandering on our own land
> We must first bring back our name, our dignity.
>
> (translated by Michelle Yeh)

FRONTIER TAIWAN

A decade of literary movements and political upheavals left indelible marks on modern poetry in the 1970s and '80s, and some of the impact extended into the 1990s. First, it set off a trend of neoclassical revival. Beginning with Yang Mu, Yu Guangzhong, and Luo Fu and continuing with Yang Ze (1954–), Luo Zhicheng (1955–), and Wen Ruian (1954–), poets much more consciously looked to the classical tradition for subject matter, allusions, idiom, imagery, and even form (e.g., modern versions of the "quatrain"). But if neoclassicism took place mostly at the thematic or stylistic level, a more profound impact was evident in the changing conception of poetry. Concern for contemporary society was for a long time viewed as the proper domain of poetry, and realism as the appropriate vehicle for expressing such concern. As the identity of the island vis-à-vis China was pushed more and more to the center of Taiwan's political and cultural agenda, poetry was encouraged, perhaps even expected, to express "the Taiwan spirit." Much work appeared in the 1980s and 1990s that either empathized with the Taiwanese people (see Liu Kexiang's "Young Revolutionaries" ["Geming Qingnian"] and "Showa Grass" ["Zhaohe cao"]) or critiqued the Guomindang (see Huan Fu's "Find an Honorific for Mosquitoes" ["Gei wenzi qu ge rongyu de mingzi ba"] and "Excuse My Rudeness" ["Shu wo maomei"]). Poetry written in Hokkien also began to thrive.

The poetry scene has changed dramatically since the 1950s. Whereas in that decade modern poets were engaged in defending New Poetry against classical verse and anticommunist discourse, neither poses a threat anymore. Whereas in the 1950s poets established the independence of poetry as a serious art form clearly dissociated from popular culture, since the 1980s they have sought to reintegrate poetry into society, either as social conscience as extolled by the nativist movement, or in alignment with the ever-growing consumer market. Neither path has taken modern poetry very far, however. Narrowly nativist or political poetry is often little more than angry venting or self-righteous declarations. Such direct comments on Taiwan's social or political issues have neither made poetry more relevant to the masses than before nor been effective in bringing about changes in society.

In contrast to the separation of poetry from song emphasized in the 1950s and '60s, beginning in the mid-1970s and throughout the 1980s there was a movement to combine modern poetry with music, to turn modern poems into melodious songs. Although a fair number of poems have made a successful crossover, the practice has not helped expand the readership for modern poetry in general. After all, songs, especially popular songs, follow certain formulas to which most poetry cannot be made to conform. Without a firm grasp of the generic differences between modern poems and popular songs, poets rarely make good lyricists. A few exceptions are Xia Yu (1956–), Lu Hanxiu (1958–), and Chen Kehua (1961–). Xia Yu's case illustrates the point well. Although she is a highly successful lyricist of popular songs in Taiwan, so far she has not made any of her own poems into songs.

Other strategies for popularizing poetry since the 1970s are associated with the media-dominated Information Age. As early as 1975, the Grass Roots Poetry Society, founded by Luo Qing (1948–), Zhang Xianghua (1939–), and others, announced one of its four principles as follows: "We realize that popularization and professionalization of poetry are two sides of the same coin. The distinction depends on subject matter and artistic devices. We hope to see a balanced expression of both without leaning toward one or the other" (Xiang Yang 1984:59). Multimedia presentations of poetry, whose major advocates include Luo Qing and Du Shisan (1950–), incorporate a broad spectrum of audiovisual forms, such as recordings, dance, mimes, drama, photography, and video. Despite various attempts to make modern poetry accessible or available to the public, it still appeals only to a select audience. Granted, a few poets have done well in the market, most notably Xi Murong (1943–) in the 1980s (later in mainland China as well). The reason, I submit, is not because her poetry inherits "realism's respect for the mundane world and its reflection of the hearts of the masses" (Lin Qiyang 1999:86), but rather because of its familiar, traditionally flavored language, romantic subject matter, and comfortable sentimentality. Its commercial success proves ever more convincingly that there is a gaping gulf between modern poetry and popular culture.

Finally, from an economic point of view, poets in the 1950s struggling to keep journals alive by pawning personal possessions has become a legend in the affluent society of Taiwan in the 1980s and 1990s. A new generation of poets has grown up to be professors (Luo Qing, Jian Zhengzhen [1950–   ], Bai Ling, Du Ye), doctors (Chen Kehua, Zhuang Yu'an [1959–   ]), or editors and publishers (Chen Yizhi [1953–   ], Yang Ze, Xiang Yang, Luo Zhicheng, Jiao Tong, Chu Anmin [1957–   ], Liu Kexiang, Xu Huizhi [1966–   ]).

As Taiwan became more urbanized—with 70 percent of the population living in urban areas, Taipei and Gaoxiong being the most populated cities—"homeland" has more and more come to mean the urban jungle, with all the ailments of late twentieth-century civilization: overpopulation, traffic congestion, air pollution and noise pollution, destruction of the ecosystem, threats of nuclear catastrophes, and so on. Many poets express their concern for the severed tie between humans and nature. Bai Ling's "Spring's Brief Visit to Taipei" ("Chuntian lai Taibei xiaozhu") sees the disconnectedness as the result of rapid urbanization. Shang Qin's "Rooster" ("Ji") juxtaposes fast-food chickens and crowing roosters. Human ingenuity has invented numerous artificial means to replace nature that far exceed nature in efficiency, such as mass-produced meats and fluorescent lights. But the artificial way of life breaks the natural cycle of day and night, life and death, and in the end brings harm to the human imagination:

> Under the artificial light
> there is neither dream
> nor dawn
>
>   (translated by Michelle Yeh)

In Chinese, the word for "imagination" (*xiangxiang*) is closely related to the word "elephant" (*xiang*). In Hong Hong's (1964–) "City Zoo" ("Chengshi dongwuyuan"), a giant elephant passes through the city, yet no one sees it as it

> gently touches
> every single thing
> (unbeknownst to us),
> departs,
> but leaves
> its imprint on the walls;
>
> disappears,
> and we forget it.

Later, we find its carcass
atop the weather station
and realize it's been standing there all along,
waiting for its kind.
                    (translated by Mike O'Connor)

The elephant's effort to get the city folk to notice its existence fails. The death of the elephant symbolizes the death of the imagination, the spontaneous passion of human beings for beauty and life expressed through creativity. The theme of the animal fables that comprise the sequence is poignantly summed up in these lines: "a small wonder in life / disappears without trace."

Small wonders are indeed hard to come by in an age in which the media turn individuals into consumers who all have the same tastes and chase after the same fads. This is the object of satire in Chen Kehua's "On TV After Dinner" ("Zai wancan hou de dianshi shang," pages 445–447). Modern life has taken on a most elaborate, impressive form but has little individuality and substance. The motif of the "hollow man" finds poignant expressions in Lin Yu's (1956–) "Name Cards" ("Mingpian," page 422) and Chen Kehua's "Bathroom" ("Yushi," page 445). In "Leaving Work" ("Xiaban"), Sun Weimin (1959–) turns the routine of a white-collar urban commuter into a powerful analogy of the isolation and indifference of modern men and women:

The commuters, as is customary, sit in their own darkness, chests rising and falling. Some take out portable cassette players to isolate themselves from the gentle, grasslike swaying of the other passengers' heads
                    (translated by Mike O'Connor)

If for Ling Yu (1952–) we are acrobats doing a balancing act between meaning and the void, for Xu Huizhi we are all fallen angels, too caught up in our desires to see the way to salvation. Erotic desire, in particular, epitomizes all desire; it is the source of happiness and sorrow, beauty and ugliness. The fact that religion, especially Buddhism, figures so prominently in the poetry of the 1990s reflects the flourishing of Buddhism and other religions in Taiwan in the past two decades and, more important, attests to the collective human quest for life's meaning at the turn of the millennium. Whether in the Buddha or Aung San Suu Kyi, Xu sees selfless idealism as perhaps the only path to emancipation and salvation.

Despite the significant transformation of the poetry scene and the broadening of the scope of poetry since the 1970s, there is an unbroken tradition in Taiwan in the poets' common concern for humanity and nature, desire for expression of individual creativity, and, above all, continuing explorations of the medium of poetry—language—whether symbolist, modernist, surrealist, realist, or postmodernist. It is through the interminable process of creation, reaction, counterreaction, interaction, and transformation from the 1920s to the present that modern Chinese poetry in Taiwan has emerged as a unique presence in world literature. To deny that history is to deny the subjectivity of this poetry. Thus, contrary to the view that Taiwan's modern poetry did not have a subjectivity until the nativist movement in the 1970s and '80s, I see a vital tradition from the 1920s to the present, made stronger by its ever-renewed ability to indigenize the alien and nativize the foreign.

Self-identity is relational by definition; the need to define oneself arises when one becomes aware of an Other. The resumption of contact between Taiwan and China since 1986 has given many Taiwanese an opportunity to visit the mainland, some for the first time, others in an emotional return after nearly four decades. Regardless of their background or reason for visiting, they get to see "China" for themselves. Invariably, such contact brings a heightened awareness of the irreducible differences that separate Taiwan from mainland China linguistically, socially, politically, and culturally. Chen Yizhi's "Broken-down Family Tree" ("Polan de jiapu"), written in 1988, presents an occasion for such comparison:

> beard pulled into loose strands, head wrapped in a scarf the
>   ancient way
> feet splash-splattered with mud—he's my cousin
> in thirty years he's never left the remote mountainside he calls
>   home
> on this occasion, he accompanies me across the river to the
>   county township
> muttering to himself as he taps the stem of his pipe:
> *there's no life in this place anymore*
> when the steamboat turns
> he coughs violently
>
> *there's no life in this place*
> the waist-thick banyan trees have been cut down
> the pitch-black mountain forest is gone
> the stone-paved road to the outside world has been dug up
> yes, and after forty years there's still no electricity
> the old people of the village are left with more and more
>   forgetting
> having no memories to hold on to
>
> in the winter of '49, his father was tossed into a nameless gully
> in '53, his brother died east of the Yalu River
> all three children born over the years
> are illiterate

in the Famine Years, they gnawed on the bark of loquat trees,
  nibbled on tupa vine
and when wolfing hunger howled in their bellies
  they filled them with lumps of white earth
and so managed to survive

inside the Sweet Potato Restaurant down by the river
I order him finless eel and a plate of stir-fried pork kidneys
he shows me our broken-down family tree
and points to a line:
"From time immemorial, all things have been one with
  Heaven . . . ."

(translated by Simon Patton)

The syntax of the first two lines is uncommon in modern Chinese. The subject of the sentence is not revealed until we have come to the end of three long descriptive phrases. In the Chinese original, the first-person narrator's cousin is referred to as "that man." Further, the first two lines use a language and images that are unfamiliar to Taiwan. Through these devices, the poem hints at the distance between the narrator and his long-separate cousin on the mainland. This psychological distancing continues in the account, in the next two stanzas, of the trials and tribulations of the family under the Communist regime, where he refers to other characters as belonging to the cousin but not to him (e.g., "his father" rather than "my uncle"). Although the narrator is sympathetic, he can only see the mainland from an outsider's point of view. He and his cousin belong to a "broken family tree" that has branched out in two different directions that grow farther and farther apart. The "China" of 1949 is not the "China" of 1999, and the "China" that left the mainland and came to Taiwan half a century ago has become an integral part of "Taiwan" today.

Cultural differences have been a major theme of much poetry in Taiwan since the 1980s, as the issue of Taiwan's identity has been at the forefront of political and cultural discussions. One immediately noticeable difference between Taiwan and China is language. While mainland China uses simplified Chinese characters, Taiwan has preserved the traditional written language. In terms of the spoken language, the Mandarin Chinese brought over by the Nationalist government in 1945 and the mix of various dialects on a small island over half a century have produced a language distinct from that on the mainland in idiom, formal and colloquial expressions, intonation, and, above all, pronunciation. The standard pronunciation on the mainland, based on Beijingese and referred to as "the common language" (*Putonghua*), requires much tongue curling, whereas in Taiwan, where southern dialects dominate, tongue curling is used much less and sometimes simply abandoned. The difference is somewhat comparable to that between "r" and "l" in American English. This significant linguistic difference is the subject of Chen Li's 1995 poem "Movement of No Tongue-Curling" ("Bu juanshe yundong").

The poem begins with three analogies: tongue curling is mentioned in the same breath with wearing a bow tie, putting on airs, and standing on ceremony. There are four tongue-curling sounds in Mandarin; trying to make them is likened to wearing jewelry that makes one uncomfortable. In other words, to curl the tongue is pretentious and unnatural. Further, in Chinese slang, "that word" (*na hua er*) is a euphemism for the phallus, but the poem equates it with tongue-curling sounds and says: "This word, that word / One can do without it" (Chen Li 1995:116). The poem gets more humorous as it introduces a tongue-twister in classical Chinese, which consists of forty-eight characters and whose meaning depends on a clear distinction between tongue-curling and non-tongue-curling near-homonyms. This is followed by a "Taiwanese" reading, which disregards this distinction and pronounces all the words without tongue curling. The poem concludes by defending the Taiwanese linguistic practice:

> . . . A good
> Tongue-twister is like a good epic
> There can only be one
>
> No constipation
> No turgidity
> No denying history
> No rejecting non-tongue-curling
>
> For example, I am a long-time *lesident* of Taiwan
> For example, the Three People's *Plinciples* is the way to unify
>   China
>
> (translated by Michelle Yeh)

When Taiwanese people come into contact with those who speak Putonghua, especially those in North China, their style of pronunciation gives away their identity and sometimes makes them objects of mockery. Chen recognizes the difference and even admits that there can only be one "good tongue-twister." In other words, when you don't curl your tongue, you ruin the classic tongue-twister. Yet he also rightly attributes the situation to historical factors. To expect Taiwanese people to speak the same way as those who speak Putonghua is to "deny history." Besides, he finds it pretentious and even sickening when a Taiwanese tries to imitate what sounds to him like exaggerated tongue curling.

The subtle gender identities in the poem are also significant. Chen equates Taiwan with the female, who does not have "that word"—the phallus *and* tongue curling—and China with the boastful male. The political overtones are clear. Chen rejects the stronger China as the norm and believes that Taiwan, though weaker, does not need to conform or aspire to that norm. Hence, the poet wants to start a "movement" to not curl the tongue.

How does a small island assert cultural distinction from a continent? This theme runs throughout Chen's 1995 book of poetry, *The Edge of the Island* (*Daoyu bianyuan*). The title itself suggests that the poet consciously assumes a marginal position as he reflects on the past, present, and future of Taiwan. As he says in the afterword: "Since 1988 when I resumed creative writing, there has been a clear trajectory of a quest for the history of the land under my feet" (Chen Li 1995:204). At a personal level, Chen is literally on the periphery; Hualian, a medium-sized city on the east coast where the poet was born and has lived most of his life, is peripheral vis-à-vis Taipei, the political, economic, and cultural center of the island. At a more general level, he is also contemplating the peripheral position of Taiwan vis-à-vis mainland China. Besides "The Movement of No Tongue-Curling," a powerful example is "A Lesson in Ventriloquy" ("Fuyuke").

腹語課

惡勿物務誤悟鎢塢鷲蕎噁岰蕙瓢瘩迼垭芴
軏杌婺鷲壑汭迕邆鎏矾籿阢靰焐唲烏焐殟扤屼
（我是溫柔的……）
屼扤焐殟靰阢籿矾鎏邆迕汭壑鷲婺杌軏
芴垭迼瘩瓢蕙岰噁蕎鷲塢鎢悟誤務物勿惡

（我是溫柔的……）

惡餓俄鄂厄過鍔扼鱷蕙餕蛋搞圖虦貁貁
顎呃愕噩軛阽鶍壑諤蚯砒砈櫨鍾岋瑘杭鰐
莩咢啞崿搕詻闗頏搕揭頏闗詻搕崿啞咢莩
齵杝瑘岋蚯鍾櫨砈砒蚯諤壑鶍軛阽顎呃愕噩
貁貁圖搞蛋餕蕙鱷扼鍔過厄鄂俄餓惡

而且善良……）

UʊUUUʊUUUʊUUʊUUUʊʊU
UUUʊUUUʊUUUʊUUUʊʊU
(I am gentle . . .)
UʊʊUUUʊʊUUUUUʊUUʊ
UʊUUUUʊUUʊUUʊUUʊU
(I am gentle . . .)

OOOooOOOOOOOOOoOO
OOoOoOOOOoOOoOoOOo
OoOOoOOoOOoOOOOOoO
oOOoOoOOoOOOOoOoOO
OooOOOOOooOOoOOO
(and kind . . .)

At first reading, the poem may seem no more than a language game, perhaps inspired and made possible by Chinese computer software (which allows one to punch in a romanization and get a long list of homonymous characters in varying tones). Lines 1–2 put together thirty-six different characters in "u" sound in the fourth tone, which are then mirror-imaged in lines 4–5. The long catalog of characters is broken up only by the inserted parenthesized line in a different typeface: "*I am gentle . . . .*" In the second stanza, there are forty-four characters in "o" sound in the fourth tone. Echoing the first stanza, the two columns of characters here (almost) form a mirror image of each other. The parenthesized line 12 completes the sentence, which begins in fragments in lines 3 and 6: "*I am gentle . . . I am gentle . . . and kind . . . .*"

What are we to make of this? First, we note the sharp contrast in typography. Lines 1–2, 4–5, and 7–11 each form a rectangular block, with a small corner of the third rectangle cut off by a single parenthesis in line 11. In terms of size, these rectangles take up much more space and look much larger and heavier than the parenthesized lines, which are less than a third of the rectangles. Second, the rectangles and the parenthesized lines have different typefaces. Also in terms of form, there is perfect symmetry between lines 1–2 and lines 4–5, but less than perfect symmetry between lines 7–8–9 and 9–10–11. Symmetry is conspicuously absent in the parenthesized lines; in fact the poet uses several devices to avoid formal symmetry in these fragments, including an odd rather than even number of lines and the repetition of "I am gentle . . ." twice in contrast to only one "and kind," thus creating a 2–1 asymmetry in the complete sentence (lines 3, 6, 12). All the line numbers of the sentence are also multiples of three, another odd number. Finally, there are the asymmetrical punctuation marks and the odd position of the parenthesis at the end of line 11.

In addition to form, there is a most dramatic contrast in sound. Whereas "u" and "o" are both fourth tone, reading thirty-six u's and forty-four o's in a row creates a hard, monotonous, unnatural sound effect. (Can we imagine the poem at a poetry reading?) In contrast to the long strings of heavy sounds, the short sentence consisting of a few simple, mono- or bisyllabic words, with an undulating cadence (due to a fair distribution of all four tones), sounds much lighter, softer, more melodious and pleasing.

Further, in terms of syntax, the thirty-six u's and forty-four o's do not form a phrase or unified image, much less a meaningful sentence. In fact, most of these characters are obscure or archaic words hardly ever used in daily speech or even in modern writing. Grouped together in this particular typographical arrangement, they create an extreme effect of defamiliarization: a Chinese reader may recognize all the words but think they look strange on the page. In contrast, although the words in the parentheses are small in number, they form a complete sentence, with the subject "I," the copula "am," and the predicate "gentle and kind." Despite its minimalist syntactic structure, this is a perfect sentence.

Finally, we note the semantic structure of the poem. The first word of both stanzas is the same character with two different pronunciations ("u" and "o") and meanings ("u" means "to loathe or dislike" and "o" means "evil"). Both words have negative connotations. Again, the contrast between them and the words in parentheses—"gentle" and "kind"—is obvious.

Why is the poem called "A Lesson in Ventriloquy"? Taken literally, the poem illustrates the difficulty for someone who is a novice in the art of ventriloquy and can only utter a single, unintelligible sound at a time. As if stuttering, he means to say "I am gentle . . ."—"I" pronounced as "wo" in Chinese—but only manages to utter "wu." If we understand the poem metaphorically, as the art of speaking without opening the mouth, ventriloquy connotes a discrepancy between appearance and reality, between outer form and inner substance, between "what you see" and "what you hear." Discrepancy clearly exists between the "u" and "o" blocks and the parenthesized fragments in the poem. The blocks have an unpleasing, strange appearance, but the sentence reveals what lies in the heart, which is gentleness and kindness. If this interpretation is valid, then the poem reiterates the universal theme of an ugly person with a kind heart. More specifically, the poem echoes a hit song in Taiwan from the early 1990s, sung by Zhao Chuan and called "I Am Ugly But I Am Gentle" ("Wo hen chou keshi wo hen wenrou"). This may not be a coincidence; the song lyrics were written by a fellow Taiwanese poet, Xia Yu, whose work Chen Li is surely familiar with.

I argue, however, that the poem has yet another meaning. In ventriloquy, one manages to make a sound without opening the mouth. In other words, the contrast between the "u" and "o" blocks and the slim parenthesized sentence implies a lopsided relationship, with the former dominant and the latter being dominated. The poem is an imaginative embodiment of the nativist poetics that Chen has been developing in his recent work. The heavy, harsh, monotonous strings of "u" and "o" sounds, with their exact, hence rigid, symmetry and their dominant presence on the page, are associated with mainland China, whose hegemony seems so overpowering but also so alien to a much smaller, weaker Taiwan. Positioned on the periphery and under disadvantaged circumstances, Taiwan nevertheless refuses to be silent and learns to have a voice of its own. The parenthesis in line 5 of stanza 2 fulfills two important functions: it interrupts the catalog of "o" sounds, thus putting an end to the perfect symmetry begun in the first stanza, and it completes the short sentence, also begun in the first stanza. Hinging on a single parenthesis, the intervention of the voice affirms a modest yet irrefutable presence against an overpowering monolith.

Along with "The Movement of No Tongue-Curling," "A Lesson in Ventriloquy" epitomizes a positive nativist poetics that envisions an open, diverse, and cosmopolitan Taiwan—in short, a cultural and artistic frontier. As an island, Taiwan is fully aware of its marginal position vis-à-vis the mainland. At the same time, however, the poet proudly affirms Taiwan's dignity as a self-sufficient world—complete, beautiful, and perfect in its own way. In contrast to the jarring u and o noises, Taiwan is music to his ear. A perfect union of form and content, "A Lesson in Ventriloquy" attests to the ultimate concern of the poet with poetic art rather than with message, political or otherwise. The bold experiment in form and language evident in Chen's recent work suggests that "periphery" has yet another meaning that goes beyond the personal and the political. On the cover of *The Edge of the Island*, we see a map of Taiwan filled in with words: the title of the book and the words "nativism + the world" (*bentu yu shijie*) and "nativism + the avant garde" (*bentu yu qianwei*), are not only repeated many times but also highlighted in different colors. Together, these phrases represent the poet's creative ideal, which is to combine nativism with a cosmopolitan, multicultural vision on the one hand and with the avant garde on the other. "Avant garde" refers to both the philosophical underpinnings and the artistic intention of the poems.

The poet's avant-gardism is in sharp contrast to some forms of nativism in Taiwan, which tend to pitch the native and local against the international and cosmopolitan, or, in more recent years, the "native Taiwanese" or *Taiwanren*—Chinese people living in Taiwan prior to 1945—against the "mainlander" or *Waishengren*—newer mainland émigrés who came to the island between 1945 and 1949. Instead, Chen emphasizes multiplicity over singularity, mutual respect and acceptance rather than privileging one subethnic group over another. The ethnic, linguistic, and cultural roots of Taiwan include at least the Portuguese, the Dutch, the Japanese, Han Chinese, and the indigenous. "The Song of the Island—For the Children of Taiwan" ("Daoyu zhi ge—gei Taiwan de haizi") begins with these lines:

The name of the island is Taiwan
Taiwan is a palette
Tongues of different shapes
let out sounds of different colors
and mix them into a colorful, beautiful island
                    (translated by Michelle Yeh)

The poem ends with a list of twenty Chinese dialects and the languages of the indigenous tribes. For the poet, Taiwan has not one but many mother tongues.

Cataloguing is a device also used in "Flying Over the Island" ("Daoyu feixing"), in which the names of all ninety-five mountains of Taiwan are juxtaposed. Some of the names are Chinese in origin, but many more are aboriginal. Personified as former classmates at primary school, the mountains gather for a class reunion and are getting ready for a group photo:

I hear them calling me together
"Keke'erbao, come down quick
You are late!"
Those standing, sitting, squatting there
Whose names I almost can't remember

They are all there, together
In the frame
Like a miniature map
                    (translated by Michelle Yeh)

The poet's own words best sum up the notion of multiple cultural roots:

Taiwan is an island full of vitality, a combination of different ethnic groups and different cultural elements—more than the so-called 'four major ethnic groups'—indigenous, Hokkien, Hakka, and mainlander. As early as the seventeenth century, Taiwan was a global stage. The Spanish came, the Portuguese passed through, the Dutch colonized it, the Japanese ruled it . . . together they have formed the uniqueness of Taiwan: a vitality born of continuous blending and tolerance. Naturally there are some pains or conflicts, but in the final analysis it is magnificently moving.

                                        (Chen Li 1995:205)

These words aptly characterize modern Chinese poetry in Taiwan, which represents a synthesis of heterogeneous forces and contending visions: aboriginal and Han Chinese, Chinese and Japanese, traditional and modern, local and global, "mainlander" and "Taiwanese," Taiwanese and Chinese. Out of this historical and ongoing process has emerged the distinct identity of Taiwanese poetry.

WORKS CITED

Amoeba Poetry Society, ed. (1985). *Selected Poems of Amoeba Poetry Society* (Amiba shixuan). Taipei: Qianwei chubanshe.

Chen Fangming. (1983). *Poetry and Reality* (Shi he xianshi). Taipei: Hongfan shudian, 1977; 3rd ed., 1983.

Chen Li. (1995). *The Edge of the Island* (Daoyu bianyuan). Taipei: Huangguan chubanshe.

Chen Shaoting. (1977). *A Short History of the New Taiwanese Literature Movement* (Taiwan xinwenxue yundong jianshi). Taipei: Lianjing chubanshe.

Chen Zhaoying. (1998). *Taiwanese Literature and the Nativization Movement* (Taiwan wenxue yu bentuhua yundong). Taipei: Zhengzhong shuju.

Chou Wen-yao. (1996). "The Kōminka Movement in Taiwan and Korea: Comparisons and Interpretations." In *The Japanese Wartime Empire, 1931–1945*, Peter Duus et al., eds. Princeton: Princeton University Press, 40–68.

Clark, John D. (1971). *Formosa*. Shanghai: Shanghai Mercury Office, 1896; reprint, Taipei: Chang Wen Publishing Company.

Ge Xianning and Shangguan Yu. (1965). *Half a Century of Chinese Poetry* (Wushi nian lai de Zhongguo shige). Taipei: Zhengzhong shuju.

Goddard, W. G. (1966). *Formosa: A Study in Chinese History*. East Lansing: Michigan State University Press.

Gold, Thomas B. (1994). "Civil Society and Taiwan's Quest for Identity." In *Cultural Change in Postwar Taiwan*, Stevan Harrell and Huang Chün-chieh, eds. Boulder: Westview Press, 47–68.

Guy, Nancy A. (1996). *Peking Opera and Politics in Post-1949 Taiwan*. Ph.D. diss., University of Pittsburgh.

Hu Shi. (1991). *Discourse on Poetry by Hu Shi* (Hu Shi shihua). Chengdu: Sichuan wenyi chubanshe.

Kuo Ting-yee. (1973). "The Internal Development and Modernization of Taiwan, 1863–1891." In *Taiwan in Modern Times*, Paul K.T. Sih, ed. Jamaica, N.Y.: St. John's University Press, 171–240.

Lai Tse-han, Ramon H. Myers, and Wei Wou. (1991). *A Tragic Beginning: The Taiwan Uprising of February 28, 1947*. Stanford: Stanford University Press.

Lee, Thomas H.C. (1996). "Chinese Education and Intellectuals in Postwar Taiwan." In *Postwar Taiwan in Historical Perspective*, Chün-chieh Huang and Feng-fu Tsao, eds. Baltimore: University of Maryland Press, 135–57.

Li Nanheng, ed. (1979). *Selected Historical Archives: New Taiwanese Literature Under Japanese Occupation* (Wenxian ziliao xuanji: Riju xia Taiwan xin wenxue). Taipei: Mingtan chubanshe.

Lin Hengtai. (1989). "A Retrospect and Prospect on Bamboo Hat" ("Li de huigu yu zhanwang"). In *The Rise of the Taiwanese Spirit* (Taiwan jingshen de jueqi), Zheng Jiongming, ed. Gaoxiong: Wenxuejie zazhi, 384–89.

Lin Qiyang. "The Corridor and the Map: A Bird's-Eye-View of Modern Poetry in Taiwan" ("Changlang yu ditu: Taiwan xinshi fengchao de suyuan yu niaokan"). *Chung-wai Literary Monthly* 28(1)(1999):70–112.

Liu Jihui. (2000). "Visual Translations of Surrealism" ("Chaoxianshi de shijue fanyi"). In *Orphan and Goddess: Symptomatic Readings of Cultural Signs of Negative Writing* (Guer, nushen: fumian shuxie wenhua fuhao de zhengzhuangshi yuedu). Taipei: Lixu wenhua shiye, 260–95.

Peng Ruijin. (1991). *Forty Years of New Literature Movements in Taiwan* (Taiwan xin wenxue yundong sishinian). Taipei: Zili wanbao chubanshe.

———. (1995). "On a Literary Debate in Taiwan around 1949" ("Ji yijiusijiu qianhou de yichang Taiwan wenxue lunzhan"). In *Explorations of Taiwanese Literature* (Taiwan wenxue tansuo). Taipei: Qianwei chubanshe, 221–39.

The Republic of China Yearbook of 1999. (1999). Taipei: Government Information Office.

Shepherd, John. (1993). *Statecraft and Political Economy on the Taiwan Frontier, 1600–1800.* Stanford: Stanford University Press.

Wang, Jing. (1980). "Taiwan *hsiang-t'u* Literature: Perspectives in the Evolution of a Literary Moment." In *Chinese Fiction from Taiwan: Critical Perspectives*, Jeannette L. Faurot, ed. Bloomington: Indiana University Press, 43–70.

Winckler, Edwin A. (1994). "Cultural Policy on Postwar Taiwan." In *Cultural Changes in Postwar Taiwan*, Stevan Harrel and Chün-chieh Huang, eds. Boulder: Westview Press, 22–46.

Wu Sheng. (1984). *Selected Taiwanese Poetry of 1983* (1983 Taiwan shixuan). Taipei: Qianwei chubanshe.

Xiang Yang. (1985). "On the Tendencies in Taiwanese Modern Poetry of the 1970s" ("Qishi niandai Taiwan xiandaishi fengchao shi lun"). In *Selected Essays of Literary Criticism of 1984* (Qishisan nian wenxue piping xuan), Chen Xinghui, ed. Taipei: Erya chubanshe, 93–142.

Xu Wangyun. (1990). "Final Battle with Time: Forty Years of Struggle of Modern Poetry Journals in Taiwan" ("Yu shijian juezhan: Taiwan xinshikan sishinian fendou shulue"). *Chung-wai Literary Monthly* 19 (5) (October): 106–26.

Yang Ziqiao. (1996). "Hokkien Poetry in the Japanese Occupation Period" ("Riju shidai de Taiyu shi"). In *Essays on the History of Taiwanese Modern Poetry* (Taiwan xiandaishi shilun), Wenxun zazhishe, ed. Taipei: Wenxun zazhishe, 79–90.

Ye Di. (1996). "The Surrealist Movement on Taiwan's Poetry Scene During the Japanese Occupation Period" ("Riju shidai Taiwan shitan de chaoxianshi zhuyi yundong"). In *Essays on the History of Taiwanese Modern Poetry* (Taiwan xiandaishi shilun), Wenxun zazhishe, ed. Taipei: Wenxun zazhishe, 21–34.

Ye Shitao. (1990). *Marching Toward Taiwanese Literature* (Zouxiang Taiwan wenxue). Taipei: Zili wanbaoshe.

Ye Zhenfu (Jiao Tong). (1996). "A Street-corner Movement of Modern Poetry—On Political Poetry in Taiwan in the 1980s" ("Yichang xiandaishi de jietou yundong—

shilun Taiwan bashi niandai de zhengzhishi"). In *Essays on the History of Taiwanese Modern Poetry* (Taiwan xiandaishi shilun), Wenxun zazhishe, ed. Taipei: Wenxun zazhishe, 459–73.

Yeh, Michelle (1991). *Modern Chinese Poetry: Theory and Practice Since 1917*. New Haven: Yale University Press.

———. (1994). Introduction to *Anthology of Modern Chinese Poetry*. New Haven: Yale University Press, 1992; paperback edition, 1994.

———. (1996). " 'Variant Keys' and 'Omni-Vision': A Study of Shang Qin." *Modern Chinese Literature* 9(2) (Fall): 327–68.

Yeh, Michelle (under Xi Mi). (1998). "The Debate on Modern Poetry in Taiwan: On 'An Incomplete Revolution' " ("Taiwan xiandaishi lunzhan: zailun 'yichang wei-wancheng de geming' "). *Chinese Literature* (Guowen tiandi) 13(10) (March): 72–81.

Yeh, Michelle. (2000). "From Surrealism to Nature Poetics: Prose Poetry from Taiwan." *Journal of Modern Literature in Chinese* 3(2) (January):119–56.

Ying Fenghuang. (1985). *A Chronology of Major Events on the Literary Scene of Postwar Taiwan* (Guangfu hou Taiwan diqu wentan dashi jiyao). Taipei: Xingzhengyuan wenhua jianshe weiyuanhui.

Zhang Mo. (1992). *Bibliography of Modern Poetry in Taiwan (1949–1991)* (Taiwan xian-daishi bianmu). Taipei: Erya chubanshe.

Zhang Wojun. (1979). "The Terrible Literary Scene on Taiwan" ("Zaogao de Taiwan wenxuejie"). In *Selected Historical Archives: New Taiwanese Literature Under Jap-anese Occupation* (Wenxian ziliao xuanji: Riju xia Taiwan xin wenxue), Li Nan-heng, ed. Taipei: Mingtan chubanshe, 63–66.

Zhao Tianyi. (1989). "Emerging from the Thorny Path: Retrospect and Prospect of *Bamboo Hat* on Its One Hundredth Anniversary" ("Cong jingji de tujing zou chu-lai: Li baiqi de huigu yu zhanwang"). In *The Rise of the Taiwanese Spirit* (Taiwan jingshen de jueqi), Zheng Jiongming, ed. Gaoxiong: Wenxuejie zazhi, 390–99.

Zhao Zhidi, ed. (1978). *A Survey of Modern Literature* (Xiandai wenxue de kaocha). Taipei: Yuanjing chubanshe, 1976; 2nd ed., 1978.

Zheng Liangwei. (1990). *Six Poets of Poetry in Taiwanese* (Taiyushi liu jia xuan). Taipei: Qianwei chubanshe.

楊華

YANG HUA

(1906–36)

Yang Hua is the pen name of Yang Xianda (Yang Hsien-ta), who was born into a poor family in Pingdong County in southern Taiwan and earned a living by teaching at private schools.

Yang's first poems were published in *Taiwanese People's Journal* in 1926 and his "Petit Poems" and "Lamplight" received prizes from that newspaper. During his lifetime he published three books of poetry and fiction. He was arrested in 1927 for violating the "public security law" imposed by the Japanese colonial government. While in prison, he wrote *Black Tide*, which contains fifty-three short poems in Chinese, under the pen name Yang Qiren. Out of work and money, Yang lived in a slum and became ill. Before a call for help to the literary community appeared in *New Taiwanese Literature*, he hanged himself in 1936.

BLACK TIDE
(seven selections)

9   Iron window!
     We have met too late!
     When we first met, a few moments of silence,
     Filled with endless sorrow.

15   Great wind!
      Don't scare people with your rustling,
      My little brother wants to sleep.

20   The narcissus is cherished,
      Planted as an offering in a porcelain pot of clear water;
      Yet she wipes her mouth and sneers
      At the lotus blossom thriving on its own in the mud.

25   Toyed with.
      Humiliated.
      How many times now?
      Though I cannot well remember,
      Of what use is it to remember well?

30   Each tragic wail of people harried by life—
      Are they bramble thorns
      Or sharp points of a snowflake-like sword?—
      Pierces my heart.

47   The flying eagle is hungry,
      Pacing the sky, it wants to swallow the stars and planets.

51   I want to free my soul from sorrow, to awaken with tears
      People's sweet dreams of love!
      I want to squeeze out my heart from the clutches of despair,
          to fill up
      The breasts of those youths who have lost their hearts.

(1927)
(translated by Kirk A. Denton)

HEARTSTRINGS
(two selections)

34   A bee dies drunk on the flowered path,
      Falling petals flutter and bury his "shell"—
      Ah, what a fine tomb of love.

45   How frightening!
      The moonlight envelops the thin shadow of the old willow,
      In the middle of the night, raindrops on broken lotus pads.

(1932)
(translated by Kirk A. Denton)

TAWNY COTTAGES

Dogs bark at guests
Mother hens call the chicks
Two or three tawny cottages
Four or five green weeping willows
Unadorned
Simple and bare
   A classical painting
   A verse of modern poetry

(published 1932)
(translated by Michelle Yeh)

SAD SONG OF THE FEMALE WORKER

Stars sparse, winds light,
Limpid moonlight shining upon her,
She rubs her face and wipes her eyes,
Thinking the day has dawned.
Daylight is work time
Don't delay, be quick, put on your coat.
Go! go! go!
She hurries to the textile factory,
But the iron gate is locked tight and she can't get in,
And now she knows the moon tricked her.
To return—the moon is sinking in the west, she's afraid she'll be
   late;

To stay—no breakfast for her, an empty stomach is all she'll have.
All is quiet, no one walks the road.
    Cold and desolate, swaying wild grass,
    Rustling wind, piercing her limbs,
    Sparse trees, the moon hangs in the treetops.
She waits and waits, but the iron gate won't open,
Gusts of frosty wind like icy water,
Oh, cold, so cold!
She hunches herself, unable to bear it much longer,
Weary and tired from waiting,
Waiting till the moon falls and the rooster crows.

(1932)

(translated by Kirk A. Denton)

楊熾昌

YANG CHICHANG

(1908–94)

Born in Tainan in southwestern Taiwan, Yang Chichang (Yang Ch'ih-ch'ang) graduated from the middle school in 1929 and studied in Japan from 1930 to 1933, upon his father's death. For most of his life he worked as a journalist in his home country.

Yang published his first poem in a school magazine in Taiwan in 1928. While a student of Japanese literature in Japan, he befriended Neo-Perceptionist writers, joined several poetry societies, and published two books of poetry in Japanese in 1931 and 1932, respectively. Of the many pen names under which he wrote, Shuiyinping was the most frequently used and best known.

In 1935 Yang founded *Le Moulin* Poetry Society with Li Zhangrui, Lin Yongxiu, Zhang Liangdian, and three Japanese poets. The name *Le Moulin* ("Windmill") was inspired partly by the French theater and partly by the common sight of windmills in Tainan. They published a poetry journal under the same name, which folded after four issues. *Le Moulin* advocated surrealism in contrast to the mainstream of realism at the time and was criticized for this reason.

In 1979 Yang published a book of collected poems, *Burning Cheeks*, which was translated from Japanese to Chinese by the poet Huan Fu in 1989 and by Ye Di in 1995. In addition to poetry, Yang published fiction, literary criticism (on Chinese, Japanese, and Western literature), and essays.

ROUGE AND LIPS

The air in the room is as deep as the bottom of a well
Her long gown rolled up to her panties
Misato caresses her curvaceous leg with a white hand
The pipe's sound, jazz, the smell of sweaty armpits, and. . . .
Awakening from a dream, I see a note: "Bye-bye" signed "M"
Rose-colored rouge, a lipstick in its case
Consciousness, defeated, flows somberly by

(1934)
(translated by John Balcom)

THE NUN

Duanduan, a young nun, opens the window.
The boundless night is growing steadily. Duanduan stretches out
her white arms and folds them tightly to her bosom. In the fearful
nighttime air, the Buddha on the altar smiles solemnly. Duanduan
awakens and grows excited. Quiet shadows; the lamps burn all night
long.

Frightened by the order of the night, Duanduan walks down the
illusory path of sex. Why aren't my breasts as lovely as those of other
young women? Why do my eyes reflect only a forgotten color. . . .

A red glass lamp continues burning. A greenish bronze clock dis-
turbs a cold heart. The main hall of the convent is as cold as a
parking lot.
In the reddish shadows, the idol moves.
The sword of Weituo, the temple guardian, flashes. The eighteenth
Arhat sits astride a fantastic tiger. Duanduan puts her palms to-
gether, feels faint, and swoons.

At the tolling of the bell at dawn, Duanduan gets up. The incense
emits fragrance. Sitting upright and looking straight ahead, Duan-
duan weeps. The sutras are chanted.

—O, Mother, Mother
Duanduan offers her virginity to the gods.

(1934)
(translated by John Balcom)

BURNING CHEEKS

In the flax-colored sunset
The gloves of the falling leaves dance
On my chest my cheeks
The wind warms itself in my pocket

The autumn mist
Sheaths the streetlights in soft petals
Together hate and regret
Flicker in a smile
Cheeks burn with loneliness

The patterned groundcover the name of which I've forgotten
Listens closely to the echo in a shell
A sand dune close by
Pities its own desolation

(1935)
(translated by John Balcom)

VEINS AND BUTTERFLIES

A gray tranquility beats in the breath of Spring
Roses shed their petals in a rose garden
Under the window, a young girl's love,
    quartz, and a specimen of the heart's
Melancholy
I play an organ as blue tears fall from my eyes

The beret's pitiful wound
The cicadas cry in the garden
A young girl lifts her veined hands at sunset

An old-fashioned corpse hangs in the wood behind the
    sanatorium
The butterfly embroidered in the folds of her blue skirt is
    flying . . .

(1935)
(translated by John Balcom)

AUTUMN SEA

On the liquid emerald of the sea
The sounds of the gulls' wings carry poetry

And fly to the window of my heart
But the green venetian blinds will never open again

Words are embroidered in the corner of a handkerchief
Crabs climb round the edge of my memory

In a rowboat's wake on the sea
Autumn colors the bored sky

I cast my hook and line in the afternoon
Catching futile time

(1935)
(translated by John Balcom)

TRAVELOGUE

Following a flock of sheep into a hawk-colored basin
Playing my flute
In the distance I hear the clip-clop of a horse's hooves
An open two-wheeled cart goes by
Headed for Parnassus, or so its white plaque says
An offering to Pan an ancient amphitheater
The antique music is a dissonant leisure land
On the street of countless flower poems and
Shining oats, eating grapes, I step over

The idle tools of a forsaken garden, tracking
The farmer's footprints

(1936)
(translated by John Balcom)

PALE SONG

In the antique sky
Moonless memories lie buried in snow-white flowers
In the seasonal wind
My poems melt one by one
Crickets cry everywhere beneath the window
Pale is the wounded soul's look
An organ plays at dusk
Scattering my poems on the wind leaving no trace
Butterflies drift
In the music of
Sickly leaves
Fluttering with fear of the whites of a suicide's eyes
I am infected by the scenery

(1936)
(translated by John Balcom)

RUINED CITY: *TAINAN QUI DORT*

1. *Dawn*

For white terror
Crimson lips emit a blood-curdling scream
Early in the morning, the wind grows still, playing dead
My feverish body is covered with bloody wounds

2. *An Attitude Toward Life*

The sun breathes into the branch tips of the trees
At night the flying moon indulges itself without sleeping
A thought slides from my body and spirit
Crosses the Strait, challenging the sky, and on a pale
Night wind flies toward
The gravestone of youth

3. *Ritual Song*

Ritual instruments
The sketch of many stars plus the song of dancing flowers
Gray brain matter dreaming of a no-man's land of dementia
Soaking wet in a ray of light like a rainbow

4. *Ruined City*

People who sign their names on the defeated surface of the earth
Blow whistles, hollow shells
Sing of ancient history, land, home, and
Trees, they all love aromatic meditations
O, dusk when autumn butterflies fly!
For a prostitute singing a barcarolle
The lament of home is pale

(1936)
(translated by John Balcom)

LOVE SONG

No matter how my heart aches
I'll never sing a song of love again
Even though it's been three years and ten

But still my song turns to love
Even as my youthful cheeks do fade
And wrinkles about my eyes have lately strayed

The wind blows
Distant roses shed faint odors through the air
As spring's footsteps nearer draw
The warmth in the land grows . . .

Butterflies skim the air languidly
All the cicadas go chirr-chirr
The gravestone—well, that is history!

(1938)
(translated by John Balcom)

SEA OF FLOWERS

Flowers and flowers
Rain down without pity
Fearfully anxious, hypocritical eyes
A woman dead among the petals!
The landscape murders expression and a pure thought
Becomes high-priced consumption
In the prism of a flower
A pale-skinned aesthetic
Leads to a brilliant tragedy

O, the sea!
O, flowers drifting on the sea!
Dancing wildly
In the spindrift at the site of an ancient city
Wet is the flower's spirit, a song on boorish lips
Spurting blood
Fruit of the Holy Spirit born of desolation
Celebrated by the fossil of solemn misfortune . . .
O, the flowers amassed
All forgotten, they rot

(1939)
(translated by John Balcom)

覃子豪

QIN ZIHAO

(1912–63)

Qin Zhi, who wrote under the pen name Qin Zihao (Ch'in Tzu-hao), was of the minority Miao ethnicity and a native of Guanghan, Sichuan. While a student at Sino-French University in Beijing from 1932 to 1935, he started publishing poems and was widely exposed to Western poetry. From 1935 to 1937 he studied economics and political science at Central University in Tokyo. After returning to China, he worked as a journalist in the military, from which he was honorably discharged in 1943. On a business trip to Taiwan in 1945, he was unable to return to the mainland due to the worsening civil war. Separated from his wife and child, he lived on the island till he died of cancer in 1963.

Qin was one of the most respected and influential figures on the poetry scene in Taiwan in the 1950s and '60s. He edited many poetry journals and poetry columns in newspapers, taught poetry courses at the Correspondence School of Chinese Literature and Art, founded the Blue Star Poetry Society, and served as a mentor to many young, aspiring poets. His complete poetry and critical essays were published posthumously.

DESERT WIND

Desert wind causes the heart of youth to age
Under the sun I chase after the shadows of my own dreams

Dream shadows fade on the distant horizon
Hope is forever buried in the bleak suburbs

In the suburbs not a bird sings
All that's left is a hushed, pale twilight

At midnight, a prisoner in an insane asylum
I portray the sweetness of life

(1934)
(translated by Michelle Yeh)

REMEMBERING

I often sink my memories
Into the bottom of a deep ocean
Yet on this sleepless night
I want to dredge up long-gone memories
From those forgotten depths

Memories are pearls
Memories are corals
The happiest memories swim
Like schools of parti-colored fish
Among ink-green seaweed

(early 1950s)
(translated by Jeanne Tai)

SEASHELLS (I)

Cocteau once said
His ears are seashells
Filled with ocean sounds
I say
Seashells are my ears

I have countless ears
Listening to the ocean's secrets

(1952)
(translated by Jeanne Tai)

GALLERY

Beyond the gallery windows wildflowers wave
    their powdery white heads
Autumn lets fall a dirge with its falling leaves
Thinking back on summer's pitiless noon hour
Like a black round fan the moon blocked out the sun's radiance
As you disappeared into the gallery's black drapes

The match's flame burned blue, staining the darkness yellow
A life blazed away, but still no sight of your final radiance
Your unfinished portrait
Ruined by brushstrokes gone awry in the gloom

Mona Lisa's smile, that I did not keep
Though a gallery's worth of mysteries remains
Venus's torso, still radiating brilliance
Beethoven's death mask, miserable in its deathlessness
Helen, brimming with tears, has gone back to Greece
I did not die by the Spartan king's cold steel
The pardoned remain behind
In eternal servitude

In the gallery, whether I am lying, squatting, or standing
A body whose psyche has been rent asunder
Pale as a stone statue from ancient Greece
    wild-haired and sightless

(published 1962)
(translated by Jeanne Tai)

BLACK NARCISSUS

Whence have you come
A fortuitous turn, a chance encounter
Not to be awaited, nor watched for
On the shores of midday dreams

I first met the Black Narcissus in your eyes
Its gleaming reflection
Wiped away my sleepy bewilderment

Second nature, not something to be captured
Profound beyond imagining
My imaginary Black Narcissus
I wish to become a devotee of that ultimate pureness
Yet already I have dissolved into sheer limpidity

Golden stamens, glistening with wondrous words
Is it an abstruse announcement, releasing my troubles
Into the dawn in your eyes?
A pure, limpid place
Only to be chanced upon, not sought
Black Narcissus, water nymph
Growing in Lethe's languid swirls

(published 1962)
(translated by Jeanne Tai)

HAIR

In the secluded room, the night turns thick like your hair
Shadows on the wall stand out like reliefs
Mountain nymphs and sea sprites
Hide in your thick hair
The hour of bliss germinates in your smile

Sprites dancing on the Muses' strings on Parnassus
Naiads frolicking in the waters of the ancient Aegean Sea
Now all hide in the mysterious depths of your hair
Holding their breath
My breath like a breeze wafts through your tresses
Listening to your heart, like a slight tremor in the earth's core

Up there on the wall is my fragmented shadow
I can make out the contemporary sad countenance of the
Flying Dutchman, adrift in the twentieth century
He will cremate the oars
Bury them in the dense stillness of your hair

And with the merry sprites
Listen to your heartbeats foretelling a good omen of death

(1962)
(translated by Jeanne Tai)

SEASHELLS (II)

Seashells, Neptune's temples
When starlight knocks at midnight
    the temple doors open
And there at the edge of the sea
    a shell calls out your name—
Ah! Beautiful daughter of Neptune

Like a shell, my house has no rafters
Like a shell, my house is small
My door opens to the azure sky
The vista rolls out, unhurriedly
    to the limitless empyrean
Through my window, night after night
    the moon and stars come calling

The sea is inside, telling a story about Neptune
Music flows, you are asleep in the sea
Asleep in the sea, the reflection of your light
    like a rainbow
Revealed in the mirror's resplendent surface
Trembling, I bow down and worship
Your forty black roses
And one red camellia

Says the sea, come float in me
Says the earth, come weigh on me
Yet here we are
Beyond space, beyond time

The lines on a shell no longer mark
    morning and evening tides
Numbers have returned to the primordial,
    the recondite

This place where we are is an alien realm
So, come float in me, says the sea
And a shell calls out your name

(published 1962)
(translated by Jeanne Tai)

紀弦

JI XIAN

(1913–   )

Ji Xian (Chi Hsien) is the pen name of Lu Yu, who was born in Hebei Province but spent his childhood in Yangzhou, which he regards as his home. He graduated from Soochow Art Academy in 1933. In 1936 he went to Japan to study painting, returning to China the following year. During the Sino-Japanese War (1937–45), Ji Xian lived under harsh circumstances in various places, including Wuhan, Hong Kong (where he worked as an editor for the *Citizen's Daily*), and Shanghai. In 1948 he moved to Taiwan with his family; he taught for twenty-six years at Chenggong High School in Taipei. He retired in 1974 and immigrated to the United States in 1976. He lives with his wife and continues to write poetry in Milbrae, California.

Ji Xian started writing at the age of sixteen. Under the pen name Louis, he befriended such poets as Dai Wangshu, Shi Zhecun, Xu Chi, and Du Heng in the 1930s, contributed to *Les Contemporains*, and founded various poetry journals. In Taiwan he created the *Modern Poetry Quarterly* in 1953, which served as a fertile breeding ground for a new generation of poets. In 1956 he founded the Modernist School and announced "Six Tenets," the second of which states that modern Chinese poetry is the product of "horizontal transplantation" rather than "vertical inheritance." In other words, foreign—especially Anglo-European—poetry rather than the Chinese literary tradition was the dominant influence on modern Chinese poetry. Throughout the 1950s and

'60s Ji Xian was a controversial figure, engaged in many debates on or beyond the poetry scene. There is no doubt, however, that he was instrumental in promoting modern poetry in postwar Taiwan. Through his charisma and polemical ideas, he influenced generations of poets and left an indelible imprint on literary history.

CITY IN FLAMES

Looking through windows of your soul,
Into its darkest recesses,
I see a city in flames, no one coming to the rescue
Only a tide of naked madmen.

I hear a sound pierce through that boundless maelstrom
Of my name, name of the lover, name of the enemy,
Names of the dead and living unnumbered.

When I answer in hushed voice
"Yes, I am here,"
I too become a fearsome city in flames.

(1936)
(translated by Denis Mair)

TO THE MAYBE MAN

Expanding and still expanding,
On top of that exploding and exploding,
An inconceivable spiral!
A spiral beyond conceiving!

On the strength of your intuition,
Your innate ability,
Maybe Man,
You pull it out of the air.
And please give me answers;
Have them be correct ones.
In the jottings of your notebook,
Write down:
The X to the Nth power of life and other inscrutable symbols.

Then we say good-bye.
Do not cry and do not linger.

When there is no more magic
And there is no God,
When all heavenly bodies have been flattened,
And icthyological specimens begin to swim,

Then, my Maybe Man,
We will have a happy reunion,
On the most dangerous edge of a planet that looks like a clock.
By that time, oh my Maybe Man,
Will you still remember how to play the mandolin?
I don't know;
Perhaps my throat has gone mute already,
No longer able to sing a waltz.

Yet we are joined into one body,
And with the speed of horses, we run,
Flailing eight pairs of futurist legs,
Casting shadows on a hard, cold ice cap that has no bounds.

                                                    (1936)
                                    (translated by Denis Mair)

SONG OF TIME NO. 2

Lie down,
Let the cavalcade of time
Go galloping
Across the plain
Of my frail chest.
I keep silent,
And hand over
All my infant dreams
For them to carry away,
Because this calvalcade
Having neither enemy forces
Nor friendly forces,
Is an inconceivable calvalcade.

                                                    (1936)
                                    (translated by Denis Mair)

MY PAGODA-SHAPED PLAN

I must use all the atoms I am made of,
My miniscule life,
And my giant heart,
To complete my pagoda-shaped plan;
Then I will stand at the apex of a cone,

Smoking strong plug tobacco and thinking,
What is more, with a genuine voice, a serene voice,
A dreamy voice,
I will declare to all contemporaries and future generations,
To all green lovers and cats,
To all mysterious telescopes,
My pagoda-shaped plan.

(1938)
(translated by Denis Mair)

STAR-PLUCKING YOUTH

The star-plucking youth
Takes a fall.

The deep blue sky laughs at him.
The great earth laughs at him.
Newspaper reporters
Bring out unbearable adjectives
And crown his name with them,
In ridicule.

A millennium later,
In a newly built museum,
A statue is displayed

Of the star-plucking youth.

His left hand is holding up the Dog Star.
His right hand is holding up Vega.
Around his waist he wears
The belt studded with three stars
Of Sagittarius, who shot him with an arrow.

(1942)
(translated by Denis Mair)

DOG HOWLING AT THE MOON

A train rolls by and out of sight, carrying a dog that howls at the
    moon.
The tracks heave a sigh of relief.

Songs with personality arise from all sides from naked girls astride
    giant cacti,
A chorus with no consistent meaning,
Discordant sounds on all sides.
Dark shadows of cacti recline on the flatland.
The flatland is a suspended disc.
The fallen train does not crawl back from the curved horizon,
But forlorn howls have struck the moon's gong and now bounce
    back
To swallow the voices of girls singing.

(1942)
(translated by Denis Mair)

SEVEN AND SIX

Holding a cane 7
Clamping teeth on a pipe 6

The number 7 has the form of a cane.
The number 6 has the form of a pipe.
So here I am.

Cane 7 + pipe 6 = myself who am 13

A poet. A genius.
A genius among geniuses.
The most unfortunate number there could be!
Ah yes, a tragedy.
Tragedy, tragedy I have come.
And so you clap your hands, you shout hooray.

(1943)
(translated by Denis Mair)

COMPOSITION IN A WINDOW

A fashion show of girls in the clouds goes floating by my window
    on a screen of azure sky:

Those are orange-colored girls kissed by the sun;
Those are peach-colored young girls;

Those girls are mascara-colored, crimson-colored, violet-
colored;

And embedded in the picture frame of the window's perfect
rectangle:
Buildings in gray, white, black, and brown colors, with roofs
showing red,
And the posture of pipe-smoking factory chimneys, the posture of
a water tower and budding trees and electric poles.

Musical notes of sparrows leap onto a staff of electric wires.

(1944)
(translated by Denis Mair)

MY VOICE AND MY EXISTENCE

I must send forth my voice, unceasingly, within my shell-covered
cosmos. The shell is tough yet transparent, like plexiglass. My cos-
mos is absolute.

I send forth my voice, because only my voice can prove my exis-
tence. All things are unreliable. All things are not to be trusted. All
things have danger: those meanings of all tempting forms and
magic spells that surround me. I must close my eyes to the beauty
or ugliness of those forms. I must remain ignorant of the depth or
shallowness of those meanings. Otherwise, the one who gets can-
celed out will surely be me—a whirlwind from any direction can
snuff me out, as readily as blowing out a match.

My voice is multifarious, like the seven colors of the sun. There are
pure colors, composite colors, appearing in endless variety. I paint
my voice with colors: indigo, orange, lemon yellow, violet, green,
turquoise, gray, and blackest black; at times I paint it with powerful
crimson and red. But my crimson is not the crimson of the Com-
intern flag. My red is not the red of their Red Square. It is the
burning essence of my life—a combustion that is irrepressible, in-
extinguishable, and fatal, yes fatal.

Simple yet complex, tranquil yet turbulent, my voice. Nearby yet
distant, fleeting yet eternal, my voice. My voice proves my exis-

tence. Therefore I unceasingly send forth my voice, within my shell-covered absolute cosmos.

(1945)
(translated by Denis Mair)

PAINTER'S STUDIO

I have a studio that is closed and cut off from everyone. Inside of it I can face the mirror and paint my naked body on canvas. My naked body is skinny, pale, and riddled with wounds: blue, purple, old and new, never fully healing, just like my hatred, never fading away.

As to who struck me with a whip, I do not know; who hacked at me with an axe, I do not know; who tightened a rope around me, I do not know; who branded me with hot iron, I do not know; who splashed acid on me, I do not know.

I only know the wish for vengeance burns fiercely in my heart.

But my only means of vengeance, which I have already adopted, is to draw my wounds over and over, to paint them over and over, in perfect likeness, then take them somewhere, to show at an exhibition, to let everyone look at them, let them also shudder in disgust, let them also know pain, and most of all fill them also with undying hatred like my own. And that is all, that is all.

(1946)
(translated by Denis Mair)

WINE DRINKER

Within a castle wall devised of jugs,
I sit silently,
Royal in bearing.

Well before the end of everyone's office hours,
I gaily arrive, the only one:
The three o'clock drinker.

I call the barkeep for the best wine,
Pour into my own cup, at perfect ease,
Ruling my complete and pure domain.

My departure and the collapse of my kingdom
Are due to the entrance of a second customer,
An invasion upon my grand solitude.

(1947)
(translated by Denis Mair)

PSYCHOANALYSIS OF PIPE SMOKING

The wreathing tendril that rises from my pipe
Is a mushroom cloud,
A snake,
A life preserver,
And the naked body of a woman.
She dances and she sings.
She sings of a dried-out river that overflows its banks,
And the extinction of a squadron of dreams.

(1953)
(translated by Denis Mair)

UNFINISHED MASTERPIECE

You are an unfinished masterpiece;
By the time you take on picturelike qualities
And give me a Mona Lisa feeling,
I have officially laid down my brush.

Because your tender right forearm
Has been stricken with terrible leprosy;
And your "Giaconda smile" has been slashed
By the knife of a madman.

(1953)
(translated by Denis Mair)

DEATH OF APHRODITE

Take the Greek goddess Aphrodite, stuff her into a
    slaughterhouse machine

cut her up
into chunks

Extract the elements
Of her "beauty"
Prepare them as specimens; and then

          in one little bottle
          after another

Display them in categories at an exhibition of relics, let the
    public enjoy them,
And get some education on top of it.

This is indeed the twentieth century: our very own.

                  (1957)
        (translated by Denis Mair)

TYPE-B BLOOD

Bath finished on a summer afternoon
Stretched out for a moment's rest
Suddenly my long lean body strikes me
With its resemblance to a Christ figure.
It too could be betrayed
Could be pierced with nails
And my type-B blood
Would also be pure and holy
It must not flow in vain
How can I let it flow in vain?
So let it flow!

                  (1961)
        (translated by Denis Mair)

BEFORE COMPLETION.* ONE

They like high speeds those greens
Being flammable, they are melancholy

---

*"Before Completion" is the name of the last hexagram in the *Yijing* (*I Ching* or *Book of Changes*).

As for the likes of decayed leaves deficient in octane
Melancholy they are not at all

Thus I often perform a clambering act
While whistling most unmusically, in sailor fashion
Inside a whole note marked with a special pause
Climbing up rigging so as to transcend

All greens and decayed leaves
All things flammable and deficient in octane
Whether melancholy or not melancholy, fond or not fond of high
    speeds
All in all I have begun again (Ah! Members of the audience
Hiss or leave early if you please
Shout loudly, keep statistically silent, or loudly applaud—
There is no public order to observe here)

Yet a cylindrical shape taken to a geometrical exponent is how
I climb up and plunge down; yet the geometrical exponent of a
    cylindrical shape is how I plunge down
And climb up . . .

(1959)
(translated by Denis Mair)

BIRD VARIATIONS

No sooner do I assume
A posture of flight, than the world
Goes into an uproar.

No end of hunters
No end of shotguns
Aiming
Opening fire.

Every bullet hole they make in the firmament
Lets through the light of a star.

(1983)
(translated by Denis Mair)

陳秀喜

CHEN XIUXI

(1921–91)

Born in Xinzhu in northwestern Taiwan, Chen Xiuxi (Ch'en Hsiu-hsi) published her first volume of poetry, written in Japanese, in Tokyo in 1970. After realizing with a shock that her children could not read her Japanese poems, Chen began writing in Chinese and published four volumes in a short period of time, which secured her reputation in poetry circles. An English translation of her work, *On Love*, was published in 1978 by the Bamboo Hat Poetry Society.

Chen's poetry is admired for its characteristic simplicity in language and unaffected style. Affectionately known as "Auntie Poet" to her colleagues, Chen served as president of the Bamboo Hat Poetry Society. After she passed away in 1991, an annual poetry prize was established in honor of her contributions.

GRAVE SWEEPING THIS YEAR

I want to hold my father and sob
but all I touch is
a cold hard tombstone

A familiar name
adorned in gilded letters, made strange
some clutch it and wail
yet it stuns me

My back to the tombstone
the mountains of my home
so majestic
push me away, into the winds of Grave-Sweeping Day

I kneel by the hyacinths
a melancholy purple
I break up the morning dewdrops with my lips
in my heart a refrain:
the tombstone is not my father
the tombstone is not my father

(published 1970)
(translated by Wendy Larson)

LOVE

A wondrous bird soars in
no set course
no one knows when   or where it comes from
it flies here not to seek a nest

the tree never takes a stance of refusal
its hands toward the skies as if wanting something
if   that bird flies onto the tree
the branches willingly bear
this most beautiful ornament
and even hope the bird will lose its wings
the tree longs to become a strong lock
because the marvelous bird on its branches
glitters more than a medal

an existence even more solid than   the setting sun at the treetop

the tree awaits a wondrous bird

(published 1971)
(translated by Wendy Larson)

TAIWAN

Shaped like a cradle, the flowery island
is Mother's
eternal loving bosom
Proud-boned ancestors
scrutinize our steps
nursery rhymes are
their oft-repeated caution
rice straw
banyan trees
bananas
waft the scent of Mother's inexhaustible milk in the air

however high the waves of the straits
however fierce the whirling typhoons
we won't forget their earnest words
as long as we march in step
as long as the cradle is sturdy
the cradle is eternal
who doesn't love the cradle Mother has left for us?

(published 1974)
(translated by Wendy Larson)

MY PEN

Eyebrows are the colony of the eyebrow pencil
round lips the territory of the lipstick
I am happy that my pen
outlines neither eyebrows nor lips

"colony," "territoriality"
each time I see these words
the sorrow of having been colonized rises in me again
count tonight's sighs

caressing my veins
surging blood moves my pen
on paper moistened by tears
it fills the page:
I am Chinese
I am Chinese
We all are Chinese

(published 1976)
(translated by Wendy Larson)

MAYBE IT'S THE WEIGHT OF A POEM

Lofty trees worry about peals of thunder
trodden grass does not envy big trees
the grass rallies its roots and leaves, awaits the call to stand up
The plum flower does not sigh over its smallness, but is happy
    with its fragrance
it envies not the glorious colors of the thorny rose
At ease with themselves, the ancients learned from nature lessons
    of peace
it is nothing unusual for dawn to shine after darkness
after frustration the age of wisdom arrives
Poetry has a powerful source of energy, a sincere loving heart
maybe a poem can topple the earth
maybe a poem can save all the people in the world
maybe a poem can release energy
to let us hear freedom and peace, live together and flourish
like the echo of an angel's call

(published 1978)
(translated by Wendy Larson)

詹冰

ZHAN BING

(1921–)

Zhan Bing (Chan Ping) was born Zhan Yichuan in Zhuolan, a township near the northeastern city of Miaoli. After graduating from high school in 1942, he went to Tokyo to study pharmacy at Meiji Pharmacy School and was certified in 1944. For most of his professional life, he taught physics and chemistry at junior high school in his hometown. He retired in 1981 and moved to Taizhong in 1987, where he lives with his wife.

Zhan Bing published his first poems in Japanese in 1941. He started learning Chinese after the war in 1945 and joined the literary society Silver Bell in 1948. He not only is a prolific poet but also has published fiction, essays, film scripts, children's literature (both drama and poetry), and even an opera. He has won numerous awards for children's literature; a well-known example is the 1963 poem "Planting Rice Sprouts," which was included in standardized textbooks for primary schools in 1989.

AFFAIR

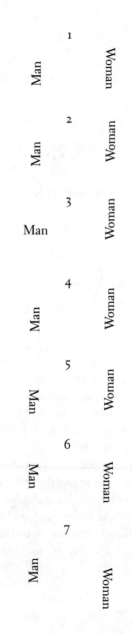

(published 1943)
(translated by Michelle Yeh)

MAY

May,
Green blood cells swim
In transparent blood vessels.
May is just such a being.

May is walking naked.
On the hills: breathing through golden hairs.
In the wilderness: singing through silvery light.
So May wanders, sleeplessly.

(published 1943)
(translated by Michel Hockx and Jim Weldon)

PLANTING RICE SPROUTS

The paddy field a mirror
reflecting the blue skies
reflecting the white clouds
reflecting the dark hills
reflecting the green trees

Farmers plant their rice sprouts
planting in the green trees
planting in the dark hills
planting in the white clouds
planting in the blue skies

(1963)
(translated by Michel Hockx and Jim Weldon)

LIQUID MORNING

In an instant,
the feeling of being newborn,
swimming in a transparent body,
no resistance at all.

At this moment,
like reading new poems I want to read

fresh sceneries
wrapped in cellophane.

For instance,
under the algaelike acacia, the tree of love,
a young girl turned fish
waving the fins of her fan.

And after that,
the *poésie* of the morning
rises toward the world of clouds
like bubbles of CO_2.

(1965)
(translated by Michel Hockx and Jim Weldon)

SEVEN-COLORED TIME

The new season has hatched.
Plants' clothes begin to breathe.
Loudly vibrating the vitreous atmosphere,
Novalis's blue flower blooms.
Like musical notes,
splendid photons drip down the corolla.
Like a solar spectrum,
seven-colored time flows from the stamen.
Ah, now
is the time for the poet to adjust the second hand of his watch.

(1965)
(translated by Michel Hockx and Jim Weldon)

LIQUID FLOWS INTO THE CUP OF THE HEART

Like looking for white snakes in green grass
I seek out the white hairs in my wife's black hair,
carefully plucking them, strand by strand—
wanting to bring back her youth

Her fragrant hair   once black and lustrous
strand by strand is turning white because of the toils of life
as I pluck out the white hairs strand by strand
my tears keep flowing into the cup of my heart

I pick up the white hairs that I cast aside lay them out on my
     palm
strand by strand those white hairs glisten with a silvery sheen
suddenly their silver needles pierce my breast—
blood from the wounds once more flows into   the cup of my
     heart

(1969)
(translated by Michel Hockx and Jim Weldon)

周夢蝶

ZHOU MENGDIE

(1921–   )

Born in He'nan Province, Zhou Mengdie (Chou Meng-tieh) graduated from the
middle school and worked briefly as a schoolteacher and a librarian. He served
in the military for seven years, and when he had to follow the Nationalist gov-
ernment to Taiwan in 1949, he left behind his wife and children. For the next
twenty-one years, he ran a sidewalk bookstand in front of a Taipei café, selling
newspapers, magazines, and poetry books (which he often gave away for free to
students). He retired for health reasons in 1981 and now lives in a Taipei suburb.

A pen name, "Zhou Mengdie" alludes to the Taoist philosopher Zhuangzi
(Chuang Tzu, 369?–286? B.C.), whose family name is Zhou, and his classic
tale of "the butterfly dream" — "mengdie":

Once Zhuang Zhou dreamt he was a butterfly, a butterfly flitting and
fluttering around, happy with himself and doing as he pleased. He didn't
know he was Zhuang Zhou. Suddenly he woke up and there he was, solid
and unmistakable Zhuang Zhou. But he didn't know if he was Zhuang
Zhou who had dreamt he was a butterfly, or a butterfly dreaming he was
Zhuang Zhou. Between Zhuang Zhou and a butterfly there must be *some*
distinction! This is called the Transformation of Things.

> (based on Burton Watson's translation in *The Complete Works of
> Chuang Tzu* [New York: Columbia University Press, 1968], 49)

Zhou is a long-time member of the Blue Star Poetry Society. His life and two books of poetry, published in 1959 and 1965, have made him a living legend on the poetry scene in Taiwan. In 1997, he became the recipient of the inaugural National Culture and Arts Foundation Award.

CALTROPS

Hugging the bitter cold
and cruel heat of the Twelfth Month,
you sleep so soundly, so sweetly,
you, flock of daydreamers,
you, with smiles hanging forever
from your wingtips.

How much innocence
will be grabbed by the greed
of hand after hand?
Where a hot mist gently encircles, here
people are, cooking and selling
the corpses of bats!

Jacket after purple iron jacket
cut down; pair after pair of black
angels' wings cut down;
daydreams petal by petal,
smiles crescent by crescent. . . .

God, did you endow Darwin with tears?

(published 1959)
(translated by Lloyd Haft)

DIARY OF A BELIEVER

Yesterdays—
yesterdays soaked through,
drenched in the shades
of Hamlet and Rudin!
Begone, begone!
My parting gift to you's a begging bowl
of nice cold compassion.

I'm the metamorphosis
of camel and sand.
Naked I lie on the back of loneliness,
letting myself be carried
on that endless distance, measureless height,

letting the sound of my footfalls
silently open in black blossoms
blooming on my chest.

Black blossoms stalking me
in smiling gloom,
the future luring me
with a blank sheet of mystery;
the blank sheet is endless,
my gloom is endless too. . . .

It's dark! Death pours me a glass
of grape wine. In the crazy, wide-awake eyes
of Omar Khayyam, I see the Eternal reflected,
and hidden behind the Eternal
my name.

(published 1959)
(translated by Lloyd Haft)

MENDICANT

A trickle of Cloud Elixir
in your begging bowl. Tracks of your feet
that rooted nowhere! The cross blossoms
on the road you speed along.
Beyond tomorrow and yesterday and today
you're burying sorrow.

Purple lilac, purple clover everywhere
like prayer beads, surrounding you with care.
Sun and moon: paired lamps
to light your soles, shoulders, back;
the robelike face of night.

The Fourteenth Month. Snowflakes fly.
The unnavigable waves of ancient legend
slumber. Ask upstream and over,
downstream and under
to show you the way.
Ask how long there's been a way.

When will the way and the sky go together?
Ask when the Udumbara's* going to bloom.
Can you glimpse, across the ties, the binds,
the drifting rings, which bubble of froth
is your name?
Ever tossing and turning on the Ganges.
Every patch of rain along the Ganges,
every drop from gulls, egrets,
shows care for you.
There'll be no going back now.
Resting your head on a snow-white wave
you say: "I've come too far!"

All the crossings
are closed, bemisted in the Fourteenth Month.
Beyond the girls, the peaches, the farewells,
you fondle an empty begging bowl.
You wonder if tonight
a falling star will drop for you
in silence, like a tear from heaven.
Like a rain of blossoms,
like the finger of a Holy One
reaching from the Other Shore . . .

(published 1961)
(translated by Lloyd Haft)

PRISONER

There'll be a patch of azaleas
blazing up from your eyes:
the fiftieth time the perennial grasses
make the change they can't help making:
green to brown and back to green again.
And I'll come looking for you
—as a broken-winged and timid butterfly—
and through a scent of tears, now red now white,
with a touch so familiar
I'll speak to you of a former incarnation. . . .

---

*Udumbara refers to a flower that blooms every three millennia, which coincides with the
birthday of a buddha.

If only I could be transformed
into that underground darkness
you're resting on! While thunder roars,
lightning tears, night cold daunts . . .
even at this distance, no heaven left to cry to,
my thought still turns on you,
solitary shadow, soul alone.
For whom can the bosom open?
Who, except the autumn weeds, knows
how heavy the blood in your heart,
how ready to be shed?

If I had known that parting
is the other side of meeting—
while the moon was haloed and before the wind
arose, I could have commanded the Long River
to go back, to the west, the source;
or given my infatuations,
spit out on a bloody handkerchief,
to the fire to burn. And stepped out of the ashes
and seen, beyond the body and within,
smoke flying, smoke vanishing.

The poisoned arrow of my plaint
has left the bowstring, shot and gone,
never to be shot back.
When will I ever roam at ease
like the biggest swans in the highest heaven?
In dreams I always see heaven falling,
see a thousand fingers, a thousand eyes,
dropping like a net
while I—mud to the left, rocks to the right—
walk straight at the screaming mouth
of a black pit. . . .

Of all impasses the most impassable!
Like a ray of cold radiance
yearning to escape from the sobbing scabbard
left behind when the sword broke.
When I roused myself and soared, riding the roc,
and died—south of the South Pole, pleasure and pain,

those kaleidoscopic cat's eyes,
opened a window for me.

A face, bleached
in the numberless night skies of the years—
my face. Blue tears gradually light up.
On the sea of your memory
the wind whirls, raising up answers.
The snow and the plum blossoms
have all gone back to winter.
Beyond the thousand mountains
a setting moon shines in solitude.
Who is it—coming again,
the familiar one, the one yet unborn?

(published 1964)
(translated by Lloyd Haft)

NINE LINES

Your shadow is a bow.
And with yourself you draw yourself
full: so full it hums.

Every day, out of the east, a sun's shaken down:
ball after ball of copper-red autumn, completed
in your wind-dried hands.

Why don't you grow a thousand hands, a thousand eyes?
—you have so many autumns:
so many selves, waiting to be shaken down.

(published 1965)
(translated by Lloyd Haft)

ON THE FERRY

Boat—carrying the many, many shoes,
carrying the many, many
three-cornered dreams
facing each other and facing away.

Rolling, rolling—in the deeps,
flowing, flowing—in the unseen:
man on the boat, boat on the water,
water on Endlessness,
Endlessness is, Endlessness is upon
my pleasures and pains,
born in a moment
and gone in a moment.

Is it the water that's going,
carrying the boat and me? Or am I going,
carrying boat and water?

Dusk fascinates.
Einstein's smile is a mystery, comfortless.

(published 1965)
(translated by Lloyd Haft)

TWELFTH MONTH

My ear membranes are rusty—soon they'll be cocoons!
Between dreams and isolation
I'm a snake! coiled in fantasies of waking up to spring.

Who knows how much time my sleep has flattened?
The night's as long as sorrow;
Cold's shell cracking inch by inch.
Where did the mail boat run aground
that set out from Subzero
carrying the Twelfth Month in bloom?

In dreams I always see snowslides,
creepers swinging from steep cliffs,
touch-me-nots no more to be restrained,
eyes closed, ruminating wind and sun . . .

while a stone lion, its face
gloomier than *Le Penseur*'s,
stands up, hops up eastward,

and roars till the dawn awakens
that makes Chaos laugh forth its tears. . . .

(published 1965)
(translated by Lloyd Haft)

SIXTH MONTH

Suddenly I wake up
to the sound of a rain of blossoms in profusion,
pounding till my shadow's soaked!
Is it a dream? Real?
Facing tonight: an upside-down
boat under a coral reef.

How much endurance will turn my bones
to an indestructible Relic? Buddha,
your heart is radiant, but the Sixth Month's heart is warm—
how many Sixth Months will I have?
Where can I park my perseverance?
Between you and the Sixth Month.

They say snakes' veins are ageless!
Even if you worked the metal of eternal night
into autumn, into winter;
even if darkness gouged out its own eyes . . .
the snake would know: from under the water
he could still cry tidings of fire.

Death whirled, dancing on my palm
till she fell, dropped like a meteor.
I want to turn around, pick her up, and put her back
but—rainbow broken, red clouds flown—
she's already become
a profusion of butterflies.

(published 1965)
(translated by Lloyd Haft)

MOUNTAIN

"If you call the mountain and the mountain does not come,
    then you must go to it."—the Qur'an

Up from the unresolved you fly,
so high, so alone,
wanting to stick your head out past the heavens,
see how your shadow
is calmer than all your thinking,
gaunter than your philosophy,
more obstinate and old.

The sorrow of Sisyphus lights up
in a symphony of thunder
and you weep like fate,
weep this day, whose day is this
and night, whose night is this?

Vague in the heights, an echo is calling you;
beyond the bitter smile of the honeysuckle
you're trembling. "If you have no crutch, then
throw away your crutch"—*that's* the sort
of madman you are.

Gales moan at your hairtips.
The cold face of time grows darker,
says there are other heavens beyond the heavens,
other clouds beyond the clouds.
Says an inch of green foxtail
is tall as the radiant points of a lion's mane.

Every rock's a fabulous mountain.
Let Caesar go back to Caesar,
God to God, you to you—
till the Eternal unfolds its full scroll of darkness
to cover the you and the Moses on your forehead.

(published 1965)
(translated by Lloyd Haft)

POLYDACTYLISM

Is it a pair of antlers
that a gazelle left hanging here?

Or is it a vacant stare, left behind
at Waiting Rock?*

Who is to say after the Five Seasons
there is no Sixth?
High in the cliffs, I faintly hear
spring on its tightrope, shivering
and again shivering.

Yesterday you were a snowdrift,
today you are spring grass
beneath the snowdrift,
hazy with awakening.
Whose is the luck-bringing magpie,
carrying in its mouth
a skyful of red clouds
on plum twigs of the Fifth Month?

From beyond the rainbow, birds
come flying;
from beyond the birds, a rainbow
comes gushing—
your hidden thoughts are a herd of sheep
that walked out over the mountainside
and know no way back home,
seeing only peak on peak
of shades of autumn.

The wind that came from cactus country
goes back into cactus
with a clang, and Contemplation's on.
From now on, after the Five Seasons
there'll be no more Sixth
till Contemplation wakens from the wind,
till nimbly as a butterfly
you waken from the wind.

(published 1965)
(translated by Lloyd Haft)

---

*Waiting Rock refers to a rock on North Mountain in Wuchang. According to the legend, a
soldier's wife stood there every day, waiting for her husband to return. She died and turned into
a rock in the shape of a standing woman.

桓夫

HUAN FU

(1922–   )

Born Chen Wuxiong in Nantou County in central Taiwan, Huan Fu also publishes prose fiction and literary criticism under the name Chen Qianwu (Ch'en Ch'ien-wu).

Like Zhan Bing, he belongs to the so-called "translingual generation" (see the introduction). With the publication in 1939 of his first poem, "A Moment on a Summer Night," he started out writing poetry in Japanese. In 1945, he was sent by the Japanese colonial government as a member of the "Taiwanese special volunteer forces" to Java and, to everyone's surprise, returned alive to Taiwan in 1946. "Carrier Pigeon," included here, is based on that experience.

After the retrocession of Taiwan to China in 1945, Huan Fu studied Chinese and a decade later was able to write poetry in Chinese. His first collection of poems in Chinese came out in 1963, and he has since published more than ten volumes. He was a founding member of the Bamboo Hat Poetry Society in 1964 and has served as editor of the *Bamboo Poetry Bimonthly*, the longest-running poetry journal in Taiwan, and *Poetry Prospect*, which he founded in 1965. When the municipal Taizhong Cultural Center was established in 1976, he was appointed director. Huan Fu has been active in promoting exchanges among poets of Taiwan, Japan, and Korea and has translated much modern Japanese and Korean poetry. He also writes fiction and critical essays. In 1979 he won the Wu Zhuoliu Literature Prize for the short story "Hunting the Woman Criminal."

WALKING IN THE RAIN

A thread of spider silk   straight down
Two threads of spider silk   straight down
Three threads of spider silk   straight down
Thousands of threads of spider silk   straight down
Surrounding me in
—a prison of spider silk

Countless spiders cast to the ground
Each turns a somersault, making a show of defiance
Then imprints my face, my clothes, with marks of sadness
I am stained all over with the marks of bitter struggle.

Ah, mother, I am so restless and homesick
I miss your gentle hands brushing away
These threads of troublesome rain that entangle me.

(1961)
(translated by Jim Weldon and Michel Hockx)

FOREST

Escaping into the forest
I stretch out my arms   like
Fir branches   straight up to the sky
I want to kick apart dead leaf piles of bad habits
But ten thousand annual rings are heavy on my heart, seal me up
In stagnant history
Vacancy fills   the space between trees

The turmoil of a century settles here
Waiting quietly for the subtropic buds to open
A new annual ring starts breathing. . . .
I am no pagan
O forest   tell me your joy
O forest   tell me your woe

(1962)
(translated by Jim Weldon and Michel Hockx)

CARRIER PIGEON

Buried in Southeast Asia
My death, I forgot to bring it back
There, islands are dotted with coconut groves
Winding beaches, and
Natives paddling dugouts at sea. . . .
I allayed the natives' suspicions
Crossed rows of coconut palms
Went into the dark dense jungle
At long last hiding my death in a corner
And so
In the midst of the second fierce world war
I lived carefree
Though I served as a heavy gunner
Fought from island to island
Showered by enemies' fifteen-millimeter shells
Target for their shooting
Hearing the sound of the enemies' movements
Still I did not die
Because my death was long since hidden in a forest corner
Only when the unrighteous warlords surrendered
And I returned to   the motherland
Did I think of
My death, that I forgot to bring back
Ah, that only death of mine, buried on a Southeast Asian island
I believe someday it will come flying, like a carrier pigeon
Come flying, bringing back news of the south

(1964)

(translated by Jim Weldon and Michel Hockx)

WILD DEER

An indelible small mole marks the deer's shoulder   just like so
many other shoulders   before its eyes all is yellow with acacia
blossom   the yellow dusk draws in   but the evening sun still
wants to reflect all ablaze the youth of the peaks and spurs   and
the ridge of Jade Mountain as always imposing and lovely   this is
no longer a temporary recline   the frail wild deer lifts its head to

look at Jade Mountain   looks at the mole on its shoulder   the
mole's wound has torn open a scarlet peony

Blood spurts out   at the speed of remembering   letting the
deer comprehend everything   with the   final   curtain   slowly
dropping   the threat of the hunter's sharp arrows weakens

Soon   blood-red twilight fills far-distant memory   the wild
deer's instincts   savor the moment of calm before death   and
recollection is a business of eternity   they   the forefathers of the
Ami tribe once had seven suns   just imagine: those seven suns
were sure to scorch the love of tawny skins   everyone sighed as
superfluous authority blighted the rich harvest of desire   so the
Ami patriarchs formed a band and went hunting   hunting the
suns up hill and down dale   —again the blood spurts out

A pure and scarlet growing peony—now   there is only one sun
now   so much ambition   so much love   belongs to the indif-
ference of the wilderness   in the indifferent reality   the trickles of
blood on the deer's shoulder flow endlessly   twitch endlessly
but the deer has had no thought of cursing in complaint   and the
wound gradually stops hurting   the shafts of light that once blazed
hot   shining on the endless tribulation of success and failure
those stories of success and failure are distant now

The knoll where the deer lies is deadly still and dark   the vast
and beautiful wildwood belongs forever to the dead   the deer is
thinking   and thinking   its misted-over cornea can no longer re-
flect those hideous faces that tyrannize the mountains   nor its
companions contending for the hind's love   oh! love   after the
exhaustion of ecstasy love drifts off to sleep   to . . . sleep . . .

(1966)
(translated by Jim Weldon and Michel Hockx)

EXCUSE MY RUDENESS

Oh Mazu
You've been sitting here so long   Your feet
Must have gone to sleep years ago
On history's sandalwood dais

The sandalwood throne
In the hall filled with incense smoke
Amid the flattery of the crowds
Has been smoked tar-black. . . .

It's very rude of me to say this
But   You ought to relinquish Your shrine
Your seat
To a young maiden
Compared to
Cosmic wars with satellites flying all over the place
That seat of Yours is . . .
Oh Mazu
If I've said the wrong thing
Please forgive me

But   do I really mean to force You
To hand over that glorious chastity
That You've preserved for over a thousand years
Your bound feet
Your sad dignity
To a young maiden?

No! But
No one should monopolize a position forever
If   I've said the wrong thing
Please forgive me
Elderly gentlemen
Of the Temple Management Committee!

(1968)

(translated by Jim Weldon and Michel Hockx)

FIND AN HONORIFIC FOR MOSQUITOS

Ceaselessly humming they fly over
To bite the back of my palsied hand
Call it a stopover
Stopover   just to draw a little life-giving blood for themselves
Just
How many mosquitos are truly helpless
How many mosquitos are worthy of our sympathy

On the back of my hand
On the bare expanse of territory
My hand is getting more and more palsied.

(1970)
(translated by Jim Weldon and Michel Hockx)

SHADOW

In the morning   shadows are long
In the evening   shadows are even longer

When the dictator sun presses down on the top of my head
My shadow can't lengthen out
It is like my fragile self-respect
My self-respect dragging—
A shadow now short now long

Shadows of different lengths   the color
Also differing   I wish for
My shadow to be longer and deeper

Now my shadow is so deep it's turned black
I know if my shadow   gets so long
That it stretches over the top of that low wall
This world will collapse
No! It's me who'll collapse
I'll end up all battered and bruised
But everything in this world will still exist

(1970)
(translated by Jim Weldon and Michel Hockx)

INCIDENT

A rain shower
sweeps by
a puddle of water on the deserted ground
reflects the quietness
of sawed-off
annual tree
rings

The veined rings
will slowly
soak in   much of
the water
then they
will come alive quietly
in desolate history books

(1983)
(translated by Michelle Yeh)

林亨泰

LIN HENGTAI

(1924–)

Born in Zhanghua in central Taiwan, Lin Hengtai (Lin Heng-t'ai) received a B.A. in education from National Taiwan Normal University and taught middle school for twenty-five years. Since he retired, he has taught Japanese at various colleges.

In 1947 Lin became a member of the Silver Bell Literary Society, which disbanded in 1949 under political repression. He published his first book of poetry in Japanese in 1949 but had begun writing poetry in Chinese a year earlier. In the 1950s he was active in the *Modern Poetry Quarterly* and played a major role, through both creative work and literary theory, in the Modernist School founded by Ji Xian in 1956. In 1964 he became a founding member of the Bamboo Hat Poetry Society and served as the first chief editor of its journal, emphasizing modernity with a local identity. Lin coined the term "the translingual generation" in 1967 to refer to the generation of Taiwanese poets who made the painstaking transition from Japanese to Chinese as the medium of their creative work. To date Lin has published five books of poetry and three volumes of literary criticism.

PHILOSOPHER

on a day of too much sunlight
a chicken balances on one leg, thinking
autumn, 20 October 1947
how can too much sunlight unbalance that leg
under a tree that has shed all its leaves?

(published 1949)
(translated by John Balcom)

BOOKS

books are piled on the desk
every time I look at them
a thought comes to mind
because most of their authors
are no longer among the living
some died of tuberculosis
some died in revolutions
some died insane
their books are nothing less than
gifts sent from the underworld
sighing with emotion
I select one
turn the pages one by one
my fingers like ascetic pilgrims
who sadly prostrate themselves at each temple

thus, I pray
I light my pipe
a thread of smoke rises as if from an incense burner

(published 1949)
(translated by John Balcom)

LANDSCAPE NO. 1

crops   next
to   more
crops   next
to   more

crops   next
to   more

sunlightsunlight shines long on the ears
sunlightsunlight shines long on the neck

(1959)
(translated by John Balcom)

LANDSCAPE NO. 2

windbreak
outside   another
windbreak
outside   another
windbreak
outside   another

but the sea   and the ranged waves
but the sea   and the ranged waves

(1959)
(translated by John Balcom)

TRACES
NO. 1

a cracked riverbed
leaves behind
faint traces in time

with no compass points
to pin space down
history shrinks into a parabola

memories that don't look back
brand the mountains
in their wrinkled valleys

NO. 2

a skein of many stories there
like roots
tangled

the horizon
dragging along its shadow
the setting sun

often winces, stealing a glance
dragging along half-ashamed
history

NO. 3

owing to the thorn's urgent demands
sharpness took shape

a point originated
in a dream from before history

evoking fleshly pain
spurting warm blood

O, the earth locked in ice and snow
is warm!

NO. 4

pile up silence
in a tomb for time

the characters have become skeletons
the setting already has turned to ashes

the theme, after flashing lightning
scurried on the open wilds of the imagination

red earth has been hammered into iron and steel
small bits of coal have been made into diamonds

NO. 5

after the fruit's flesh is
slowly eaten

a longan pit
is then tossed away

like an eye it stares
out of a garbage heap

resentfully eyeing its peeled
skin littering the ground

NO. 6

without language
this world
would probably hold no surprises

with no surprises
this world
would probably lack love

without love
this world
would probably be easy to part with

NO. 7

on a resplendent street
a crowd of shadows
hides in the bright light

a man-made moon
hanging on the wall
is a fragile object of glass

silently buried
underneath pleasure
is the moment never to awaken again

NO. 8

at the edge of pain there is no pain
but an itch
even a kind of pleasure

at the heart of pain there is no pain
but a heat
to make one sweat

only one who observes pain feels pain
but it is poetry
that strangely enough brings tears

(1982–1983)
(translated by John Balcom)

杜潘芳格

DU PAN FANGGE

(1927–   )

Born in Xinzhu in northwestern Taiwan, Du Pan Fangge (Tu P'an Fang-ko) (Du is her husband's last name, Pan her maiden name) received a Japanese education through high school. A devout Christian and mother of seven, she started writing poetry in the 1960s and joined the Bamboo Hat Poetry Society shortly after it was founded in 1964. In 1992 she became the first recipient of the Chen Xiuxi Poetry Prize. She has published seven books of poetry to date and is among the first in Taiwan to write modern poetry in an ancient dialect spoken by the Hakka people in southeastern China. Among the poems included here, "Paper People" and "Womb" are written in Hakka, the rest in Mandarin.

REBIRTH

Yellow silk ribbons
and
black silk ribbons

my death
a rebirth
with a bow tie of
soft, pink silk ribbons

(1967)
(translated by Michelle Yeh)

PAPER PEOPLE

Everywhere on earth are people made of paper
Swaying to and fro in the autumn wind.

But I am not a woman of paper;
My body is the temple of God,
I entrust my heart to God,
Who fills me with heaven-sent enlightenment
And endows me with abilities and strength.

The island of Taiwan is full of paper people.
I search and search everywhere
For a true human being like me.

(1970)
(translated by Michelle Yeh)

BEYOND THE MULBERRY TREE

When butterflies perch, their wings close up neatly and upright,
Yet moths spread open their wings, like airplanes.

Legend has it that flying moths are carriers of human souls.

Mulberry twigs covered with saw-toothed leaves,
Through the tiny interstices I gaze at the distant hill.

I see angels in twos and threes smiling brightly.
Papa, I see you smile too.
Death, after all, is not frightening;
It takes you to a better place.

Through the tiny saw-toothed interstices between the mulberry
    leaves, I gaze
At the high hill far, far away, with the eyes of a seventeen-year-old
    girl.

(1985)
(translated by Michelle Yeh)

UNDER THE POMELO TREE

A newly hatched butterfly
Comes from the north riding on a spring horse

Sparkling sunlight bounces off its mane

In the south grows an emerald green pomelo tree

Travelers on earth
How can blood and words truly connect?

Those bluish words that turn pale from fatigue
Those words my ancestors never really heard
Let them bury the lush green pomelo tree

Yes
Butterfly, flap your wings

(published 1990)
(translated by Michelle Yeh)

WOMB

A womb
Gives birth to myriad forms of life
What is a womb?
It is a transit station.

(published 1990)
(translated by Michelle Yeh)

洛夫

LUO FU

(1928–)

Luo Fu (Lo Fu) is the pen name of Mo Luofu, who was born in Hengyang, Hunan Province. He joined the military during the Sino-Japanese War (1937– 45) and moved to Taiwan in 1949. After graduation from Cadre Academy in 1953 and a brief stint in the marines, he worked as a news editor at a military radio station. From 1965 to 1967 he was assigned to a post in Vietnam. He retired from the navy in 1973 as a commander; the same year he also graduated with a B.A. in English from Tamkang University. He has been a full-time writer and translator since.

Luo Fu started writing in mainland China in the mid-1940s. While stationed in southern Taiwan in 1954, he founded the Epoch Poetry Society with Zhang Mo and Ya Xian and served as the editor of the *Epoch Poetry Journal* for more than a decade. Like Ji Xian, Luo Fu was a controversial figure involved in many literary debates in the 1960s and '70s. His poetry has been immensely influential in Taiwan and China.

CHIMNEY

Standing alone under a pale setting sun
Black hair lifted by the wind,
  but a slender shadow stands still
It is a little cool below the city wall,
  a little lonely
I am a chimney longing to fly

Head lowered, I gaze at the long moat
The water brimming, meandering for thousands of years
Who has had me imprisoned?

Every afternoon I gaze up
At the white clouds' footprints in the sky

I yearn to travel afar; Oh! that long river, those blue mountains
If I could be a wild crane chasing the clouds
Or even a fine speck of dust
But I'm just a shadow cast below the city wall
—yielding loneliness to others

(1956)
(translated by John Balcom)

DEATH OF A STONE CELL
(four selections)

1   Simply by chance I raised my eyes toward the neighboring
        tunnel; I was stunned
    At dawn, that man rebelled against death with his naked
        body
    Allowed a black tributary to roar through his veins
    I was stunned, my eyes swept over the stone wall
    Gouging out two channels of blood on its surface

    My face spreads like a tree, a tree grown in fire
    All is still, behind eyelids only the pupils move
    Move in a direction most people fear to mention
    And I am a bitter pear tree, cut down
    On my annual rings you can still hear wind and cicadas

2   In reply to those who knock, the brass ring answers with the
         glories of the past
     My brothers will come and drink the anxiety filling my brow
     Their thirst and hunger like an indoor plant
     When I squint, metallic sounds
     Clang inside the walls, fall on the guest plates

     Afterward it's an afternoon of debate, all sorts of filth is
         revealed
     Language is just a pile of dirty laundry
     They are like wounded beasts unable to find permanent
         shelter
     If the tree's silhouette were sundered by the sun
     Its height would make me feel as solemn as when I face the
         setting sun

3   Like tree roots subject to nobody's will
     But still struggling to lift the darkness filling the mountains
     Like wild strawberries indifferent to eugenics
     Allowing their offspring to wander over the marsh
     Scolded by servants, I finished many dawns

     Oh, you grower of grapes on the rock, the sun leans over
         you
     When I reach to deeper strata, clutching lively root hairs
     Then I'll gladly drown in your blood
     To be the skin of your fruit, the bark on your stems
     I'm humble as the number on a condemned man's back

4   Joy, it always resembles someone's name
     A weight concealed within, at the edge of the unknown
     Grain creates a crisis in the embryo of an illicit marriage
     They say the demeanor of my tongue
     Is enough to cause insanity in all the piranhas of the
         Amazon

     Therefore all change is predictable
     Everyone can find the fingerprint of a name after it is teased
     Everyone has a few customs like receding footsteps

If your laughter rings untrue
Then I'll kill all songs, including the joy

(1965)
(translated by John Balcom)

BEYOND THE FOG

An egret
Reads *Les Nourritures Terrestes* in a rice paddy
It circles a certain point, swirling like fog
Lowering its head by chance
It snaps up a cloud on the water's surface

Contemplation is nothing more than
Pondering whether or not the sun is a nihilist
Lifting its left leg, it wonders
If its body should swing into the fog
Or beyond the fog

It spreads its wings and the universe follows, drifting upward
Dawn is a song, short and bright
Igniting itself in the fog
If the horizon line rises to bind you
It can only bind your wings, not your flight

(1966)
(translated by John Balcom)

FISH

Anyway, only a petal of the setting sun remains in his eyes
There'll still be time tomorrow to break the mirror
He stands reverently at H-town
A poplar flies around him
Casually looking up, he sees
Bone ashes drifting from a chimney
Or is it butterflies?

He wrings his hands and ponders
As the whiteness beyond the window becomes a myriad of colors
He is the sole hero of a thousand tales
Washing his hands may only create another woe

Turning his palms up . . . look!
Scales but no fins
What kind of fish are they?

Later, squatting under the eaves
He eats a fruit called the moon
Spitting the crushed seeds into the sky; they become stars
On the ice-cold tip of his tongue
Is the pure scent of burnt snow
Later he kicks a stone, waltzes
Along the wall, around the mouth of a dried-up well
And looking down
He no longer sees his own face

(1968)
(translated by John Balcom)

GOLD DRAGON TEMPLE

the evening bell
is a small trail
    travelers take
    down the mountain
ferns
along steps of white stone
chews its way all the way down

if this place were covered with snow . . .

but all that's seen is
a single startled cicada rising
to light the lanterns
one by one
all over the mountain

(1970)
(translated by John Balcom)

THE WOUND OF TIME

1   Pale is the moonlight's skin
     But the skin of my time slowly blackens

Peels away layer by layer
In the wind

2   A raincoat from before the war hangs behind the door
A discharge order in the pocket
The night-blooming cereus on the balcony
Blossoms in vain for one night
The wound of time continues festering
So serious
It cannot be cured even by chanting a few lines of the
    dharani mantra

3   Some say
Hair has only two colors:
If not black then white
What then the tomb grass, green then yellow?

4   Our kites
Were snatched away by the sky
None have returned in one piece
The string is all that remains in our hands
Broken yet unbroken

5   Pain
Proves we age in time
Roots warm the sleeping soil
The wind blows
One by one the bean pods burst

6   At times I vent my anger before the mirror
If only
All lights in the city were extinguished
I'd never find my face there again
I shatter the glass with my fist
Blood oozes out

7   We sang war songs on the boulevards that year
Heads high, chins up, we proudly entered history
We were stirred to the quick
Like water
Dripping on a red-hot iron
The names on our khaki uniforms
Were louder than a rifle shot

But today, hearing the bugle from the barracks nearby
I suddenly rose, straightened my clothes
Then sat down again, dejected
Softly keeping time with the beat

8   Reminiscing about the old days
     When we fought with our backs to the sea

     . . . .
     Twilight falls
     Horses gallop away
     An old general's white head
     Is seen
     Slowly looking up
     Out of the dust

9   Wading through the water
     Our bodies made of foam
     We suddenly raise our heads
     The twilight sun, beautiful as distant death

     On the water's surface
     Reflection of a giant bird of prey
     In a flash it's gone
     Can we swim the sea within ourselves?

10   In the end I took out all the bottles
     But it didn't help
     With what little wine remained
     I secretly jotted a line in the palm of my hand
     It suddenly froze
     As severe winter broke in my body

     The fire is dying, am I supposed to feed it my bones?

                                        (1979)
                          (translated by John Balcom)

SHARING A DRINK WITH LI HE*

Stones shatter
Heaven is startled
Frightened stiff, the autumn rain freezes in mid-air
Beyond my window, I suddenly see

---

*Li He, or Li Ho, is a late Tang poet who lived from 791–817.

A traveler on a donkey arrive from Chang'an
On his back a cloth sack of
Horrifying images

Before his arrival, lines of poetry
Fell like hail
Beyond my window, I again hear
Xihe, the charioteer, tapping on the sun
Oh, such a thin scholar
So thin
He resembles an exquisite wolf-hair writing brush
His large blue gown billows in the wind
Welling into thousands of waves

I mull over quatrains, quatrains, quatrains as if
I were chewing five-spice beans
In your impassioned eyes
Is a jug of newly brewed Hua-tiao wine
From the Tang dynasty to the Song to the Yuan to the Ming and
    to the Qing
At last it is poured into
This small cup of mine
I try to stuff the seven-character quatrain that you are most proud
    of
Into a wine urn
I shake it up, then watch as the mist rises
Language dances drunkenly, rhymes clash chaotically
The urn breaks, your flesh shatters
Screeching ghosts are heard on a vast plain
The howls of wolves are carried over thousands of miles

Come, sit down, let's drink together
On this blackest night in history
You and I are obviously not from among the run-of-the-mill
We aren't troubled by not being included in
    the *Three Hundred Poems of the Tang Dynasty*
Of what use are the nine grades of official rank?
They are not worth bothering about

Weren't you hung over that year?
Vomiting poetry on the jade steps of noble houses

Drink, drink up
The moon probably won't shine tonight
For this once-in-an-eon meeting
I want to take advantage of the darkness to write you a difficult
    poem
Incomprehensible, then let them not understand
Not understand
Why after reading it
We look at each other and burst out laughing

(1979)
(translated by John Balcom)

BECAUSE OF THE WIND

Yesterday following the riverbank
Strolling slowly I came upon a place
Where reeds stooped to drink
In passing, I asked a chimney
To write for me a long letter in the sky
Though carelessly writ
My heart's intent
Shone like the candlelight at your window
Still somewhat obscure
That cannot be helped
    Because of the wind

It matters not if you understand my letter
What matters is
You must, before the daisies wither
Quickly lose your temper, or laugh
Quickly find that thin shirt of mine in the trunk
Quickly face the mirror, combing your soft black charm
Then light a lamp
With a lifetime of love
I am a flame
To be extinguished any moment
    Because of the wind

(1981)
(translated by John Balcom)

THE CRICKET'S SONG

Someone living abroad once said: "Last night I heard a cricket chirr and mistook it for the one I heard in the countryside of Sichuan."

From the courtyard
To the corner of my room the cricket sings
Chirrup, chirrup
Suddenly it jumps
From a crack in the stone steps
To the pillow where, white-haired, I lay my head
Pushed from the edge of yesterday
To this corner of the world today
The cricket is heard but not seen
I search everywhere for it
No trace in the blue sky
No sign in the earth
Even in my breast I can't find that little ticker
The evening rain lets up
The moon outside my window
Delivers the sound of woodcutting
The stars roil
Chirrup, chirrup
The cricket's song is like a purling rill
Childhood drifts downstream
Tonight I'm not in Chengdu
My snoring is not a longing for home
And the chirrup in my ears weaves an unending song
I can't recall the year, the month, or the evening
In what city or village
Or in what small train station I heard it
Chirrup, chirrup
The one I hear tonight surprises
Chirrup, chirrup
Its song
Meanders like the Jialing River beside my pillow
There is no boat for hire so late at night
I can only swim with the current
The waves at the Three Gorges reach to the sky
Monkeys cry on both shores

Fish
Spicy fish on a blue porcelain platter
Chirrup, chirrup
Which cricket is it that really sings?
The Cantonese one seems the loneliest
The Sichuan one, the saddest
The Beijing one, the noisiest
The Hunan one, the spiciest
But
When I wake
It's the cricket in Sanli Lane that
Sings the softest and most dearly of them all
Chirrup, chirrup

(1985)
(translated by John Balcom)

METAPHYSICAL GAME

Grasped then cast
The die spins
A frightful whirlpool
The gods are silent

The hand opens
Begins to sweat
Heaven and earth
Black and yellow
In a bowl
    falling
        rolling
            rolling
                spinning
As the stars lose their footings and fall
Their startled cries can be heard
From a black hole in the Milky Way

Sides with indented marks
Roll
Jangling rate of probability
Motion equals limitless vitality
Existence in all its forms

Around and around on the wheel of existence
Around and around it goes
Turning, crawling
On that sorrowful course

Before the hand opens
The gods are silent
The gods are silent
When the temple bells ring out
One after another
The universe, held in the palm of the hand,
Slowly shrinks into
An egg
A stone
A cube
Of rolling uncertainty
No one can say
What will be lost
Yesterday's boundless sea
Tomorrow's mulberry orchard
Or the observing sky
Of eons of endless change
In the hand
As yet unopened
Rages a tempest
The struggle between life and death
Or just a metaphysical game
A classic filled with typographical errors
Neither to be believed
Nor denied

Released
It falls
Spinning
A seductive whirlpool
Software and hardware
Analysis and reason
The Book of Changes and astrology
All useless for knowing
How our lives are arranged—
Where we will board ship
Where we will disembark—

And even more useless for determining
If those deep red marks are
Scars or birthmarks
Thrown casually
It rolls and spins
Rolls back to the very beginning
The universe
Primeval chaos
Veiled in mist
The gods silently
Looked down at
A frightful whirlpool

(1985)
(translated by John Balcom)

MAILING A PAIR OF SHOES

From a thousand miles away
I'm mailing you a pair of cotton shoes
A letter
With no words
Containing more than forty years of things to say
Things only thought but never said
One sentence after another
Closely stitched into the soles

What I have to say I've kept hidden for so long
Some of it hidden by the well
Some of it hidden in the kitchen
Some of it hidden under my pillow
Some of it hidden in the flickering lamp at midnight
Some of it has been dried by the wind
Some of it has grown moldy
Some of it has lost its teeth
Some of it has grown moss
Now I gather it all together
And stitch it closely into the soles

The shoes may be too small
I measured them with my heart, with our childhood
With dreams from deep in the night

Whether they fit or not is another matter
Please, never throw them away
As if they were worn-out shoes
Forty years of thought
Forty years of loneliness
Are all stitched into the soles

*Author's Note: My good friend Zhang Tuowu and Miss Shen Lianzi
were engaged to be married when very young, but because of the war
they were separated, unable to communicate with each other for more
than forty years. Recently a friend managed to deliver a pair of cotton
shoes to Zhang. The shoes were made and sent by Miss Shen. Tuowu
received them as if receiving a wordless letter full of unspoken
thoughts from home. He wept, beside himself with grief. Today
Tuowu and Miss Shen have both grown old, but their love is
everlasting. This poem was written from the point of view of Miss
Shen, and for this reason the language has been kept simple and
clear.*

(1987)
(translated by John Balcom)

BEIJING SYCAMORES

After liberation
The rows of sycamores on Chaoyang Gate Avenue
Occupied the Beijing
Fall

Though transplanted from France long ago
Their coughing still sounded of home
The grammar of their wind-borne talk fell by the wayside
After free verse was shunned
The sycamore leaves wrote
Nothing but some
Rhymeless rustling

(1989)
(translated by John Balcom)

FUNERAL FOR A POEM

I consigned a love poem
Locked away for thirty years in a drawer
To the flames

In the burning fire
The words cried out
The ashes were silent
But it had faith that one day
The person for whom it was meant
Would read it on the wind

(1989)
(translated by John Balcom)

I BUY AN UMBRELLA JUST TO LOSE IT
(A HIDDEN-TITLE POEM)*

I am going to buy an umbrella
Buy a black one—grimly unexpressive. It's
An unending, boring day of rain. An
Umbrella and why we all need one, that's
Just what the No-Noists are discussing in a Ch'eng-tu tea house.
To stay dry, they conclude, is simply a pretext for the truth—i.e., to
Lose
It

(1992)
(translated by John Balcom)

SILENT PUMPKIN

From an uninhabited place, the vines
Come flooding in
The pumpkin vines grow longer
While my poems
Get shorter and shorter

The pumpkin is silent
Because there is nothing to say
Its belly gets bigger and bigger
When cut open,

---

*Luo Fu's hidden-title poems are a form of acrostic poem, in which each word of the title must begin a line. Luo Fu published a collection of forty-five such poems in 1993.

Half is very sweet
Half tastes like last night's osmanthus
What does that mean?

(1996)
(translated by John Balcom)

羅門

LUO MEN

(1928–)

Luo Men (Lo Men), *men* meaning "door," is the pen name of Han Rencun, who was born on Hainan Island and graduated from the American Civil Aviation Research Center in China. For many years he worked for the Civil Aviation Bureau, Ministry of Transportation, and is now retired. He lives in Taipei with his wife, Rongzi; their home is well known as "House of Lights."

Luo Men published his first poem in the *Modern Poetry Quarterly* in 1954. He is a long-time member of the Blue Star Poetry Society and has served as editor of its journal. He has received numerous literary awards, including "The First Literary Couple" with Rongzi from the Philippines. To date he has published eleven books of poetry and five volumes of essays.

THE FOUR STRINGS OF THE VIOLIN

At childhood, your eyes are like the azure sky.
Grown up, your eyes are like a garden.
At middle age, your eyes are like the rough ocean
Now that old age has arrived, your eyes become the home of
    sadness,
Silent like the theater after curtain-fall deep in the night.

(1954)
(translated by Shiu-Pang Almberg)

SHRAPNEL — TRON'S MISSING LEG

A postcard flown in
Made twelve-year-old Tron walk up the steps leading to the
    clouds
While the priest trod on the red carpet
    And the bullet in a beeline darted

If it had been a thin cloud skimming across the lake
    It would have skimmed forth a sort of smile on Tron's face
If it had been a single wing flying in from the green fields
    It too would have flown into Tron's birdlike age

But when the swing rose, a rope snapped
And the whole azure sky tipped in behind the sun
The swing did not complete the pirouette on the skating rink or
    the ballet stage afar
But got ground like a gramophone disc under the broken needle

*Author's notes: Tron was a little Vietnamese girl whose leg was blown
off by shrapnel during the Vietnam War, as reported in the December
1965 issue of* LIFE.

(1965)
(translated by Shiu-Pang Almberg)

WINDOW

Pushing hard   my hands flow like a current
   Forever myriad hills and rivers
   Forever eyes that cannot turn back

My gaze afar
Turns you into a bird with a thousand wings
Forsaking the sky   no longer on your wings
My listening
Turns you into a flute with a thousand stops
Its sound reaching as far as eyes gazing into the past

Pushing hard   I get trapped and locked up
                       In transparency
                          (1972)
          (translated by Shiu-Pang Almberg)

A WILD HORSE

          Raising its forelegs like lightning
           Producing a peal of thunder
             It then put them down
               And what came
                 Was a spatter of rain
              That chased the winds
        Galloping in through the landscape
        Rushing out through the landscape

Except for the horizon
   It has never seen any rein
Except for mountains where clouds and birds sit
   It has never seen any saddle
Except for rainbows in the sky and rivers on earth
   It has never seen any bit
Except for the smoke in the bleak desert
   It has never seen any whip

At the very thought of the stable
It would tear even the wilderness asunder
At the very thought of vastness

All its four legs would be wings
 Mountains and rivers take flight together
 Where the hooves land flowers cover the ground
 When the hooves lift stars cover the sky

(1975)
(translated by Shiu-Pang Almberg)

WHERE LIGHT LIVES

Light has no wall around
Nor has light's abode
The house of light is only a place on the deck
Traveling through time and space
It carries nothing but
An art gallery in its eyes
And a concert hall in its ears
Thus its hands can be free
      To embrace the earth
Its feet can relax on the horizon
Its head can rest high in the starry sky
 Turning the world into wandering clouds
 Floating past with the flow of light
 The moon is the dam
 The sun is the shore
Go up and you'll find the very home of light

(1979)
(translated by Shiu-Pang Almberg)

RUNNING AWAY

In the lens-grinding workshop of the sun and the moon
I can clearly see
The road running away from streets and lanes
 And wilderness coming to meet it
The tree running away from the potted plant
 And woods coming to meet it
The bird running away from its wings
 And skies coming to meet it
The man running away from his name card
 And haze and clouds coming to meet him
The road and the tree the man and the bird

Running away *en bloc*
And the horizon fetching them all back on a leash again

(1979)
(translated by Shiu-Pang Almberg)

THE OLD MAN SELLING FLOWER POTS

Every day
He pushes a cartload of years
    To display for sale at the entrance of the lane

Sitting outside the pots
Vacant for thirty-odd years, he too is
        An old flower pot
Staring at the flowers and the soil of his native land

Birds of paradise bloom on rooftops
Clouds unfold at the horizon
Eyes open in distant views

At a peal of police sirens
He leaves, pushing the ever-heavier wheels
Someone saw him whistling lightheartedly
        Rolling an iron hoop

(1981)
(translated by Shiu-Pang Almberg)

THE CITY—SQUARE EXISTENCE

The sky is drowned in the square urban well
Hills and rivers dry up outside the square aluminum windows
What shall eyes do?

The eyes look out
Through the cars'
Square windows
And find rows of square windows
        Of high-rises
        Staring back

The eyes look out
Through the rooms'
Square windows
And find rows of square windows
                    Of apartments
                        Staring back

Eyes fail to look out
                    And windows too are blind
                        On square walls
            They can only resort to dining tables
                        And mahjong tables
                To look for square windows
Searching here and there they all find
                        Their escape at last
            In the square window
                Of the TV set

                                (1982)
            (translated by Shiu-Pang Almberg)

UMBRELLA

He leans against the apartment window
Watching umbrellas in the rain
    Move into many
    Solitary worlds
He comes to think of a huge crowd
                Every day with tides of people
                Going from buses and subways
Holding themselves, to go home and hide
                    Behind closed doors

Suddenly
All the rooms in the apartment

                    Run out into the rain
                Shouting aloud that they are
                    Also umbrellas

Astonished he stands
    Tightly holding himself like an umbrella
    Nothing but the sky is an umbrella

Rain falls inside the umbrella
Outside there is no rain

(1983)
(translated by Shiu-Pang Almberg)

YEARS OF POETRY
—FOR RONGZI

If the bluebird didn't come
How could the woods and fields under the spring sun
  Fly into gorgeous April?

If not for June, treading a trail of blossoms
And radiance, that in flame has become
  Cremated into that phoenix,
How could summer at one stretch of its wings
  Turn the maples on both hills all red
And hand over all brilliance and beauty to autumn?

The swan on the quiet dusky country
  Has left behind the last petal of pure white
    To light up the sweet gentle winter
      Grab a handful of snow
    A handful of silvery hair
    A handful of light from mutually gazing pairs of eyes
All being rivers flowing back to April
And poetry sent back to April

*Postscript: With the chimes from your childhood memories, at 4
o'clock in the afternoon on Thursday, April 14th, 1955, we trod along
the red carpet in church, treading the light in the house of light and
entering the long long years of poetry. All I would like to say to you
from the bottom of my heart is in this poem.*

(1983)
(translated by Shiu-Pang Almberg)

READJUSTMENT OF TWENTIETH-CENTURY SPACE
FOR EXISTENCE

Apartments and country places
  Sit at the extremes of freeways
    And stare at each other

Going on in this deadlock
Is not as wise as slowing down
For the mountains have hilltops
  Houses have rooftops
And heaven would not give in to anyone
  Nor be lower than anyone
  No way
Those were the words of birds and planes
  On their way up there

In the days to come
As long as the freeways
 Are thoroughfares
There will be people bringing their idyll into town
  And people driving their city to the country
   Since soil and carpet have walked into
    The same pair of shoes
  And landscape and cityscape are equally pretty
    In the same pair of eyes
Everybody will crowd into the TV set
 Not knowing each other
But becoming faces all the more familiar

        (1983)
    (translated by Shiu-Pang Almberg)

WHO COULD PURCHASE THE HORIZON?

Pull over here
All the rays, shining here and there,
 From the sun, the moon, the stars, and the lamps.

Pull over here
All the routes, running here and there,
 Of cars, ships, and planes.

Pull over here
All the lines, straight and curved, drawn here and there
 By painters' hands.

Pull over here
The views and visions hither and thither
In everybody's eyes.

All, pulled and gathered,
In the end
Is no more than that vast horizon going afar
   Leading heaven and pulling earth
      On a leash

(1991)
(translated by Shiu-Pang Almberg)

蓉子

RONGZI

(1928–)

Rongzi (Jung Tzu) is the pen name of Wang Rongzhi, who was born into a Christian family in Jiangsu Province. She married the poet Luo Men in 1955 and worked at Taipei International Telecommunications Bureau until 1976, when she retired. She now lives in Taipei.

Rongzi started publishing poetry in 1951 and was one of the first women poets to publish in the postwar period. She later joined the Blue Star Poetry Society. To date she has published ten books of poetry in Taiwan and China.

TO MORNING
—A LOVE SONG

I wonder why the nightingale has restrained her song
    And when the morning star retired.
Why don't you tie a bell to your nimble feet
    To wake me early from deep slumber?

Let the morning breeze blow away my heavy drowsiness,
    And let me with the jade cup of my life
Drink to my heart's content the sweetness of morning.

The space of morning is wide and free.
    Following its gait, blithe and proud,
I wish to take up a bamboo basket
    And gather rainbows from the great earth.

Oh, why don't you tie a bell to your nimble feet
    But let me sleep till I wake from deep slumber
When the morning light has spread all over the hills?

It dawns on me that your beauty has a thousand faces
    And I wish to study your countenance.
—The sun is soon overhead.
    Where can I seek your traces?

(published 1953)
(translated by Shiu-Pang Almberg)

NO MORE BLOSSOMS FLY IN OUR CITY

No more blossoms fly in our city   in March
Everywhere crouches that gargantuan construction beast—
Sphinx in the desert   watching with sarcastic eyes
And the urban tigers howl
From morning till dusk

From morning till dusk
Are the rain of smog   the thunder of urban noises
The discord between gears
And the strife between machines
Time is shattered to pieces   Life fades all the while. . . .

Night falls   Like a huge venomous spider, our city
Spreads its shimmering web of temptation
Trapping the footsteps of pedestrians
Trapping the lonely hearts
And the void of night

Often I sit alone in the dreamless nightscape
And watch the nocturnal city below   like
A gigantic diamond brooch
Displayed in the window of the commission house
And waiting to fetch a high price

(published 1965)
(translated by Shiu-Pang Almberg)

A GREEN LOTUS

A faint echo too becomes the past   Looking up
One sees only the cold starlight   illuminating the horizon
There's a green lotus   in the watery field
Meditating and humming, under the moon and the stars, in
    solitude.

The thing in itself is to be appreciated
And laudable is the fragrance   A green lotus
Has the haze of moonlight   and the classic beauty of stars
    sinking in a lotus pond
Through all that mud and marsh, staying so fragrant and
    fabulous!

Quiet thoughts spread wide   Veils for the face
Deter strangers from looking at each other
There's shape in the shadow   and shadow in the water
A lotus, still and silent, watching the firmament.

Purple is going into dusk   a long window facing the setting sun
Even though your lotus pad is full of dewdrops   you never weep
Still a luxuriant green   still a soft flame
Rising   from light cold ripples.

(1957; revised 1968)
(translated by Shiu-Pang Almberg)

UMBRELLA

The debut of a fluttering bird
Makes continuous flaps   with arcs of a bat's wings
Joining to form a perfect circle

A green little umbrella is a lotus pad
The red is the morning sun   the black the evening clouds
Umbrellas of different colors are blossoming trees
That can walk. . . .

An umbrella is held to shield off the sky
Screening the hot sun   screening the rain
Screening the transparent notes of simple nursery rhymes
A little world of its own, free and at ease

I hold an umbrella   to open or shut at will
When shut it is a stick or staff   when open a flower or a bower
In which is hidden a quiet me.

(1976)
(translated by Shiu-Pang Almberg)

WHEN ALL LIVING CREATURES GO BY

The great earth lies like a brown bodhisattva
A single hazy light seeps through the distant sky

The winds are zither strings
Whose footprints are those countless traces on the sand?

Listen, all of a sudden the zither changes its tune
Those familiar tracks of yours have veered
So the winds play another key and similarly
Wipe out the shoeprints of former generations
—When all living creatures go by

(1982)
(translated by Shiu-Pang Almberg)

THE INSECT WORLD
— PORTRAIT OF THE GRASSHOPPER

I sit alone at the tip of summer's bough
Tilting my legs high up   I am also
A reigning king facing south.

It's high summer   and
My kingdom prospers
I am reluctant to exchange my green world of plenty
for the polluted world of Man!

They—
Have to swallow the exhaust of smog   and
Sulky air of their own kind
While I get to enjoy twinkling drops of nectar
In the company of happy fragrant flowers.

(1983)
(translated by Shiu-Pang Almberg)

向明

XIANG MING

(1928–)

Xiang Ming (Hsiang Ming) ("toward light") is the pen name of Dong Ping, who came from Changsha, Hunan Province. In 1944 the spreading War of Resistance against Japanese invasion drove him out of his hometown, and in 1945 he enrolled in Central Air Security Academy in Guiyang, Guizhou Province. In 1949 he moved to Taiwan with the military, from which he was honorably discharged as a colonel in 1984. After a brief stint as an electrical engineer, he worked as an editor for various newspapers and journals.

Xiang Ming started writing poetry in 1951, studied with Qin Zihao in 1953, and published his first collection in 1959, followed by five more over the decades. He served as the chief editor of the *Blue Star Poetry Journal* from 1985 to 1992 and cofounded the *Taiwan Poetics Quarterly* in 1992. In addition to poetry, he has published prose and children's stories.

DAWN AT PROSPERITY CORNER

I take a deep breath in the rose-colored light of early morning
How close they seem: the foothills of Dadun Mountains
I don't dare to look up
To look up and touch the metallic clouds

Stretching out the right hand
Is the Pacific, a huge slice of thin silver
When you stretch out, by chance,
You scoop up a lens of aquamarine

Leading toward the west; how much the West is weighed down
The dense clouds over the isthmus are brewing up the dawn
You can't see any farther
Beyond that, in the distance, only nightmares

Now, we are just beginning to read the sea
Now, the sea is instructing us
Not until you have thoroughly read one page of the early dawn
Can you greet the day's schedule, spry and happy.

(1962)
(translated by Eugene Eoyang)

TUMOR

You are the kind of tumor
That lurks deep inside the body
That one wants to get rid of once and for all
A kind of terminal disease
That's prolonged and incurable
Except in ashes and death

You're definitely allergic to more than pollen
Between summer and fall
When the cicada casts off its coil
You go into a spasm

Besides, you're as stubborn as a callus on the hand
Peel off one layer

And another
Is already incubating.

I absorb the quintessences of Nature
You suck them out of me
I hold lightning in my mouth
But you roar out the thunder
My breast seethes fire
You turn it into a lamp

In the end, all you want is
To make me as thin as the thinnest paper
On the paper whatever it is
The days and months have swept past
In the end suddenly welling up in tears, and letting out a
    shriek—
This becomes a poem.

(1975)
(translated by Eugene Eoyang)

IVY

You are a growth of ivy, made scraggly by wind and soil that's
    fallow
With the kind of fragility that causes worry
When the electric guitar next door makes a racket

Yet you, surprisingly, are not accustomed to using your ears
You reach out multitudinous
Grasping palms
Using broken tiles as your home
Using antitheft windows as a ladder
With red trumpetlike flowers blaring out
Upward
Upward

Yet, incredibly, you do not know
Upstairs it's the fourth floor

Even though the moon is setting
It glows over the ancient horizon

(1977)
(translated by Eugene Eoyang)

THE SETTING SUN ON MANILA BAY

Before it can cry out in pain
That setting sun hovers in mid-air over Manila Bay
Hurried by the twilight
Leaps into the sharp knife edge slicing sky from sea
From the shore, lined with coconut trees
Blood hot as fire
Boiling all of Manila Bay
Into a deep beet red

How majestic an ending
I think of a common sight by the roadside
Filipinos wielding machetes
Their knife edges almost as keen
At once chopping down to roll on the ground,
One after another, coconuts as ripe as the setting sun
Indeed, they were also cut down so suddenly
They didn't have time to cry out in pain

(1987)
(translated by Eugene Eoyang)

POSSIBLE

Evening approaches; it's about to snow
It's possible that the flock of geese will stop honking
Filth as far as the eye can see
It's possible that, for the moment, we can cover things up
We pile up a snowman
It's possible my eyes see him melt, like tears, into a pool of dead
    water
Three loud roars
At the front of the eaves
Icicles almost breaking off or about to break
Resonating to the sounds and falling down
It's possible that they will disintegrate or shatter

If
Going down the road we can track
And hunt down
Three or five fugitive verses
For a volume of peppermint-flavored
Late Tang poetry titled *Clearing After Snow*
Why not? Nothing's
Impossible.

(1991)
(translated by Eugene Eoyang)

ROLLING A STEEL HOOP

Early, very early, there was a dream
A steel hoop looped in a circle barely a foot across,
Guided by a short bamboo stick
Perfectly straight and smooth;
Chasing agile childhood,
Rolling until it wobbles off by itself, on none other
Than the tortuous pebble-strewn paths by the old houses
The forlorn wooden bridge trembles and shakes when walked on
So unsettling and dangerous
The pace of the feet and the torque in the wrist
Excited and interested
It's as good as Mom's cooking
We never get tired
When the hoop slips out of one hand
I catch it with the other to maintain the momentum
As if the entire globe
Were just this hoop creeping around at my feet
Steady now, let me
Hurry it on along.

(1991)
(translated by Eugene Eoyang)

余光中

YU GUANGZHONG

(1928–)

Born in Nanjing, Yu Guangzhong (Yu Kwang-chung being his preferred spelling) matriculated at Nanjing and Amoy Universities in China. He received a B.A. from National Taiwan University in 1952 and an M.F.A. from University of Iowa in 1959. He has taught at various universities in Taiwan and Hong Kong and was twice a Fulbright scholar in the United States, in 1964–66 and 1969–71. He is Chair Professor of English at National Sun Yat-sen University in Gaoxiong, Taiwan, where he was also Dean of the College of Liberal Arts from 1985 to 1991.

A prolific and versatile writer, Yu has published fifty books; eighteen are poetry and the others are collections of lyrical essays, literary criticism, and translations (of Oscar Wilde, Ernest Hemingway, Anglo-American poetry, Turkish poetry, etc.). A dozen or so of his poems are well known either as popular songs or as textbook selections, most notably, "Nostalgia," "Nostalgia in Four Rhymes," and "A Folk Song." Recipient of all major literary awards in Taiwan, including the National Literary Award in Poetry, he was president of the Taipei Chinese Center, PEN International, from 1990 to 1998.

WHEN I AM DEAD

When I am dead, lay me down between the Yangzi
And the Yellow River, and pillow my head
On China, white hair against black soil,
Most beautiful, O most maternal of lands,
And I will sleep my soundest, taking
The whole mainland for my cradle, lulled
By the requiem that rises on both sides
From the two great rivers, two long, long songs
That on and on flow forever to the East.
This the world's most indulgent, roomiest bed
Where, content, a heart pauses to rest
And recalls how, on an icy Michigan night,
A young man from China used to look
Intensely toward the East, through
The darkness to the dawn of China.
So with hungry eyes he devoured
The map, eyes that for seventeen years had starved
For a glimpse of home, and like a new-weaned child
He drank with one gulp all the rivers and lakes
From the mouth of Yangzi all the way up
To Boyang and Dongting and to Koko Nor.

(1966; revised 1998)
(translated by Yu Guangzhong)   •

THE DOUBLE BED

Let war rage on beyond the double bed
As I lie on the length of your slope
And hear the straying bullets
Like a whistling swarm of glow-worms
Swish by over your head and mine
And through your hair and through my beard.
On all sides let revolutions growl,
Love at least is on our side.
We'll be safe at least before the dawn;
When nothing is there to rely upon,
On your supple slope I can still depend.
Tonight, let mountains topple and earth quake,

The worst is but a fall down your vale.
Let banners and bugles rise high on the hills,
Six feet of rhythm at least are ours;
Before sunrise at least you still are mine,
Still so sleek, so soft, so fully alive
To kindle a wildness pure and fine.
Let Night and Death on the border of darkness
Launch the thousandth siege of eternity
As we plunge whirling down, Heaven beneath,
Into the maelstrom of your limbs.

(1966)
(translated by Yu Guangzhong)

GREEN BRISTLEGRASS

Who, after all, can argue with the grave
When death is the only permanent address?
When all the condolers have left,
What if the undertaker's back door
Faces the south or the north?
The coach looks always ready for exile,
And none can dissuade it from the trip.
So-called immortality
May prove nothing but an empty password
For whoever must travel at night,
Even if it works and convinces.
None ends up taller than the bristlegrass
Unless his name soars to the stars
To join Li Bai or Rilke
         while the rest
Is left behind beneath the grass.
Keep names to names, dust to dust,
Stars to stars, earthworms to earthworms.
If a voice calls under the night sky,
Who, indeed, is going to answer
Except a glimmer from above
Or a cricket from below?

(1967)
(translated by Yu Guangzhong)

IF A WAR IS RAGING AFAR

If a war is raging afar, shall I stop my ears
Or shall I sit up and listen in shame?
Shall I stop my nose or breathe and breathe
The smothering smoke of troubled air? Shall I hear
You gasp lust and love or shall I hear the howitzers
Howl their sermons of truth? Mottos, medals, widows,
Can these glut the greedy palate of Death?
If far away a war is frying a nation
And fleets of tanks are ploughing plots in spring,
A child is crying by its mother's corpse
Of a dumb and blind and deaf tomorrow;
If a nun is squatting on her fiery bier
With famished flesh singeing a despair
And black limbs ecstatic round Nirvana
As a hopeless gesture of hope. If
We are in bed, and they're in the field
Sowing peace in acres of barbed wire,
Shall I feel guilty or shall I feel glad,
Glad that I'm making not war but love,
And in my arms writhes your nakedness, not the foe's?
If afar there rages a war, and there we are—
You a merciful angel, clad all in white
And bent over the bed, with me in bed—
Without hand or foot or eye or without sex
In a field hospital that smells of blood.
If a war O such a war is raging afar,
My love, if right there we are.

(1967)

(translated by Yu Guangzhong)

NOSTALGIA

When I was young,
Nostalgia was a tiny stamp,
Me on this side,
Mother on the other side.

When I grew up,
Nostalgia was a narrow boat ticket,

Me on this side,
Bride on the other side.

But later on,
Nostalgia was a low, low grave,
Me on the outside,
Mother on the inside.

And at present,
Nostalgia becomes a shallow strait,
Me on this side,
Mainland on the other side.

(1972)
(translated by Yu Guangzhong)

WHEN NIGHT FALLS

Once I looked through the city's fanciest shops
Just for a graceful desk lamp
With a firm stand, a slim upright post,
And a classical shade trimmed with lace,
Like a parasol soft with yellow halo
To offer me such gallant shelter
Against the night, the dark downpour
Of the night. Just for a cozy lamp
To share night after windy night
All in the aura of fellowship.
For when night falls, the lamp stands on my side
With history out there on the night's side,
And in between an endless whirlwind blows.
Is night, then, for the bed or the lamp?
Is it with the asleep or with the awake?
In the end will always come a time
In utter silence and solitude to face
Whispering ghosts up on the walls, to face oneself
And shoulder all the dark weight of night.
The asleep are launched on a thousand pillows
To be ferried to a thousand dreams.
The awake keep watch over the same night
That closes in on us, and in ceaseless silence
It seems we've been sleepless thousands of years.
And the lamp by the elbow, candle's child

And torch's remote heir, seems to have shone
Through the long night that spans the centuries.
Yet, however deep the night and loud the snore,
A few lamps will always shine and drill
Holes through darkness to echo the stars
That shone before the patriarch torch.

(1977)
(translated by Yu Guangzhong)

THE CRYSTAL PRISON
— ON A WATCH

Uncountable unless under a magnifying glass,
Handled with care by tweezers only,
Such dutiful and skillful little slaves:
By what mischievous sprites, from where,
And with what tricks, were you kidnapped
To this curious device of a crystal prison?
Shut behind the round steel gate, waterproof,
Day and night, to a pressing beat, push
Around the center of quietude,
Push all the golden wheels of a mill
That grinds the heartless flow of centuries
Into years and months, days and hours,
And hours into fine flour of minutes,
Of minutes and moments and seconds.
So out it drips stealthily, through the gate
Called "waterproof." This is the tiniest
Factory, that, tick-tock-tick, knows no rest.
If you doubt it, gently press your ear
Down to your wrist and closely listen
To the slaves' songs in the crystal prison,
Time's ever-chewing, gnawing monotone
When wheels meet wheels, teeth fitting zigzag teeth.
Are the prison songs, you ask, happy or sad?
Happiness or sadness is for you to tell—
A sad, slow tune or a brisk, happy tune.
Listen, the turning wheels are neither sad
Nor happy, even though rivers flow
From your wrist. Gently put your ear down
To the two pulses racing day and night,

Warm blood racing against cold steel,
Blood running faster, seventy-six beats to sixty.
At first the young blood runs at a hundred and forty,
The carefree hare jumping way ahead,
But the steely steps are closing in.
Lay your ear to your wrist and carefully listen.
Which pulse taps the rhythm of your life?

(1978)
(translated by Yu Guangzhong)

A TALE ON THE HILL

Sunset says, behind the dark writhing pines,
That scribble of a burning cloud
Is the signature he left,
Changing from fiery red to ashy purple,
Valid for the evening only.
Some homeward birds
Flying over for a closer look
Are soon lost in the twilight, no, the dark,
With not a bird coming back.
This tale is most prevalent
In autumn among the hills.

(1979)
(translated by Yu Guangzhong)

EVENING

If evening is a lonely fort,
The west gate open to sunset glow,
Why are all the travelers,
Who hurry on horseback,
Allowed only a passage out
And never an admission in?
And, once out, they're all ambushed,
When sunset clouds switch to black flags
And the west gate shuts behind.
Often I turned to ask the garrison,
But was answered only by bats
Flitting up and down an empty fort.

(1982)
(translated by Yu Guangzhong)

THE SPIDERWEBS

Dusk is a sneaky spider
That steals across the water,
Trotting on its multiple legs,
Not a trace on the tranquil sea.
You never know where, for sure,
The landing is to be,
And find only too late,
At a surprised backward glance,
That we have all been captured
In the vastness of its webs.

(1984)
(translated by Yu Guangzhong)

THE PEARL NECKLACE

Rolled away in the recesses of memory,
The precious years that we had shared,
Never expected to be recovered,
Were displayed on a blue porcelain plate
By the salesgirl of the jewelry shop,
Who came up to us and, smiling, asked:
"Would this one of eighteen inches do?"
So thirty years were strung along:
Dear years, where a year spanned hardly an inch,
Where each pearl, silver and shimmering,
Warm and full, was calling back
A treasured day we spent together:
Each pearl a fine day dewdrop,
Or on a wet day a raindrop,
Or a bead in a rosary told
And retold on days of mutual longing.
So the thread goes all the way
Through the sun and the moon, around your neck,
And in eighteen inches through our joint life.
(September 2, 1986, on the poet's thirtieth wedding anniversary)
(translated by Yu Guangzhong)

WHAT IS THE RAIN SAYING
THROUGH THE NIGHT?

What is the rain saying through the night?
The lamp upstairs asks
The tree by the window,
And the tree by the window asks
The car down the lane.
What is the rain saying through the night?
The car down the lane asks
The road to the horizon,
And the road to the horizon asks
The bridge up the stream
What is the rain saying through the night?
The bridge up the stream asks
The umbrella of my boyhood,
And the umbrella of my boyhood asks
The shoes wet inside out.
What is the rain saying through the night?
The shoes wet inside out ask
The frogs croaking all around,
And the croaking frogs ask
The fog falling on all sides.
What is it saying, the rain, all night?
The falling fog asks
The lamp upstairs;
And the lamp upstairs asks
The man under the lamp;
And the man under the lamp
Looks up and asks:
    Why is it still raining
    From antiquity till tonight,
    From a drizzle to a downpour,
    From the eaves to the ocean shore?
I'm asking you, snail-slow moss,
What is the rain saying through the night?

                    (1986)
        (translated by Yu Guangzhong)

THE LANGLOIS BRIDGE
— ON A PAINTING BY VAN GOGH

A clanking drawbridge with rattling chains
Joining the banks of the canal:
Was this where once you trudged across
To a gas lamp, sooty and yellow,
To meet the family of potato-eaters
Hunched around a greasy table?
Did you really cross the bridge
To the *wanen* who grudged you love,
To pits even deeper than hell,
To Rachel's scream and Gauguin's scorn,
Flashing a razor in your hand,
To the asylum's endless corridor
Beyond the sanity of common men,
To Lamartine Square's scorching heat,
The loneliness of roadside cafés
And the lonelier haloes of moon and stars,
To the golden fields when July came on,
The swooping crows and the surging corn?
Yet what you lifted to the sun
Was not a brush but a gun.

The bang that didn't startle the world

Till after a century the echo came
Bringing five million across the bridge
To flood hotels, restaurants, museums
And jostle in long waiting lines to see
What none, except your younger brother,
Had cared to turn and look at:
    The sunflowers,
    The irises,
    The starry night,
    The whole splendor of a new world.

(1990)
(translated by Yu Guangzhong)

管管

GUAN GUAN

(1929–   )

Guan Guan (Kuan Kuan) is the pen name of Guan Yunlong, who was born in Shandong Province. He worked as an engineer at a military broadcasting company before becoming a part-time actor in film, television, and theater and a full-time writer.

Guan Guan started writing poetry in the 1960s and is a long-time member of the Epoch Poetry Society. He attended the International Writing Workshop at University of Iowa in the 1970s. To date he has published two books of poetry and four volumes of prose. His poetry is characterized by the use of Shandong dialect and disregard for sentence divisions.

COUSIN RAT

Negroes come dancing out of a drum. Stamping upon your head. From the room upstairs. From this stained-glass window shattered by a trumpet. They dance out with such grinding hips. Such a song of pure fluidity. Such menstrual lips. Splashing on the bared teeth of your eyes. Your eyes that clamp onto cancer, gonorrhea. Up there over the high-voltage line. Below the warning siren. Such huge breasts raised in place by a crane. A bomb of some kind, held in by a silk sash.

Up on a billboard.

Between buildings and jet airplanes. Your face pinched by constant tics. Your stretched throat. Your tired-out shoes.

"Fire! Help, fire!!"

At last your sewer-slinking tail gets run over for good. A shining red truck. You flee. You flee into the door of ravenous thighs. In the zone where beds meet money.

You keep surveillance over the face of a wristwatch. Plead with the face of a watch. Look ahead to the face of a watch. Figure how many cc of true feelings remain after penicillin. After you turned 15. Your younger sister was swatted away by a sheet of newspaper. The beautiful machine that swatted you. For machine and love of country you went on a hormone-buying spree.

This was right. Once Berry went away. This was right.

Underneath a billboard.

At the rifle range, the target breakfasts on bullets. (It ruminates on good years of eight-course dinners.)

It swears at the measly menu. It mutters about the prices.

Tanks are munching on grass. Munching on briar roses.

Cannon barrels are sipping on stars. Sipping bats.

Bayonets are harvesting wheat. Harvesting wild chrysanthemums.

Barbed wire is tangled up with vines, slicing at wind falling in love with a view of ocean.

A downpour falls and passes. Only a police dog is there to enjoy the moonlight.

Between a rifle and a grave. Bullets deserve your approval. Though none qualify as lucky omens.

(1959)
(translated by Denis Mair)

THE RAVENOUS PRINCE

I keep wanting to get myself an ice-shaving machine. I'll crank it
and whip out an ocean or two. Chill my wife's favorite mixed fruit
into an ice dessert. A beautiful assorted platter. Then my wife and
I (she wearing her red quilted jacket) will dig in. To go with our
cocktail tête-à-tête.

We whittle away at the rainbow of ice. Paste it on the wall of our
bellies. Hold an art exhibition for tapeworms. What is left we put
in a rouge case. The kind with several shades to prettify people's
faces. Then we lop off a chunk of sun and chop it up with chunks
of night. So we can eat gloomy sun. Let it do an air-raid drill in
our stomach. Have an affair. Give birth to some gloomy little suns.
Give birth to a brood of piglets. Then I'll mince some moon with
some ocean. Get a taste of salted moon. Invite tapeworms to make
love on a bed of salted moon. Whistle a tune. Watch the flesh get
its baptism. Reduce man and beast to shavings. Chew slowly on
them for flavor. My wife says, Why not give some to a saint so he
can taste it?

   Then with vehemence we chill missiles and satellites in the
gelato. At this point we sic dogs at their abashed legs. Like crazy
we chill dance steps and grins into the mixture. To watch their
embarrassed performance. We vehemently chill an emperor in his
connubial bed. To watch him plow away in embarrassment. He'll
think he will be there until wheat harvest time. Fiercely we chill
spring, summer, fall, and winter. To watch how even time can be
embarrassed. And watch a death-reporting wristwatch read its own
obituary.

   And then we join anger and melancholy and laughter together.
And eat them up. Then we go to sleep side by side. Let any of them
complain to the United Nations if they will, or wherever else.

   We are children of ice. We are snowmen.

And we know. We know we are eating the sun.

(1959)
(translated by Denis Mair)

LONG STREET

Still all these freshly painted little mouths. Still these shoes strolling over pavement. Still this twilight kissing mouths of skirts.
Oh Lord
What to do about this afternoon?
What to do about this long street?

Oh Lord
If a sedan chair trailing ribbons were carried past, what would be inside? What would be sitting inside? Windows glower at each other. What could they be glowering at? Those melodies crushed by the wheels of cars. Don't take them for leaves whose divorce was decreed by wind. Don't take them for murdered leaves. Don't take them for vagrant leaves trampled by porters.

Oh Lord
Utility poles cannot change to betel trees; the base of a marble wall doesn't get pregnant with dandelions. On the fragrant lawn in the park. Certain skirts have kissed it on certain nights. It has been watered by drops of blood. Hair has gotten tangled. They come to amble on the green, to tread the soft grass. Make a feast of spring's naked body. At least not to let her be a cement slab.

Oh Lord
In the gelato shop a palm tree grows, bearing coconuts of sun. It hides sexy slacks from view. It hides perishable ice. I try crawling past two skirts, wishing to pluck a rose. A virgin rose. Or a tuft of grass. Grass that has never seen a streetlight. My sole temptation the bit of true feeling in a silk sash. Beyond that I do not claim to know. Even when it comes to models with demure eyes. When it comes to pretty feelings that breed upon gift wrap. To a haggard carnation in the trash heap. To a liquor bottle burning with thirst.

Oh Lord
The wall of this cheap hotel has no hitching rings for horses. His Eminence the Circuit Commissioner passed through and once slept in this bed. That woman also slept here. She has slept with barbarians from all frontiers. She has slept with several foreign currencies. Ah! Those magotty spring days, all bunched on the phoenix head on your *cheongsam* slit up the thigh.

Oh Lord
If I win the lottery
I will buy a red-lacquered coffin
And lay it down at the end of this long street
To be a boat for children to play in
Or a den for wild dogs
Or for flocks of sparrows to land on
Or to hell with it

Or maybe . . .

(published 1961)
(translated by Denis Mair)

TALKING ABOUT THE "EMPEROR QIANLONG TRIPITAKA, CARVED ON KNOT-FREE UNBLEMISHED SLOW-CURED BLOCKS FROM PRIME PEAR TREES FELLED IN WINTER"

A complete Buddhist tripitaka, called the Emperor Qianlong Edition, on which carving began in the eleventh year of Yongzheng's reign (By that time he had murdered his brother the prince and tortured the upright minister Zheng Yin to death. That was when champions of justice like Lü Liuliang and Gan Fengchi and Fourth Missus Lü were crawling over walls and jumping from roof to roof in "Swordsmen of the Yongzheng Reign" and in "Arson at Red Lotus Temple" and in "Razor Garotte.") The carving went on until the fifth year of Qianlong's reign. (That was when the Gold River region was pacified [really wiped out], and the Muslim queen died forlornly in the emperor's rear palace.) Who knows why they got it in their minds to carve this salvation-bringing, pain-relieving, greatly compassionate compendium of sutras? How did the bloody hands of two emperors bring themselves to take up knives and carve this compendium of sutras?

Four hundred fifty carvers. Every single one was adept at martial arts; well-known swordsmen gathered from across the empire over a collection of scriptures. One hundred thirty-one devoted monks came to do the proofreading. Who knows if they found a bloody taint between the lines from the bloody talons of Yongzheng and

Qianlong? This must have been the *Peach Blossom Fan** of Buddhist sutras!

Seventy-nine thousand thirty-six woodblocks. Who knows how many thousand knot-free unblemished pear trees were killed? The price of pears must have gone through the ceiling in those years. A lot of people didn't know the taste of pears. I wonder if his fine Majesty had pears to eat? (Ah, so many fewer "raindrops spangled on pear blossoms in spring"; so many fewer "blossoming pear trees overshadow the crabapple." His majesty sure couldn't do without a blossoming pear tree to overshadow the crabapple tree in his harem!)

The blocks weighed four hundred tons. Four hundred tons of pears would make good eating for a whole lot of people. Eighty thousand ounces of silver were spent. How many tons of wheat could eighty thousand ounces of silver buy?

None of this is important. This set of scriptures has made it through four hundred-odd years since Year Five of Qianlong's reign to become a national elder—that's what's important!

Who knows how many people these sutras saved? How many bandits? How many robbers? How much greed, anger, delusion, and pig-headedness? How many monks did these sutras save? How many Taoist priests? How many fishermen, woodcutters, gentlemen farmers did they save? How many heroes and good fellows did they enlighten? How many imperial relatives did they awaken? How many moonstruck boys and pining girls did they wake up?

Anyway, if those pear trees hadn't been carved into the tripitaka, you can bet they wouldn't have lived for four hundred years. They would have been burned sooner or later by the "Red Spear Syndicate" or the "Cutlass Gang" or the "Heavenly Peace Kingdom" or the "Allied Armies of the Eight Powers" or the "Boxer Rebels"! Four hundred fifty expert carvers would have gone hungry; one hundred thirty-one devout monks couldn't have spent time beneath a votive lamp, burning the midnight oil!

The Peach Blossom Fan is a drama written by Kong Shangren in the seventeenth century about the destruction of the Ming dynasty at the hands of the Manchus in 1644.

How many people's worth of rice would eighty thousand ounces of silver get you? After all, a man can't turn into a scripture compendium; a man ends up as shit! Unless you happen to be the female corpse excavated from Mawangdui that wore a suit of jade armor!

Seventy-nine thousand thirty-six blocks of pear wood meant the death of how many pear trees? How many flowers bloom on a pear tree each year? How many pears grow? How many flowers bloom from a scripture compendium? How many pears grow out of it? How many monks and nuns can a pear tree save?

I'm telling you, this is the most fascinating question. Who can answer this question?

Do you want the tripitaka? Or do you want pear trees that bloom and grow pears? Do you want an antique, or do you want pear trees that won't last four hundred years?

The great river hurries eastward. Waves have washed away the gallant figures, and not-so-gallant ones too. Blossoms and pears quickly turn to manure. Give those seventy-nine thousand antique woodblocks a few more four-hundred-year spans, and they'll be manure too.

"Huineng, Huineng, nothing exists after all; what is there for red dust to defile?" "Tell me, Rector, what are you?" "What is there for red dust to defile? Nothing exists after all."
    "Ah!"

"Nowadays all we see is muddle-headed tyrants who kill people. We never hear of emperors who carve a tripitaka after their killing." "Mama Rat had another brood; the littering problem gets worse each generation."

"You're talking nothing but bullshit!! A lot of bullshit!!"

(1993)
(translated by Denis Mair)

商禽

SHANG QIN

(1930–   )

A native of Hong County, Sichuan Province, Shang Qin (Shang Ch'in, "Shang bird"), pen name of Luo Yan, also known as Luo Ma, was forced to serve in the Nationalist army in Chengdu in 1945. As a reluctant young soldier, he traveled all over southwestern China, and in 1950 he went to Taiwan with the army, from which he was honorably discharged in 1968 as a sergeant. From 1969 to 1971 he attended the International Writing Program at University of Iowa. Over the years he has held a number of jobs, ranging from clerk, gardener, and owner of a noodle eatery to editor for *China Times Weekly*. He retired in 1992 and now lives in suburban Taipei, spending most of his time reading, writing, studying Chinese color woodblock prints, and collecting antique ink stands and porcelain.

Shang Qin was first exposed to the works of Lu Xun and Bing Xin when he was locked up in a storage for attempting to run away from the army. He collected folk songs in Yunnan and Guizhou Provinces and started writing poetry. In 1955 he published his poems in the *Modern Poetry Quarterly* and joined the Modernist School shortly thereafter. He has also been closely associated with the Epoch Poetry Society. Shang Qin was the first poet in Taiwan to take a serious interest in surrealism, which had a profound influence on his prose poems in the 1950s and '60s. To date he has published four books of poetry in Chinese; individual collections have also appeared in English, French, and Swedish translations (see the bibliography).

THE ANTHILL

I walk behind others, snap up the splinters of air that have been cut by the men's knife-edged trouser creases and the shavings of air that have been planed off by the women's mouths, and try to sew them together; but I cannot cleanse the air that has been polluted by their hair.

Then the dog that follows me picks up my sighs and uses them as chewing gum, and the melancholy of the dog is carried away by the ants at the foot of the wall and used to build an anthill.

(published 1957)
(translated by N.G.D. Malmqvist)

THE LADDER

When I look out through the window in front of my desk I see a little concrete shed with a flat roof, situated about twenty-five meters from the window. It used to serve as a garage but now stands abandoned. Last winter someone, I don't know who, leaned a bamboo ladder against the shed and the ladder was one third taller than the roof.

Outside the window grow a few stunted cherry trees. In winter I can see the water marks and the cracks in the walls of the little shed through the sparse branches of the trees, and that helps me to retain a certain sense of reality. But when winter passed and spring quickly took its place, the profuse blooming and untimely withering of the pale cherry blossoms never troubled me—and now without my being aware of it summer has arrived.

One afternoon I sit at my desk, utterly overcome with boredom. Holding on to the lower edge of the desk, I lean backward in my chair. At that moment a scene suddenly presents itself before my eyes. I can no longer see the little shed, with its stained and cracked walls, which is hidden behind the dense foliage of the cherry trees, but above the highest branches of the trees I see—oh, the bamboo ladder is still standing there, and that part of the ladder that sticks up above the roof of the shed stands there unsupported. Just now the sky is blue as the sea and at this very moment a white cloud slowly sails past the uppermost rung of the ladder. At the same time an idea takes shape in my brain and I say to myself: "What the devil! How could such a preposterous idea enter into my head?" While I sit there and reproach myself, my colleague, Mr. Chen, who has been standing behind me since I don't know when, says:

"What's the matter? Thinking of someone again, are you?"

"What the devil!" I say, pointing at the ladder and the cloud, "can't you see?" At that very moment the ladder suddenly begins to move—someone is probably carrying it away.

"Hold on! Hold on!" Shouting like a madman and with complete disregard of the danger he jumps across my desk and out of the window and falls flat on the ground, all the while shouting madly: "Hold on! Hold on!" I can only lean my head on the desk and sigh.

(1957)
(translated by N.G.D. Malmqvist)

THE MAPLE TREE

A little boy pointed at a tree by the roadside and asked me: "What kind of tree is that?"

It was in the third month of the year and I replied: "A tree."

The trunk and the branches of the tree were silver-gray and the green leaves were as tender as the little boy's small hands. But my answer didn't satisfy him; in a fit of anger he tossed his head and cried: "Tree? What kind of tree?" How could I answer him? It was in the third month of the year, you see, so I said: "You are too young, my little friend.—How old are you?"

"Six and a half," said he.

"Good," I said and patted his head, which was covered with long, fine hair. "I'll tell you in six months' time, when you are seven."

Six months passed as if they had swum over a small pond. The maple trees revealed their goose-red webbed feet and let them dance in the wind. But the long-horned grasshoppers and the crickets had already robbed me of the boy's friendship—he never returned to ask me what kind of tree it was.

One evening when twilight set in I picked up a scarlet leaf from under the tree and said to an old man who happened to pass by: "This is a maple leaf."

The old man gave me a look typical of the grasslands in autumn and replied indignantly: "I know!" And then he joined the leaf piles whirling in the westerly wind and walked away with heavy steps.

(1957)

(translated by N.G.D. Malmqvist)

THE GLOVES

One day when I had finished work and returned to my bedroom, I first pulled off one of my gloves and threw it on the bed. I then pulled out a cigarette from the packet and stuck it in my mouth. Just as I had lit the match and was preparing to inhale, I suddenly found myself staring through the black smoke curling above the flame at the rough and once-white glove, which had been colored red by red earth, black by black earth, and red-brown by a mixture of red and black earth.

At that moment, as it had left my hand, the glove was naturally quite empty and flat. The index finger was bent and formed an angle of thirty degrees, the little finger I couldn't see, as it was squashed and hidden under the ring finger and the middle finger; it looked indeed as if the glove had lost one finger—oh, how it must suffer from feelings of loneliness and pain. I hurriedly shook my hand and extinguished the match, pulled off the other glove, and in great haste threw it beside the glove on the bed.

The other glove landed on its back with spread-out fingers, deprived of strength. The tips of the fingers pointed at the first glove, with which it formed a right angle, from a distance of about ten centimeters. To say that the gloves were resting wouldn't do, since they were actually quivering. There they lay, a pair of rough and red-brown gloves that had once been white. What better symbol than these gloves of total hopelessness, utterly empty sadness and a human being who has reached the utmost degree of degradation? Not even a widow who dances a slow waltz with an overcoat.

(1957)

(translated by N.G.D. Malmqvist)

A FAUN'S AFTERNOON

1   _____

   _____

2   An eight- or nine-year-old boy sits beside a pond about three meters broad, filled with water so dirty that it reminds you of a lens in a pair of sunglasses, and shouts at two water buffalos that are wallowing in the water: "Woo! Woo!" at the same time pulling with all his might the ropes that pierce their nostrils. One of the two buffalos gives him a look filled with disdain, while the other tosses its head, spurting out dirty water through its nostrils, and these are the only replies the boy gets.

A wind of the third degree blows over the grassland in the vicinity.

The little boy starts to beat the surface of the water with a slender bamboo rod and at the same time points toward the grassland, which is billowing in the wind. "Ah, my forebears, my ancestors, come up here and look! See how green the grass is, and how tender! But ah, the grasses are fleeing, trying to escape the God of Wind who is pursuing them! How tall the grass is! If it isn't beaten down by the huge wheels of the God's chariot, you won't even have to lower your heads to graze it. . . ."

But the two buffalos don't even glance in his direction; they toss their heads sideways, stir up some mud from the bottom of the pond with their tails, and toss it in the air, as if waving their hands and saying: "Mind your own business!"

The little boy suddenly lets go of the bamboo rod and the ropes and runs quickly toward the wind; once he has reached the grassland he pulls up a handful of long grass, hurries back to the pond, puts the grass in his mouth, chews on it, and then tries to persuade them with his mildest voice: "Oh, my dearest, come here! This grass is so tender and so sweet!" Then he sniffs at the grass and says: "Oh, how fragrant! Come here! Come and eat! Oh, my darlings, how tender it is, and how sweet!" At the same time he pulls the ropes.

One of the buffalos, which seems to have smelled the fragrance of the grass, begins to get up, but the water, shining and black as asphalt, caresses the huge grayish-red belly of the buffalo with its warm and soft hands. Having turned its head and gazed at the boy and the grass in his hands, the buffalo suddenly rolls over on its side: the black water is forced to the sides of the pond and then rushes back and embraces the buffalos, as if they were newlyweds reunited after long separation; the water covers the backs of the buffalos and swells around their necks. But the little boy comes down flop beside the pond.

3   We all know that if the boy hadn't lost his flute (ah, but we don't know how he lost it!), he probably wouldn't have had to go to all this trouble. He sits there by the side of the pond, now looking at the two buffalos that wallow in the dirty water, now looking at the grass that is about to flee from the grassland, crying bitterly until the sun with a smile goes down behind the mountains and in re-verse order gives the chromatic lights back to the sky.

(1958)
(translated by N.G.D. Malmqvist)

GIRAFFE

After the young prison guard noticed that at the monthly physical check-up all the height increases of the prisoners took place in the neck, he reported to the warden: "Sir, the windows are too high!" But the reply he received was: "No, they look up at Time."

The kindhearted young guard didn't know what Time looks like, nor its origin and whereabouts, so night after night he patrolled the zoo hesitantly and waited outside the giraffe pen.

(1959)
(translated by Michelle Yeh)

OVERDRAWN FOOTPRINTS
— IN MEMORY OF THOSE DAYS WITH YA XIAN
AT ZUOYING

This is perfect. If I must withdraw every hand gesture in my previous life under this cold weight, if I must repeat every word that I've spoken, every laugh, in this timeless space, just as I promise to— that I will withdraw every footprint I left in my previous life—but there's no need. This is perfect.

This is great. No more "time." No more words. Shadows are touchable water weeds. This path is no longer a path. Wild mustard green and burdock. This is already the roof ridge. "Between Indian strawberry and Aaron's Beard." Wonderful. Pushing aside the weight and coldness of the moonlight, I withdraw my footprints. Footprints return to themselves. . . .

Tonight in the midst of existing without "time" and words I come to the tree-shaded path where we used to see each other off many times. ("Is my old friend coming tonight?") Tonight is my old friend coming? I pace back and forth. When the Milky Way slants to the east, I vaguely sense time rising in my substanceless body: a newborn child proclaims by crying—the rooster has crowed. And I know only too well—that when it comes to those footprints, I have already overdrawn.

(1963)
(translated by Michelle Yeh)

PIGEONS

All of a sudden, I close my right fist tightly and pound it on my left palm. "Pow!" How empty the wilderness is! Yet in the morbid sky a flock of pigeons flies by: are they in couples or singles?

With my left hand I hold my loosening right fist, whose fingers slowly stretch yet, unable to go all the way, can only turn around and around in my palm. Ah, you innocent hands that have worked but are to keep on working, have killed but are to be killed in the end, how you resemble a pair of wounded birds. Yet in the dizzy sky a flock of pigeons flies by: are they in couples or singles?

Now I use my left hand to caress my trembling right hand gently, but the left hand trembles too, making it look even more like a woman pitying her wounded partner, a grief-stricken bird. So I use my right hand to caress my left hand gently . . . perhaps those flying in the sky are hawks.

In the anemic sky, not a single bird. Innocent hands tremble from leaning on each other, hands that have worked but are to keep on working, have killed but are to be killed in the end, let me raise you up high, how I wish to release you—like releasing a pair of healed birds—from my arms!

(1966)

(translated by Michelle Yeh)

THE DOG

Each time I look through the slats in the louvre window I watch this little road, which runs alongside the river and which doesn't as yet qualify for the name of street, until darkness falls and watch the dim light of the street lamp, which is lit I don't know when, turn bright, and I keep on watching until the man walking his dog appears in the circle of light thrown by the lamp.

Each time I have to wait until the man has almost reached the lamppost before I can see the gray dog that trots behind him. The closer the man gets to the lamppost, the more closely the dog follows him. Once the man stands right beneath the lamp, the dog disappears. I imagine that for some reason or other it is raising its hind leg against the post; but once the man walks past the lamppost, the dog suddenly overtakes him. The dog gets farther and farther away until the man is beyond the boundaries of the lamplight.

A man who owns such a trusty and interesting dog is indeed to be envied.

One day I am struck by the thought that I would like to say hello to that man, and I leave my little wooden hut. On my way toward the lamppost I realize that I too have a trusty dog following behind me and that the dog suddenly overtakes me when I walk past the lamppost. It runs farther and farther away until it disappears outside the circle of light.

(1976)

(translated by N.G.D. Malmqvist)

THE MOSQUITO

Ever since my colleague got married, I may be said to have taken over the little wooden hut that he had built himself on the bank of the river. But at practically the same time I took over a hutful of mosquitos.

Ever since I replaced the original louvre windows with screen windows, I have been deprived of the pleasure of observing how the shadow of myself that the lamp used to throw on the windows turned into a puppy.

In order to expel the hordes of small creatures from the first territory that I had ever owned, I immediately installed a screen door.

But doors have to be opened.

A number of uninvited guests eventually avail themselves of this opportunity to slip in. Even though I am particularly careful, a single mosquito may disturb my peace. But what disturbs me most of all is neither their humming and buzzing nor their bites.

It is rather that this heart of mine cannot tolerate the presence of others. Once I have a feeling that another living creature is present in the hut, I get restless; I can neither write nor read—I can't even think. When in vain I have tried to kill them or drive them out with the aid of books and articles of clothing and they have disappeared, I can only sit there and wait until they reappear. When at long last I detect a mosquito crawling on the screen door, I think: "OK, if you want to get out I'll oblige you!" But when I get to the door it has already fled into the dark recesses of the room.

Disgusting! The hatred in my heart is beginning to torment me.

At that moment a wily plan is beginning to take shape. I strip down to my underpants. As I am well aware that mosquitos aren't particularly fond of light, I place the stool at a fair distance from the lamp, where there is still sufficient light for me to see clearly. Absolutely still, I murmur under my breath: "Hey, come and eat!" I think in my heart that a mosquito isn't a human being who requires a great deal of pressing.

But I was wrong: mosquitos don't understand human speech, it's true, but nevertheless they are not so stuffy. If my exercise a while ago hadn't made my skin smell of sweat, the mosquito certainly wouldn't have accepted my invitation. I think someone once said: "An evil smell emanates from a man whose heart is full of hatred."

And mosquitos are creatures attracted by foul smells.

In the end it arrives, silently and quietly, but not at the place where I want it to land. I notice a pain in the calf of my leg, feel how the skin throbs of its own accord, and am just about to move my leg around when the mosquito has flown away.

It's enough to make me irritated. But the more irritated I become, the more I have to restrain myself. And I remind myself of the fact that mosquitos always attack those parts hidden from view. I therefore continuously shift the position of my legs on purpose, while at the same time I slightly wave my right hand, until the mosquito, deprived of an alternative choice, lands on my left upper arm, which I keep perfectly still.

"Good!" I don't know whether it's because the mosquito has heard my silent cry of triumph that it suddenly conceives of flying away. Even though it lands again on the same spot it still seems somewhat timid. All the time I exhort myself to show restraint and be patient and try as hard as I can to hold my breath. It seems as if the mosquito already has enough confidence in me to take a little stroll among the sparse downy hair on my upper arm. Of course I know that it is looking for a suitable spot to attack.

I have already started to feel a slight pain in the skin and I can see the spot where it has sunk its sharp snout. To begin with, the feelers on either side of its mouth are slightly curled against the skin and by then the sucking mouth has quite clearly penetrated still deeper, as only the feelers can now be seen above the skin.

This is a common mosquito of a kind that frequents human habitations, but it belongs to a species that breeds among the grass, not in stagnant, foul-smelling water. It's rather large and quite unlike the tiny spotted mosquitoes you find up in the mountains. It may indeed be said to be very attractive, and the well-formed and smooth wings on its back are a dazzling gray.

It's no exaggeration to say that the shape of the mosquito is attractive. Its belly is elongated without being emaciated, and it's adorned with alternating black and white stripes. Most beautiful of all are the six long legs. Each leg, which is about twice as long as the body, is divided into three sections of different length and thickness. When the mosquito is standing up, the four front legs present a picture of a well-balanced composition; and furthermore the various degrees of inclination of the three sections of the legs, which fully accord with the laws of mechanics, give the viewer a sense of complete stability.

But what are most fantastic are the two hind legs. Look at them now, raised high in the air, a movement that is adjusted to the inclination of the body of the mosquito when the sucking mouth is penetrating deeper and deeper into the skin. The tail of the mosquito is now raised and the entire body forms an attractive angle of fifteen degrees against my skin. The two hind legs move continuously in a rhythmic fashion, probably as a result of the exertion involved in sucking blood.

In this way the belly of the mosquito, which originally was clearly marked by black and white stripes, is beginning to expand and assume an indeterminate color. What I actually observe are expansion of the stripes: those that originally were black turn reddish brown, and those that were white change to pink, and while this happens I continually restrain myself and endeavor to be patient.

That's it! You have already sucked my blood into your belly.

This situation reminds me of the blood tests in the army. When the nurse pierced the skin in the crook of your arm with her needle, she would ask whether you felt any pain and you would at the same time watch the red blood rise in the syringe. The difference is that a blood test is an "event," while the fact that a mosquito is sucking my blood into its belly under no circumstance can be considered an "event." I am sure that you don't get this. What I vaguely perceive is that this is an exchange of life. The pity is that this exalted perception is so transient. When the stripes on the mosquito's belly have disappeared entirely and have been replaced by a reddish brown color and I am struck by the deep sensation that the mosquito has become intoxicated by my blood, I can almost hear myself cackle viciously, deep inside.

The mosquito is actually drunk, it has become intoxicated on human blood.

The swelling belly of the mosquito isn't only reddish brown, it also shimmers in the glare of the lamp. The mosquito is indeed drunk. Its two hind legs, which are raised in the air, not only have ceased to move but seem to have lost their power and droop feebly. But the mosquito has no intention of leaving after having eaten its fill. It is really drunk. Excellent!

In this situation a member of the human species who is several tens of millions times larger than a mosquito naturally doesn't need to resort to strong measures. I slowly raise my right hand, put out the index finger, and press it lightly against the body of the mosquito. When I rest my finger on the mosquito I can feel the resilient belly, and I can even measure the temperature of my blood in-side it.

When I remove my finger, the mosquito has ceased moving. Its sucking mouth is still buried deep in my skin. The rascal is far too greedy and self-indulgent. What I cannot fully understand is if it is because I don't want to soil my hands with blood that I don't apply enough pressure to make its belly burst, or whether it is because I fear to see that the blood of the mosquito is in fact my own, or whether it is for some other reason.
In any case the mosquito isn't dead yet, it has merely fainted.

Pinching it between my thumb and my index finger, I lift up the mosquito and place it on the palm of my left hand.

I am rather sorry for the mosquito for having fallen into my trap.

Perhaps I ought to set it free, if it could be revived?

I begin to suffer from remorse. I have fed a mosquito with human blood, infected by hatred. Will that hatred be propagated if the mosquito should suck the blood of another human being? If this mosquito should breed a new generation of mosquitos, would they be driven by hatred to suck the blood of humanity? Of course, all this is baseless speculation. The most rational explanation is that even though my heart for a moment was filled with hatred, this hatred would probably be dissolved when the blood was sucked into another existence.

But in the end I refuse to set the mosquito free. I quickly make a paper ball and imprison the mosquito in it. In all seriousness, even if hatred can be transmitted, there is no reason to believe that humankind would be lacking in that feeling. And as to heredity, mosquitos will continue to suck blood, even though they are not motivated by hatred.

What really worries me is that the awareness of sorrow, which is a uniquely human characteristic, may be transmitted to the insects.

(1982)
(translated by N.G.D. Malmqvist)

ELECTRIC LOCK

Tonight the streetlights where I live went out at midnight as usual.

While I looked for my key the kind-hearted taxi driver aimed his headlights at me as he backed up. The ruthless glare projected the inky silhouette of a middle-aged man onto the iron gate. It was only after I had found the right key on the chain and inserted it straight into my heart that the good fellow drove off.

Then I turned the key in my heart with a click, pulled out the delicate piece of metal, pushed the gate open, and strode in. Soon I got used to the darkness inside.

(1987)
(translated by Michelle Yeh)

MOONLIGHT
—IN MOURNING OF SOMEONE

An eyewitness recounts: "At the beginning I was simply stunned by what he was doing, when I saw him walking above the tips of silver-grass swaying in the breeze, wondering if he wasn't indeed Bodhidharma! He raised his cane high, shoved both of his arms outward and hard, as if he were roaring; maybe he thought he was Moses parting the Red Sea. Though the stream was shallow, there were caverns left by illegal excavations. But I didn't hear any sound of water; it was early morning on the sixteenth day of the month, the moon was especially full, the sky was very blue, so there was no reason why he could not reach the other shore."

Neither his clothes nor even his shoes were wet. According to the autopsy report, he was drowned by moonlight.

(1987)
(translated by Michelle Yeh)

THE CAT WHO WALKS THROUGH THE WALL

Ever since she left, this cat has been coming in and out of my place as she pleases; doors, windows, even walls can't stop her.

When she was with me, our life made the sparrows outside the iron gate and windows envious. She took care of me in every way, including bringing me with her hands the crescent moon on nights when there was a power outage, and emitting cool air by standing next to me on humid summer nights.

I made the mistake of discussing happiness with her. That day, contrary to my usual reticence, I said: "Happiness is the half that people don't have." The next morning, she left without saying good-bye.

She's not the kind of woman who would write a note with lipstick on the vanity mirror. She didn't use a pen either. All she did was inscribe these words on the wallpaper with her long sharp fingernails: "From now on, I will be your happiness, and you mine."

Since this cat started coming in and out of my place as she pleases, I have never really seen her, for she always comes at midnight, leaves at daybreak.

(1987)
(translated by Michelle Yeh)

SNOW

I fold a letter from the back, it's whiter on this side, a good thing that man doesn't like to write on both sides. I fold it and fold it again, then fold it diagonally into a cone, then cut it with a small pair of scissors, cut it and poke it, then

I've always thought snow is made this way: I open the cut-out letter, it's a good thing that man's handwriting is so light that it doesn't show through, white, spread out, a six-petaled snowflake lies on a yellow palm of hand.

Yet in the sky three thousand kilometers above or even higher, a group of angels are at their wits' end when they are faced with the littering bodies on a big square below, and as the temperature suddenly drops below zero, their arguments and sighs gradually crystallize and fall one by one.

(1990)
(translated by Michelle Yeh)

ROOSTER

Sunday, I sit on an iron bench with a missing leg in a quiet corner of the park to enjoy the lunch I bought at a fast-food place. As I chew, all of a sudden it occurs to me that I have not heard a rooster crow in a few decades.

With the bones I try to put together a bird that can summon the sun. I can't find the vocal cords, because they no longer need to crow. Their work is incessant eating and they produce themselves.

Under the artificial sunlight
there is neither dream
nor dawn

(1993)
(translated by Michelle Yeh)

RAILROAD CROSSING

The alarm bell sounds, the train is coming. My daughter in my arms pushes me away and turns her head around. The rumbling sound covers up the ringing of the bell, whose red eyes keep on blinking. This is how the gaze in my daughter's eyes is carried away by the train. She doesn't even know what distance means.

At the same time my gaze is frozen too, because this city is suddenly cut up: the breathing, the air, the clamor, the wailing—all cut into two halves until the security rail rises. And the other half of my nostalgia for this city lives on.

(1997)
(translated by Michelle Yeh)

張默

ZHANG MO

(1931–   )

Zhang Mo (Chang Mo)—*mo* meaning "silence"—is the pen name of Zhang Dezhong, who was born in Wuwei County, Anhui Province. He attended middle school in Nanjing and during the Sino-Japanese War (1937–45) moved around between his hometown and Nanjing. In spring 1949 he went to Taiwan via Shanghai and joined the navy, in which he served for more than two decades.

Zhang Mo cofounded the Epoch Poetry Society in 1954 with Luo Fu and Ya Xian while they were stationed in Zuoying in southern Taiwan. To date he has published ten books of poetry and four volumes of literary criticism, and has edited numerous poetry anthologies. For nearly half a century Zhang has dedicated himself to the compilation of modern poetry archives, including poetry collections, periodicals, critical studies, and historical documents. He has made a unique contribution to the understanding and study of modern Chinese poetry in Taiwan.

A SONG WITH NO MELODY

Out of the moon in the branch tips flow
sparks of fire
Out of the sparks of fire flow
two shores covered with thin grass
Out of the two shores covered with thin grass flow
clouds in relief
Out of the clouds in relief flows
the still sleeping earth
Out of the still sleeping earth flows
an as-yet-unfinished ink-splash painting
Out of an as-yet-unfinished ink-splash painting
rapidly flows
An empty horizon line where no soul walks
I'm Yang Pass where the song of parting never ends

(1972)
(translated by John Balcom)

I AM A GLASS OF UNLIMITED VOLUME

Standing on the face of time
A layer of cold light faintly floats
Sinking as you draw near
Rising as you move away
I am a glass of unlimited volume

Piercing its clear pupils
To grasp the moving fluid
As if to glimpse everything
Exposed under the sun's rays
There is nothing after all
Other than a huge stemless glass

I am delighted that the world surges like waves
Fortunately, I am a glass of unlimited volume

(1975)
(translated by John Balcom)

ODE TO A SHABBY ROOM

the silverfish
slowly
paint
on the spines of traditional
string-bound books

Andersen's Fairy Tales, which stands to one side
and
Mickey Mouse, who fights indefatigably for justice
ferociously savor
the silent aroma of alcohol

and Li He serenely
dozes how many times
and Ryunosuke Akutagawa gleefully tosses away
a fool's life

night surges
through a small path in Neihu
the name of which is of no consequence
violently I bite chunk after chunk
out of my own shadow

(1977)
(translated by John Balcom)

SHAKE THE HEAD, WAG THE TAIL: A SEVEN-STORIED PAGODA

On the very top of the pagoda
I reach out and grab a few sluggish white clouds
Wring them out
So that the sky won't rustle so

Then I stealthily take
The obscure sound of birds
In an airtight cage
Down to the sixth floor
Their melody hums with the wind chimes under the pagoda's
    eaves

Descending to the fifth floor
There sits a naked monk
Begging bowl in cupped hands
His eyes closed in meditation
Oh, the sounds of nature
Loudly a flock of winter jackdaws is heard
from beyond the borders
Invigorated, lined up on the fourth-floor spiral staircase
Skipping and jumping, skipping and jumping
One by one down to the
Third floor
Second floor
First floor
With its maddening crowd

A sudden storm, the pagoda
is unable to withstand it
Shakily, with the horizon on its back
Despondency and darkness on its back
It departs

(1995)
(translated by John Balcom)

THE FUTURE: FOUR VERSIONS

I see
the world
gently swaying on a mulberry leaf

I see
humanity
softly crying in a broken jar

I see
history
shining wearily in an ancient temple

I see
the future
suddenly crouching there in a coffin

(1995)
(translated by John Balcom)

瘂弦

YA XIAN

(1932–   )

Ya Xian (Ya Hsien, "mute strings") is the pen name of Wang Qinglin, who was born in Nanyang, He'nan Province. He joined the military and moved to Taiwan in 1949. After graduating from Cadre Academy, where he majored in drama, he served in the navy. In the 1960s Ya Xian was invited to the International Writing Program at University of Iowa and later earned an M.A. from University of Wisconsin, Madison. He has been the chief editor of the *Epoch Poetry Quarterly, Young Lion Literature and Art*, and, for many years, the literary supplement of the *United Daily*. He is retired and divides his time between Taiwan and Canada.

Ya Xian had a meteoric writing career. He started writing poetry in the 1950s, reached the zenith of creativity in 1957–60, and stopped writing completely in 1965. The brevity of this period, however, affects neither his status nor his influence as a major poet in Taiwan and, indeed, in modern Chinese poetry as a whole.

UMBRELLA

An umbrella and I
And heart disease
And autumn

I walk holding my roof over my head
Droplets make dampening remarks
Jump about on this domed roof
Having no song to sing

Even in autumn
Even with heart disease
Having no song to sing

Two frogs
Held by the split-open soles of my shoes
Sing out with each step I take

Although they sing for now
I have nothing to sing about

Umbrella and I
And heart disease
And autumn

(1956)
(translated by Denis Mair)

SHRINE OF THE VILLAGE GOD

Far far away
by a bleak and desolate shore
the Big Dipper reaches down its ladle to fetch water

presenting it to Night
to brew into dark port wine

Night
bids the wings of a bat
to carry the wine to the Village God

In tiny bowls before the censer
in the shallow earthenware jar
the wine keeps making a fuss
waiting for someone to come and drink it

But the wasps keep complaining
(their home is too cramped)
living as they are in the Village God's ear

What the little squirrels love most of all is to eat
any old candle ends they may steal in the Shrine

The wine calabash mutters in the grass
what kind of poet is he
who doesn't drink wine

the wine keeps making a fuss

the Village God silently smiles a bitter smile
(he has smiled like that for several hundred years by now)
ever since that day
no single drop of wine has moistened his beard

ever since the Village God's wife
died in the wind
died in the rain
died under the naughty scythe of the boy cutting grass

(1957)
(translated by N.G.D. Malmqvist)

FUNERAL PARLOR

Vultures take flight from behind the church
Flowers have been placed about our necks
(Mama, why won't you come?)

Boys trim whiskers for the last time
Girls put on their last dab of rouge
There will be no more going to dances

Cane gripped in the hand will tap earth no longer
Light and shade cavort no more across glasses on the nose

Nor lavender kerchiefs enwrap sweet strawberries on excursions
(Mama, why won't you come?)

The "Desideratum" beneath the pillow
Takes too much strength to read a second time
The secret of life is secreted after all
In this long, pitch-black, wooden box

Will spring come tomorrow?
We ride a litter to the crossroads
To see what scenery we might see

Will tomorrow be our birthday?
We wear clothes of such fine white silk
Hearts skip as the boatman rows to grandmother's bridge

Yet vultures take flight behind the church
What is the pastor's pipe organ weeping about?
What are the nuns chanting in a drone?
(Mama, why won't you come?)

How nice that she promised to plant for us
A little alder tree on Memorial Day,
I do not love that rustling sound
So terribly forlorn and all.

Ugh! What is wriggling in the sockets of my eyes?
Why do worms have to get involved?
Besides, there are no tears for them to drink
(Mama, why won't you come?)

(1957)
(translated by Denis Mair)

THE MOUNTAIN GOD

The hunting horns have shaken down last year's pine cones
the plank road rumbles under the hooves of the pilgrims' donkeys
when the melting snow streams like silver threads from the
    spinning wheel of the Weaver Maid
the Shepherd Boy sharpens his new scythe on the stone Buddha's
    toes

Spring, ah, spring
under the bodhi tree I feed a traveling stranger's horse

The outcrops breathe hard under layers of stone
the sun sets the forest on fire
when the old hag Malaria hobbles away to the little inn to peddle
    her bitter apples
life leaks from the red eye sockets of the weasel
Summer, ah, summer
I bang the rusty knocker against a sick man's gate

Rustic songs clown around in the baskets on the peasant girls'
    backs
with crying voices the wild geese beg the clouds to wait
when the decrepit evening sun brushes away his golden beard to
    suck the persimmons in the grove
even the red leaves are large enough to hold all four lines of a
    quatrain
Autumn, ah, autumn
on the misty river I help a fisherman cast his net

The woodcutter's axe sings in the deep valley
frightened stiff, the wild cat in the deserted village hides in the
    old peasant woman's sleeve
when the north wind whistles in the chimney
old men in leather boots lined with sedge whip their tops on the
    frozen pond
Winter, ah, winter
together with a beggar I warm myself by a brazier beneath a
    cracked bell in an old temple

(1957)
(translated by N.G.D. Malmqvist)

BABYLON

Plantain juice washes the princess's hair
a silver chain fetters the parrot to its peg
golden pheasants are left to pace the cold tiles of the palace roof
white leopard skins cover the marble floors of the corridors
I am a dark-skinned slave girl

Frightened awake by horses' hooves, the scolded earth at the
    border
listens to sad complaints of faraway sister nations over broken
    promises
blinded prisoners of war shackled in stone reliefs
in the winter evening ward off the shifting sand with their shields
I am a bleeding foot soldier

Pour port wine on the scaffolds of date wood
fill the beggar's iron bowl with gold coins
add oil to the copper lamps on the altars of the gods
light torches on the Star Terrace to call back the star of the Swan
    that has lost its way
I am a white-headed sacrificial priest

The prince cools his lean shoulders with a palm-leaf fan
bloody toeprints sink into the long paved alley
like an antelope yearning for fresh cool water
a palanquin just now passes the fountain
I am a carrier shouting to disperse the crowd

All wailing will have to wait until tomorrow
today we have work to do

(1957)
(translated by N.G.D. Malmqvist)

SPRING DAY

Oh, Lord, the *suona** has already sounded
Winter is as empty as the sleeve of a man who has lost one arm
dark and endlessly heavy

Oh, Lord
Let us on the sundial see
the shadow of your gown
let us on the tips of the grass
on the tender pistil of the violet
seek your bloody footprints

---

*A *suona* is a Chinese brass instrument, similar to a trumpet.

We also long to hear your new songs
streaming from the twelve stops of the wooden flute
from the dialogue of wind and sea

Oh, Lord, the *suona* has already sounded
let the white sprites
(they have knitted a woolen winter cap for the mountaintop)
from the rivers, from the creeks
return to their old homes by the lake

Give the young boys a grass slope where they can roll their
    copper hoops
Give the young girls a piece of dry ground where they can spin
    their tops
command your sun, oh Lord
to descend on the old woman's stick with dragon-head handle
warmed by your rays

Oh, Lord
spread fresh flowers on the road that the sedan chair has passed
moisten their lips with the juice of fragrant grass
let them kiss each other

Do not build ferries for those who have none
let them test the temperature of your rivers
let also thorns, thistles, and jujube trees
prick them, that they may feel a sweet pain

The *suona* has begun to sound, oh Lord
place your voice on our vocal cords
when we draw
the tasseled curtain of the sedan chair
and find Spring seated inside

(January 1957, after reading Rilke)
(translated by N.G.D. Malmqvist)

THE BUCKWHEAT FIELD

The cuckoo was calling, in the woods
calling like a haiku
that year Spring was in the low grass
musicians, three-stringed lutes, folding fans

ah, happy Spring
(she waited for me in Luoyang
waited for me in the buckwheat field)
calling, like a haiku
the cuckoo in the woods

The jasmine was blooming in the park
blooming like a pointillist painting
that year Spring was in Paris
the Seine, old bookstalls, Hugo
ah, a beautiful Spring
(she waited for me in Luoyang
waited for me in the buckwheat field)
blooming, like a pointillist painting
the jasmine in the park

The raven was perching on the Cross
perching like Edgar Allan Poe
that year Spring was in Kentucky
red soil, stagecoaches, Valley of the Dead
ah, a sad Spring
(she waited for me in Luoyang
waited for me in the buckwheat field)
perching like Edgar Allan Poe
the raven on the Cross

(1957)
(translated by N.G.D. Malmqvist)

SHIP RATS

Catching sight of the lights on the western shore of Luzon
recalls memories of our gray buddies over there
happily sharpening their teeth

In Manila there are a great many bakeries
The year was 1954
there once was a black girl
who swapped a kiss for half a walnut kernel

She now lives in the cubbyhole where sails and ropes are kept
looking after the children

dreaming, the swell of the sea her pillow
she doesn't care much for a housewife's chores

The Chinese captain was rather opposed to that marriage
even though I promised never again to chew the pockets of his
    Western suit
or the red spines of his logbooks

My wife always says that we were smart to have escaped that time
perhaps we no longer have to fear the cat

But I say, what's even worse
are those reefs
that we know about
but the captain doesn't

But of course, we needn't worry about which way the wind will
    blow tomorrow
as long as we can sharpen our teeth today

           (August 12, 1957, on board a ship outside northern Luzon)
              (translated by N.G.D. Malmqvist)

THE BEGGAR

I wonder what it'll be like when spring has arrived
what'll the snow be like
the robin and the puppies, when spring has arrived
what'll they be like then

As before, the temple of the God of War
as before, washed socks will be hung to dry on the long-shafted
    spears
as before, a beggars' jingle here, a beggars' jingle there
jujube tree, jujube tree
the sun that belongs to us all will shine, shine
on that jujube tree

But what's most important is
that I don't have a single copper
to give to my memories, as crushed as dead lice
to give to my straw sandals, worn out by the streets

to give to my desire of slaughter
hidden among the battlements of my teeth

Each and every door is closed to me, when evening comes
people begin to love only the fences they have themselves built
it's only the moonlight, the moonlight that has no fences
fills my broken old earthenware bowl with charitable milk, in the
    evening
when evening comes

Who has struck his own profile on the golden coin
(Yee-ya-ya! A beggar sings this)
Who has thrown his ceremonial tablet in the dust
(Yee-ya-ya! A beggar sings that)
Jujube tree, jujube tree,
the sun that belongs to us all will shine, shine
on that jujube tree

Spring, I wonder what it'll be like when spring has arrived
the snow, the robin, and the puppies
and my knotty stick, will it bloom
and what'll it be like when it does

(1957)
(translated by N.G.D. Malmqvist)

RED CORN

In the years of the last emperor the wind kept blowing
blowing on a string of red corn

It was actually right beneath the eaves
that it was hung
as if the whole North
the sadness of the whole North
were hanging there

Recalling those afternoons when we played truant
snow had chilled the private schoolmaster's ruler
my cousin's donkey was tied beneath the mulberry tree

Recalling the time when the *suona* began to sound
and the Taoist priests kept chanting
Grandfather's spirit had not yet returned from the capital

Recalling the cricket's calabash stacked away in the padded jacket
a tiny bit of cold, a tiny bit of warmth
and the copper hoops rolling over the knoll
in the distance we saw Grandma's buckwheat field
and burst into tears

It was actually that kind of red corn
that was hanging there for a long long time
right beneath the eaves
when the wind was blowing, in the years of the last emperor

You will never understand
that string of red corn
the way it was hanging there
and its color
not even my daughter who was born in the South will understand
not even Verhaeren

Recalling the present
I have already grown old
strings of red corn are hanging
under the eaves of memory
the winds of 1958 will keep blowing
strings of red corn will keep hanging there

(1957)
(translated by N.G.D. Malmqvist)

SALT

Second Granny surely never met Dostoevsky. In spring she cried out only these words: "Salt, salt, give me a handful of salt!" Angels were singing in the elm tree. That year none of the sweet peas blossomed.

The Minister of Salt led a camel caravan by the edge of the sea seven hundred miles away. No seaweed had ever been reflected in Second Granny's sightless eyes. She cried out only these words: "Salt, salt, give me a handful of salt!" Giggling angels shook snow down on her.

In 1911 Party* members entered Wuchang. But from the foot-
binding cloth hanging from the elm tree Second Granny doddered
into the panting of wild dogs and the wings of vultures. Many voices
drifted away on the wind: "Salt, salt, give me a handful of salt!"
That year almost all the sweet peas put forth white blossoms. Dos-
toevsky never did meet Second Granny.

(1958)
(translated by Michelle Yeh)

FLORENCE

An entire afternoon
spent sitting
under the patterned parasol of a macaroni stall
dressed in a shining jacket
the China Sea
waits for me beside the sole of my right shoe

Just as yesterday
having gotten up into the horse-drawn carriage, I ask myself:
where shall I go?
in this wind of blue satin
even sorrow is borrowed

But something, whatever it might be
must be hidden in between poverty and the life-prolonging
    chrysanthemum
In Palazzo degli Uffizi
Rafael is dying every minute

When I finally pass the bridge
I pull a blade of grass to chew on

---

*"Party" refers to the Nationalist Party, or Guomindang, founded by Dr. Sun Yat-sen. It
launched the eleventh campaign in the city of Wuchang, Hebei Province, in 1911, which suc-
cessfully overthrew the Qing dynasty.

trying hard to remember a face
and her expression when she ate a spring roll that year

(1958)
(translated by N.G.D. Malmqvist)

THE MONASTERY

Jesus never once visited our monastery, but last autumn he walked
as far as the other side of the pagoda. When he had listened to the
sound of the beats on the wooden fish outside the meditation hall,
to the voices of the nuns reciting the sutras, and to the murmur of
the bodhi tree, he turned around and walked into the wilderness.

He was suddenly struck by the insight that this was China, the
wilderness of China.

Those people, said Jesus, they simply have no idea where Jerusalem
is. In their minds the Pharisees do not resemble the Huns. Poplars
that grow here could never be carved into a beautiful cross, al-
though—although the oats in the fields have the same kind of
flowers.

That entire winter Jesus slept in Bethlehem, where he dreamed of
dragons, dreamed of Buddha, dreamed of the Nestorian tablet,
dreamed of lutes, of prickles and thorns, dreamed of dreamless
dreams, dreamed that he never once visited our monastery.

(1958)
(translated by N.G.D. Malmqvist)

ABYSS

*"I want to live, nothing else. At the same time I've discovered
discontent."*

—Jean-Paul Sartre

Children often lose their way in your hair,
The first spring torrent, hidden behind your barren pupils.
Fragments of time shout. The body displays a carnival of the
    night.

In the venomous moonlight, in the delta of blood,
All souls stand erect, and pounce on the haggard face
Drooping on the cross.

This is absurd. In Spain
People wouldn't even throw him a cheap wedding cookie!
Yet we observed mourning for all, spent the whole morning to
    touch a corner of his shirt.
Later his name was written on the wind, on a banner.
Later he cast us
Leftover life.

Go look, fake sadness, go smell putrid Time;
We are too lazy to know who we are.
Work, take a walk, salute the wicked, smile, and be immortal—
They are the ones who cling to mottos.
This is the face of the day; all the wounds whimper, teeming
    viruses hide beneath the skirts.
Metropolis, scales, paper moon, mutterings of power lines,
(Today's notice pasted over yesterday's notice)
The anemic sun trembles now and thén
In the pale abyss
Sandwiched between two nights.

Time, Time with a cat's face,
Time, strapped to the wrist, semaphoring.
On a rat-wailing night, those killed long ago are killed again.
They make bow ties with cemetery grass, grind the Our Father to
    a pulp between their teeth.
No head will rise among the stars,
Or cleanse the crown of thorns with gleaming blood.
In the thirteenth month of the fifth season, heaven lies below.

And we build monuments to honor the moths of yesteryear. We
    are alive.
We cook oatmeal with barbed wire. We are alive.
Walk through billboards' sad rhythms, through squalid shadows
    on the cement,
Through the souls released from prisons of ribs.
Hallelujah! we are alive. We walk, cough, debate,

Shamelessly occupy a corner of the earth.
Not much is dying at the moment,
Today's clouds plagiarize from yesterday's.

In March I hear cherries hawking.
Many tongues shake loose the debauched Spring. Blue flies
    nibble at her face;
Her legs swish between the high slits of the *cheongsam*; she longs
    for someone to read her,
To go inside her body to do work. Except for this and death,
Nothing is certain. Living is a wind, living is the sound on the
    threshing ground,
Living is a pouring out at them—women who love being
    tickled—
Of the desires of an entire summer.

In the night beds sag everywhere. The sound of feverish light
Walking on broken glass, a confused tilling by coerced farm
    implements,
A translation of peach-colored flesh, a horrible language
Pieced together with kisses, a first meeting of blood with blood, a
    flame, a fatigue,
A gesture of pushing her away.
In the night beds sag everywhere in Naples.

At the end of my shadow sits a woman. She is weeping,
A baby is buried between Indian strawberry and Aaron's
    Beard. . . .
The next day we go watch the clouds, laugh, drink plum juice,
And dance away the remnants of our integrity on the dance floor.
Hallelujah! I am still alive. Two shoulders carry a head,
Carry existence and nonexistence,
Carry a face wearing a pair of trousers.

Whose turn is it next time? I wonder. Perhaps the church rat's,
    perhaps the sky's.
Long ago we said good-bye to the much-hated umbilical cord.
Kisses imprinted on the mouth, religion on our faces,
We each carry our coffin as we wander about.

And you are the wind, the birds, clouds in the sky, a river without
    end,
You are ashes standing erect, death not yet buried.

Nobody can pluck us up from the earth. We see life with our
    eyes closed.
Jesus, do you hear the thriving jungles humming in his brain?
Somebody is drumming under the sugar-beet field, somebody is
    drumming under the myrtles . . .
When some faces change color like chameleons, how can rapids
Retain reflections? When their eyeballs stick to
The darkest pages of history!

And you are nothing.
You do not break your cane on the face of the age,
You do not dance with dawn wrapped around your head.
In this shoulderless city, your book is pulped on the third day to
    make paper.
You wash your face with night sky, you duel with your shadow,
You live on inheritance, on dowry, on the faint cries of the dead,
You walk out of the house, then walk back in, rubbing your
    hands. . . .
You are nothing.

How can you make the legs of a flea stronger?
Inject music into a mute's throat, or let blind people drink up the
    light?
You plant seeds on the palm of your hand, squeeze moonlight
    from a woman's breasts
—You are part of the dark night revolving around you,
Bewitchingly beautiful, they are yours.
A flower, a jug of wine, a bed of seduction, a calendar day.

This is an abyss, between the pillows and the sheets, as pale as an
    obituary couplet.
This is a tender-faced gal, this is a window, a mirror, a tiny
    powder compact.
This is laughter, this is blood, this is a satin bow waiting to be
    untied.
That night Maria on the wall ran away and left behind an empty
    picture frame;

She went to look for the Styx to wash away the shames she had
    heard.
But this is an old story, like a carousel lantern: senses, senses,
    senses!
In the morning when I hawk a basketful of sins on the street,
The sun pierces my eyes with spikes of wheat.
Hallelujah! I am still alive.
I work, take a walk, salute the wicked, smile, and am immortal.
I live for living's sake, watch clouds for the sake of watching
    clouds.
Shamelessly I occupy a corner of the earth. . . .
By the Congo River lies a sleigh;
Nobody knows how it slid that far.
A sleigh that nobody knows lies there.

(1959)
(translated by Michelle Yeh)

THE CATHOLIC NUN

She somehow feels that something is calling her from far away
this mackerel-colored afternoon
when her fingers have completed a full round of the rosary
she somehow feels that there is something

But the sea lies on the other side of the ferry station
it is afternoon, she is sitting there
the bugles in the barracks always keep blowing like this
while she is sitting there

Perhaps the wind will rise tonight, outside the wall
the plaintive mandolin will drift all the way down the road—
something like this seems to have been written down in a book
what happened to the protagonist afterward

A vague guess. And she gets distracted . . .
closing her eyes she leans for a moment on the night
at the same time pushing the carnations on the piano farther
    away from her
since they make her heart ache

(1960)
(translated by N.G.D. Malmqvist)

THE COLONEL

That was simply another kind of rose
Born of flames
In the buckwheat field they fought the biggest battle of the
     campaign
And his leg bade farewell in 1943

He has heard history and laughter

But what is immortality?
Cough syrup, razor blade, last month's rent, so on and so forth
While his wife's sewing machine engages in skirmishes
The only thing that can take him captive, he feels
Is the sun

(1960)
(translated by Michelle Yeh)

DIVA

At sixteen her name made the rounds in the city
Forlorn but lilting syllables

Those almond-colored arms needed a eunuch to guard them,
That little topknot was ravishing to men from Manchu times.

Is that an air from "Spring in Jade Hall"?
(Each night the courtyard filled with faces nibbling melon seeds!)

"How I wee . . ."
Her hands bolted into a cangue.

Some people tell
Of an affair with a White Russian officer in Jiamusi.

Forlorn but lilting syllables
All the matrons cursed her in every city.

(1960)
(translated by Denis Mair)

ANDANTE CANTABILE

The necessity of tenderness
the necessity of affirmation
the necessity of a drop of wine and sweet-scented osmanthus
the necessity of decently watching a woman walk past
the necessity of admitting at the very least that you aren't
    Hemingway
the necessity of wars in Europe, of rain, canons, weather, and the
    Red Cross
the necessity of taking a walk
the necessity of taking the dog out for a stroll
the necessity of peppermint tea
the necessity of rumors, which every night at seven o'clock

whirl about like dried grass at the other end of the Stock
    Exchange. The necessity of
revolving glass doors. The necessity of penicillin. The necessity of
    assassinations. The necessity of evening papers
the necessity of dressing in trousers of French velvet. The
    necessity of betting on horses
the necessity of inheriting one's aunt's money
the necessity of a balcony, the sea, and smiles
the necessity of laziness

But what is looked upon as a river must continue to flow on and
    on
such is always the way of the world—always:
the bodhisattva Guanyin lives on that faraway mountain
poppies grow in the poppy field

                                                    (1964)
                            (translated by N.G.D. Malmqvist)

COURTYARD

No one can pull him back from the place behind the power
    plant
From wife, from wind, from after-dinner chatter
From the autumn courtyard overgrown with foxtail

No one can pull him back from hours after work
From little sister's letter, from velvet cape, from cold cream
From the whole bind he is in, leaning on porch with face in
  hands

No wish to lead an offensive into Hungary
Or write all evening in a stack of red notebooks
At the cusp where darkness is welded to dawn
Not thinking of what some say "might be"

So sleep, my ocean

If she were taken with weeping
If she insisted on seeing the bad side
If she brought up the old matter about her cousin
Just sleep, take your own rest
My embracing sea

(1964)
(translated by Denis Mair)

SONG OF THE ORDINARY

On the farther side of the caltrop patch is a primary school,
  beyond that
is a lumberyard,
Next door is Auntie Su's garden, planted with lettuce and corn
To the left of three maples are some other things
Farther on is the Postal Bureau, a tennis court, and straight
  westward is
the train station
As for clouds drifting over clothes hung out to dry
As for sorrow perhaps hidden somewhere near the train tracks
It is always this way
May has come already
Accept these things quietly, do not make a fuss

At 5:45 a freight train passes
The river ties lovely knots under bridge pilings and moves on
When grasses set forth to take over that far graveyard
The dead never gawk or stare

Most of all
On a terrace
A boy is eating a peach
May has come already
No matter whose roof eternity nestles under
Accept these things, do not make a fuss

(1965)
(translated by Denis Mair)

RESURRECTION DAY

She walks southward on Dehui Street
Since September she has been far from joyful
Before the war she loved someone
The particulars are not clearly known

Maybe it was the river, or the stars, or the evening
Or a bouquet of flowers, or a guitar, or springtime
Or a certain not very clear mistake, for which the blame is hard
    to fix
Or maybe some other things

And all this can hardly constitute a song
Even so, she walks southward on Dehui Street
Now and then she lifts her head
To glance at a row of toothpaste ads

(1965)
(translated by Denis Mair)

辛鬱

XIN YU

(1933–　)

Mi Shisen, who writes under the pen name Xin Yu (Hsin Yü), was born in Hangzhou, although his ancestors came from Cixi, Zhejiang Province. In 1948 he ran away from home and enlisted in the Nationalist army in Beijing; he moved to Taiwan in 1950 and was honorably discharged in 1969. Since then he has been engaged in promoting science education through the publication of *Science Monthly*.

Xin Yu started writing poetry in 1951, having been inspired by fellow poet Sha Mu. He joined the Modernist School in 1956 and later associated himself closely with the Epoch Poetry Society. To date he has published six books of poetry, in addition to fiction, essays, and television scripts. He has served as the chief editor of the *Epoch Poetry Quarterly* since 1996.

THE SONG OF THE SOIL

1   Sun-pointing sunflowers stubbornly withstand the buffets of
         wind and rain
     Testimony, day after day, to the radiance, the majesty of the
         sun
     And the verdant forest is forever like a colorful circle
     That knits together the rhythms of the heart of the earth
         with the harmonies of heaven
     Creating a natural and subtle pulse

     And then there is the mute magnificence of the many-tiered
         mountains
     The soft suppleness of many-cadenced rivers
     Amid the fecund and multifold fellow feeling
     Man's copious main theme stands out over all
     Manifesting ultimate power and grace

2   On the garden walkways and the pathways in the field
     They inscribed their brilliance and undying strength
     In their footprints with creative hands
     Again and again, molding and casting
     My body in the lightning and the thunder

     They plough me with the resuscitations of the spring sun
     Plant in me the powerful fragrances of the summer sun
     Dye me with the delectations of the autumn sun
     Cover me with the distant aloofness of the winter sun
     —Refining reality, burying illusions

3   Whether your fate is fixed or a matter of chance
     Without ulterior motives
     I open my heart to the flora and fauna
     Allowing people, in augmented joy
     To build an even more beautiful future

     Do not mark me with the exhalations
     Made rancid and corrupt by gold and diamonds and cash
     Nor stalemate me with pseudo-truths and rigid formulas
     I would rather, in the midst of the work of reclamation and
         construction
     Let myself loose in the freedom of the sky

4   I willingly accept the dissection and analysis
In the narrow-mouth jar of human wisdom
Let me be marinated into a dessert
Or side dish   Let my taste buds
Lightly touch my forehead and my lips like the petals of a
      flower

Then blood and tears flow from my eyes
I hope, in the foreseeable future
To hear the sound of suckling
Just as the sky is the loving mother to myriad stars
I will build a sleeping cot for everything under the sun

                    (published 1967)
             (translated by Eugene Eoyang)

THE ZANZIBAR LION

The gums were numb
On the tongue, the exhalations from a forest grove
Stemming from a dream
As if a call from someone unfamiliar
Assailed the ear
Whereupon I circled the tree three times
Just so I could let out one good belch.

I circled the tree. Circled it a fourth time.
Afterward, Manon and I played that game
Afterward, I chewed on beef jerky
Afterward, I circled the tree
And put the prairie behind me,
Abandoning the strong wind over my head

Dust to dust ashes to ashes
I am a lion from Zanzibar
A place where national parks
Are a throwback to civilization

My brothers, wouldst thou be dozing
A bald eagle is circling very low in the sky
The runaway wetlands are deep in the earth
But those humans are by my side

Along with their guns and their generic winks
A flurry of raging scurrying
Fire

I circle the tree
After a belch slides out from the throat
I bite into that beef jerky
Play that game

And will the humans be satisfied?
My brother and I look at each other
In that sector of the sky, what seems to be both here and not
    here:
A mass of black cloud.

(published 1971)
(translated by Eugene Eoyang)

A LEOPARD

a lone
leopard   at the edge of the vast grassland
crouched
not knowing why

so many flowers   fragrant
so many trees   green
the firmament opens
and envelops everything

this leopard
   once roared
   and stalked
no longer knows what fragrance is in a flower
nor what green is in a tree

not knowing why
crouching   a leopard
   the stillness of the sky
   the forlornness of the forest

the vast grassland
d i s a p p e a r s

(published 1972)
(translated by Eugene Eoyang)

SEEN AT THE SHUNXING TEAHOUSE

Plopped down on the side of Zhonghua Road
The thirty seats in this teahouse
One next to the other
Unaware how desolate they are

But he is one who knows

At exactly ten o'clock, he reports in
And sits on a hard wooden bench by the side
A cup of strong Longjing tea
That doesn't quite dispel last night's carousing

Soy sauce-flavored watermelon seeds, peanuts
Plus two packs of Long Life cigarettes
Yes, he knows
     That's all he will ever get

No! There is still the heroism of youth
That flows from his hoary weather-beaten face
His flitting frown a dagger
One mighty bellow   to shout down the dust

He is one who knows   loneliness is
Past midnight
The thirty seats in this teahouse
One next to the other . . .

(published 1977)
(translated by Eugene Eoyang)

THE SPEECH OF STONES
—FOR HUMANS

People leave. The room is empty.
There is a slice of lovely silence.

I sit in a corner of the museum
Gently   exhaling a breath,
Thinking: Oh, to go home!

For many years a guest in an alien land
Who knows how often I've wept to myself?
Musing on the vastness of the world   time without end
In a wink . . . see Yungang enveloped in mist
But I can't quite make out the scene.

"Long time no see" — My yellow-skinned relatives!
Tonight I will not dream
I will stay awake   in your attentive gaze
Your familiar voice   lingers in my ears
I say: It's good to be home

Don't turn on the lights! Let me leave open
The windows of my heart in the pure pitch-black darkness
With the sheen of silk.
Gradually let me extend a hand out
From the inner layers of my life. Let it out.

Let it knock
At the doors of your houses: Knock knock
Knock knock   at each and every house
I knock to bestir my relatives
My long-separated relatives: Wake up!

Wake up!   The collected echoes of history
In this solitary shout
I gnash my teeth
And say only this:
"LET ME GO HOME!"

(published 1983)
(translated by Eugene Eoyang)

鄭愁予

ZHENG CHOUYU

(1933–)

Zheng Chouyu (Cheng Ch'ou-yü), pen name of Zheng Wentao, was born into a military family in He'nan Province and as a child traveled all over China with his father. He grew up in Xinzhu in northwestern Taiwan and graduated from National Zhongxing University with a B.A. in foreign languages and literatures. He received an M.F.A. from University of Iowa and for many years has been teaching Chinese at Yale University.

Zheng started writing poetry in the early 1950s. The lyricism of his work from the '50s and early '60s has made him one of the most widely read Chinese poets in Taiwan and China. Many of his poems from that period have been made into songs. After a hiatus of ten years, he resumed writing in 1975; to date he has published a dozen books of poetry.

LIFE IN THE MOUNTAINS

Ever since I came to the mountains, my dear friend,
My days have turned around—
Going always from dusk to dawn.

Every night, I brush past the shoulders of dark boulders
To stand on the howling peak
And sing. Here alone but undaunted I can be high-sounding.

Displayed above is the poet's family tree.
   Oh, the blood relation of wisdom needs extension.
   So I carve transparent names deeply in the whole sky
And sing. Here alone and undaunted I can be high-sounding.

                         (1952)
               (translated by Shiu-Pang Almberg)

MISTAKE

I passed through the South of Yangzi
The face waiting at the turn of seasons, like a lotus flower,
blooms and wilts

Without the east wind, the willow catkins in March do not flutter
Your heart is like the lonesome little town
Like its streets of cobblestones near nightfall
When footfalls are silent and the bed curtains of March not
    unveiled
Your heart is a little window tightly shut

My clattering hooves are beautiful mistakes
I am not a homecoming man but a passing traveler. . . .

                         (1954)
               (translated by Shiu-Pang Almberg)

IN DREAMLAND

The forest is at my feet and my cottage is still up there.
The fence having come in sight is hidden again at the turn of the
    path.

Someone should be waiting by the door,
Waiting for the new books I bring and the zither repaired.
But I bring only a jug of wine,
For the one waiting has already left.

Clouds on my path and on my clothes,
I'm in someone's vague thought.
Up here I find neither birds' song nor flowers' smiling faces.
I'm in a cold dreamland. . . .

The forest is at my feet, but my cottage is still up there.
The fence having come in sight is hidden again at the turn of the
     path.

(1954)
(translated by Shiu-Pang Almberg)

WATERY LANE

Too high are the surrounding hills, making the clear sky
Look like a window painted blue . . .
We draw a curtain of clouds
To make shade and a fringe of rain

I used to love the chimes of bells
But now for your sake I worry about rain or shine in the little
     yard
Forget it
Who cares if our union in this life is rooted in eons of wisdom
Now that you and I have been destined to meet
Like two little fish in this watery lane

(1955)
(translated by Shiu-Pang Almberg)

BUDDHIST CHANT

After three thousand years of wandering
He has at last taken off his wanderer's shoes on the westernmost
     peak
And the gate is closed   Intermittent knocking is heard on the
     animal-head ring
Who has returned   standing on the front steps?

Who has returned, having trailed every star and holding his bowl?
Then an ancient hoary male voice is heard
Sounding from the jingle of the inverted bell

Now that he is back at the mountain gate   he takes his time
    entering
He recalls the ferrying   the drinking   and the pecking
And turns around to look once more
At the world of six times seven
(Oh   bells and drums   the wondrous forty-two syllables of the
    magic *tara*)
The evening prayer of the first day begins in holding the incense
Letting the wooden fish swim forth from the lotus under the
    tongue
My soul
Is neither far nor near

(1957)
(translated by Shiu-Pang Almberg)

SKYLIGHT

Every night, the stars come to my tiled roof and draw water
I lie on my back at the bottom of the well. What a deep well!

Ever since there's the skylight
    I feel as if I could tear off the ice and snow covering my body
    —I am the spring in the northern land that cannot be denied

All stars are pretty, taking up by turn the week's seven nights
And what about the little blue star of the south?
The water from the fountain spring is already swaying within the
    four walls
And the jingling earthen jar is not yet drooping.

Oh, all stars are pretty
But there's only one name that sounds in my dreams
A name as free and easy as running water . . .

(1957)
(translated by Shiu-Pang Almberg)

STOPPING AT A MINOR STATION
—A DEDICATION

Two trains meet at a minor station four hours past midnight
Many of the two rows of windows along the two trains face each
    other
By chance, someone draws the blinds, failing to see what place it
    is
This is a minor station. . . .

Could there be two people sitting by windows facing each other
Ah, old mates from childhood long apart
Meet on the road both going toward dawn but in opposite
    directions
But this is a deep cold night at year's end, blocked by wind and
    rain
Besides, like a traveler's dreams, these are days of no surprises

(1957)
(translated by Shiu-Pang Almberg)

STILL LIFE

Leaning askew   is a row of languid books
In straggling heights   a ladder for soul-searching
Sweetness flows down   and gets contained   in the last cup
Enticing the bee's legs   is the pale-yellow fake honey

Rainwater begins to erode the mural   a scroll of
An overcast sky in worn-out glaze   A stultifying
Empty bed   is a spread of soft gray snuggling up to me
And I am merely a human exhibit
An exhibit   for sale and not for sale

I am also a still life in the company of wood and wind
On dismal days   I am an open book
With the title page already turned last night

(1957)
(translated by Shiu-Pang Almberg)

MORNING

The song of birds has knocked on my window, sounding like
    glazed inverted bells
All through the night raindrops have moistened the blue monk's
    habit in my dream
Now hanging from the tall banana tree outside
Early morning, like a little girl on tiptoe, has come
To peep at the tonsure of my youth with a kind of regret
A touch cool to the skin, saying, "Oh, to go home now!"

(1957)
(translated by Shiu-Pang Almberg)

AFTERNOON

The woodpecker pecks incessantly, like the footsteps of someone
    crossing a bridge
The whole afternoon the woodpecker pecks
While the hillock has already shifted its shadow to the other
    shore of the rivulet
We too have sat through the afternoon and walked
With sounds like footsteps across the bridge, traveling far
As far as the home of the setting sun—Oh, yes
We shall stay the night on the other side of the sky, where there
    are no stars

(1957)
(translated by Shiu-Pang Almberg)

PURE CLARITY

Drunken, I let the silent night flow in my body
And, plugging my ears, I let mystery echo in my body
The scent of flowers oozes from my skin
At this most beautiful moment I let myself be worshipped
And accept a sacrifice of flying streamers from a thousand
    families

The stars hang down in strings, making the wine overflow
    between my lips
The fog is still and cold like praying eyes

Numerous eyes casting their gaze across my hair
I wish to return, brushing the vegetation off my body
I have returned to being a range of green hills lying supine

(1959)
(translated by Shiu-Pang Almberg)

BORDER INN

The autumn territory is divided under the setting sun
At the border, yellow chrysanthemums stand in silence
And he has come from afar, drinking soberly
Outside the window is a foreign country

He longs to step out and in one stride attain homesickness
That beautiful longing, within the reach of a stretching arm

Perhaps it'd do no harm to get drunk
(He is an enthusiastic taxpayer)

Perhaps he should sing aloud
And do more than the chrysanthemums
Merely standing by the border.

(1965)
(translated by Shiu-Pang Almberg)

THE TEMPLE BELL

I heard the temple bell again
And took it for the Galway left on the gramophone overnight
Dewdrops glided down the pine window
And split the spectrum of the morning sun into seven different
    whites

The last of which I'm drinking
The milk in the glass
But the nun who brought the milk left before dawn
And shut the door

(1984)
(translated by Shiu-Pang Almberg)

GUESTS OF SNOW

The red leaves become sparse . . . autumn rain comes seven days
    out of ten
But overnight the north wind brought
An invitation from snow

So I get busy with clothes against the chill, while my wife, afraid
    of winter, and
Our winter-loving children get their gear ready
For frolic in the snow. I fill the tank . . . and we set out northeast
To become guests

To be received by snow all over the sky, and all the way
To return greetings of welcoming smiles
Sparse woods and farmhouses stand in fresh postures, as if waiting
And not quite. Distant hills too
Have turned heaven and earth's lasting marriage into a new affair

But I hesitate, when we arrive at the snowy plain that looks like
    my native place
There's no path . . . nor do I have the heart to tread on the soft
    tender skin of new snow
How could I say "virgin beauty," newfangled words, to describe
    age-old "love fright"?
Ah, children!

(1984)
(translated by Shiu-Pang Almberg)

白萩

BAI QIU

(1937–)

Bai Qiu (Pai Ch'iu), pen name of He Jinrong, was born in Taizhong in central Taiwan. He learned Japanese first and started studying Chinese in 1946, a year after the retrocession of Taiwan to China. He graduated from Taizhong Business School and has worked for years in interior design. Having lived in Tainan and Taipei, he now lives in his hometown.

Bai Qiu started writing poetry in 1952 and won a prize at the first poetry competition sponsored by the Chinese Literature and Art Association in 1955. He was associated with all the major poetry societies in the 1950s and 1960s, including the Bamboo Hat Poetry Society, of which he was a founding member and editor of the society's journal. To date he has published nine collections of poetry and a book of literary criticism. He is also an accomplished calligrapher who exhibits his work regularly.

ARMCHAIR

Arms always held open
In a big, dark room, it stands out
In the slanting light, in front of me
Something seems to leap forward
Out of the darkness

Its squat frame, tensed, like
A catcher waiting for the ball
in the twilight mist on the playing field
Like a will, nakedly
Awaiting the roaring impact of a star

Loneliness breeds silence in life,
on this earth, it's
A body without a voice —
Its unyielding form becomes
A shining sentence

Standing there in silence

(1964)
(translated by John Balcom)

SKY

The sky must have a mother's warm bosom.
So broad, the warmth of blood can be felt,
always ready to
Comfort.

And Ah-huo lies wounded in the trenches
Shattered like a flower. His dying eyes look up
at the sky
Filled with resentment for life

Born unwillingly
Dying unwillingly

Then with difficulty he raises his gun
To shoot the sky dead

(1968)

(translated by John Balcom)

CRY

A cry leaks out of the morgue
There is no one inside
But a cry is left
In a room that has died countless times

The sunlight looks in at the window
The face of the morgue is clearer than ever
One living cry is left
In a world of absolute death

A drop of blood still struggles
In the tenaciously sucking proboscis of a fly

(1968)

(translated by John Balcom)

WEIGHT

Awakening
I find a vine spread over the ground
Heavy with fruit

What else can I say?
I'm a stratum of rock
With a man's tenacity
And you are just
A tiny, tiny seed

A small crack
A little warmth
Has spread now and become
The whole weight of my life

(1969)

(translated by John Balcom)

GEESE

Still we live and must fly
In this boundless sky
The horizon forever receding far ahead
Leading us on, ever in pursuit
It ought to be near but when we look up,
it is always just as far away

It's the same sky in which our forebears flew
The vast emptiness like an unvarying exhortation
Our wings like theirs beat against the wind
A continuation of their will
descending into an unending nightmare

Between the black earth
And the bottomless blue sky
The future is just the horizon line
Leading us on
In our pursuit we slowly die off, die like
a cooling sunset
Still we fly high in the boundless sky
As solitary as a leaf in the wind

And the frigid clouds
Coldly stare at us

(1969)
(translated by John Balcom)

CANARY

Lock the whole world outside the bars
That stranger can't be trusted
Those prying eyes
And eavesdropping ears

Forget existence
In a corner of this vacant place
Idle away life
Idle it away without regret

(The dawn light leaking from the sky
Strikes and hurts its wings)

Life untrusted
Sing for no one
Free the blood in its breast
Drop by drop

Oh, my only canary
Every day plucks feathers from its wings
Every day spits blood with its song

(1969)
(translated by John Balcom)

VINE

You sleep, a bed of vines
Dreaming
You still tightly twine around me
So weak, it's as if
Someone must support you

But the sea keeps calling me from afar
Boundless freedom is there on her bosom
Yes, your bedroom is my death cell
And the unsleeping bird of night
Rebukes me for betraying the sky

Awake, I watch you
Thinking how you always need someone
to support you
But if I detected the smell of someone else
on you
I'd go mad

Oh, I'd best let you tie me down!

(1969)
(translated by John Balcom)

THE SQUARE

The crowd disperses noisily
                back to bed
to embrace sweet-smelling women

Still the bronze statue upholds its principles
arms raised in a call to action
facing the empty square

But the wind
impishly scatters the leaves
to erase the footprints

(1970)
(translated by John Balcom)

SILENT GECKO

Awakening from a poem
        That lingering gliding sound
Is a restless moth
        Flitting around the closed room

Its companion has been frightened away
It alone flutters in a dream

The gecko has eyed it for a long time
And has moved into a good position
After a few pauses
It strikes swiftly and silently

For some reason I cry out in sorrow
Feeling caught in the belly of reality

(1970)
(translated by John Balcom)

葉維廉

YE WEILIAN

(1937–)

Born in Zhongshan, Guangdong Province, Ye Weilian (Yeh Wei-lien), also known as Wai-lim Yip, moved to Hong Kong at the age of twelve. He received a B.A. from National Taiwan University, an M.F.A. from University of Iowa, and a Ph.D. in comparative literature from Princeton University. For many years he has been professor in the Department of Literature, University of California, San Diego.

Ye started writing poetry and was active on the Hong Kong poetry scene in the 1950s. While a college student in Taiwan, he was closely associated with the Epoch Poetry Society. He developed his poetic theory, which relates modernist poetry to Taoist aesthetics, in the 1960s and '70s; it was highly influential in Taiwan. Ye is also a prolific literary scholar and translator of classical and modern Chinese poetry.

FUGUE

I

North wind, am I to bear this one more year?
Streets shiver along the walls
Romances, cold sorrows, from the frontiers
Disclose to me these:
Patience of mountains   Erratic breath of outlands
Chronic neighing of Tartar horses
Bonfires in war and farming in spring
Plants that transcend all knowledge
Immaculate snowfalls   Grand cathedrals and palaces
All plunge into the scandals of gods
In our youthful days
The song goes:
              The moon will rise
              The sun will sink
Quick, quick, do not get lost in the sun
Have you forgotten the oracle of the dragon?
It may slip again from the jade balcony
Into this single sycamore among
Compacted houses   Yesterday
Or is it today?
Beside the river, the deep-flowing river
and dark-shimmering rushes
I see a cloud of crows gather around a drifting of lives
                              But where to?
The winds bring the barking of dogs into winding back alleys
The poets are dead   The Vixen reappears
Is the one-eyed seer still living?
The north winds roar   In the cold street in the flying dust
I vaguely recognize this is the bus to my native land
Tables, mats, and wines proudly invite me
To look at the stars—fugitive ideas on flowers
And intentions in myths
                    We go sightseeing

II

My feet and my hands collide together   In the rushing coach
Stumps uphold the body of winter
In the rush, the fire burns the translucent days of the past

In the rush, the tree-lined boulevard tempers the translucent
    days of the past
A line of thatched huts and flying birds embrace
My skyward solitude   I go in search of
Vespers and festivals within a tent   a beach
A kitten rains in apricot days   and smoke from wild ferns
In the first frost shortly after my vigorous hands
Caressed a holy face
                    Standing up, he
Imitating the ancient prophet:
                          By the Twelve Branches
                                It comes true
                                It comes true
I wait for you to bring you to the golden dynasties of Tang,
    Yu, Xia, Shang, Zhou

The earth holds a full load of floating-sinking memories
We were the great book read into the world
We were the children on the vastest plains
We were the giant of sky-reaching ranges
The earth holds a full load of floating-sinking memories

Glimmering Mars appears and strolls over our gardens
A man with disheveled hair sings
                        I want to see the land of Lu*
                        Mount Tortoise hides it
                        And I have no axe or hatchet
                        To Mount Tortoise, what can I do?
Warm southerly winds
Woes-soothing southerly winds
Grains-increasing southerly winds
                        In early winter
                        In whispers
                        In sickbed
The fire burns the translucent days of the past
The boulevard tempers the translucent days of the past
We drink to the flowering chrysanthemum   make a flute from
    reeds
And play a stanza from the fugitive song

---

*Lu is the birthplace of Confucius and a symbol of Chinese culture.

III

Do you not see people seeking for their children
    the embryo of man?
Do you not see people seeking from abrupt waterfalls
    an ode of stone?
Do you not see people seeking in the jingling of spears
    communion with the heavens?
Against the maple, the willow, the wind, and the wine of the poet
There is the speech of cliffs   the hurrah of the sea
The soundless pit of the sky as we remember
A source turns into a pond
   or gets into plants
   or gets into human bodies
   real or unreal
   abstruse or void
We simply walk down the steps   No monsoon
Nor ill-omened events coming on
Let us brood over a tale: A peach or a desire
Which spoils the moral of the celestial court? O how boring
Let me tell you the legendary charm of a white mouse . . .
                  But on craggy precipices
Or on rocky ruins of a long wall
What can we make of the world?
               We have admired
Millions of flowers, trees, and bays of water, far and near
What can we make of the world?
              We have made and remade
Rhymes, rhythms, meter, tones, ballads, etc.,
What can we make of the world?
Board a congested bus   stop at the crossroads
Look here and there   wait for a butterfly
Wait for a supreme seer   wait for a knight on horseback
Pass by
   How many faces
   How many names
Flouted by trees and buildings
My good friends? They are far away
I stop and scratch my head
Night brings down a galaxy of chilling rains

                        (1960)
              (translated by Wai-lim Yip)

PASTICHES FROM TAIWAN COUNTRYSIDE
(four selections)

4. *Sunset and white egrets*

Ruler-straight horizon
Divides the scenery
The lower panel is broad ink strokes of mistiness
The upper panel is endless dreamy drunken red
Dots and dots of flying flashes
Now rising now falling like musical notes
Are silently playing
The sunset

Welcome back!
Egrets, white, wing to wing
   wing upon wing

6. *Deep night visitor*

Night sinks deeper
Following the fragrance of the cassia
I walk the entire narrow lane
And arrive at the Temple of the Tutelary God
Beside a big banyan tree
When laughter of girls washing by the well
Has subsided
I tiptoe
To the side of the well
And, in a fast move,
Pull up from the well
A bucket of glittering stars

8. *Glazed sun*

Caught in the mud ditch
The sun
In one stroke
Glazes the thick murkiness

Into a stretch of
Ceramic brightness

9. *To stay the sunset*

In order to stay the sunset
Children bathing in the stream
Cup their hands and bail water
Toward the sky

Golden ears of grain
As in fairy tales
Transparent birds
Flap their wings in mid-air

(1981)
(translated by Wai-lim Yip)

QUEST

Perhaps we have waited too long.
All journeys are a circle
(You said you knew)
Return to a pure beginning.
In spring: forest trees show their first green.
Some fierce animals appear.
In deep nights: dark water gurgles.
Some specks of ghostly fire drift around.
You departed from the east to the west, losing your way. . . .
Anticipation is
A line in the distance
So thin, so small, so fine
Between seen and unseen.
Notes of flutes stretch on and on
Toward that distant beginning
Long forgotten
Chaining you.
Every time you said: We have waited too long,
You opened your heart's window.
The air all at once was filled with the tenderness of earth,
As if that happy moment had already arrived.

Birds, like bouquets and bouquets of light,
Exploded out from the tree like a fountain.
You ran to embrace it
And suddenly stopped short.
Are you all ready?
After the fusion of this moment
And then
And then, separation and death.
You responded philosophically:
Eternal happiness is—
Eternal quest, following the wings of
Pain. . . .
In the surging springtime,
In the clear river water,
Between the shadows of two banks of peach blossoms,
There is some prowling, there is some calling.
Invading the spring coldness is
Your familiar fragrance,
Such a soft and small line of fragrance
Chaining you.
Thus, you open your heart's window again. . . .

(1981)
(translated by Wai-lim Yip)

TRAVELING IN SPRING

The souls of azalea flowers
Are trapped
Below the dark canal under the tar thoroughfare

The windblown ways of willows
Swing in the
Memories of a distant past

We travel together
On the dust-raising New Birth Road South
In search of
Dreaming about
Those familiar petals-red and leaves-green in the vague air

The old bell of National Taiwan University
As if to echo the turning wheels of bicycles

Rings, rippling waves
Reach us in the present
In a journey, anxious and pressing.

Distance
Like one's age—in the mist
Is a network of lines that defy undoing
A mere dot of light
Occasionally
Brightens from the lukewarm past

Wisteria, a stretch of flowers
Flash by the car window

We travel together
Inside the restless humming of engines
Talking about a kind of cold
Talking about a kind of heat
And how they break out from rigid frames
To stimulate a kind of frisking
A kind of total unfurling
From the fountain of surging feelings
Between monotonous gray shadows
Under the chase of speed
And how to find out from it
Those words, engaging, disengaging, between getting and losing
In the cold
To let them slowly warm up
To let them slowly take on color. . . .

The quiet cries of azaleas
Fade in the dust of cars
The fine combing of windblown willows
Becomes invisible in the dense opaque sunlight
We travel together
Toward the past
Toward the future
That runaway road
Now bright, now dark

(1985)
(translated by Wai-lim Yip)

林泠

LIN LING

(1938–)

Hu Yunshang, who writes under the name Lin Ling, was born in Sichuan and grew up in Xi'an, Nanjing, and Taipei. After she graduated with a B.S. in chemistry from National Taiwan University in 1958, she went on to earn a Ph.D. from University of Virginia. For years she was engaged in chemical medical research in the United States. She is retired and lives in New Jersey.

Lin started writing poetry in the early 1950s and published her first poem, "The Wanderer," in 1952. She was an active member of the Modernist School and has served on the editorial board of the revived *Modern Poetry Quarterly* since 1982. To date she has published two books of poetry.

AFTER THE SHOW IS OVER

An icy liquid, in an overflow of fervor
spills out from a heap of melting snow
—after the show is over—
I walk out too, following them
out, also like a drop in their midst . . .
dispersed

Such a chilling thought
who can find
a flock of sheep lost in the open country?
(perhaps cold forms in this way)
I turn up my collar
though there is no wind, all is still

A bat with no eyes
flies out of the dark, then throws itself onto another
darkness, without any pointless hesitation

(1955)
(translated by Michael Day)

THE MAN WHO KNOCKED AT THE OUTPOST

The man who knocked at the outpost
does not stop below the tower
the man who knocked wears a dark gown
whip in hand, faces in, looking around into the distance
every gate shut tight, only
the eastern wall's silver-whiskered watchman dozes
with eyes of memory, sizing up the arrival from far away

The man who knocked
does not stop below the tower
he never stays in any place
horse hooves make no sound. The long long whip
—when he leaves—
unexpectedly covers a moat, which has never known mist, with
    fine sand

The man who knocked left a dry branch
and the remains of a fire amid the wild growth beyond the wall

they fly up on the wind, and fall
but dreams of rest are not to be found
in the bags of the man who knocked

(1956)
(translated by Michael Day)

NONMODERNIST LYRICISM

That land is not fit to live in
but I call it home.
It endowed me with the first
longitudes and latitudes of life, to the north of the Tropic of
    Cancer
It is the original soil
I repeatedly set foot in,
but ultimately leave

I remember, there
cattle of one color are not sacrificed, in the wilderness
brocade and silk are not written on, in the starry sky
blood
is not smeared on the lips—
an oath must be written with bones
but the modernist subjected to bone-whipping
is unwilling, also unable
to express emotion

I mean to say, to express emotion so recklessly
    (I'm saying, ahh, so recklessly)
as an infant lifts a foot, alone
in the last blooming field of late spring
there is an urgency that cannot be tabooed—
I'm saying, like an infant's isolation
    by sleep
by the years:
From all profane knowledge
concepts and classical texts
and being the apprentice of—
lofty mountains and open country; make the heaven-sent wind
stop, take a ferry across the wide river
let the divine wind

guide you, everything proper for harmony
   or improper
self-restraint and indulgence

   (I'm saying . . . and I'm saying
   a sworn
   modernist is unwilling
   also unable
   to express emotion)
Even keeping quiet won't do
   reticence is the highest degree of vehemence
   vehemence is the highest level of soundlessness
Even if it's blankness
that won't do either. Blankness
has followed time, tangling together
taking on form. (Easy to touch
   hard to lay out the corpse)
It consumes and corrodes
my unstrung tension
plasticity and tenacity
   in a very small place
laid with a checked cloth
twenty-four by twenty-five
—there, former days are soil; I cultivate
with aged seeds
and a mistaken time sequence
but today it's a dormant bed, rest; the forbidden chamber
of my tempting dreams

There, every night, I arraign
intense emotions from the distant past
and consider
their release—
or execution: The ultimate
unpardonable
execution . . . if there can be found
a killing ground by a river
next spring, after the Waking of Insects
on the first nice day

hang, draw, and quarter me.

                  (1981)
         (translated by Michael Day)

FOR LIN LING*
—AS A GUEST IN FRANKFURT, 1991

An elderly couple once parted before this door.
Cast away by children, they each had to
go their own way, to seek separate abodes.
Later it was said the man went to Holland
and boarded a boat; and the woman . . .
too old—coming down in the world is hard—
wearing an old leather jacket altered by her
mother in childhood, she stands on a snow-
covered hill, a Swiss farmer passes by and takes
her for a sheep, helps and gives
her land too, and a new home is found

(1998)
(translated by Michael Day)

TWO OR THREE HOME REPAIRS IN SPRING

This banister   suddenly wobbles for no reason: Can it be
the flock of crows suddenly rising outside the window   surprised
the irrepressible spring day
in the treetops; are the tricolored cherry buds
for the speed with which they fall
giving some hint of a brief life?

If not   it is the restless scent
on the grassy hill; a fallen book of poetry
splashed paint   the color brown
drips into the ripped-open chest of a young Hutu girl:
old news of nineteen ninety-four   a fresh scar in ninety-eight
a burnt-yellow stack of papers darkly weathering
in the grass   young soul-vested chrysanthemums and
dogwood

(and my brown girl softly sings
Rwanda ah lovely lovely Rwanda . . .)

---

*A good-humored self-portrait.

Hidden   behind the long stair
I indulgently select
this fragmentation unexpectedly executed on the blue sky
a slant perspective   the posture of a bird's-eye view
and history —
the crystal clarity through which its echo filters
and ultimately   like a termite I leave my sawdust

(1998)
(translated by Michael Day)

夐虹

XIONG HONG

(1940–   )

Xiong Hong (Hsiung Hung) is the pen name of Hu Meizi, who was born in Taidong in southeastern Taiwan. A precocious child, she began writing at the age of fifteen; much of her early work appeared in the *Blue Star Poetry Journal* and won her the accolade—coined by Yu Guangzhong in 1957—of "the Muse's favorite daughter." She has published three poetry collections since 1968.

A Buddhist all her life, Hsiung Hung has led a deeply religious life and has written many Buddhist *gathas* or paeans since the 1980s. The mother of two, she has also written children's poems. With a B.A. in art from National Taiwan Normal University and an M.A. from Chinese Culture University, she works as a designer.

THINKING WITH FIRE

so, life leads to a road where there's nothing to wait for
lined on both sides with marvelous architecture
enormous towers with staring compound eyes often filled with
    songs of joy
and small melancholy rotundas

so, sinking to the bottom of the jade cup quivering with shock
are two eye-catching rubies in the necklace of time past:
March and July

if the fortress stacked with dreams caught fire
I would stand there blankly in the rain
watching somebody
beside herself thinking of
somebody else

(1960s)
(translated by Simon Patton)

DARK ASSOCIATIONS

the dusk: eyes that have wept
watching me, all feeling in flames

and ultimately, that which is visible
and that which is not—
the flames of the five thousand colors go out as one
    (you could not bear my trust)

in darkness, the forest trail; in darkness, the wide bridge
    while the demon hand that conducts fate is already arranging
(the minute hand chases the hour hand, sure to overtake it)
is already arranging—
in darkest night an even darker death at a quarter past seven

with a shock I realize that the dark moment is over
what is done can't be undone
    even if you look to the west, regretfully

(1960s)
(translated by Simon Patton)

I'M ALREADY ON MY WAY TO YOU

you stand beneath colored lanterns on the other side
the orchestra hushed, I long to wade across this circular pond
across this sheet of blue glass painted with water lilies
me, the lone soprano

me, alone, the sculptor's hand
sculpting an immortal sadness

a sadness that lives forever inside a smile
the orchestra hushed, globe of the world spinning only east or
     west
I pray for the point where today and tomorrow meet
on the glossy paper of eternity

but the glow of the lanterns hasn't moved, stepping your way
I'm already on my way to you
the orchestra hushed
and me, the lone soprano

(1960s)
(translated by Simon Patton)

JAR

it brings you no sadness, porcelain water jar
there on the table as in ancient times, or by a limpid spring
you feel no sadness, drinking the sweet coldness it holds

in a deep forest, translucency about to drip from a million leaves
you wander by, trapping the pure liquid in your jar
one by one poems take shape

pouring forth at any time, the music never stops beating its wings
I am a single white feather in its midst

expectation is arranged on my table, as if it were ashore
you wade through heavy leaden time to
make off with this jar

(1960s)
(translated by Simon Patton)

RIPPLES

I suddenly think of you:
not the you in the aftermath of disaster
   or when all the flowers were gone

why—if they have a direction—do
the tides of humanity run toward separation?
and why doesn't time's flowing light lead to you
when a million lamps go out?

that childish first day, like the blade of some stunted grass
then a verdant plain, falling barren
all the grass and trees scorched by your million burning seconds
of passion

I should have only sculpted your likeness in glass perhaps
never in concentrated thought
you should have told me long ago perhaps
that there were no temples, no images of the gods anywhere

I suddenly think of you, but not the you of this moment
no more radiant starlight, no more brocade splendor
not in the most beautiful dream, nor in the most dreamlike
   beauty

a sudden thought
but so faint now the sadness
like ripples left
in the wake of a faraway boat . . .

(1960s)
(translated by Simon Patton)

LIFE

bright yellow rape flowers
sway beyond the screen
sunlight
a small child on a bicycle
has no idea of the joy of living
except after grave
illness

(1975)
(translated by Simon Patton)

楊牧

YANG MU

(1940–)

Wang Ching-hsien, who writes as Yang Mu, was born in Hualien on the east coast of Taiwan. After receiving a B.A. in English from the Christian Tung-hai University and completing mandatory military service, he earned an M.F.A. from University of Iowa in 1966. He went on to study comparative literature with the late Shih-hsiang Ch'en at University of California, Berkeley, from which he received a Ph.D. in 1970. He is a professor of comparative literature at University of Washington, Seattle. Since 1996 he has also served as Dean of Humanities and Social Sciences at National Dong Hwa University in his hometown.

Yang Mu started writing poetry while in high school and published his first book of poetry, *By the Water's Edge*, in 1960. Under the pen name Ye Shan, he was first known in the 1950s and 1960s for his sensuous, classically flavored poetry, although he was equally interested in symbolism and high modernism. The adoption in 1972 of the name Yang Mu signaled a new direction in his poetry, toward bolder artistic experimentation on one hand and critical reflections on history, philosophy, and social reality on the other. Yang Mu is a leading essayist, a prolific editor, and a highly respected literary scholar who publishes in both Chinese and English. To date he has published twelve books of original poetry in Chinese and two volumes of poems in English translation (see the bibliography).

NEWS

None. At the harbor I measure my paleness
with a compass

On the road home dead birds
with wide-open, laughing eyes
A rifleman wipes sweat from his brow in the teahouse
watches the scenery . . .

For the ninth time we talk about the clouds
but the dim-witted girl is always beautiful—
even though the slab's green moss is crushed
and chimneys are reckoned
she still loves to laugh, she's still so beautiful

For the hundred and seventh time we talk about the clouds
Yes, she still loves to laugh, she's still beautiful
there are still dead birds on the road
the rifleman still wipes sweat from his brow in the teahouse
watches the scenery . . .

                                                    (1958)
              (translated by Michelle Yeh and Lawrence R. Smith)

FOOTSTEPS

Walk with me into cicadas humming, into fretfulness
Count horses on the entablature
dust-kicking chestnut horses
Calculate age by the river's edge
Sleeper, your hands are pythons

He walks, a shifting shadow, slowly rises
through the palace
to where I sit cross-legged
leaving that empty space to me
yesterday's me

The spot where you drew water from the river
I turn to stare
A blue gourd floats

so do the traveler's lips
Give me ashes, loneliness in clamor
A rosary from the future moon and stars
Counting the beads, you put out the light I sought

North-northwest, beautiful fire watcher
coming from the forest, do you hear stars howling in the east?
The moon to the right, we cross the river at high speed

(1959)
(translated by Michelle Yeh and Lawrence R. Smith)

FLOWING RIVER

No flaming pomegranate in May, spring passes quietly
Setting a ribbon afloat, a hyacinth sits on the slope
Darkness falls around me, mountain wind leaves little behind
but a corner of dusky sky, its lacy clouds, and willow catkins
I lean against a felled tree
whose rustling flows endlessly on

I won't sing anymore, my dear
Spring has turned me into a young girl in a red dress
chasing the bright butterfly of a chiming bell
In sadness I lie down, become a new grave
listen to the vibrating bell from the other side of the river
Spring passes, quietly taking me away

(1962)
(translated by Michelle Yeh and Lawrence R. Smith)

IN THE MIDNIGHT CORNFIELD

1   In the midnight cornfield
my head on the river's dam, I dream
of spring partridges
taking flight from the bank
like clouds emerging from hills. Twilight
a wine shop's fading banners trail—
sadness from the chimney of a paper mill
reflected in the brass-stand mirror
"My eyes are dim, love is like
a napalm bomb" burning away

your arms, your shoes, your book of fairy tales
In the midnight cornfield
you lay your head languidly
on the chilly river's dam, always thinking
of a city where golden apple trees have died, our city
On a snow-drifting, wine-sipping winter night
someone knits a pair of wool socks for you
and wipes coffee stains from the candle stand
the gesture of an aged hand
a farewell song
your dagger, your dagger
your water bag, your water bag

2   Or on the streets after the shops have closed
on the revolving city walls
a bell is ringing
On a distant island, the bell rings
while you sit reading a letter
and listen to the motor's sound
Well water
churns your shadow
and breaks subterranean stars and clouds
"My eyes are dim, flowers fall
on my night-dreaming bed, my eyes . . ."
Many spring lamps
many banished rainy nights
thinking about Dryden's *All for Love*
on the bookshelf by the window
footprints in the yard, the corner of a shirt, brass bells
He is a wild goose of no return, dust of no return
that flaps up and falls
a window that opens and closes

(1965)
(translated by Michelle Yeh and Lawrence R. Smith)

SCREEN

First, the wall's particular mood
maturing behind warp and woof of satin and paper
like a crop anticipating autumn
an allusion reaches from the painting on the screen

transmitted through a teapot
snagging with a smile
knocking over landscapes and butterflies
in swift vehicles and

sojourns at inns. Forlorn
guilty, packing, a familiar tune
Don't know the mood when the sun sets and dew falls
I paint my eyebrows
while you head for the wine shop

(1967)
(translated by Michelle Yeh and Lawrence R. Smith)

THE SECOND RENUNCIATION

Still the sound of reed catkins
grinds with ripping
force over a cup of remaining wine, streets aslant
This return did not meet the winter month of drifting wind and
    snow
Where the bell chimes, a flock of crows arrives
to ask about an untimely death at the Buddhist monastery. Yes

in my memory you are a collapsed stone Buddha
You still smile, but brambles grow like enticing potted plants
behind your ears, under your arms. You were muddiness on the
    South Mountain
born of chance kneading, even returning to green moss now
you have enjoyed centuries of fragrant incense, the midnight
    wooden fish
Monastic scandals constantly brought to your sight
You are no god—

They say I committed murders for you
must've been before I went over the pass
and now I've forgotten . . . or only vaguely recall
When I escaped, floating clouds saw me off to the mountain's
    joining
When I left, he still sat on the peak with flustered faces. . . .
His dejection at departure was caused by drunken sickness and
    autumn melancholy

and at that time you just stood coyly in the sound of bells and
    drums
gazing down at a few praying men and women
waiting for me to return, dig wells, grow vegetables for those
    greedy monks

(1969)
(translated by Michelle Yeh and Lawrence R. Smith)

FLOATING FIREFLIES

1   Poisonous scorpion fluids and thorny
    shadows cover my complexion when tides fall
    To the east of the broken bridge, black hair spreads out
    Dressed as a tired homecoming man
    I pull the oars
    and row into what seems an unfamiliar bay

    A torn map of the constellations in my pocket
    a howling wind
    Through the dense foliage I see
    my enemy sipping tea after food and wine

2   This orange-scented village deserves to be
    burned down . . . a ribbon of smoke surrounds the ancient
        well
    until frogs croak loudly
    We wake up on ashes
    birds vanish into the clouds
    It is quiet all around

    My eroding bones are in an awkward state of phosphorus
        deficiency
    Before and after rain I get
    melancholy and homesick. At moments like this
    a firefly always flits up from the old mansion's ruined garden
    nimbly, shyly
    It must be my enemy's
    only daughter, my wife whom I killed by mistake

3   The story has no ending
    Cymbals strike on All Souls' Day

peach trees grow as usual

When sharpening a knife makes me sweat
the hillside turns pale, the river ripples as the boat sinks
the wine sours at the bottom of the jug, tears reflect
a flock of migratory birds in the fresh, familiar frost

My mourners are scattered in foreign lands;
some become blacksmiths, some peddle medicinal herbs.

(1969)
(translated by Michelle Yeh and Lawrence R. Smith)

ETUDES: THE TWELVE EARTHLY BRANCHES

1. *Rat*

Prostrate, we wait
for midnight—shapeless midnight
except for a bell chime
coming like childhood
from three streets away

Turn and pay homage to long-absent Aries
Kneeling like a field sentry in the dark
I advance northward
Louisa, please face the Earth God
worship him the way I worship your sturdy shoulders

2. *Ox*

NNE¾E Louisa
fourth watch, chirping insects occupy the peninsula I just left
Like Aldebaran, I search the wide-open
valley, a bamboo grove on the other side

Hunger burns on combat lines
Fourth watch, the intermittent lights of vehicles
quietly flash
across your raised thighs

3. *Tiger*

Gemini daybreak. Listen
to the earth's raging tears
Listen, my crawling comrades
unclean melons
Listen, east northeast and north
exploding spring, incendiary shells, machine guns
helicopters chopping up the morning fog. Listen

Louisa, what does the Persian rug say to you?
What does the Asian mud say to me?

4. *Hare*

Please face east when the Crab
shows an array of autumn hues with its many-legged obscenity
Versatile

My metamorphosis, Louisa, is incredible
Patterns of wilderness embroidered on my clothes
swallow baby girls like nightfall
I slaughter, vomit, sob, sleep
Versatile

Please repent with me toward the east
toward the hares of next spring
running and leaping over streams and death's bedding
Please testify with all the pleasures of your senses
Versatile

5. *Dragon*

Lion in the west (ESE¾S)
Dragon is the occasional East in legends. Now
we can only define a constellation of ecstatic groans
with complete nakedness

East southeast south, Louisa
you who bleed profusely
and suffer so much
are my most allusive
bitterest
secondary star

in the constellation of the Leech
that I define

6. *Snake*

Or leave me with your dew-drenched morning flowers

7. *Horse*

Louisa, the wind's horse
gallops along the shore
Provision was once a rotten shell
I am a nameless water beast
lying on my back all year long. Libra at noon
in the western hemisphere, if I am overseas . . .
in bed, cotton sways on the brimful plain
Libra hangs over the corpse-floating river of lost dignity

I hold the distorted landscape
with my groin. A new star rises from the south
Can my hair and beard be heavier than a shell, Louisa?
I love your smell as you kneel toward the south
like a sunflower moving with time
longing for an unusual curve, oh Louisa

8. *Ram*

"I'll be your fullest winery."
In the afternoon Capricorn sinks into
the shadow of the old continent. High like Taurus at fourth watch
I suck and press the surging vines

Surging vines
the harvest flute slants west
Is Louisa still feeding doves on the porch?
Slanting to the west, poisonous stars
please cover me with her long hair

9–10. *Monkey-Rooster*

Another dashing arrow
45 degrees oblique:
the equestrian archer falls, embracing an armful of moonlight

Rise, rise, rise like the monkey, please
I am a weeping tree by the river
the hesitation of Capricorn
The sun has set to the west

11. Dog

WNW¾N
Fill me with the water of the seven seas
Din at first watch ambushes a square
a drizzling rain falls on our rifles

12. Boar

Louisa, please hold me with all the tenderness of America
accept me, a fish of wounded blood
You too are a shining fish
rotting in a polluted city. Louisa
please come back to life in the olive orchard
and lie on your back for me. Second watch
a dewy olive orchard

We have forgotten a lot
a steamboat brings back my poisoned flag
The eagle hovers like a vulture for latter-day carnage
North northwest and west, Louisa
you will scream
when you find me dead upon my victorious return
lying cold and stiff on your naked body

(1970)
(translated by Michelle Yeh and Lawrence R. Smith)

LET THE WIND RECITE

1   If I could write you
     a summer poem, when reeds
     spread vigorously, when sunshine
     swirls around your waist and
     surges toward your spread

feet, when a new drum
cracks in the heat; if I

rocking gently in a skiff
riding down to the twelfth notch
could write you an autumn poem
when sorrow crouches on the riverbed
like a golden dragon, letting torrents and rapids
rush and splash and swirl upward
from wounded eyes; if I could write you

a winter poem
a final witness to ice and snow
the shrunken lake
the midnight caller
who interrupts a hurried dream
takes you to a distant province
gives you a lantern, and tells you
to sit quietly and wait
no tears allowed . . .

2   If they wouldn't allow you
to mourn for spring
or to knit
if they said
sit down quietly
and wait—
a thousand years later
after spring
summer would still be
your name—
they'd bring you back, take away
your ring
and clothes
cut your hair short
and abandon you
by the edge of the enduring lake—
then at last you'd belong to me

At last you'd belong to me
I'd bathe you
and give you a little wine

a few mints
some new clothes
Your hair would
grow back the way it was
before. Summer would still be
your name

3   Then I'd write you
a spring poem, when everything
begins again
So young and shy
you'd see an image of maturity. I'd let you shed tears freely
I'd design new clothes and make a candle for your wedding
    night

Then you'd let me write
a spring poem on your breasts
in the rhythm of a beating heart, the melody of blood:
breast images and the birthmark metaphor
I'd lay you on the warm surface of the lake
and let the wind recite

(1973)
(translated by Michelle Yeh and Lawrence R. Smith)

ZEELANDIA*
—TAINAN, TAIWAN

1   The enemy side has entered the muggy droning of cicadas
I look up from below stone steps; dense broadleaf trees
open into a bed of wind—
giant cannons have rusted. And I don't know how to calmly
    ravish
her new blue flowered dress
in the history of stampeding gunsmoke

A bright expanse delights me
like a European sword boldly piercing through

---

*Zeelandia is the seventeenth-century Dutch name for Tainan, an ancient city in southwestern Taiwan.

a fallen torso. We go up the steps
drum in the troops, but when I
loosen her row of twelve buttons
I find what welcomes me still are her familiar
cool breasts asserting a birthmark
Enemy ships deploy on the sea
we sweat and get out of the rain

2   Enemy ships are busy preparing for attack at dawn
we sweat as we set up defenses
Two pillows build a cannon mount
cicada droning fades away, the subtropical wind
churns into a swaying bed
To begin with you are a water beast from another land
so smooth, so clean
your limbs more slender than ours

Your accent sounds crisp too
it's a cry for help when ramparts crumble
and false as a dried-up well
Whenever I bend over, I hear your
endless empty echoes

3   The giant cannons have rusted, gunsmoke
vanishes in history's broken pages
but I, worried, caress your waist
Once more the row of glossy green broadleaf trees
waits for me to lie down and name it slowly

Seen from the bell tower
it's one of your slanting pendants
each pearl is a battle
bullet holes from fierce fighting all over the trees

In my embrace of sulfur smoke, Holland's body
rolls like a windmill

4   Counting in silence, I slowly loosen
the twelve buttons of the new dress
In Zeelandia sisters share

a dress that falls off easily in summer: the wind comes from
    the strait
and teases the open butterfly collar
where I thought I'd discover an archipelago of spices. But
    who would know
what appear before me still are
those cruel mint-scented breasts. *Ihla*
*Formosa,** I've come to lie on
your bed of cool wind. *Ihla*
Formosa, I've come from far away to colonize you
but I have surrendered. *Ihla*
Formosa, Ihla
Formosa

(1975)
(translated by Michelle Yeh and Lawrence R. Smith)

SOLITUDE

Solitude is an ancient beast
hiding in my jagged rock heart
A stripe on his back that changes color—
I know it's a protective device for his species
Loneliness in his eyes, he often stares at
distant floating clouds and yearns for
celestial shifting and wandering
He lowers his head and muses, allowing the wind and rain to
    whip
his abandoned ferocity
his wind-eroded love

Solitude is an ancient beast
hiding in my jagged rock heart
When it thunders, he moves slowly
laboriously, into my wine cup
and with adoring eyes
looks at a twilight drinker
I know at a moment like this he regrets

---

*In the sixteenth century the Portuguese called Taiwan *Ihla Formosa* (beautiful island).

having left his familiar world
and entering my cold wine. I lift the cup to my lips
and with kindness send him back into my heart

(1976)
(translated by Michelle Yeh and Lawrence R. Smith)

FORBIDDEN GAME 1

Noontime
leaves sway gently outside the screened window
swaying to an ambiance, an incomprehensible romance
(The G string is hard to control, she says, her hair falling to the
    left)
Head lower, her ring finger presses music from a Granada wind
Chanting the rosary inside the window, a nun raises her head—
a wanderer's horse saunters by in the distance
The horse trots so slowly; she has counted twelve rosary beads
The wanderer vanishes over the horizon. So Lorca says . . .

The papaya trees near the ranch
are rapidly bearing fruit. The noontime air
seems to carry an abundant stillness
Twelve years seem still too—
she's finally learned to control the G string, even
the beautiful timbre of the note

Then I hear, I hear the sound of a chinaberry growing
and at the same time dropping fruit: at first
the span between leaving the branch and touching the ground is
    short
seven years, twelve years later, it has gotten longer and longer
(We measure it with silken threads of spring rain, but I
can hardly endure the span of separation)
The moment the chinaberry plumbs through the octave
then another moment—a low, bitter dripping sound
one lower than the first, more bitter
than the first

At last it hits the ground. She raises her head
and sees me listening gloomily to the invisible leaves
swaying gently outside the screened window. At noon

a white cat naps on the balcony
Last winter's dried leaves gather before the steps
dried leaves from years ago pile up in my heart
"I've finally learned to control the G string," she says, "like
    this—"
with a smile; her ring finger presses easily, like a prairie
a Granada wind. . . .
The poet opens the door and walks to the intersection. Quiet
    noon
suddenly a cluster of gunshots; Lorca
is speechless as he falls

People push open the windows to look
knocking over several pots of pansies
Under the fierce sun the prostrate chinaberry is one octave lower
ending a short-lived grand romance in silence

(1976)

(translated by Michelle Yeh and Lawrence R. Smith)

FORBIDDEN GAME 2

In a faraway place, behind the maple grove turning red
a river swells after a fresh shower
I can hear the sound of trout breathing each other in
hear the evening smoke report on autumn's abundance
and desolation. But a serene mood
is louder than all these sounds
more solemn too—in a faraway
faraway place

Allow me to rethink the question of time. "Music"
you say as you lay your left hand on the octave, "is a temporal
art. What about spatial arts?
And combinations of time and space? And . . ."
And the uplifting, ecstatic joy of the union of time and space
and spirit. Sometimes
I can't help facing a river swollen after a fresh shower
after the maple grove and evening smoke
before serenity

Sometimes you can't find my traces
(even if you try very hard), sometimes

night falls slowly on this side of the valley
A bugle echoes through the fortress. I walk a path
leading directly to death and eternal life
You may be able to find it on fantasy's
prairie, on the edge of dream
in tears, in blood

I find it hard, hard to believe this is a dead man's song
floating in a simple, moving legend
accompanying rumor (a bugle
echoes through the fortress): people stand around and listen
till pounding cavalry hoofbeats surround the town
getting closer and closer . . . then the people
innocently disperse

"There is the joy of the union of time and space
and spirit," the poet says
"an uplifting, ecstatic joy"
In a faraway place
a river swells after a fresh shower
and looks serene
But I hear a mood more serene, more sonorous
than any sound, a slight rage real
as a low cry, on the edge of dream and memory
in tears, in blood

How do you forget that reality—
across the preparation of reeds, whispers of stars and trees
homework of the moon and sea—how do you forget a street
some fruit and wine (even
if you can)? I can't imagine
the gunshot that leads to death and eternal life
when I enter the maple grove
turning red, I cannot imagine

this is a dead man's song, floating in
a simple, moving legend
accompanying rumor—
a bugle echoes through
the fortress

(1976)
(translated by Michelle Yeh and Lawrence R. Smith)

FORBIDDEN GAME 3

Try to remember
the great concern in Granada
try to remember your language and pain
green winds and green horses, your
language and happiness—your occasional happiness—
beyond the grove by the awakening riverbank
a donkey's hoofbeats at this moment are louder than wine and
    harvest

She wishes to talk to you, with multisyllabic words
she wishes to talk to you (with gestures too)
She inquires about the direction of the church
though this doesn't mean a young person like her
already understands religious Granada
Saint Michael, please protect
this good, curious girl
bring her up

teach her to hear—as she listens to the bell chime—
history's deeper sigh
recorded in an obscure place in the textbook
on the other side of the olive stained-glass window—
the peasants' sweat
the soldiers' blood
Teach her to recognize the row of fig trees on the riverbank
A wind once came from the assembled fortresses
and persecuted a boy who left home on Sunday
(his love as pure as his cap
he could recite Lorca's new poems)
The boy once lay dying under a row of beautiful
fig trees, too soon to shed
a peasant's sweat and a soldier's blood

Teach her to listen and know all this

Then you can give her back to me
a radical heathen
We'll spend the whole winter
studying rhetoric and semantics then

forgetting rhetoric and semantics. We'll
spend the spring traveling
discussing Granada's myths and poetry
in a tavern throughout the night. We'll
do field work and interviews
and together spend the long summer vacation
collecting folk songs and proverbs. And autumn
will find us inside a red-leafed window
wiping away peasants' sweat and soldiers'
blood; the little donkey's hoofbeats will
be louder than wine and harvest

You will love such a good, curious girl
Saint Michael, try to remember
that great concern

(1976)

(translated by Michelle Yeh and Lawrence R. Smith)

FORBIDDEN GAME 4

Chilly sunlight brightens up a rain gutter
It's so quiet: the residents may be reading morning papers
no exciting news
can destroy this morning's emptiness
Hovering slowly, surviving mosquitos
trace shiny vectors. There's not even a breeze

I sit at Granada's edge
meditating on the poet's bleeding heart
A guitar leans in a corner of the tavern
in the lingering warmth of last night's fire
I say to myself: "Music is at best
ornamental to the story, so are melody and rhythm"
When the music's lost (for example, now)
the story is still there, the hero still alive
so is the one he said good-bye to
now combing her hair in a flowering garden

If music is really fit for defining love
is love merely ornamental to life?
So I sit wondering, a few gray pigeons on the street

strutting and pecking around. There was bleeding there once
"Love, when it vanishes (for example
this moment, or tomorrow, or next year)
can life go on?" Someone insists
love is the whole of life

Still thinking
I sit at Granada's edge
A donkey comes up from the other end of the street
followed by a bleary-eyed man—
last night he spread six rumors. Yet
"when love vanishes, life can still be
finished out." Delighted, I move toward this conclusion
Heros are still learning cross-country warfare and demolition
even if he gets killed in a foreign land or only
executed by the cavalry in the morning, the once-leaping
life still lives in a place farther than Granada
the one he once said good-bye to still
combs her hair in a flowering garden

This conclusion satisfies me
as I lift my head to look at the chilly sunlight
brightening up a rain gutter. I get up from the desk
Someone picks up a guitar in some corner of the house
and repeats a faraway grand romance
Delighted, I walk toward the pecking pigeons
The man with the donkey (last night he'd
already spread six rumors about me)
turns around to beckon me with bleary eyes—
the guitar suddenly stops

a cluster of gunshot . . .

(1976)
(translated by Michelle Yeh and Lawrence R. Smith)

SOMEONE ASKS ME ABOUT JUSTICE AND RIGHTEOUSNESS

Someone asks me about justice and righteousness
in a neatly written letter
mailed from a town in another county, signed

with his real name, including social security number
age (outside my window rain drips on banana leaves
and broken glass on garden walls), ancestry, occupation
(twigs and branches pile up in the yard
a blackbird flaps its wings). Obviously he has
thought long without reaching an answer to this important
question. He is good at conceptualization, his
writing is concise, forceful, and well-organized
his penmanship presentable (dark clouds drift toward the far end
    of the sky)—
he must've studied calligraphy in the Mysterious Tower style. In
    elementary school, he
probably lived in congested public housing in a back alley
    behind a fishing harbor
He spent most of his time with his mother, he was shy and
self-conscious about speaking Mandarin with a Taiwanese accent
He often climbed the hill to watch the boats at sea
and white clouds—that's how his skin got so dark
In his frail chest a small
solitary heart was growing—he writes frankly
"precocious as a Twentieth-Century pear"

Someone asks me about justice and righteousness
With a pot of tea before me, I try to figure out
how to refute with abstract concepts the concrete
evidence he cites. Maybe I should negate his premise first
attack his frame of mind and criticize his fallacious way of
gathering data, in order to weaken his argument
Then point out that all he says is nothing but bias
unworthy of a learned man's rebuttal. I hear
the rain getting heavier and heavier
as it pours down the roof and fills gutters
around the house. But what is a Twentieth-Century pear?
They were found in the island's mountainous region
a climate comparable to the North China plains
Transplanted to the fertile, abundant virgin land
a seed of homesickness sprouted, grew
and bore flowers and fruit—a fruit
whose pitiful shape, color, and smell was not mentioned in
    classics
Other than vitamin C its nutrient value is uncertain

It symbolizes hardly anything
but its own hesitant heart

Someone asks me about justice and righteousness
They don't need symbols—if it is reality
then treat it as such
The writer of the letter has an analytical mind
After a year in business management, he transferred to law. After
     graduation
he served in the army reserve for six months, took the bar exams
     twice. . . .
The rain has stopped
I cannot comprehend his background, or his anger
his reproach and accusations
though I have tried, with the pot of tea
before me. I know he is not angry at the exams, because they are
     not among his examples
He speaks of issues at a higher level, in a precise, forceful
well-organized manner, summarized in a sequence of confusing
questions. The sun trickles onto the lawn from behind the
     banana trees
glitters among old branches. This isn't
fiction—an immense, cold atmosphere persists
in this scant warmth

Someone asks me a question about
justice and righteousness. He was the neatest boy in his class
though his mother was a laundry woman in town. In his memory
the fair-skinned mother always smiled even when tears
streamed down her face. With her soft, clean hands
she sharpened pencils for him under the light
Can't remember clearly, but it was probably on a muggy night
after a fiery quarrel his father—his impassioned speech and heavy
     accent that even his
only son could not fully understand—
left home. Maybe he went up to the mountains
where the climate resembles the North China plains to cultivate
a newly transplanted fruit, the Twentieth-Century pear
On autumn nights his mother taught him Japanese nursery
     rhymes
about Peach Boy's conquest of Devil Island. With sleepy eyes he

watched her rip out the seams of old army uniforms
and scissor them into a pair of wool pants and a quilted jacket
Two water marks on the letter, probably his tears
like moldy spots left by the rain in the corner. I look outside
Earth and heaven have cried too, for an important question
that transcends seasons and directions. They have cried
then covered their embarrassment with false sunlight

Someone asks me a question about
justice and righteousness. An eerie spider
hangs upside down from the eaves, bobs in the false
sunlight, and weaves a web. For a long while
I watch winter mosquitos fly in a dark cloud
around a plastic pail by the screen door
I have not heard such a lucid and succinct
argument in a long time. He is merciless in analyzing himself
"My lineage has taught me that wherever I go I will always
carry homesickness like a birthmark
But birthmarks come from the mother, and I must say mine
has nothing to do with it." He often
stands on the seashore and gazes far away. He is told that at the
    end of the mists and waves
There is an even longer coastline, beyond them, mountains,
    forests, and vast rivers
"The place that Mother has never seen is our homeland"
In college, he was required to study modern Chinese history and
    he memorized the book
from cover to cover. He took linguistic sociology
did well in labor law, criminology, history of law, but
failed physical education and the constitution. He excels in citing
    evidence
knows how to infer and deduce. I have never
received a letter so full of experience and fantasy
fervor and despair with a cold, poignant voice
a letter that strikes a perfect balance between fervor and despair
asking me, politely, about justice and righteousness

Someone asks me a question about justice and righteousness
in a letter that permits no addition or deletion
I see the tear marks expanding like dried-up lakes

In a dim corner fish die after failing to save each other
leaving white bones behind. I also see
blood splashing in his growing knowledge and judgment
like a pigeon released from a besieged fortress under fire—
a faint hope of the exhausted yet persevering resistance—
it breaks away from the suffocating sulfur smoke
soars to the top of a stench-filled willow tree
turns around swiftly and darts toward the base of reinforcement
    troops
but on its way is hit by a stray bullet
and crushed in the deafening encounter, its feathers, bones, and
    blood
fill a space that will never be
and is quickly forgotten. I feel
in his hoarse voice that he once
walked in a wasteland, crying out
and screaming at a storm
Counting footsteps, he is not a prophet
He is no prophet but a disciple who has lost his guide
In his frail chest that pumps like a furnace
a heart melts at high heat
transparent, flowing, empty

(1984)

(translated by Michelle Yeh and Lawrence R. Smith)

FROST AT MIDNIGHT

'Tis calm, indeed, so calm, that it disturbs
And vexes meditation with its strange
And extreme silentness.

—Samuel Taylor Coleridge

Like pushing aside layers of reed stalks, at summer's end
when the aroma of firewood through chimneys wafts gently in
    the air
comes to me creeping low, on a soft breeze—a calling
unfolds delicately, yet seems just around my eyelids—
when the swaying clumps of duckweed, their color stirs up bits of
    memory

when the long-tailed dragonfly flies toward me, hesitant
and trembling toward me, it hovers above the twilight-dyed
    ripples
and tries to land on a thorny water plant
scattering powdery pistils, making the dusk return to the swiftly
changing moment when I push aside layers and layers of reed
    stalks
like pushing aside layers and layers of reed stalks at the end of
    that faraway summer

So I see, like the last ashes in an incense burner
in front of the already dim altar that insists on shouting
in silence, trying hard to elevate the instant to an eternal memory
in my faint unease like transparent moth wings flapping
outside the window, sound of dried, broad leaves like hearts,
    blowing about one by one
circling in the wind before falling at random into the cool shade
    of the empty courtyard
I see an expanse of light on the startled pond at summer's end
lingering at ease, softly chanting a long, ancient tune, intending
    to
turn fate into luck when frogs croak at intervals in the lonely
    hour
when crickets besiege childhood wilderness, when I push aside
    layers and layers of reed
stalks to find time slowly transcending summer's end

(1985)
(translated by Michelle Yeh and Lawrence R. Smith)

FOR NO REASON

Sitting among dry cicada husks
you start worrying
for no reason
Past, present, future . . .
the future?
Hair lightens with each washing
skin translucent from love
you're behind in your piano practice
Suddenly you realize the tea's getting cold
a moment

of bewilderment
In the yard
chrysanthemums seem smaller. You close your eyes
not wanting to look at them, but recall your childhood
of surprising crabapple red, peacock
blue, perilla purple, peony yellow . . .
the sound of scissors cutting and wrists
bumping on wooden bolts of fabric
Then you think: When I am old
will I be able to unfold as easily
as satin brocade on a slick surface
to unfold, to spread out, with such dazzle?

(1991)
(translated by Michelle Yeh and Lawrence R. Smith)

THE TRAVELER'S HEART: A VARIATION

"The great river flows night and day,
In the traveler's heart, sorrow never ends."
—Xie Tiao (464–499)

Quietly I gaze, and note how
heavenly bodies take turns passing before me
how their countless hues fill my weakening heart
how sounds, spreading in all directions, get louder and more
    varied—
are the competing lights trying to block me?
I concentrate on capturing
gathering it all into my bosom, whether
loneliness or sorrow, this moment when I face the

great river. In the wind I wave with a sentimental gesture
at the row of drooping willows that tremble in thunder and
    lightning
But I stand alone, at the intersection of time and space
my gray hair wandering in the direction
of the slowly darkening sky, toward an eventual compromise
affirming that all the gains and losses are nothing but emptinesses

The great river flows night and day
Do not tempt the books or the sword that I have long neglected

I look left and right, and all I see are reeds in the haze
nodding their heads for no reason. Instantaneously all sounds and
     colors
cease to be, yet the universe is moved, looks at me with tear-
     glistening eyes
and grasps the dynamic particles near and far so that they cannot
stir me with their momentum, the compelling will of the Creator
or with the instinct for adventures

the desires and longings . . .
Perhaps because of it all
I am not allowed to sigh in the dark
or cry in the shadow of being abandoned, left behind
deprived of love and caring:
The great river flows night and day

(1992)
(translated by Michelle Yeh)

THE PROPOSITION OF TIME

Look closely at my gray hair under the light:
Were last year's snowstorms unusually fierce?
At midnight, when I sat alone between the tumbling sky and
     earth
I say, with a hand on my chest, I missed you

Maybe you worry about the stars in the sky
some will be expelled from Capricorn when spring arrives
But I recognize them each time I look in the mirror
they have long found a home on my temples
Maybe you care about the cassia tree
in the moon: Is it wounded
or will it bloom? So you ask
I never think about it before autumn comes
If Wu Gang* dies from fatigue, I will take his place

------

*Wu Gang and the cassia tree in the moon refer to a Chinese myth reminiscent of the Greek myth of Sisyphus. For his offense Wu was made to chop down the cassia tree, which immediately grew back where it was cut.

See the morning dewdrops rolling on the sunflower leaves
trying to balance themselves between veins
Jade and pearls adorn the back of your hair like philosophy and
    poetry
only prettier than dewdrops, and more concerned

Fish-scale nebulae in the northern hemisphere cast their
    reflections
on the surface of the sea where mackerel swim. Quietly
I look for a navigation route, and muster all my strength
to display time on the proud beach of my forehead
In old age I will still play the piano for you
like this, I will send you on a voyage to Byzantium—
when the end is near, there will be tranquility
"Über allen Gipfeln . . ."

(1993)
(translated by Michelle Yeh)

A TALE
—TO THE TUNE *METAMORPHOSIS* 2
BY PHILIP GLASS

If the tide, at the speed of memory, unceasingly
if I, with the same heart, if the tide, just once
during all the nights and days when we are apart
told the story from beginning to end—
a circular tune, a meandering
discourse, about life and death, highs and lows
an answer to a call coming from afar

On the surface of the steadily cooling sea
like the frail breaths of white birds who, deep into the season
fly over the faint wakes of passing ships
if the tide once did
if I, with the same heart

(1994)
(translated by Michelle Yeh)

SOLITUDE, 1910
(LEO TOLSTOY: FROM ASTAPOVO . . . TO SONYA)

What kind of heated will ignites the apples of my fading eyes
    repeatedly
in the cold night, and at last
the moment when the train disappears with a long whistle and I,
    lost, stand
near the end of the railroad tracks in the midst of rapidly
    evaporating steam and fog
Sigh, Sonya, Sonya my love
my love has been extinguished, cut off
and so has my hate

I have lost the power and the determination to conjure up
your face, your voice, your graceful concern and indifference
Under the light brown hair as you grow old
your smooth, insouciant forehead will display nothing, yet
even now, I am almost lost
in your tender smiles and reproaches
in your habitual sulking and fears

Only in your diary
do I exist, and will live on haphazardly—
I can still be moved by a cup of tea
from the past; I still linger, when the dusky twilight
creeps near and envelops the window where I sit alone
I still remember how, sadly, I come to slowly
from some philosophical concepts, with a hand on my chest
pieces of paper scattered across the floor

But I can't recall much else, maybe
the bright yellow blooms swaying on the prairie
like stars at the roof-corner of the train station, yellow flowers
that spread endlessly along the roadside, sparkling on the prairie
we once saw—how they shine by the corner of the roof
as I think of some such names
tones, strokes of handwriting, traces of
complete solitude

(1994)
(translated by Michelle Yeh)

張錯

ZHANG CUO

(1943–　)

Also known as Dominic Cheung, Zhang Cuo (Chang Ts'o), pen name of Zhang Zhen'ao, was born in Macao, although his ancestral home is Huizhou, Guangdong Province. After graduating from a Jesuit middle school in Hong Kong, he earned a B.A. in Western languages and literatures from National Zhengzhi University, Taiwan; an M.A. in English from Brigham Young University; and a Ph.D. in comparative literature from University of Washington, Seattle. Since 1974 Zhang has taught in the Departments of Comparative Literature and East Asian Languages and Literatures at University of Southern California, Los Angeles.

Zhang began writing poetry in the 1960s and to date has published eleven collections. He started out as a modernist, but in the 1970s he renounced modernism and turned to realism, addressing social issues in a simpler language. His mature style, which blends the lyrical with the narrative, has won him several prizes in Taiwan. The theme of his recent poetry is a persistent quest for homeland, identified as Taiwan, which nevertheless leads to restless wandering.

AUTUMN REMINISCENCE

Raise your head out of meditation, the trance starts with the scent
    of hair roots
following the breath of a breeze
you appear in the light of autumn—
gorgeous, and bright
some say you are wasting away
it is an announcement of autumn's relaxed descent
A mood of falling leaves
in the hues of a scarlet season
remembering Mu Dan, and his lines:
"Your eyes see the conflagration,
you cannot see me, though I light for you;
Ah, what burns is only a ripe age,
yours, mine. We, parted as if by a range of mountains."
A noon like a gray pigeon in the courtyard of an old temple
an ugly relief of an oldster's head holds
a lamp that will never be lit!
A little solemn and sacred, like a witness
all previous pain and sorrow
could vanish in a traded glance
or mutual concern, even love
Thereupon in all seasons
stubbornly, we persist in a rose garden
and silently embrace in a world beyond the reach of words
containing all gingko trees, cotton roses, and birds of paradise
(another type of bright genealogy of light)
This merciful, cruel autumn!
brings tears and joy, alarms and excitement
a tiny bit of greedy expectation too
from the start quietly all along
the persistence of suggestion.

(1992)
(translated by Michael Day)

THE DISTANCE OF WINTER

When the ground beneath a gingko is gold,
I know cold-faced autumn absolutely cannot be held.
The words of wind brush by, an exchange of heat and cold,

Leaving behind a translucent space.
I begin to know—
Already it is the distance of winter.
There is a fog rising from the haze behind my eyes
In the distant gloom, so near
And coldly pretty,
Despair big with contradiction and expectation
Lingering in the desolation of autumn and the provocation of
    spring;
There's a dampness, not last night's feeling of spring,
But the great gray sea of winter.
That is a billowing poignant refusal,
Just as if amid the endless years
Trying to stop the unstoppable
Seasons that breezily arrive then drift away.
You ask me how to let winter keep its pure identity,
I reply, with a pale face, a twinkling frost on my temples,
And a leopard of Hemingway
At Kilimanjaro, pure white ice and snow!
That is another kind of persistence and transparency,
Another type of winter distance,
Silent, and far beyond reach.

(1992)
(translated by Michael Day)

WORDS OF A GOOSE CATCHER*

With a hopeless love we turn into a flame that lights our path
sealed into an earthen jar, by night we wade

---

*"Words of a Goose Catcher" is based on the tenth-century *Taiping Compendium*, which thus notes the life of wild geese and the technique of goose catching: "Wild geese spend the night on the banks of rivers and lakes, on sand beaches and shoals, moving in hundreds and thousands. One mighty one resides in their midst and has slave geese surround him and police the area. Southerners have a method of catching them: when the sky is dark, or when there is no moon, they conceal candles in earthen jars and several people carrying clubs steal forward with bated breath. When they are almost upon the geese, they lift the candles a little way out of the jars, then hide them again. The slave geese raise the alarm, frightening the big one too. In a short while calm is restored and then men move forward again, again raising the candles. The slave geese are frightened again. The whole process is repeated four times, by which time the big one is angrily pecking the slave geese. The candle carriers slowly close in and raise the candles again, but now the slave geese are afraid of being pecked and do not respond. Then, lifting their candles high, the men with clubs enter the flock, striking out around them, harvesting a great many geese."

into a lake where a flock of wild geese rests, intentionally
    announcing our presence
a mystery of nature, goose slaves compete to cry in alarm
raise a tumult on a thousand sandbars
later they settle down—
nothing but a fight of light between moon and stars.

Finally we reach the edge of the formation of geese
entrapping them in an inescapable dragnet
until one large goose wails, breaks through the net
then, we keenly sense the wretched sorrow of
the instinct to escape, the dutiful looking back
no look is so despairingly met
so absolute, yet futile
awakening a thousand years of poetic promises to never part
even the unthinking chivalry of a double death!
With the fall of the Jin,** the Mongols continue south
fools and idiots rendezvous and tryst
the powerful and the rich pay a million for a nice pot, a hundred
    pieces of gold for a courtesan
husbands and wives of similar ilk separately fly away
to the South of vast waters, soft sand, and tall grass
one body sinks, trussed
how can the other fly into a thousand mountains and snow at
    dusk?
In the night, we seem to hear a song
an intermittent query—
I ask the world . . . love is . . .

(published 1993)
(translated by Michael Day)

**The Jin Dynasty was destroyed by the Mongols in 1234. The poet Yuan Haowen (1190–1257) wrote the famous song lyric that begins with the line: "Ask the world what love is." It was based on a real-life incident: on the way home from a state examination, Yuan met a goose hunter and learned that during the course of the hunt a goose had escaped but its partner had been caught in the net and died; the escaped goose wailed mournfully and would not leave, and finally, it threw itself at the earth and died. Touched by its faithfulness, the poet bought both geese and buried them in Goose Mound.

IN IMITATION OF THE ANCIENTS

"Moving, moving, always moving on"*
The hardest thing to while away is repose
Torrents of rain in the plum-blossom season
Still dodge behind innumerable sultry afternoons
Lush silvergrass grows in the courtyard
In a provocative pose, as to the river, grass in the wake of a prairie
    fire
Long ago after waiting or expectation is turned to ash

A promise that can't be kept is a lie
Leaving never to return is to be parted by death
What really cuts us off is not a path
But two hearts incapable of trust!
That evening as I rushed for the night train
I thought of a song about
An illusory butterfly, night rain
Tapping on a window
Yet love is my permanent faith
Though the road is long and hard, and meetings unknown
My night will forever be your day.

(published 1994)
(translated by Michael Day)

---

*From the first of the "Nineteen Ancient Poems," a collection of poems by unknown authors from the turbulent time of dynastic transition in the second–third centuries A.D. The cited poem expresses the sorrow of a conscript's wife.

THE SECRET GARDEN

"We are a pair of scissors
who come together to cut."
　　　　　　　　—Anne Sexton

Hand in hand in tacit agreement
we walk into a secret garden of negation
the subject of blooming is exceptionally clear
but the ending of wilting is vague
Like a song with teardrops—
"A life of decline, a withering rose
a lifetime of beauty all for this love."
But you must know,
getting together is easy staying hard
staying together is hard
abiding even harder.

We seek to capture scattered shadows and light
holding the pure purple blossoming of summer in reserve
we resist the hungry gloom of autumn
another kind of drizzly afternoon
grasping your hand
impossible to age with you
"This kind of emotion is unnameable
I strip off my mask of many years, follow you in crime
to again know this world."
But after recognition what is there?
And what after staying together?
many of life's idiocies lie in wait
all to prove a language of constancy!
You should know—
"Though in the public eye the mountains and rivers remain un-
　　changed
there can be no return to the same tableau."
A face of wind frost
the withered look of a tree
everything seems to be in the secret garden, you and me,
and all the reckless accomplishments of the flowers.

　　　　　　　　　　　　　　(published 1994)
　　　　　　　　　　　　(translated by Michael Day)

吳晟

WU SHENG

(1944–   )

Wu Sheng is the pen name of Wu Shengxiong, who was born in Xizhou, Zhanghua County, in central Taiwan. He graduated from Pingdong Agriculture College in 1971 and has been a biology teacher at Xizhou Junior High School ever since. In addition to teaching, he farms in the fields.

In the 1980s Wu Sheng was a leading nativist poet and he remains best known for his depictions of rural Taiwan. He was invited to attend the International Writing Program at University of Iowa in 1980. To date he has published five books of poetry and four volumes of essays. "Rainy Season," included below, is written in Hokkien.

RICE STRAW

In a dry wind
Sheaths of rice straw tremble
In an abandoned field

On an afternoon that is cool
Not for lack of warm sunlight
The old people of my village wither away
In crumbling courtyards

And finally, who remembers
That the old people of my village
Like a sheath of rice straw
Once sprouted, flowered, and bore fruit

From sprout to sheath of rice straw
Is the chronicle of life for everyone in my village

(1972)
(translated by John Balcom)

RAINY SEASON

Have a smoke
Have a drink
Damn this miserable weather

Shoot the bull
Flirtin' with somebody else's girl
Damn this miserable day

Bitch and grumble
Figure your pay and what things cost
Damn this miserable life

When it ought to rain it don't
When it ain't supposed to
It rains without lettin' up

Does as it pleases
Pourin' down rain
Damn, just gotta go on livin'

(1972)
(translated by John Balcom)

PREFACE TO *VIGNETTES OF MY VILLAGE*

Long, long ago
The people of my village
Began to look up with hope
The sky of my village
Is so indifferent
Indifferent blue or gray

Long, long ago
My village lay in the mountain's shadow
A vast ink painting
Dark and troubled
Pasted on the faces of the people of my village

Long, long ago
For generations on this piece of land
Where no wealth or prosperity grows
Where no miracles are ever produced
My ancestors wiped away their sweat
And brought forth their fated children

(published 1972)
(translated by John Balcom)

THE LAND

Bare-armed, who cares about the latest fashions?
Barefooted, who cares about being poetic?
Wiping sweat away you chant your own poem
Intoning your own verse
Who cares for affected literary moods, much less
Becoming part of history?

Lines of awkward footprints
Are written on the honest soil
Along the broad fields our ancestors

Sweat over
Never contending, never arguing,
silently waiting

If flowers blossom and bear fruit
Who can ask for anything more?
If blistering blights
Or violent storms come
Erasing those bitter footprints
There is no sadness, no regret,
they will continue

No swords or knives are worn
There are no learned discussions on virtue and wisdom
Be content today hoeing and plowing
Someday, when you are forced to stop
You'll willingly lie down to be a part
Of the broad earth

(1975)
(translated by John Balcom)

ANIMAL SPIRIT TABLET

In my village there is a slaughterhouse, at the entrance
of which is an animal spirit tablet.

The tablet says: "Spirits begone!
Do not come back, do not return
Each one hurry
Find a new abode
Do not come back, do not return!"

Every festival the butchers come from all around
To fearfully burn incense and make offerings
Why don't you just accept it
You are beasts born for slaughter
Why not resign yourselves?

Oh, pigs, dogs, fowls, and beasts
There's no need to cry, to accuse, or
Be surprised—on one hand they worship
On the other, they butcher and pray for peace
There's nothing wrong with that

There's no need to cry, to accuse, or
Be surprised—they butcher
They worship, fearing the return of your innocent souls
To demand life. Pigs, dogs, fowls, and beasts
Spirits begone!

(1977)
(translated by John Balcom)

IN THE WOODS OF A FOREIGN COUNTRY

I have never heard a wind
That conveys such an urgent message
I have never heard a bird song
Calling with such distant homesickness
I have never heard a river
Whispering with such tender longing

In the woods of a foreign country
I pace the riverbank every day at dusk
Stirring up the sighing leaves covering the ground
I guess they also know, I have
So many concerns to express

As I stroll, as if in a trance
All sounds
Become thousands of words
Mumbled again and again
Like swaying willows on the riverbank
Entangling me

Those youthful words
How many years has it been? We haven't brought them up again
Not because they have faded, nor because they are forgotten
But out of bashfulness
In this unpoetic daily life of worrying about daily needs
They are concealed deeper than ever
In the debts that drag on from year to year
In every quarrel and angry outburst

A few days after leaving home
It seems like it's been ages

Every day around dusk in the woods of a foreign country
All sounds
Often become thousands of words
Mumbled again and again
Like swaying willows on the riverbank
Entangling me

(1981)
(translated by John Balcom)

I WON'T DISCUSS IT WITH YOU

I won't discuss the art of poetry with you
I won't discuss those complicated and ambiguous metaphors
Let's get out of the study
I'll take you for a walk over the length and breadth of the land
To see all the new shoots
And how they struggle in silence to grow

I won't discuss life with you
I won't discuss those profound and abstruse philosophies
Let's get out of the study
I'll take you for a walk over the length and breadth of the land
To touch the cool, clear river water
And see how it irrigates the fields

I won't discuss society with you
I won't discuss those heartbreaking strifes
Let's get out of the study
I'll take you for a walk over the length and breadth of the land
To visit farmers here and there
And see how they wipe their sweat away tilling the land in silence

You've lived a long time in the noisy bustling city
Poetry, life, and society
You've already argued about them a lot
This is the busy season for sowing
And you've paid us a rare visit
I'll take you for a walk over the length and breadth of the land
To appreciate the spring breeze
And how it softly blows over the earth

(1982)
(translated by John Balcom)

THE WORST THING ABOUT WRITING POETRY

The worst thing about writing poetry
Isn't racking one's brains
Isn't the sleepless pursuit
Isn't the toil of choosing the right words

The worst thing about writing poetry
Isn't working on a poem
for long lonely years
And not receiving any response when it's done
Nor is it the little fame
That invites the jeering of peers

The worst thing about writing poetry
Isn't the mind's feeble attempts
To contain the crashing waves
Of poetic emotion

The worst thing about writing poetry
Isn't looking life's imperfection in the eye
Yet being unable to do anything about it
Nor is it having to bear the pains of life
That constantly weigh you down

Even if it hurts, still you must patiently
Seek the bloodstains

Perhaps the worst thing about writing poetry
Is not knowing any other way
Besides writing poetry
To combat the immense sadness of life

(1997)
(translated by John Balcom)

李敏勇

LI MINYONG

(1947–   )

Born in Gaoxiong in southern Taiwan, Li Minyong (Li Min-yung) received a
B.A. in history from National Zhongxing University. Having held various posts
as teacher, journalist, and editor, he now works in the business world and lives
in Taipei.

Li has been active on the poetry scene since the 1960s. He has served as
chief editor of *Bamboo Hat Poetry Bimonthly*, president of *Taiwanese Literature
and Art*, and president of the Taiwanese PEN. To date he has published seven
books of poetry. Li is also a prolific literary critic, essayist, and translator of
world poetry.

MEMENTO OF THE DECEASED

Your handkerchief sent to me from the battlefield
Your handkerchief like a flag signaling cease-fire
Your handkerchief that causes my tear marks to ever expand
Piercing the territory of my heart with the sharpness of shrapnel

Your handkerchief sent from the battlefield
Your handkerchief like a final verdict
Your handkerchief that triggers the decay of my youth
Burying me with the thundering roar of a landslide

A pale
Memento of you
A sealing tape
Across my sunken breasts

(1969)
(translated by Michelle Yeh)

PRISONER OF WAR

Major K has no motherland
When taken prisoner of war
He declared himself stateless

On the day he was set free
As people from his motherland drew near
He silently wished
To put himself in their hands

Armaments are forbidden
Armaments are not forbidden
There is no motherland anymore
The motherland is still here

Major K has been made the subject
Of an experiment in dual cognition
One day sooner or later
It will be your turn or mine

Quietly the world wipes its tears
Quietly the world wipes its tears

(1973)
(translated by Denis Mair)

ASPIRATION OF POETRY

Our search is for words that have not been ruined
To pursue the genuine in a false land

Power is a ringleader who compels
The wraiths of politics to twist our language

With deliberate care
We clear a place for each injured word
And let words join into a force of resistance

Let language come to life again
So we may have sufficient strength
To capture the doers of harm

(1990)
(translated by Denis Mair)

TILTING ISLAND

Within the black box of power
The army conducts its ceremonies of rule

Shadows of rifles and cannons
Suppress the land and people

Shaken until it tilts, the island
Raises a battle cry in the storm

A republic of dreams is sprouting
Watered by blood and tears

(1990)
(translated by Denis Mair)

DEATH REPORT

The newspaper
Carries news of a criminal executed by firing squad
Popping of rifles
In the glimmer of dawn
A body falling to the ground

Blood spills on the ground where the criminal fell
The blood
Is quickly covered by triggermen
But the blood has soaked in
And become one with the ground

On that spot one death sentence after another
Has already been carried out
The spilled blood has been clotted
Giving the dirt a red-brown color
Making the dirt thirsty for more blood

Because of this thought
My hands begin to tremble
The newspaper falls
I see blood flowing from its pages
Clotting on the floor

Whose blood is it waiting for?
This apparition of blood on the floor?
I ask myself
But the cold floor acts as if nothing happened
The newspaper rests on its silent surface

(1991)
(translated by Denis Mair)

READING POEMS ON A LATE-NIGHT AIRLINER

Returning home from my travels
Flowers pressed in my passport go between pages of a book

Pressed on my heart is the mark of a far land
Sunset highlights fir trees at a field's edge

Nighttime on an airline flight
Carefully reading poems by Szymborska

Some people only like common poems
She says

I am another type of person
I hear a deer running fleetly in the book of poems

A hunter runs in pursuit
Through a forest that hides reality

Szymborska is a Polish poet
I am a poet from Taiwan

By means of translation
We hold a conversation in poetry

I use the language I write in
To read the lines of her poem

"Forgive me, distant war
Forgive me for taking these fresh flowers home."

"Forgive me, gaping wounds
Forgive me for this scratch on my finger."

I open the porthole cover
Look for small stars in the night sky

Beneath a certain little star
Szymborska brings clumsy words alive

By light of that same star
I dream of a new land

With the power of poetry
We attempt a kind of revolution

When consciousness is awakened
Who says it is not possible?

"Maybe the weight of a single poem
Can tilt the earth."

A departed woman poet from Taiwan
Gives encouragement with these lines.

But my countrymen
Are more fond of haughty words

Fast asleep on an airline flight
Their usually silent mouths are open

Each of them a fallen tree
A forest moving through air

(1997)
(translated by Denis Mair)

羅青

LUO QING

(1948–   )

Luo Qing (Lo Ch'ing), pen name of Luo Qingzhe, was born in Qingdao, Shandong Province, and moved to Taiwan with his family in 1949. He received a B.A. in English from Fu Jen Catholic University and an M.A. in comparative literature from University of Washington, Seattle. He has been a Fulbright professor at Washington University in St. Louis and is currently a professor in the Department of English, National Taiwan Normal University.

Luo Qing is a versatile artist, well known for his poetry as well as his paintings. Like his older contemporaries, such as Yu Guangzhong and Yang Mu (who was his teacher at the University of Washington), he lives the dual life of a poet and an academic, writing both creative works and literary criticism. In addition, he enriches this textual life with a vibrant career in the visual arts. His poems and paintings often are presented together in complementary sets and in both media. Luo is constantly experimenting with the limits of the materials and genres, in ways that defy not only native aesthetic conventions but also international ones. He is perhaps best known in both media for his playful, often zany, attitude toward established forms. To date he has published twelve books of poetry in Chinese, a collection of poems in English (see the bibliography), two volumes of essays, nine books of literary criticism, and three books of art historical criticism.

THE INVISIBLE MAN

I stand here and look at you; you don't look at me
I stand there and look at you; you still don't look at me
I patiently stand in all the corners, in all the spaces
Looking at you—you never look at me

Only you can see me, but you don't even look
You don't look at me because no one can see me
No one can see me because
You don't look at me

You don't look at me, therefore I don't exist
I don't exist, then you don't exist either, so there
Neither you nor I exist, well then, no one . . .
No way to exist

Yet, just suppose everything in everything
Approaches the danger of not existing
Would you still not give a damn about looking at me
About taking a look at me

If so then I might as well stand here quietly, or stand there
Stand in all the interiors, looking at you, looking at you
I might as well look at you and see you as everything, see
    everything as you
I might as well look at you and at everything, seeing it all as me

(1971)
(translated by Joseph R. Allen)

HEAVEN'S REVENGE

. . . the third watch begins and
With a lunge that stirs a gust of wind
I leap over your walls, outer then inner
To peer down into your intricately designed rooms

Seizing the chance, I merge with the flakes of falling snow
And float down soundlessly into your shadowed, forbidden
courtyard

I hide among the wispy bamboo that you planted with your own
hands,
Becoming your bodyguard, rifle shouldered in a near doze
It is I—come to murder you

Snow. Lying in secret ambush on the elegant roof tiles
Below the tiles, your warm, delicate bed
Blood. Thickly congealed on the cold hill of unmarked graves
Below the hill, my long-lost parents

If you would like to listen closely to the sound of falling snow
Then listen for my footsteps coming slowly toward you
My footsteps are silent, as silent as my shadow, and my shadow
Fearless and carefree, keeps bumping into your high-priced
antiques

Just now I bumped into that narrow-necked vase that you treasure
more than life itself
I'll let her, since she is so cold and void, protect me, conceal me,
rebelling against you

If you want to dream about petals and seeds that have fallen from
that vase
Then dream about me.

The me of your dreams
Along with your heart and your bedroom are alike
Blacker than the night
The you caught in the gaze of my eyes
Along with my eyes and my dagger are alike
Flashing with light
In rhythm with your warm and steady breathing
I raise the sharp and gleaming blade—drive it into your chest,
softly rising and falling
For an instant, everything around . . . with the universe caught in
silence
Is so alluring and beautiful
(1972)
(translated by Joseph R. Allen)

THE AVENGING GHOST
—TALKING WITH PU SONGLING*

A sullen wind entices music from the lute strings
Rotten leaves scuttle toward the sheltering arcade
Strange clouds, bizarre stars
Paper windows, white as snow, grate like grinding teeth
The wooden gate stands slightly ajar, smiling a thin, silent grin

Suddenly, the murky clouds swallow the moon
And everywhere the earth is sunk into darkness
In this darkened void a single paper lantern
Floats up and down, round and round it goes
Lamp but no shadow
Light but no flame
Leisurely it roams
Through the pavilion, into one bedroom, then another
Putting out the light, one by one, of the faces
Terrified, mouth-gaping, wide-eyed faces

And then it is deadly quiet
Quiet like blood.

Oozing slowly from the skin of the four walls
Suddenly from deep within the entryway
A thin piercing laugh rises—
Rises like a strand of fine wire
Puncturing the layers of dark
Drawing forth a burst of flame, a strange wind

The heavy smoke smothers the dust piled thickly on the beams
The ashes cover the creaking furniture like shrouds
Tongues of flame lick the blood-spattered ground
Like tears, the drops of blood awaken the quiet, fearful courtyard

Above the courtyard wall
The round moon reemerges

---

*Pu Songling was the author of the eighteenth-century classic, *Strange Tales from the Liao Studio*, a collection of supernatural stories.

Hanging there cool among the roaring flames
Silently shining into the dark corners of the wall

And there sticking up from the dirt
A pale, emaciated finger
Beckons you
Ever so slightly

(1976)
(translated by Joseph R. Allen)

ONCE MORE LOOKING OUT AT THE DEEP BLUE SEA AFTER LOOKING OUT AT THE DEEP BLUE SEA MANY TIMES BEFORE

On the calm and sweeping sea
There seems to be nothing at all

On the sea where there seems to be nothing at all
There is in fact simply nothing at all

It is just because there is after all nothing at all
That we know there was originally nothing at all

But on the calm and expansive sea
Is there actually nothing at all?

On the sea where there is nothing at all
Of course there is nothing at all

On the calm and sweeping sea
There is predictably completely and naturally nothing at all

Author's note: Cao Cao's first poem in the "Walking out of Summer's Gate" sequence, titled "Looking out at the Deep Blue Sea," was written in the seventeenth year of the Jian'an reign (C.E. 212). It goes like this:

Eastward we approach Stele Mountain
From there looking out at the deep blue sea
How peaceful and broad are its waters
Alpestrine spires stand on the mountain isle
Trees grow in profusion
The myriad plants are abundant

The autumnal winds sigh
Heavy waves surge
The course of sun and moon
Seems to start from there
The river of stars burning bright
Seem to rise from its depths
How very fortunate
That songs enchant intent

Also note: *This is the first poem I wrote*
              with a Chinese word processor
              Since the characters for "alpestrine spires" were not
              contained in its memory
              when I came to write the above note
              I had to create them with the character-graphics
              program

(1985)
(translated by Joseph R. Allen)

CÓRDOBA

1. It Must Be Made of Salt

I really would like to say

That Córdoba, white against the sky,
Is a city of sugar cubes
But I can't, and I won't
Write it that way

2. Tangerine Streetlights

There in Córdoba

The cobbles click as donkeys lightly tread
. . . along cobblestone streets
And tangerines so orange
. . . under the dark green leaves

The yellow light illuminating
And reviving . . . the dark road home
     For all the night travelers
        . . . returning to their hotels

3. Porcupines Under the Lemons

There in Córdoba

Under the lemon trees we
Gaze up at all that tangy fruit
Bumping against each other in the windless night
Bringing out the countless, soundless stars

To shine on us below
Like porcupines
Under the lemon trees

4. Knocking Alight

There in Córdoba

We spread wide our hands
To push open the narrow lanes
Knocking open the carved frames of windows
Along the surrounding walls

We call out to awaken
Each and every lamp within those very windows
Knocking alight
The long road snaking up the mountain

And at the end of the road
At the highest place on the mountain
We knock alight
The whole starry night

5. Olive Man

There in Córdoba

We take our wine
With the songs of wandering minstrels
Music as salty as salted fish
And as bitter as bitter absinthe

As brutal as the noonday sun
And as tart as midnight lemons
In the end all is turned into
Green olives bursting open

Caught in the throat
Burning like
too many glasses
Of cheap liquor

6. Coffee Annotations

There in Córdoba

In a little restaurant
We are having our breakfast
With a vagrant who introduces himself
With dirty and tangled hair

Smiling at everyone
With his broken shoes
And praising the talents of the baker
With his beard full of bread crumbs

Every once in a while
He dips his brown finger
Into the deep black coffee
To annotate and amend our lives

7. Dreams and Trash

There in Córdoba

When the evening bell tolls
Each ring drops into our drinks
Like an ice cube
Translucent and sparkling cold

There it stirs up lines
Of dream bubbles

To be inhaled into the lanes
Like straws of wheat

To those dark
And winding lanes
Dawn comes like a still and silent
Street sweeping machine

Through its immense silver straw
It inhales the trash blowing along the streets
As well as all the tattered dreams that hang and flap in the wind
Above the window frames

8. *Doors Within Doors*

There in Córdoba

Each door
Is different:
A different color
Or a different shape
A different size
Or a different thickness
And each door handle
Is different

And so are
Their knockers
And even the small doors
In the main doors are each of its own kind

And in those small doors
Are windows, large and small,
Opening onto
Accidently revealing
A dark and quiet courtyard
hidden in our hearts
Perhaps pristine, or filthy
Well kept, or run down

(1991)
(translated by Joseph R. Allen)

I REFUSE
—A CRITIQUE OF FALL

Oh, Fall, damn Fall,
I can see you from afar
You are coming after all

But I refuse
To invent for you
Any sort of metaphor

I wouldn't want to say
That you are a carpet woven out of red and yellow leaves
Or a wire net knitted from the black branches of trees

Nor would I say
That you are a harvest basket brimming with fruits and grains
Or a bronze brazier holding the ashes of tattered blossoms and
    wilted grasses

I just couldn't say
That you are the chilling words from the wagging tongues of
    falling leaves
Incited by the bawdy poet's drunken face, purple blotches among
    the red

No way could I say
That you are perfume factory upon perfume factory burned down
    by a mad,
Middle-aged arsonist, lawless, godless, and on the most-wanted
    list
I have never said
That you are abstract impressionism infused with minimalism
Or romantic realism with a touch of terrorism

I would not dare say
That you started a French Hair Revolt in China with its billion
    plus people
Or a Cultural Revulsion in France with its white frost and
    countless red maples

Even less would I dare say
That you are the red October Revolution that was launched from
    within the green watermelons of June
Or the white waves of the May Fourth student protests that arose
    from within the blue
Mediterranean Ocean of March

No, I absolutely will not recognize
You as a member of some underground party who likes to brush
    lightly against
My fifty-year-old right shoulder with the single last leaf

Oh, Fall, damn Fall,
I can see you from afar
Can see you coming after all

But I refuse to call
Out to you
In any sort of way

For although I should have, at the very least,
More than forty different ways
To damn you till your head hangs between your legs

I refuse to do so, definitely refuse
Because, you see, it's still
Spring

                                                            (1996)
                                    (translated by Joseph R. Allen)

PLEASE JUST WINK

Although Taipei is filled with
Many, so many cars
And people
and animals too

Still I just must invent
One more little car
And a person
And an animal too

Quietly I would place them
Those little things
In sprawling
Taipei

A car with headlights but no engine
A person who can walk but cannot talk
And there would also be an avileporophidia possum*
Who casts no shadow but can imitate the calls of birds

If here in Taipei
You happen to hear, or see, or even meet them
Please just wink
And smile

(1996)
(translated by Joseph R. Allen)

QUATRAIN

Every tree, yes, every one, is one—
A living, growing quatrain;
Birds hopping . . . through its branches:
Marks of moving punctuation!

(1997)
(translated by Joseph R. Allen)

---

*Qiuyu, a mythical animal with the body of a rabbit, a bird's beak, the eyes of an owl, and a snake's tail. It closes its eyes when it sees someone.

蘇紹連

SU SHAOLIAN

(1949-)

Born in Shalu in central Taiwan, Su Shaolian (Su Shao-lien) graduated from Taizhong Teachers College in 1970 and has been an elementary school teacher since.

Su was a founding member of the New Tide Poetry Society in 1968 and the Dragon Race Poetry Society in 1971. In 1992 he cofounded the *Taiwan Poetics Quarterly*. His first book of poems appeared in 1978, followed by six more, all in the 1990s. Su is well known for his prose poetry and has also won prizes for his children's poetry.

BEAST

On the dark-green blackboard I write the character "獸" and its phonetic transcription *shou*. Then I turn to face a whole class of primary school students and begin explaining to them what it means. After a morning of painstaking effort, they still haven't gotten my drift, staring at me blankly and driving me up the wall. The dark-green blackboard behind me is a jungle, and there—written on it in white chalk—crouches the character "beast" yowling at me. I pick up a duster and am just about to rub it out when it dashes off into the jungle. I head off in pursuit, chasing after it everywhere until the platform is covered in chalk dust.

I come running out of the blackboard and stand there, my clothes ripped to shreds by the beast's claws, traces of blood on my fingernails, the buzz of insects in my ears. As I look at myself, I can't believe what I see: I have turned into a four-legged vertebrate covered in fur. I snarl at the class: "This is what a beast is! This is what a beast is!" The students all burst into tears, terrified.

(1974)
(translated by Simon Patton)

PEELING A PEAR

The right hand holds a small, shiny knife. Walking away from the entrance to the alleyway, my features black as pitch, I get closer and closer to the luscious pear in my left hand with every step I take. Turning the knife, I cut on an angle to remove the peel, listening to the screams of the pear tree. Layer by layer, the pear skin falls away to reveal white, juicy flesh. A sweet smell fills the air, but the knife in my right hand is covered in blood.

In the meantime, the left hand has been fuming with rage, its five digits curled in toward the palm and pressing tightly, sunk into the flesh of the pear, squeezing hard, destroying it soundlessly. Only later do I find that there's no pear at all—only a fist gradually unraveling like layers of peel.

(1974)
(translated by Simon Patton)

PHOTOCOPIER

My wife lay down flat and I rolled down on top of her, wet with the ink of life. Next morning, finding a photocopied reproduction of my body, complete with scrawny limbs and a sunken chest, on the sheet beneath her, I asked: "Are you perhaps a photocopier that will reproduce my image for the rest of your life?" She burst into tears, not answering.

In the course of these nightly reproductions, my body image—subject as it was to the traumas of living—appeared to my amazement in countless layers on the bed, shriveled and misshapen. In the end, the image sat up and opened out into a very, very old me.

(1975)
(translated by Simon Patton)

MIXED BLOOD

On a crinkled, yellow morning, I found my name huddled with its kin of unknown skin colors in a household registry book, and held tightly by another name. I scolded that name: "Su Shaolian! Why are you holding my name?" Startled, the three-character name *Su Shaolian* let go, covered its face with its hands, and started weeping. Soon my name followed suit, tears wetting the household registry.

Only because there was nobody by that name did the three characters *su shao lian* attach themselves to my name, my nationality, my tradition, my lineage, and how wrong it was of me to abandon them!

(1975)
(translated by Michelle Yeh)

SHADOW BURIAL

Down a gutter that runs the length of the wall, I conduct a band of late twentieth-century shadows. As each of them is reflected in the dirty water, they make a double row of shady figures walking in silent procession. They carry a coffin in which my own rapidly vanishing shadow is lying. I lead them in the funeral rites: past the doors of houses that weep, past schools that weep, past the town hall that weeps, past the weeping dawn.

Before the burial, my shadow fades in its coffin until only a mouth remains. All of a sudden, the mouth begins to speak: "You are the first person to make it into the twenty-first century, for that will be a century without shadows." I see the last of my shadow finally disappear: my crying is all that's left.

(1977)
(translated by Simon Patton)

SLEEP DEEPLY, SHORE

On the shore, late one evening
I enter the water quietly
and swim off toward a limpid, sober land beyond the sea.
I am an accomplished swimmer, my stroke is graceful.
Stars look down wide-eyed in startled envy,
and appreciation shows on the full, round face of the moon.
I am a spirit swimming beneath the night sky.

No human being will see me.
I don't need any experience
or a name
or clothing
or heavy burdens,
because at this moment I am leaving the shore behind.
Mother, I've left the shore.

There are so many young men like me!
Their corpses float
all around me:
those of boys I went to school with
and those of my friends.
I have joined them—
a steady stream of tears,
a steady stream of infinite yearning.

I'm a long way from you now, shore.
You must sleep deeply.
I beg the tidewaters not to beat you,
ask the seashells not to disturb you with my messages,
implore the lights not to shake you from your rest.
You must sleep deeply

because in your embrace you hold the cities and the country.
However, all these I have left behind,
including you, shore of China.

I have drifted so far.
In the turning of the earth
the sky stays forever silent,
nor can I say anything.
I am like a floating log
or an empty bottle.
There is nothing sad about all this.
I wish myself far away,
ashore on some virgin continent.

The sea grows colder and colder
till it stops frozen on the tip of my nose.
With a smile on my face, I sink.
You, shore of China, have lost another of your people
but do not wake suddenly. Sleep deeply,
because my family lives on,
lives on, on your
surface.

(1984)
(translated by Simon Patton)

THAT HORSE LIKE MOONLIGHT

I turn over on my other side
as if to discover that horse like moonlight
slowly turning its head, wading through water toward me
it comes ashore at the far end of the bed-mat

I spend a sleepless night tossing and turning
waiting wide-eyed for its arrival
that horse like moonlight, it stands on the mat already
I spend a night of repeated dreams tossing and turning
wading through a thousand miles of water, horse hooves on the
    shore
should also leave the sound of their stride on my body
the thin bed-mat floats through the night
and carries me as I lie on my side

floating on water, in the night sky
with that horse like moonlight

I too can feel
that the moonlight is damp, it falls gently
drenching the mat, streaming into the water at the other end
as I lie on my side; I no longer dare turn over
for if I did
the long-accumulated, eye-brimming moonlight
would all come spilling out

let me get through the night without closing my eyes
eyes fixed on that horse like moonlight

(1998)
(translated by Simon Patton)

簡政珍

JIAN ZHENGZHEN

(1950–   )

Born in Taipei, Jian Zhengzhen (Chien Cheng-chen) graduated from National Zhengzhi University with a B.A. in Western languages and literatures. He went on to earn an M.A. in foreign languages and literatures from National Taiwan University and a Ph.D. in comparative literature from University of Texas, Austin. Currently he is a professor in the Department of Foreign Languages and Literatures, National Zhongxing University.

To date Jian has published six volumes of poetry and four books of literary criticism in Taiwan and China. He has also served as chief editor of the *Epoch Poetry Quarterly*.

SECRET

Open the drawer, and a
crow flies out, turns into
the print, large and fine, on the morning paper
the telephone rings, the various sounds
inside the receiver grow many
waving fingers
a portrait
leans crookedly against a lamppost
a handkerchief that sopped up sweat
sinks ponderously in the wind
the sound of a helicopter on regular patrol
scatters a flock of startled pigeons
and what echoes back
is the tick-tock of a wall clock

(1988)
(translated by Andrea Lingenfelter)

ON THE GREAT WALL

Are you cold?
The wind that comes from who knows where
pierces the icy chill of every dynasty
bores into the enlarged pores of your skin
You can't keep your hair neat
Randomly it twists into a bun
Randomly it is blown about
into every style of the twentieth century
Forty years have passed
Does that give you the right to stand on this ancient wall
wallowing in emotion
like a diva bemoaning her personal suffering?
Maybe you've seen the cracks in the gray earth and stone
But in former lives these stones were a pile of yellow earth
long ago traded away to the vast desolation
along with countless bodies rendered phantom

Are you hot,
climbing the steep stairs

and stepping into sweltering history?
Perhaps you've seen sweat become channels
that drown sweating men?
The mountains and rivers those two feet walked over
became an earthen wall
and before the blisters on those feet had healed
there at the foot of the wall
were composed echos of a finale
The round bright moon always hangs from either end of a
    shoulder pole
like a brilliant white and somber face,
looking ahead to the future and back to the past
Earth and stones were piled up
Did they say it was so
that future generations could stand in the moon palace
and regard this sinuous wound in the world of men
with admiration?

That year, countless women
took limp twigs
in the moonlight
and hung themselves, their slender bodies
casting long shadows
and making a tranquil composition of chilling beauty
that appeared to float upon the waters
Though the waters could not contain the press of corpses
or the songs of farewell
that caused the waves to rise up

Voices grow cold in the wind
We pass through the indistinct history of this ancient wall
Our swollen ankles
return from History
the world overturned beneath our feet
Many souls, restless for a thousand years,
stand guard at the passes, and under the bridge,
directing us back to the present
back to these
banners
that flap in the wind

(published 1990)
(translated by Andrea Lingenfelter)

MEMORY

A needle shuttles in and out of the fabric
in the dancing candlelight I
try to discover what is troubling my mother
Vague sentences
cut short by a sleepless rooster
It's like a button that won't fasten
and is simply let be
Afterward, we wait together
for daybreak after the typhoon
The photograph of my late father on the wall
hasn't taken back its smile
We help each other sort out our feelings
spreading some on the table
but the insects that bore through the table legs
have already gotten started

(published 1991)
(translated by Andrea Lingenfelter)

READING A LETTER

I wait until dark to read the letter
so that a shaft of light coming out of the darkness
can illuminate the waiting
Of everything
beside the letter paper:
a blank sheet of writing paper,
a telephone and
a letter opener

The blade shines coldly
I see, in the shadow of the lamp
a striped mosquito circling around
I drive off the growing chill by reading the letter
Maybe the mosquito has heard the news of autumn outside the
    window
It alights on my left hand, which holds the letter
My heart is itching
but the mosquito must pay

for the itching of my hand
A trace of blood, neither large nor small,
soon obscures
the nickname you call me by

Suddenly, I give a start
You, over a thousand miles away
are certainly at this moment
watching the rise and fall of air outside your window
Maybe a clear river
is afloat with hard-to-decipher reflections
Maybe white snow on a mountaintop
is tinted already with early morning light
Maybe the surrounding red maples
Bear a little-known bloody radiance

(1996)
(translated by Andrea Lingenfelter)

白靈

BAI LING

(1951–)

Bai Ling (Pai Ling, "white spirit") is the pen name of Zhuang Zuhuang, who was born in Taipei. He graduated from Taipei Institute of Technology and received an M.S. in chemical engineering from Stevens College of Science and Engineering, New Jersey. Currently he is an associate professor at Taipei Institute of Technology.

Bai Ling joined the Grape Orchard Poetry Society, founded in 1962, and later the Grass Roots Poetry Society in the 1970s. In 1985 he cofounded the Poetry's Sound and Light Workshop with fellow poets Luo Qing and Du Shisan and experimented with multimedia presentations of poetry. He is also a cofounder of the *Taiwan Poetics Quarterly*. To date he has published four books of poetry, in addition to prose and literary criticism.

CHILDHOOD YEARS, PART 1: THE 1940S

With shells exploding in the background, the skies are dotted
With one after another stalk of cotton candy
A tank askew on its side, and planted in the paddies: an airplane
How much fun these toys would be if only we could move them!
My mother foraged for food everywhere with me on her back
In a clump of reeds, she came upon a human arm
My mother shrieked out, picked me up in her arms, and ran
    about wildly—
Even though I turned back several times to look, I couldn't tell
If it wasn't my sister's smashed-up doll

On the road, my childhood companions were all howling
Their gaping mouths each an open pit
And the artillery kept offering us—popcorn.

(1983)
(translated by Eugene Eoyang)

SPRING'S BRIEF VISIT TO TAIPEI

When spring paid Taipei a brief visit
She ambled over, sneaking through the city gates
At that time Taipei had no window grates
    So spring would often beckon at the windows of each home
    Would help the young roadside grass to straighten up
    Tell each flower to open its mouth only after brushing its teeth
    And never let itself convey the least bit of filth

    Those days, Taipei didn't have too many tall buildings
    So spring didn't have to climb too high
    Those days, Taipei didn't have too many water faucets
    So spring often went to the Tamkang River to wash her hands
    Those days, early morning was a time for gymnastics in Taipei
    So when spring sauntered out, she had no need of a face mask
    Those days, Taipei didn't have many motor engines
    So spring wasn't startled by a sudden noise
    Those days, zebra-striped crosswalks were enough to stop
        traffic
    So spring was not afraid to be turned topsy-turvy by the wind
    Those days, spring wouldn't miss traffic signs, even if she had
        to wear glasses

You didn't need to drive a car to be honked off by a horn
Nor worry about dumping garbage and being fined by the
    EPA
Those days, yawping spring would often wear miniskirts
For everyone to see, and people would start whistling

Those days . . .
Those days, you wouldn't find spring sleeping in the public park
    Nor parking on the road dividers
    Nor squatting on flower pots, to "fertilize" them
    Nor going up and down in an all-glass elevator
Those days, spring wouldn't climb over the walls
    No need to see one's own name upside down on the shutter
    No need to beckon children through a keyhole
    No need to put on a TV show for every household

Spring—ah!—Spring came to Taipei for only a brief visit
And then she left
She's an old hag now, walking all this time on bound feet
She said, if she walks any slower, she might be crushed by a
    mountain of garbage

Spring: the old antique, she hasn't changed much for the better.

(1986)
(translated by Eugene Eoyang)

LIP ROUGE

We're in the room, reading . . .
A fog moves in   even the window loses its way
On the windowpane, I trace out
Several little trails where the water condenses
And then I ask you, with your freshly made-up mouth
To plant, at the start of each trail,
A kiss, the imprint of your lips.

By the time we brew tea   the fog has lifted
At the top of the landscape
Stops a
Yawning sun.

(1991)
(translated by Eugene Eoyang)

KITE

Getting up in the world, how high can a fragile hope hover in
   the sky?
The length of one's life, surely it's full of these *coups de théâtre?*
The gossamer line, as if the sky and I were at a tug of war
Higher and higher, almost out of sight
Along the riverbank, I begin to pull the sky down, running fast.

(1993)
(translated by Eugene Eoyang)

零雨

LING YU

(1952–)

Ling Yu (Ling Yü) was born in Taipei County. She received a B.A. in Chinese from National Taiwan University and an M.A. in East Asian languages and literatures from University of Wisconsin, Madison. She divides her time between Taipei and Yilan, where she teaches at National Yilan Institute of Technology.

Ling Yu wrote fiction before she turned to poetry in the early 1980s, when she became editor of the revived *Modern Poetry Quarterly*. She has since published four volumes of poetry. In 1991–92, at the invitation of Professor Helen Vendler, she was a visiting scholar at Harvard University.

SINCE YOU CAN'T ADVANCE YOU CAN'T RETREAT EITHER (FROM "THE TRUNK SERIES")

Go into the right side of the trunk
turn right, and there's the village of memory
Go into the left side of the trunk, turn left, and there's
the exit that takes you forward

The middle is your prison cell
Every day you sit up straight
collecting toys
Each drawer contains
a calendar
Each day you must resolve
one contradiction, and you practice being on time
to the bathroom. On time to the office building

you practice running home
before darkness falls, so as not to be caught out
in the dusk

so as not to walk through the wrong door

(published 1992)
(translated by Andrea Lingenfelter)

NAMES VANISHED FROM THE MAP
(five selections)

Kungtung Mountain

I walked far away in a dream and then I came back. First light
gone, getting close to noon, imitated a bird
imitating a human voice. Just as before
a house by the road, tiny insects
imitating a human voice
strode up a wooden staircase, swung
in the mirror. Dreamed until midnight

Fought as far as Kungtung, every last soldier
This was as far as the old man got
There was snow in summer, many men lost feet

and others lost hands
Those who lost their heads
were all left on Kungtung. Today
the old man has lost his admission ticket

Kongtong. The number of hotels here keeps growing
some people collect admission tickets, souvenirs
and there is also a reenactment of that year's battle
Push the map to the north
the north
is already nearing the horizon as distant
as the sky

People with birthmarks on their faces are searching for relatives
as are people with tattoos
Those marks ring their eyes, as if
they'd been born with the third eye, or
they had dreamed too much

Dogs howl
A certain kind of dream often appears
on nights when the moon is full. Stride up
a wooden staircase, peer
at my own shadow
Now the moon with edges gnawed sharp by the dogs
is like a malevolent dream, wandering far enough away and then
turning back around

Mount Peng

It is still a long way to Mount Peng
Dreams walk on the ground, beneath clusters of windows
they flee

Huge volumes of refugees surge onto Mount Peng. In late
    autumn
blue-colored birds are hunted
mounted on sheet iron
on a section of trunk taken from a sapling
—its two young footprints
have left imprints on his chest—and
a length of flame as swift as a foal

Blue-colored bird, its feathers are the first to die
and then its two eyes and then its speech
From a chilly ferry, Mount Peng
is not far
People intent on their journeys take over every
winter nest. So goes
the dream. Dreaming that the blue-colored bird
spreads its wings and flies away from the woods and even looks
    back
and speaks to the dream

Yang Pass
    —Delighted to See Daybreak After a Sleepless Night

At first a large bird—for reasons unknown to me—came shrieking
across the way and then something with wings swiftly
brushed past the corner of the house and daybreak that white
    horse majestically
burst into the room and lifted its luminous brow

I went to a village and then another
village, passing through, exhausted
yet unable to sleep
each day my records show
that this extraordinary horse appeared. But
the best kind of horse, or those said to be the best
come from Yang Pass in the west where there is at least
one that has wings and what's more it understands
human speech

And for a long, long time I didn't
open my mouth to speak, even if you plied me with wine
pressing urgently and what's more several times people even cut
my feet with ropes

Yuyuan
    —According to an ancient legend, Yuyuan, or the Abyss of Yu,
    was where the sun went when it set.

Went to Yuyuan to visit the imprisoned sun

Those wings that chafed at their lot were its
crime

Its wings furl up a corner of the darkness, bleeding
Sharp arrowheads fastened tightly to its vital parts
It says, even in my dreams it hurts
to breathe

And even if it got rid of its wings, even if
the sky could not bear
a head, dreams go on
My neck is still listening intently: the daylight
passing through dark night
calls to me

Zhao Pass
   *—Riding the #208 Bus and Thinking of Wu Zixu Crossing
   Zhao Pass*

Left hand pressing the window, a night full of snow and ice
right hand pressing the window
a night full of snow and ice, a night
full of snow and ice. Covering up Zhao Pass

And then, strand by strand, my hair turns traitor
my face is everywhere, behind
fugitive wheel ruts, while pursuers are still searching
the barking of tracking dogs draws closer and closer
and in the mirror, I am already a grandfather

Someone calls out my childhood name, hoping
I will be recognized, to add
to the severity of these barbs

Tonight I want to cross Zhao Pass, by a path
over the most treacherous topography, and to embrace
that warmest of strangers
the watchman—coolly
he sizes me up, as if
the temperature of the snow were the same as my heart

Lanpini Garden
—*According to legend, Maya, Sakyamuni's mother, held on to the*
  branches of the Tree of No Sorrow with her hands, and the Bud-
  dha was born from the right side of her body.

Mother, her gaze passed over
Me, passed over the limbs
Of the Tree of No Sorrow
I was born. The sky
Was as before, sometimes daylight and sometimes
Night

I walked down a narrow lane, in the darkness
Many shadows returned to their place of birth
From my time in mother's womb, I already knew
How to meditate

A cart followed me, casting off
A bundle. Swiftly it disappeared
Into a dark alley
I didn't open it, it was
My only scripture
I know

I walked in a narrow lane
Time was right behind me, dogging my heels
I didn't say good-bye to her
Mother
Her gaze passed over me, passed over
The horizon that grew more distant with each passing step

Sometimes it is daylight and sometimes
Night, in solitude
I return to my mother's tear-wrapped womb
—That primeval warm
Turbulence—
I am inside, meditating

(published 1992)
(translated by Andrea Lingenfelter)

THE FAMILY OF ACROBATS

1   two hands grasp two feet
       leap forward   (toward the front of the square)
       somersault back   (buttocks facing the most crowded
                         part of the square)
       somersault forward   (in the most crowded part of the
                         square
                         ever shrinking ever smaller)
       somersault back   (ever shrinking ever smaller)
       somersault forward   (ever shrinking)
       jump back   (ever smaller)
       . . . .

       being stepped on   (only the eyes are left)
                         (the square is obscured by
                         buttocks)

2   pressed up against the spot just under the ribs
       braced against a pole
       that end of the pole braced against
       a spot
       the spot just under the ribs

       the spot just under the ribs
       has a little weight because it has a little
       weight and so they hover
       spreading open pairs of arms, pairs of legs

       they hover because of
       a pole because it is pressed up against
       the spot just under their ribs

3   right hand flies up high in the air
       cuts through cuts through   cuts
       through the brick's weakest
       point

       exploding brick flies off
       in every direction and with the sharpest
       body flies up to find
       the right hand

4   a mouth, spitting out
flames. for the darkness on all four sides
for the darkness coming
too soon for

it incites you. from within the body
spontaneous combustion in a winding passage
scuttles out and crosses the square for

everyone who catches fire recognizes
his fellows

5   what sort of person sweeps through this square
with the speed of flight?

two arms outstretched to embrace
then emptiness extends its hand

is it the rope moving?
or is it the flesh?

(always wearing a smile)
on a set street corner
embracing each other's body
then brushing past each *other* and gone

is it the speed?
or is it an actual embrace?

landing in her partner's place
(always wearing a smile)
each one casting a sidelong glance
at the empty space left by his partner

6   between head and arm. flames are wings. turn
head. arms
balance. find direction
swing between the stairs and
the street. a hunchback
moves toward the dusky square
swinging. a distant flock of doves
takes flight and links up with their arms

turn. flame. turn. all of the wings
fly toward the sky. arms. all of the arms
lift. heads lift. conveying
a belief in Pure Land. lift. flames. lift
wings. the doves return to roost in their cages

all of the hunchbacks walk away from the dusky square

7   I know Fate entirely   how to
     grasp a pair of hands

     right hand flings off sadness left hand
     flings off happiness right hand flings off
     sadness left hand flings off happiness
     sadness happiness sadness happiness
     right hand left hand right hand left hand
     sadness happiness sadness happiness sadness sadness
          happiness happiness
     right left right left right right left left
     hand hand hand hand hand hand hand hand

     I know nothing of Fate   how to
     grasp a pair of hands

8   some dozen hands certainly some dozen hands reach out
     pulling me pricking me pummeling me poking me
          pinching me

     I retreat to a dark corner and retreat again to a dark
     corner a dark corner dark

     corner to examine my flesh. my flesh it
     bears no wounds only spontaneously I have grown
     wings I have grown wings

     I spring out to the sound of applause I spring out and
     I leave the self I was yesterday back there I simply
     leave the self I was yesterday

     back there

9   and with that the bindings are loosened
     leaving behind a length of palsied rope

push open the door and push open the door again beyond
   the door is a door
the world of a door open the door and open the door again
   and walk down
a cramped stairwell and open the door
and open the door again. walk down a cramped stairwell
and open the door and open the door again. above
there is the world of a door—push open the door
and open the door again and look into the distance beyond
   the door at unreachable regions
and push open the door
push open the door again

feel a length of rope in the darkness
and slowly bind yourself

(published 1993)
(translated by Andrea Lingenfelter)

FREEZE-FRAME IN THE MIDST OF WAR
(two selections)

All of the Babies Have Disappeared

Bombs. Exploding in babies'
private parts   All of the babies
have disappeared

A face made of skin and resembling a rapidly ripening
fruit hangs from the limb of a tree

The tree's branching limbs are like a mother's desperately
   outstretched
arms. Too late
because of the sudden weight these arms
bow and shudder

Where Is My Head?
   —Taken from the Myth of Xingtian

In the department store next to a busy part of town
such a tall mass grave

. . . . .

heads bowed, all of the brothers are searching
for heads

In a dark alley the enemies are still tracking someone down
and the road is strewn with surveillance equipment. With our tits
we keep watch on our surroundings, navels dripping saliva,
dressed up like ordinary people out shopping

the maggots on the heads are like rows
of tears, and because of our visit
their seething quickens—unfamiliar heads

because of the proddings of memory they twist and are distorted
and even more strangely
take on a resemblance

(published 1996)
(translated by Andrea Lingenfelter)

陳義芝

CHEN YIZHI

(1953–)

Chen Yizhi (Ch'en I-chih) was born in Hualian on the east coast of Taiwan. After graduating from the Chinese Department of National Taiwan Normal University, he completed an M.A. at New Asia Research Institute in Hong Kong. At present he is chief editor of the literary supplement of the *United Daily* and a lecturer at several universities.

Chen published his first poem at the age of seventeen, and his first book of poetry, *Setting Sun, Rising Smoke*, appeared in 1977, followed by six more over the years. He has also published a study of gender awareness in the poetry of postwar Taiwanese women.

TAIWAN RAINS

the water buffalo settles quietly
clear stream waters flow gently over its legs hooves belly back
just like Taiwan, a huge rock set down in the middle of the sea
rain like buffalo fur streams down
falling on its black-brown soil
its porous skin

it chews away on last winter's plentiful grain scent
plunging its head underwater in the rain and then joyfully lifting
    it again
it looks out into the smooth distance, at peace with the world
following the low ridges between fields and the muddy
    rectangular plots
like a farmer squatting beneath a tree at noon to eat his midday
    meal
delineating spring plains covered in misty, gray drizzle
from riverbanks of green, tongue-wagging grass

ploughs and harrows are brought out:
acre after acre of farmland kicks up its feet and rolls over
making the eyes of innocent childhood open wide
15°C and a monsoon wind blowing in from the northeast
the ancestors gave clear indication of the beginning of spring
water in irrigation channels surges into the fields, vapor rises from
    the earth
wooden trowels tenderly embrace the sprouting rice
like mischievous children

the early-ripening sugarcane cherishes sweetness in its heart
plump white radishes long to remove their heavy mud jackets
when bananas put on their smiling faces, pineapples confess their
    green, astringent affections
heaven and earth in harmony, a beautiful first lunar month
rain pours into fields from almanacs
flows from childhood dreams beneath the pen

longan trees burst out in fine, tiny white flowers alongside Muddy
    Stream
the mangos of Gaoxiong get ready to receive the kisses of bees

the lotus-mist fruit in Pingdong signed their contract with early
     summer long ago
while I—come from far away
mount a turbulent wind at the stroke of midnight and ascend
in the beginning was the rain:
that dearest of brothers

(1985)
(translated by Simon Patton)

BROKEN-DOWN FAMILY TREE

beard pulled into loose strands, head wrapped in a scarf the
     ancient way
feet splash-splattered with mud—he's my cousin
in thirty years he's never left the remote mountainside he calls
     home
on this occasion, he accompanies me across the river to the
     county township
muttering to himself as he taps the stem of his pipe:
there's no life in this place anymore
when the steamboat turns
he coughs violently

there's no life in this place
the waist-thick banyan trees have been cut down
the pitch-black mountain forest is gone
the stone-paved road to the outside world has been dug up
yes, and after forty years there's still no electricity
the old people of the village are left with more and more
     forgetting
having no memories to hold on to

in the winter of '49, his father was tossed into a nameless gully
in '53, his brother died east of the Yalu River
all three children born over the years
are illiterate
in the Famine Years, they gnawed on the bark of loquat trees,
     nibbled on *tupa* vine
and when wolfing hunger howled in their bellies
they filled them with lumps of white earth
and so managed to survive

inside the Sweet Potato Restaurant down by the river
I order him finless eel and a plate of stir-fried pork kidneys
he shows me our broken-down family tree
and points to a line:
"From time immemorial, all things have been one with
    Heaven. . . ."

(1988)
(translated by Simon Patton)

THINKING, WORRYING (I)

someone asked me
why a single red flower at the tip of the branch?
I said it's like the fate of the puppet
always a hand pulling strings behind his back

someone asked me
why this endless succession of doors
I said it's to calm people down
all these sideways-glancing hearts

someone asked me how to get to
the top of the mountain, the edge of the forest, the end of the
    rainbow
I said the sun rises in an early morning thunderstorm
dreaming is one way out . . .

but nobody asked me
what color are fairy tales, really?
and nobody answered
like waiting for a string of prolonged notes?

a car climbs over hills like a beetle
beneath a sea-blue sky a train crosses the plain
twilight has hoisted weariness
in the harbor an enormous oil tanker vanishes
in the wink of an eye

the world appears to be populated
in fact it is not

pen in hand, I behold in my mutterings
the mad flight of the mind's tumbleweed

(1992)
(translated by Simon Patton)

WHALE

1   Innumerable small ripples follow in the wake of my
        thought:
these are my followers.
In order to learn something of the vastness, they
are forever caressing my brow with their fingers.

How limpid my ideas—
wayward yet amenable children!

2   I spout a column of water at the blue sky
as if proclaiming aloud
a declaration to seize possession of an island.

Through me the atheists
catch their glimpse of God.

3   The long wings of a thousand gulls glide across the dawn
in search of me.
Like kites on their strings,
they patrol the ocean for me.

The journey lies wherever they soar;
the fish school wherever I voyage.

4   Heaven and earth are like an upturned bowl.
Who in the depths of the ocean is using sonar?
Is it the rolling dice of fate
concealing a secret code in their jingle?

Solitude, you too I know dwell in this vortex of surging tides
bearing the load of my inexhaustible tears.

(1993)
(translated by Simon Patton)

AN ALZHEIMER'S KIND OF LOVE

all because of a lapse of memory
he parked his car in a place where he had once seen fireflies
not noticing how dark it was
how bright the headlights of his car, wanting

to fly like a firefly from the city
to its outskirts, and only come down
in front of a window level with a sloping hill
a flight made possible by the absence of coordinates

at that elevated window he meets a star
in the middle of writing a letter, and asks:
Are you still writing that same old note?
that part of a letter once forgotten

again on that unillumined slope he meets with
an eloquent wind
and once more he inquires: *Is this our story?*
how fine life sounds, how sad it is in fact

there's no one about
apart from the sweet-scented osmanthus it does seem that
someone did once walk this way
yet left nothing discernible behind

the plot is as unlikely as a movie
with effort he tries to picture the start of the road
he once turned to retrieve something he'd dropped
retracing the route, returning to where he was
the object recovered, but what of the road?

left alone in the darkness hitting out at fireflies
darkness: an exam hall he has never been inside
listening attentively to the unfamiliar cry of a baby, in the
    doorway of his home
bewildered, he passes by before he can name it

now, Alzheimer's disease is a notice board for missing persons
looking for someone who has finally grown old

and cannot tell whether the stars are indelible tears
on a letter or in somebody's eyes

owing to a lapse of memory he parked his car
in the green blur of a morning mountain track in the year 2012
there he seemed to catch a glimpse of himself, but after a
    moment's distraction
the next thing he knew it was anxious sunset

everything in the intervening eighteen years—forgotten
by the year 2012, the stories people tell each other
and his many encounters with himself
have vanished for the sake of that catastrophic scattering of
    fireflies

(1995)
(translated by Simon Patton)

ENTOMBED WARRIOR

When you enter my dark, silent pit
I watch you expectantly
looking for me
in response to the prompting of my dreams
Just like all those years ago when thousands and thousands of
    troops and horses
held their breaths in anticipation
I call out to you

A foretaste of the army's ferocity had
already come, tripping across fire
Roof-beams snapped, the ceilings of earthen chambers sank
In the instant I called
I threw off my head, turning to gaze
at the wounds of all those annihilated souls

The flexed arm of my former incarnation is jolted heavily against
    a stone wall
Maimed feet like the wrath of heaven curl into
tokens of destiny
I see you frown, confronted with
the 108 pieces of my body

imprisoned 22 centuries ago inside a dream's
unease

When smoke and dust suddenly filled the air and misgivings
    appeared on all sides
I thought of you, convinced
that one day you would make your way into my dark and silent
    pit
in search of me
dispelling the unwoken dreams of my former self

You come to make two holes for my eyes
to clear a passage for my breath
Separated by memories of a vast and indistinct eternity
you will pass on to me a filament of human warmth
and teach me to remember
the roads of twenty-two centuries I wished to walk but never did
the shame of twenty-two centuries I hoped to avoid but never
    could

Vast and indistinct eternity had all its causes planted in
that instant of massed troops and horses
when I held my head up high without dread
but in a moment of distraction
before I had a chance to call you
fate arrived at last

"The paths of the world are treacherous. One must take care!"
And so I was imprisoned by the darkness in
a fortress unknown to the world
imprisoned in a pose of unremitting waiting, second by second
What remains unbroken
is a love condensed in time

Twenty-two centuries of waiting can't be exchanged for
a single lifetime, not even impermanence
However, this world has always been waiting for you
to recognize me
by that single link of feeling
between mortal human bodies

(1997)
(translated by Simon Patton)

渡也

DU YE

(1953–   )

Du Ye (Tu Yeh, "to ferry") is the pen name of Chen Qiyou, who was born in Jiayi in southern Taiwan. He received a Ph.D. in Chinese literature from Chinese Culture University and now teaches at National Zhanghua Normal University in western Taiwan.

Du Ye started writing poetry in the 1960s and is a member of the Epoch Poetry Society. To date he has published eleven books of poetry in addition to many volumes of literary criticism and lyrical essays.

FROG

On the road home, the brightest headlights on earth that I have
ever faced allowed me to capture the moment of your leaping in
the air, but by the time you softly floated down, you had already
been crushed by speeding darkness. All I heard was the sound of
spring being torn to pieces. After that gentle car had sped off with
a roar, I squatted to carefully examine you lying there embedded
in the tire tracks on the cold, wet, desolate mountain road. Smiling,
you looked like a thin, shiny piece of paper.

Then I too took off with a roar. There at road's end, I first heard a
single frog croaking; then I heard the croaking of thousands of your
fellows surge forth. They squatted there in my darkened eyes, in-
sistently inquiring about spring and your whereabouts.
     But it was too late for all that . . .
     I immediately turned my back on those frogs in the dark
     I, with no home, held back my tears, not daring to answer them
                                            (published 1977)
                                  (translated by John Balcom)

SNOWFIELD

It was when we were stranded on the second floor of the library, in
the silence amid the old-style thread-bound books, that you asked
me about the origins and development of the traditional song lyric.
You immediately rose into the air; suddenly I drifted to the farthest
snowfield. Head hanging, I wept. Then I faced into the wind, every
scattered page of my book floated toward your shining tower, and
I shouted:
     "but . . .
     (The snow silently drifts away)
what about the origins and development of our love?"
                                            (published 1980)
                                  (translated by John Balcom)

VERMILION CABINET

Early spring 1988
The 41st anniversary of the February 28th Incident
I specially buy an old cabinet
Vermilion, like the blood of our forebears
I clean it, dry it, and touch it with great care
The same as I treat my ancestors

I put it in the living room
I put my modern history books inside
I put my Taiwanese history books inside
I put all of Taiwan's sufferings
Inside

I close the door
The door creaks
Closing Taiwan tightly away inside
The same as I treat my ancestors

I stare at the airtight cabinet in silence
I realize that all the sufferings aren't really locked up
In the heart of the cabinet
I find that all the sufferings are
Here with me
Vermilion blood, the blood of Taiwan
In my heart

(published 1988)
(translated by John Balcom)

A WISH

In my locked room
I think of them
No sky
No earth
No ray of light
I instruct them to open their textbooks
I write everything on the blackboard
The lights then go on one by one
In the glowing light

I look at them
Merely for a hawk
Or an egret
I too wish to create a blue
Sky
Where they can fly

Merely for a few flightless chickens
And ducks
I must labor to produce a magnificent
Land
Where they can stand

Let those that can reach the sky
Carry a lamp
And those left on the ground
Let them carry a lamp too
And go on living

(published 1989)
(translated by John Balcom)

UNIVERSAL LOVE, NOT WAR

I was studying the philosophy of universal love
And putting it into practice
Peaches stood at the border of my heart
Crying so that Mozi was helpless
She accused Orchid of snatching her territory
Of stealing my heart
Orchid scratched Peaches
Later Little Plum joined
The fray
In my tiny heart
They created
A Warring States period of love

Together, they destroyed Mozi's system
I seemed to hear
Mozi, in a sweat, shouting:
"Not war, not war."

(published 1990)
(translated by John Balcom)

LI BAI

After a bottle of Shaoxing wine
My wife becomes two
After a second bottle
She becomes three
Three bottles down
My wife disappears
How wonderful
The swaying ground
Is filled with stars
The delirious sky
Is lined with bottles

Late at night
All is quiet on the western front
The wine gone
Sobriety
Returns
My shoes are on the bed
I'm under the bed
My wife
Is in my ears

(published 1990)
(translated by John Balcom)

THE TILAPIA IN THE SKY

The tilapia and its children
Stand up to the fishhooks of mankind

The water is filled with hypocritical bait
And cold-eyed hooks
Day and night the tilapia ponders
Existential problems
Since aquatic creatures
Have no tears

And since they cannot live in their old home
The tilapia, unable to shed tears, has no choice but

To take its countless children
And like the birds
Fly far away
To a place high in the sky
Where there are no fishhooks

(published 1995)
(translated by John Balcom)

陳黎

CHEN LI

(1954–   )

Chen Yingwen, who writes under the name Chen Li (Ch'en Li), was born and raised in Hualian, on the east coast of Taiwan. He graduated from the English Department of National Taiwan Normal University in 1976 and has since been a middle school teacher. In recent years he has also taught creative writing at National Dong Hwa University in his hometown.

Chen started writing poetry in the 1970s, under the influence of modernism. He turned to social and political themes in the 1980s, and in the 1990s has explored a wide range of subjects and styles, combining formal and linguistic experiments with concern for indigenous cultures and the formation of a new Taiwanese identity.

To date Chen has published seven books of poetry. He is also a prolific prose writer and translator. In collaboration with his wife, literary critic Zhang Fenling (Chang Fen-ling), he has translated the work of a large number of Latin American and East European poets into Chinese, including Neruda and Szymborska. In 1999 he was invited to Rotterdam Poetry International.

THE LOVER OF THE MAGICIAN'S WIFE

How can I explain to you this breakfast scenery?
Orange juice falls off the fruit tree, and then flows along the river
    into cups;
sandwiches are conjured out of two beautiful roosters.
The sun always rises from the other end of the eggshell, in spite
    of the strong smell of the moon.
The table and chairs are just hacked off from the nearby forest;
you can even hear the leaves crying.
Maybe walnuts are hiding under the carpet, who knows?
Only the bed is stable.
But she's so fond of Bach's fugues—the magician's wife whose
    fickleness is due to
people's incredulity. You can't but stay up the whole night fleeing
    with her.
(I'm most likely the one who pants after her, dog-tired . . .)
I'm afraid after she wakes up she'll play the organ, drink coffee,
    and do her calisthenics.
Alas, who knows whether the coffee is boiling in the hat?
It's my turn, perhaps, to be the next garrulous and verse-parading
    parrot.

(1976)
(translated by Zhang Fenling with Chen Li)

THE LOVE SONG OF BUFFET THE CLOWN

Simply because half the world's sorrow is resting on his nose,
Buffet the Clown stays awake the whole night. He laughs,
radiating light as dutifully as a street lamp.
No other machine is more awkward; he hangs a hammer on his
    breast to guard, to watch over time,
as if his hands rather than his legs were the clock hands of
    infantile paralysis.
Our righteous Buffet knows no hunger.
He lives frugally, keeping his figure slim for the numerous
    affectionate ladies on the balcony.

His hat is a weathercock whose paint is chipped,
chasing the dandruff of dreams day and night.
His eyelashes are the illegitimate children of pelicans.
His sighs are the female cousins of crows.
But how proud the neck covered with lipstick marks,
persisting in its slenderness more gracefully than a giraffe.

Simply because half the world's happiness is resting on his nose,
Buffet the Clown stays awake the whole night.
He laughs, he laughs, behind the eyes as sour and yellow as
    lemons.
For the tiny eyedrops of love
he must cry, must pretend to cry sadly.
No more honest magic can ever be seen.
He presses a curved glass wand close to his ears
to turn the evil curse into grape juice and make it flow into his
    mouth.
But you must forgive him for his speeding heartbeat;
timid Buffet is at best half a great rope-walker,
dancing shakily before the slanting electric guitars.
Ha, when the ladies and stars are frustrated in love,
Buffet the Clown reads the moonlight
and imitates a broken clockwork orange, singing silently.

Simply because half the world's superiority is resting on his nose,
Buffet the Clown stays awake the whole night.
He cries, he laughs, in the upside-down dressing mirror.
For the sake of the ladies' bright spirits
he adorns himself carefully, rubs laboriously
and polishes his wits as if they were worn-out shoes.
And without his knowledge dust moves into his hair,
wrinkles of desire crawl up his baby face like a giant spider . . .
Ha, Buffet the Clown has no mask.
Buffet the Clown has no Oedipus complex.
He must get angry, must get jealous,
must write his love poems on every disposable advertisement like
    a forgotten hero,
and on the great morning—
march into the printing house of sunshine with all the vermiform
    appendixes in the city.

(1978)
(translated by Zhang Fenling with Chen Li)

IN A CITY ALARMED BY A SERIES OF EARTHQUAKES

In a city alarmed by a series of earthquakes, I heard
a thousand black-hearted jackals say to their children,
"Mother, I was wrong."
I heard the judge cry
and the priest repent. I heard
handcuffs fly out of newspapers, blackboards drop into a manure
     pit. I heard
literary men put down their hoes, farmers take off their glasses,
and fat businessmen take off their clothes of cream and balsam
     one by one.

In a city alarmed by a series of earthquakes,
I saw pimps on their knees returning vaginas to their daughters.

(1978)
(translated by Zhang Fenling with Chen Li)

LISTENING TO *WINTERREISE* ON A SPRING NIGHT —FOR FISCHER-DIESKAU

The world is getting old,
laden with such heavy love and nihilism.
The lion in your songs is getting old too,
still leaning affectionately against the childhood linden tree,
unwilling to give in to sleep.

Sleep may be desirable, when
the past days are like layers of snow
covering human misery and suffering.
It may be as well to have flowers in one's dream,
when the lonely heart is still seeking green grass in the
     wilderness.

Spring flowers bloom on winter nights,
boiling tears freeze at the bottom of the lake.
The world teaches us to hope, and disappoints us too.
Our lives are the only thin sheet of paper we have,
covered with frost and dust, sighs and shadows.

We dream on the fragile paper—
none the lighter for all its shortness and thinness.
We grow trees in the dream that has been erased time and again,
and return to them
each time we feel sad.

I am listening to *Winterreise* on a spring night.
Your hoarse voice is the dream in my dream,
traveling along with winter and spring.

Author's note: In January 1988, I heard Fischer-Dieskau, the famous German baritone, singing Schubert's song cycle, Die Winterreise (Winter Journey) *on satellite TV. Ever since I was a teenager, I have listened to Fischer-Dieskau's recordings of numerous German songs, and I have never got tired of* Winterreise. *On this occasion, on a quiet midnight, I saw the performance of so many familiar songs, such as "Der Lindenbaum" ("The Linden Tree") and "Frühling-straum" ("Dream of Spring"), coming out of the throat of the sixty-three-year-old singer, along with the voice of time. I was moved to tears. How much love for art lies in Fischer-Dieskau's aging voice, which reminds one of a life full of vicissitudes!*

(1988)
(translated by Zhang Fenling with Chen Li)

THE RIVER OF SHADOWS

Every day, from our teacups
flows a river of shadows.
The places spotted with lipstick marks
are the constantly vanishing
riverbanks.
A houseful of tea fragrance allures us into sleep.
What we drink may be time,
may be ourselves,
may be our parents, who have fallen into the cups.

We catch from the silty bottoms of the cups
last year's scenery:
a mountainful of jasmine,
flowers blooming and falling.

We watch the cold river boiling once again,
warmly dissolving the descending darkness.

Then we sit drinking tea from the cups that
brighten up like lanterns. We sit
on the bank as high as a dream,
waiting for the tea to turn into the river,
for the trees to blossom and bear fruit,
till we, like our parents, are incarnated
in a fruit,
a camellia,
vanishing into the river of shadows.

(1992)
(translated by Zhang Fenling with Chen Li)

THE EDGE OF THE ISLAND

On the world map on a scale of one to forty million,
our island is an imperfect yellow button
lying loose on a blue uniform.
My existence is now a transparent thread,
thinner than a cobweb, going through my window facing the sea
and painstakingly sewing the island and the ocean together.

On the edge of the lonely days, in the crevice
between the new and the old years,
the thought is like a book of mirrors, coldly freezing
the ripples of time.
Thumbing through it, you'll see pages of obscure
past, flashing brightly on the mirrors:

another secret button—
like an invisible tape recorder, pressed close to your breast,
repeatedly recording and playing
your memories and all mankind's—
a secret tape mixed with love and hate,
dream and reality, suffering and joy.

What you hear now is
the sound of the world:
the heartbeats of the dead and the living

and your own. If you cry out with all your heart,
the dead and the living will speak to you
in clear voices.

On the edge of the island, on the boundary
between sleeping and waking,
my hand is holding my needle-like existence:
threading through the yellow button rounded and polished by
the people on the island, it pierces hard into
the heart of the earth lying beneath the blue uniform.

(1993)
(translated by Zhang Fenling with Chen Li)

MICROCOSMOS
(ten selections)

1   A great event on the desolate
winter day: ear wax
drops on the desk.

2   A parade in honor of death:
strolling shoes working shoes sleeping
shoes dancing shoes . . .

3   On a night cold as iron:
the percussion music of two bodies
that strike against each other to make a fire.

4   All the sorrow of night will be turned into golden
ears of rice by daylight, waiting to be
reaped by another sorrowful night.

5   "Which runs faster, grass or dust?"
after a spring shower, beside a deserted railway,
someone asked me.

6   Having constantly broken world records,
our lonely shot-putter throws his head out
in one put.

7   The white skin turns a mole
into an island: I miss
the glistening vast ocean inside your clothes.

8   Sandals throughout the seasons: do you see
     the free verse my two feet write, treading
     upon the blackboard, upon the dust?

9   The story of marriage: a closet of loneliness plus
     a closet of loneliness equals
     a closet of loneliness.

10   A rondo now forte now piano:
     the flush toilets of the nihilistic republic are playing
     their mumbling national anthem again . . .

(1993)
(translated by Zhang Fenling with Chen Li)

AUTUMN SONG

When dear God uses sudden death
to test our loyalty to the world,
we are sitting on a swing woven of the tails of summer and
     autumn,
trying to swing over a tilting wall of experience
to borrow a brooch from the wind that blows in our faces.

But if all of a sudden our tightly clenched hands
should loosen in the dusk,
we have to hold on to the bodies of galloping plains,
speaking out loud to the boundless distance about our
colors, smells, shapes.

Like a tree signing its name with abstract existence,
we take off the clothes of leaves one after another,
take off the overweight joy, desire, thoughts,
and turn ourselves into a simple kite
to be pinned on the breast of our beloved:

a simple but pretty insect brooch,
flying in the dark dream,
climbing in the memory devoid of tears and whispers
till, once more, we find the light of love is
as light as the glow of loneliness, and the long day is but

the twin brother of the long night.

Therefore, we sit all the more willingly on a swing
interwoven of summer and autumn, and willingly mend
the tilting wall of emotion
when dear God uses sudden death
to test our loyalty to the world.

(1993)
(translated by Zhang Fenling with Chen Li)

THE WAR SYMPHONY*

兵兵兵兵兵兵兵兵兵兵兵兵兵兵兵兵兵兵兵兵兵兵兵兵
兵兵兵兵兵兵兵兵兵兵兵兵兵兵兵兵兵兵兵兵兵兵兵兵
兵兵兵兵兵兵兵兵兵兵兵兵兵兵兵兵兵兵兵兵兵兵兵兵
兵兵兵兵兵兵兵兵兵兵兵兵兵兵兵兵兵兵兵兵兵兵兵兵
兵兵兵兵兵兵兵兵兵兵兵兵兵兵兵兵兵兵兵兵兵兵兵兵
兵兵兵兵兵兵兵兵兵兵兵兵兵兵兵兵兵兵兵兵兵兵兵兵
兵兵兵兵兵兵兵兵兵兵兵兵兵兵兵兵兵兵兵兵兵兵兵兵
兵兵兵兵兵兵兵兵兵兵兵兵兵兵兵兵兵兵兵兵兵兵兵兵
兵兵兵兵兵兵兵兵兵兵兵兵兵兵兵兵兵兵兵兵兵兵兵兵
兵兵兵兵兵兵兵兵兵兵兵兵兵兵兵兵兵兵兵兵兵兵兵兵
兵兵兵兵兵兵兵兵兵兵兵兵兵兵兵兵兵兵兵兵兵兵兵兵
兵兵兵兵兵兵兵兵兵兵兵兵兵兵兵兵兵兵兵兵兵兵兵兵
兵兵兵兵兵兵兵兵兵兵兵兵兵兵兵兵兵兵兵兵兵兵兵兵
兵兵兵兵兵兵兵兵兵兵兵兵兵兵兵兵兵兵兵兵兵兵兵兵
兵兵兵兵兵兵兵兵兵兵兵兵兵兵兵兵兵兵兵兵兵兵兵兵
兵兵兵兵兵兵兵兵兵兵兵兵兵兵兵兵兵兵兵兵兵兵兵兵

---

*The Chinese character 兵 (pronounced "bing") means "soldier." 乒 and 乓 (pronounced "ping" and "pong"), which look like one-legged soldiers, are two onomatopoeic words imitating sounds of collision or gunshots. The character 丘 (pronounced "qiu") means "hill" or "mound."

兵 兵 兵 兵 兵 兵 兵 乒 兵 兵 兵 乒 兵 兵 兵 乒 兵 兵 兵 乒 兵 兵 兵 兵
兵 兵 兵 兵 兵 兵 兵 乒 兵 兵 兵 乒 兵 兵 兵 乒 兵 兵 兵 乒 兵 兵 兵 兵
乒 兵 兵 兵 兵 兵 兵 乒 兵 兵 兵 乒 兵 兵 兵 乒 兵 兵 兵 乒 兵 兵 兵 兵
兵 兵 兵 乒 乒 乒 兵 乒 兵 兵 乒 乒 兵 兵 乒 乒 兵 兵 乒 乒 兵 兵 兵 兵
兵 兵 乒 乒 兵 兵 乒 乒 乒 兵 乒 乒 兵 乒 乒 乒 兵 乒 乒 乒 兵 兵 兵 兵
乒 兵 兵 兵 兵
乒 乒 乒 乒 乒 乒 乒 乒 乒 乒 乒 乒 乒 乓 乒 乒 乒 乒 乒 乒 乒 乒 乒 乒
乒 乒 乒 乒 乒 乒 乒 乒 乒 乒 乒 乒 乒 乓 乓 乒 乓 乒 乒 乓 乒 乓 乒 乒
乒 乒 乒 乒 乒 乒 乒 乒 乒 乒 乒 乒 乓 乓 乓 乓 乓 乓 乓 乓 乒 乒 乒 乒
乒 乒 乒 乒 乒 乒 乒 乒 乒 乒 乒 乓 乓 乓 乓 乓 乓 乒   乓 乓 乓   乒
乒 乒   乓 乒 乒 乒   乒   乓   乒 乓   乓 乓   乓 乒
乒 乒   乒 乓   乒   乓   乒   乓   乓 乒 乒   乒   乒
        乓 乒   乒   乒 乓 乒   乒   乒   乒   乓   乒   乒
乒   乒 乒   乒   乒   乒
        乒   乒   乒   乒   乒
                乒   乒

丘 丘
丘 丘
丘 丘
丘 丘
丘 丘
丘 丘
丘 丘
丘 丘
丘 丘
丘 丘
丘 丘
丘 丘
丘 丘
丘 丘
丘 丘
丘 丘

(1995)

FORMOSA, 1661

I've always thought that we are living on the cowhide
though God has granted my wish to mix my blood, urine,
and excrement with this land.
Exchange fifteen bolts of cloth for land as large as a cowhide?
The aborigines couldn't possibly know that a cowhide could be
     cut
into strips and, like the spirit of omnipresent
God, encircle the whole Tayouan island,
the whole Formosa. I like the taste of
venison, I like cane sugar and bananas, I like
the raw silk shipped back to Holland by East India Company.
God's spirit is like raw silk, smooth, holy, and pure.
It shines upon the youngsters from Bakloan and Tavacan
who come daily to the youth school to learn spelling, writing,
praying, and catechism. Oh Lord, I hear their Dutch
smell of venison (just like the Sideia language
I utter from time to time in my sermon).
Oh Lord, in Dalivo, I have taught fifteen married women and
maidens to say the Lord's Prayer, the Gospel, the Ten
     Commandments,
and grace before and after meals; in Mattau, I have taught
seventy-two married and unmarried young men to say
various prayers, to know the main religious doctrines, to read,
and by sincerely teaching and preaching catechism, to start
enlarging their knowledge—oh, knowledge is like a cowhide
that can be folded and put into a traveling bag to carry
from Rotterdam to Batavia, from Batavia to
this subtropical island, and be unfolded into our Majesty's
     agricultural land,
the Lord's nation, cut into strips of twenty-five *ges*,
which length squared forms one *morgen*, and then three and four
     zhanglis.

In Zeelandia, between the public measurement office, the tax
     office,
and the theater, I see it flying like a flag, smiling remotely
at Provintia. Oh, knowledge
brings people joy, just like good food and myriad
spices (if only they knew how to cook Holland peas).

Oranges, with sour flesh and bitter skin, are larger than
    tangerines. But they don't know that
in summer the water tastes even better than lovemaking when
mixed with salt and smashed oranges. In Tirosen,
I have acquainted thirty married young women with various
    prayers
and simplified key items; in Sinkan, one hundred and two
married men and women have been taught to read and write (oh,
    I
taste in the Bible in romanized aboriginal languages
a taste of venison flavored with European ginger).
Ecclesiastes in Favorlang, the Gospel according to Matthew in
    Sideia,
the marriage of the civilized and the primitive. Let God's spirit
enter the flesh of Formosa—or, let the venison of Formosa enter
    my
stomach and spleen to become my blood, urine, and
excrement, to become my spirit. I've always thought that we are
living on the cowhide, although those Chinese troops are
    approaching
on junks and sampans with large axes and knives
attempting to cover us with an even bigger
cowhide. God has granted my wish to mix my blood,
urine, and excrement with the aborigines'
and print them, like letters, on this land.
How I wish they knew this cowhide, in which new spelling
words are wrapped, can be cut into strips and thumbed into
pages, a dictionary loaded with sounds, colors, images, smells
and as broad as God's spirit.

Author's note: Bakloan, Tavacan, Dalivo, Sinkan, Tirosen, and Mattau are names of communities of the plains aborigines in Taiwan. The Sideia language and the Favorlang language are dialects of the plains aborigines (Sideia is also called Siraya). Zeelandia was a city built on Tayouan island (now called Anping, in Tainan) by the colonists during the Dutch Occupation period (1624–1662). Provintia was a fort they built. It is said that the Dutch offered to exchange fifteen bolts of cloth with the aborigines for a cowhide-sized piece of land. After the agreement was made, they "cut the cowhide into strips and encircled land more than one kilometer

*in circumference" (see Lian Heng, A General History of Taiwan).
"Ge" was a measuring unit used by the Dutch, equaling about twelve
feet five inches. Twenty-five ges squared equals one morgen. Five
morgens make one zhangli.*

(1995)
(translated by Zhang Fenling with Chen Li)

DIALOGUE

—For Hikari Oe*

At the concert celebrating the sixtieth birthday of the conductor
Seiji Ozawa, I hear the new duet by Hikari Oe, mentally retarded
son of the novelist Kenzaburo Oe. The aging Russian cellist in
exile, the gorgeous Argentine woman pianist. They are conversing.
How do shadows weave a crown of laurel, how does imperfection
contain the beauty of a flower? In life's earth, stone, cloud, rain —
lights, of language and music. Flying over the river of Time: "Wan-
dering, drifting, what am I like?"** Exile, return, suspension, res-
olution. C string and chromosome, pain and love. On my video
player whose right speaker is out of order so whenever it replays
noises interfere incessantly, I hear so clearly a breeze blowing across
fine grass on the riverbanks, my chest suddenly broadens as stars
reach down. On my solitary transnational journey in the afternoon,
I gladly pull out the passport issued by a fellow traveler from an
earlier time:

"The moon rushing forward, the great river flows."

(1996)
(translated by Michelle Yeh)

---

*Hikari Oe was born with a brain hernia in 1963 and did not speak his first word till the age
of six. At thirty-two he started writing music; he has since become an internationally acclaimed
composer. In his 1994 Nobel lecture, Kenzaburo Oe (b. 1935) described his own writing as a
coming to terms with his son's condition and referred to "the exquisite healing power of art."
"Hikari" literally means "light," and "Oe" means "great river."

**The question "Wandering, drifting, what am I like?" and the last line of the poem are
direct quotes from "Thoughts on a Night Journey" by Du Fu (712–770).

BUTTERFLY AIR

"The fluttering of ten thousand butterfly wings in the Southern
    Hemisphere causes a
typhoon in the summer mid-day dream of a woman near the
    Tropic of Cancer, who was chased by
love but betrayed love . . ." I found this sentence
in the meteorology book with color illustrations lying on the
    dressing table in your room.
Ah, the terrace of memory with metallic walls and glass floor,
where I once entered but later lost the key and could not
get in. With a navy blue eyebrow pencil you highlighted
in the book: "The staple food of the butterflies is love poems,
    especially
sad ones, ones that cannot be swallowed in one gulp and need to
    be chewed over and over . . ."

I mull over ways to reach you again: Dismember yesterday,
hang it up and let it float outside your building like a spider? Or,
    on the wings of
one butterfly stamp after another, deliver a parcel of longing and
    despair
to your door? Your smooth, tightly closed metallic walls make
    every single
crawling insect trying to climb up slip and fall off the
    building . . .

So I wait for the fluttering of butterfly wings in the Southern
    Hemisphere to cause a
typhoon in your summer mid-day dream, to allow the butterfly
    shadows secretly issued by sorrow
to flap and strike the doors and windows of your heart, and let a
    question mark,
a comma, in the incompletely digested poem stir up your
    memory
like a tiny screw, pop the top of the old perfume bottle sitting on
    your
nightstand, so that you can hear anew the chirping insects,
    barking dogs, singing clowns
without a nose that we once heard together and are stored inside,
so that you can smell anew the perspiration and scented mud that
    we once rolled on:
at the bottom of a deep lake a summer night's conversation that
    cannot be stopped.

Now our hearts are as far apart as the two poles of the globe,
    although my eyes,
like a thumbtack, still fix on the longitude and latitude of where
    you are on the map.
I can only write a poem, a sad poem, to make the butterflies in
    the Southern Hemisphere fight for food
and make them flutter ten thousand wings so as to cause a
    typhoon
in the summer mid-day dream of you, behind metallic walls in a
    tall building near the Tropic of Cancer.

(1996)
(translated by Michelle Yeh)

TUNNEL

From a distance your weeping
drills a tunnel in my body.
This morning I return to the familiar darkness,
enter the cell of honeycomb that belongs to me,
waiting for sorrow to drip like honey.

In amber-colored time I solidify,
feeding on imaginary death, on soft candy
of emptiness. Your weeping
is a soundless inscription on my ear;
at the end of the tunnel it sparkles into

a translucent rain tree.

Look for its shape, not for its entrance.
A tunnel passes through a life of grief connecting you and me.

(1997)
(translated by Michelle Yeh)

ON THE ISLAND

1   A hundred-pacer snake stole my necklace and singing voice.
    I will go beyond the mountain to get them back.
    But Mother, look!

He has torn my necklace up, cast it down to the valley,
and turned it into starlight flowing all night long.
He has compressed my singing voice into a teardrop,
falling on the silent feathered tail of a black long-tailed
    pheasant.

2   Our canoe has drifted from the ocean of myth to the beach
    tonight.
Our canoe, my brother, has landed anew, along with this
    line of words.

3   A fly has flown onto the sticky flypaper below the goddess's
    navel.
Just as the day hammers gently on the night,
my dear ancestor, hammer gently with the unused Neolithic
    tool between your thighs.

4   We do not die, we just grow old,
we do not grow old, we just change plumage,
like the sea changing its bedsheets
in the stone cradle, at once ancient and young.

5   His fishing rod is a rainbow of seven colors,
bending slowly down from the sky
to hook every swimming dream.

Ah, his fishing rod is a bow of seven colors
that aims at every black-and-white fish flying out of the
    subconscious.

6   Because the bees buzz underground,
we have earthquakes. Yet earthquakes
can be sweet, if a bit of honey should
seep through the cracks of the
earth's crust, through the cracks of the heart.

7   She stood singing on a rock with her brother on her back;
the god who heard the singing voice fetched her to heaven.

But she felt like eating millet, so she asked her father
for three grains to sow them in heaven.

"On hearing thunder, just picture me
threshing millet."

At the sight of lightning, we'll assume
she has threshed open her homesickness again.

8   Her body, unopened by desire,
is a cement room without doors and windows.

"Drill a hole through my wall, Mother.
Numerous fleas are anxious to rush out of the dark ages,
out of my soft, swelling *hahabisi,*
to receive the baptism of light."

9   Under the giant Harleus's crotch hid a rapid transit system.
His eight-kilometer-long penis is the most flexible viaduct,
crossing swiftly running dales, crossing mountain ranges,
stretching from Village Hikayiou to Village Pianan.
Fair girls, while you enjoy the ecstasy of free transportation,
    beware
that his fleshy bridge may suddenly turn its direction
and creep into your dark tunnels.

10   The day is too long, the night is too short,
and the valley of death too far away.
My dear sisters, leave the taro fields
to men, and sweat to ourselves.
Let's put the hoes on our heads like horns
and become goats, to take shelter from the sun under trees.

You are a goat,
and I am a goat.
Away from men, away from toil,
we play and enjoy the cool breeze in the shade.

*Author's note: The black long-tailed pheasant is a rare bird found in
the Taroko Gorge National Park. There is a legend about the origin
of the Amis: a brother and sister sought shelter from a deluge and
drifted to the east coast of Taiwan on a canoe. According to the Atayal
myth of the creation, there were a god and a goddess in very ancient
times who were ignorant of lovemaking until one day a fly landed on
the private part of the goddess (the Amis have a similar myth).*

According to a Saisiyat legend, old people could recover their youth simply by peeling off the skin. An Ami myth has it that the rainbow was originally the seven-color bow of Adgus, the hunter who shot down the sun. There is an Ami legend about how earthquake was formed: the people living on the ground cheated those living underground by exchanging hemp bags filled with bees for goods. The Paiwan have stories about a girl singing on a rock with her little brother on her back and being delivered to heaven because she aroused the gods' sympathy and affection. A Bunun legend goes like this: once upon a time there was a beautiful girl whose private part (hahabisi in the Bunun language) was a little swollen but tightly sealed. Her mother cut it open with a knife, and out sprang numerous fleas. There is an Atayal legend about the giant Harleus, who had a tremendously long penis. He stretched it out as a bridge for people to cross flooded rivers, but he got lustful at the sight of pretty girls. A Puyuma legend goes like this: two girls were close friends. One day they worked in the taro field on the mountain. It was so hot that they took shelter from the sun under a tree. Rejoicing, they put hoes on their heads and were turned into goats.

(1998)

(translated by Zhang Fenling with Chen Li)

COMPOSITION

I cultivate a space
with loneliness, with breath.
Two or three plastic bottles on the floor,
a laundered pair of orange panties
dripping from the stainless steel   dripping.

I cultivate orange smell,
shampoo, wings of a glider.

I cultivate a word in lower case
veronica: cloth with the holy face of
Jesus; a bullfighting pose (with both feet
planted, the bullfighter slowly moves
the cloth away from the attacking bull).

I cultivate a closet in which hang a pair of black jeans
and a blue T-shirt.

I cultivate a laptop computer awaiting the input
of the sea and a range of waves.

I cultivate a gap:
isolating me from the world
and leading me to your human world hanging under the belly
    button.

I cultivate the tortuous, complex nation-building history
of a newest, smallest country.

(1998)
(translated by Michelle Yeh)

楊澤

YANG ZE

$(1954-\ \ )$

Yang Ze (Yang Tse), pen name of Yang Xianqing, was born and raised in Jiayi in southern Taiwan. He graduated from the Department of Foreign Languages and Literatures, National Taiwan University, and went on to earn a Ph.D. in comparative literature from Princeton University. After a brief stint of teaching at Brown University, he returned to Taiwan to assume the chief editorship of the literary supplement to *China Times*.

Yang was a member of the National Taiwan University Poetry Society and published his first book of poetry in his senior year. With three books of original poetry to date, Yang has exerted significant influence on younger poets.

FUGUE OF VIOLENCE AND MUSIC
– TO JETHRO TULL

The window's shadow keeps moving, dusk, six o'clock
the bugle call returns on time from the hunting woods
the silvery-white bugle call – and the dead
baron, will he feel all this? The sound of people, of horses
all of it quickly filtered by twilight. As this is a fugue
of violence and music, I faintly hear
candles moving, and nails being hammered into a coffin at
    midnight.
From afar I see that at dawn, on the grass in the cemetery,
people are reenacting the dead baron's funeral
the lute strings' excitement and their grief: this is a minstrel
    singing –

This is a minstrel singing: it makes the land sink into the sea, and
    the sea
sink into wasteland, and on the wasteland grows the rose's song
violence and hammering, a melancholy hammering, like a bugle
    call –
as desolate, as entreating, as futile: flute, triangle, electric guitar.
This is one part of singing, this is all of
existence – all of joy, all of misery
all of spring, all of love . . .

The window's shadow keeps moving, dusk, six o'clock
I sit down to wait, embracing deathly stillness even more
    complete.
Night, solid as a castle, solid as death itself, is about to
soar and sway in the chime of evening prayer; but love,
let love not think about these things. Time is but
a wounded migrant bird in the bell's sudden, formidable embrace
knocked down into our loving hands.
On love, and on time, by the light of the flames
let me write you a song:
faith, dreams, distant civilization; let my explanations
be one with the short month of May, the bright and beautiful
month of May. . . .

(1977)
(translated by Maghiel van Crevel)

UNDER A SCORCHING SUN, A STIFLING NOON, I STARED

Under a scorching sun, a stifling noon, I stared—
at my shadow on the asphalt road, thinking and crying
madly walking, oh, like a city with sunstroke
groaning and moaning beside a fire truck's foam . . .

Because these are years lived in the wind, flying
dust in your eyes and mine
brews tears. At dusk
I stand at the skyscraper's windows, and see
a great crowd of people just like me
dragging a useless body, hurriedly walking
at dusk, discontented with all of reality.
I feel as if trekking in solitude through a desert of old,
dust is flying, I am like a minister in exile
trekking in solitude through a desert of old . . .

Because these are years lived in the wind, in the wind I
hang my head, I shed tears: "Even if
the sages were to return, they could not
deliver me from this pressing grief . . ."

Under a fierce and scorching sun, I stared—
my soul floating upward and dispersing like blue smoke in the air
"Endless showy flowers on Cold Food Road
A scented carriage tied to the tree outside someone's house."
Because these are years lacking in faith,
I madly walk, oh, like the sages of old:
a city with sunstroke groaning and moaning beside a fire truck's
    foam . . .

(1977)
(translated by Maghiel van Crevel)

THIS IS THE SPRING OF CYNICISM

this is the spring of cynicism; we
hide ourselves in the folds of a dry, cold smile
carrying fake flowers from walks taken with our lovers

(In Liverpool, someone hangs himself with a white necktie; but
    what
has that to do with me?)

this is the spring of cynicism, we
wake up in the middle of the night to sob like children, in spite
    of ourselves . . .
I've been to a few of General X's dinner parties
cautiously, humbly bearing in mind my age and status, and
    soon—
I got to know everyone in the city

(this is possible, in China: a poet I know sold his surplus
    personality
for a position as a lowly government clerk . . .)

this is the spring of cynicism—but there's no dearth of delight:
demons from hell like Oxhead and Horseface, dog-mouth ivory
I am busily erasing mottos that will make people blush from
    every book
busily sticking Band-Aids on the injured eyes of every mirror
but I hear a seemingly cynical voice that says:
"There is more between two points than just a straight line
for our ideals, My Child, we exercise restraint and give way
give way, go around and still advance . . ."

(on the bank of the Congo sits a sleigh—sits a sleigh,
for no reason at all . . .)

(1977)
(translated by Maghiel van Crevel)

RAINY DAY—WOMEN #12 & 35

autumn freshness in the human world, a rainy day
and in the evening twilight one cannot but sigh wistfully
aimlessly standing at a bus stop on the way home, looking
at buildings under construction across the street, while in that
    light rain
one lonely mercury streetlight after another lights up
two, three gaudily dressed women walk by through the rain at
    dusk

lips pursed, racing to meet their appointment with life
on a red brick road where no sages will come back to life, I
    glimpse
someone sucking on a Kent cigarette with lowered head
time, stunned and inauthentic, is like
a huge diamond ring on the ring finger
wet and glimmering in the rain

overnight, that man's hair and beard turned gray; I
am lost among roadside dynasties, full of untimely feelings . . .

the city night explodes in a wild burst of nearby rock 'n' roll
and in neon-red rain I am shot dead by billboard stars
the world is sinking in a sea change
all the way down into the center of the evil night
someone stoops to pick up her lipstick
I realize that your and my city
left lying at the roadside
is a cigarette butt that won't be lit again

(1978)
(translated by Maghiel van Crevel)

CLEAR DAY—WOMEN #12 & 35

when night disappears at the entrace of the alleyway
the sunlight smells as if it's slow in coming, outside
the French windows, between the bushes that line the street
and the parked cars
there's a woman hawking
steamed stuffed buns in a local accent
as people's reflections in car windows walk on

a generous, gentle breeze strokes the branches, behind a wall
the ground is covered in flower petals
waking up from a dream at noon, in between
days to come and days gone by
two young women that no one knows
walk past a green mailbox on a street corner

when, oh when will the lotus bloom?
it will bloom in March.

and if not in March, then when will it bloom?
school's out, and three girls race ahead
red hats, yellow schoolbags, white socks
hair in braids flying under a clear sky

but the way of the sages has truly never
once been practiced in this world

(1978)
(translated by Maghiel van Crevel)

OUTSIDE IS THE SNOW

outside is the snow
is the snow fluttering and flying
 the snow that loves the roaming life like I do
 whose wandering the earth has led to regret
outside is the snow of a strange land

outside is the snow
is rain and snow riding each other
 the rain that loves to cry like you do
 whose disenchantment with the world has led to awareness
outside is the snow of a foreign country

outside is the rain is the snow
is rain and snow that rustle
 in the eaves and gutters of strangers
 on the closed road by the lake
outside is the fierce rain and snow of spring

outside is the rain is the snow
is rain and snow thick and fast
 desolate rainstorms like your eyes
 foggy snowstorms like my forehead
rain and snow that reach back to previous lives

 "in wild confusion, now joined and now parted"
 not afraid to turn to mud we go down
 and in the dream arrive anew
 on that evil earth, our home . . .

(1983)
(translated by Maghiel van Crevel)

NIGHTLY HOMECOMING

People of Taipei on your way home at night:
should you find yourselves tripping over me in pitch-black
    dreamless arcades
please dispel all doubts, the one lying there drunk is indeed me

           (1990)
    (translated by Maghiel van Crevel)

LIFE IS NOT WORTH LIVING

Life is not worth living.
Before today, I have perhaps
already felt a sense of foreboding.
Before today, before the moving pattern
on your skin, like that of a young animal, before
the quince in the dark
the highly perfect terrace and stars
before the night—the night of the magic flute
and the unicorn that belongs to all lovers:
when the magic flute shrieks
when it shrieks through the rooms and finally cools down
and the bugle call returns to that very last
that very first dawn over the plains . . .

Life is not worth living.
Before today, I've had that feeling.
Before today, before my being relative
and your being absolute—like the wild hare's
sincere, courageous, passionate love instinct
and then (making it hard not to doubt you)
a many-sided, impure temperament
that tends toward the sentimental, that tends toward speed
and toward an illusion-fostered
bit of indulgence and madness.

Life is not worth living at all.
Long before today, before books,
music, and painting—right from the start
I've had that gloomy feeling.
Green light, blue roses

spliffs, and Zen,
I dream of you: scooter girl
acting like the headless rider from a painting
carrying your thick black hair, racing
away toward dawn over the plains . . .
And when the magic flute shrieks
when it shrieks and finally turns cold
the magic potion of love and death is but
like sunset over the ocean —
eternal violence
and madness . . .

Life is not worth living.
Before the elephants running on the shore
and the ocean and the distant sky grow old together:
a young animal darkly licking its wounds
only to safeguard
your sentimentality from beginning to end
I am willing to take the hilt for the knife
be an indefatigable
ever-defeated swordsman
and like a groundhog, I will
diligently go on living
although before your illusions
my nothing, before
your cave, my light—
although life is not worth living.

(1990)
(translated by Maghiel van Crevel)

LET ME BE YOUR DJ

a.   in utterly empty and deserted streets
      parasol trees shrug off their sighs
      please come quick—to find me at the midnight middle-age
          bar
      let me be your DJ

b.   there's still parking at the entrance of the alley
      please come quick—to find me at the wee hours bar
      let me be your DJ

c.   as usual the sun will rise day and night revolving
like a giant turntable forged from melancholy
when you and I exert ourselves climbing tomorrow's steep
   slopes
our field of vision is yesterday's abyss
please come quick—to that bar, refuge of illusions
let me be your DJ

d.   and still the sun will rise day and night revolving
like a giant turntable that will never grow mossy
Cat Stevens, Jim Croce, Jim Morrison
times of anger and nothingness
silhouettes of youth impatient and insane: looking back—
and the waves of life are now a thing of the past
please come quick—to find me at the bar before dawn
let me be your DJ

(1990)
(translated by Maghiel van Crevel)

羅智成

LUO ZHICHENG

(1955–)

Born in Taipei, Luo Zhicheng (Lo Chih-ch'eng) graduated from the Department of Philosophy of National Taiwan University. After working as editor for *China Times* for two years, he went to study at University of Wisconsin, Madison, where he earned an M.A. in East Asian Studies and completed course work in the doctoral program. Since returning to Taiwan, he has assumed various editorial positions at newspapers and magazines and has taught at several universities. Active in the media, including television and advertising, he is now the publisher of the travel magazine *To Go* and teaches at Soochow University, Taiwan.

Luo published his first book of poems, which he not only self-financed but also designed and illustrated, in 1975. He has published five books of poetry, two books of prose, a volume of critical essays, and various translations. Already an established poet in the 1970s, he has continued to influence poets of a younger generation.

FATHER

"I have always wanted to write a poem for you
but the secret of the love between us
is family property that must not be squandered."

One day we will go to the banks of the great lake, and
while He is busy sorting and counting all the fish
we'll help Him sort and count the fragrant flowers and the
     waterbirds.
When the stars arise, having washed their hands and faces,
with our wandering souls, we'll
help Him survey the soil.
Then, squatting on the generous gaze
of the ridges in the fields
we'll chat with a perfect silence that carries the rustle of leaves
in the wind, our serene smiles slowly turning with the night skies.
One day we will be born from the fields
plowed by our sons
never again to sing sadly of the flesh,
our blessing passed on to posterity's
indomitable forehead—
had we not stopped the scorching sun long ago
it would have cast their shoulders like iron;
had we not stopped the floods long ago
they would have given them trunks full of
severely frowning wisdom.

One day we will go to heaven
to open up wasteland
in between constellations, fencing off our fields
compiling our county annals
cultivating our vegetable gardens.
At that time, please watch me
my silver forehead melting in deep sleep.

The livestock are drinking beside my pillow
the village women are knotting fishnets from the light of the
     waves.
On the banks of the great lake
even if night's curtain were drawn tighter, it could not cover

this vast and fertile earth—look
at that distant dawn, where night can't make ends meet.

Father: and our family
will thrive, trees in a forest
like towering masts on the sea of time.

(1978)
(translated by Maghiel van Crevel)

DARLING LETTERS
(five selections)

1   before growing up, we must
     let our love unfold

2   like a drunken magician
     with lively words and phrases
     cooking a soup brimming with flavor and aroma
     it doesn't matter whether it's poetry
     my quest is for a taste of beauty and nutrition

3   coming back to life happens every day

     by a black fly washing its feet, my thinking
     is stirred into rippled waves
     in a dreamland thin as the cicada's wings
     now sinking now floating
     I am washed up on the shores of darkness
     clinging to matters of great concern
     this morning
     I have awakened yet again

4   that suitcase needing to be packed anew every day, full of
     diaries, street names, insomnia, and exam papers
     at some time in the past
     I lost it on the way

     I need to write them anew every day

5   I will allow you to lie to me
     at least another thousand times

—from your sincere eyes, who would still crave
those trite true facts?

(published 1979)
(translated by Maghiel van Crevel)

THE WOLF

The wolf
there's something sad about it.
Driven from paradise, forever
forced into pursuit, but hopelessly so,
rummaging through chests and cupboards, to discover . . .
But there is no one to listen to its story.

Cold dewdrops cover
hairy hot limbs:
after a night of mad running
talons and fangs still rage
with the energy of the swell after a storm.

There is a loneliness that never gets tired,
a loneliness whose gaze lights the first rays of morning
while feverish, hot breath stirs hollow body cavities.
The wolf
has a sadness about it.
It does not share—
it does not share in other people's dreams.
Its vigorous life is not dedicated to any goal.
The wolf neglects itself like
a king drawing up a list of those to be banished.

The wolf attacks, and bites
The wolf always turns its back on
the awestruck stares of a herd of deer—
because deer don't understand:
wolves
have their soft spots too.

(1986)
(translated by Maghiel van Crevel)

THE GREAT RAINS OF '93
—TO THE ETERNAL "LAST READER"

This year's spring rains
are the beginning of an ice age that will blossom in 20,000 years
but nobody has noticed.
I myself and, in two days' time,
Reader A reading this poem in the damp open-air store are the
    only exceptions.
We are concerned that this city, before even
reaching the peak of its civilization
will get stuck in the snowy season of deep, unending sleep
and that all scenery and garbage of the subtropics
will turn into oilfields and coal mines for the next civilization
and long, long before the next civilization
on this afternoon
I and Reader A who has not yet read this poem
find shelter from the rain in a bar widely known for its bleak
    humanist spirit
carrying under our arms an umbrella we've had no time to open
    and a
newspaper forever worried about recession
with an expression on our faces just like
a flag drenched through and through.
Flags will normally yearn for storm, not balk at being blown into
    folds
but if drenched a flag will end up as one great sticky bundle
seemingly harboring some sign
or thought
or scheme
conning its way into this evil environment
that lies between the late twentieth and the late nineteenth
    century
or between the previous ice age and the next.
As for us—the estrangement between me and Reader A
is a result of the fact that
we don't know that all the while we've been shoulder to shoulder
    as nonvoting delegates
and our weary eyes conceal a mutual longing.
In two days' time, Reader A in the open-air store will
be reading this poem, and briefly

feel attracted by its message
without ever realizing that he's met with Author A
at civilization's every evil hour . . .

(1993)
(translated by Maghiel van Crevel)

THE BOOKSTORE OF MY DREAMS

We are awed and fascinated by the jungle
that is this bookstore.

In a district in decline
behind a number plate forever overlooked by the postman
hundreds of miles of bookshelves of all descriptions and
stone tiles, wood paneling, and
muddy corridors
congested, sprawling
stretch knowledge all the way into
the reaches that electricity has not yet reached:
covered in cobwebs, in mystery miasma,
the foyers of mice and moths, sewers,
carpets in knee-deep water and
secret rooms with keys forever lost . . .
And bookshelves, tens upon tens, carrying huge animal samples,
ruined flags, family emblems,
windows sealed shut, drawers with memory loss
gape and gawk at us, putting on display
the savage face of human wisdom . . .

Nobody, not even the eighty-nine-year-old third-generation
    storekeeper, Mr. L.,
nobody knows the bookstore's true dimensions—
not even Professor T., who last year, in pursuit of some
    remaindered book,
was submerged forever in the quicksand of letters,
or the critic who, after many years, came bursting back out of a
    mural
or the new breed of bats that had sunk their teeth into his
    neck . . .
Really, even in the tightly guarded stack rooms at the eastern end
    of Section B

in the shrubbery mostly made of biographies and fables
we will occasionally run into the
skeleton of one who lost their way . . .

We are fascinated by the labyrinth
that this bookstore truly is!
In an age filled with breathless change
we are close to tears when singing the praises
of that immovable, insoluble, unrevealing iceberg
and to read—
to read those rare, abstruse souls
and those indefatigable daydreams
is the ritual sacrifice of our youth . . .

Like a giant beast deep in hiding
from behind a quiet shop front the bookstore engages with the
    outside world
but beyond its range upon range of bookshelves
it is still growing
like a newborn star in its energy, its violence
and its unimaginable possibilities . . .

Toward evening
we always hear, far and near,
the sounds of woodwork coming loose, of stealthy, silent steps,
of aborigines moving furniture among broken bamboo slips and
    torn paper. . . .
These fearful things I have long ceased to fear.
On tiptoe I pick out a *flora* from the Yin dynasty
and through the gap on the shelf comes the sound of water.
I turn the pages in concentration
sitting straight as a sundial
tiny as an ant
and then exchange it for another book
curious, searching, reading
until knowledge closes its doors . . .

(1994)
(translated by Maghiel van Crevel)

向陽

XIANG YANG

(1955–)

Xiang Yang (Hsiang Yang, "facing the sun") is the pen name of Lin Qiyang, who was born in Nantou in central Taiwan. He received a B.A. in Japanese and an M.A. in journalism from Chinese Culture University. He worked as chief editor of *China Times Weekly* and of the literary supplement of the *Independence Evening Post* before becoming executive editor of the latter publication. In 1997 Xiang Yang left the media to pursue a Ph.D. in journalism at National Zhengzhi University. He has taught at Jingyi University in recent years and is now Deputy Publisher and Executive Editor of the *Independence Evening Post*.

Since the mid-1970s Xiang Yang has been active on the poetry scene. He cofounded A Gathering in the Sunshine Poetry Society in 1979 and was among the first in Taiwan to write modern poetry in Hokkien, of which "Nine to Five" is an example. He attended the International Writing Program at the University of Iowa in 1986, helped establish the Taiwanese PEN in 1987, and served as its vice president in 1990. A prolific writer, he has published five books of poetry, two English translations of selected poems (see the bibliography), five volumes of essays, another five of literary criticism and social commentaries, and children's stories.

TRAIN STATION

Isn't it like
That small red flower
Standing timidly in the deep gloom
Under the golden gingko grove of home
Soaked in the rain last autumn?

Away from home this spring, from the train at dusk
I see an egret
Flap its ash-white wings
Soar among crimson clouds
And disappear!

(1976)
(translated by John Balcom)

MY CARES

Floating clouds sink their gloomy faces
In a small pond reflecting verdant trees and blue sky
And the pond sends the circling ripples with the wind
To swimming fish
My cares are the willows pacing around the shore

Departing night urges tomorrow to stay
Leaves flutter down through the mist
But joy and sorrow remain silent forever
There, in the reflection of the bridge railing
The surprise encounter of the fish and the leaves

(1978)
(translated by John Balcom)

SEED

I'll just stoop, listening as the twigs and branches wither
Unless I resolutely break from this beautiful and reliant corolla
As all the fragrances, the bees, the butterflies, and the yesterdays
    are
Scattered by the wind. Only by rejecting the protective
    camouflage of green leaves
Will I be able to wait for the soil's fearsome blast

But if I choose to dwell on a mountain slope,
    then the open wilds will be closed to me
If I settle at the seashore, then I'll lose the cleansing stream
Between heaven and earth, so broad yet so narrow
I drift, I fly, I float to find a suitable place
To settle, take root, and be fruitful

                  (1978)
        (translated by John Balcom)

AUTUMN WORDS

No longer can the leaves cling to the withered limbs
Falling in droves they speed to the heart of the cold lake at dawn
Someone with an umbrella walks the dew-drenched shore
From the forest all that is heard is a falling
Pine cone, a startled cry

Is this how you come? Ripples
And echoes linger over the quiet water
The duckweed suddenly parts
Leaving the mountain's reflection kissing
The blue rain-washed sky, and autumn is deeper

                  (1979)
        (translated by John Balcom)

NINE TO FIVE

This job has got me down
Up early to stand in the cold
Waiting for the bus, shake your head
Stamp your feet, look at your watch
Wait, wait, wait
The bus so crowded, nearly makes you faint

This job is a pain
Working hard every day
Gotta watch the boss's moods
Don't dare cross him
Just work, work, work

Killing yourself for
a few bucks each month

This job has got me down
Sometimes you've gotta work
till late at night
Listening to the clock, counting
the minutes
Time just drags on and on and on
When the sun comes up
you're ready for bed

(1982)
(translated by John Balcom)

UNIFORM

They all wear the same uniform, their arms
All swing in unison, they all march to the same
    step
On a road of lush spring grass; they are satisfied
To close ranks, their eyebrows, mouths, and
    shoulders
Forming a line to carefully measure the silent plain

Even the wind dares not cough. They
Chop down the conceited trees, prune away
Leafy branches and flowers; finally they all
Look up and shake their heads, for naturally, as
    keepers of this earthly garden, they
Cannot force uniformity on the clouds in the sky.

(1984)
(translated by John Balcom)

LESSER FULLNESS OF GRAIN[1]

Splash! A frog jumps in the pond
Startling the drowsy crows in the trees
The water lily pads tremble
Ripples ring outward over the water
Spreading the tranquility
Alone sits the lotus
On this stifling summer afternoon
Even the clouds are loath to appear
In a column, ants carry bread crumbs
Walking rhythmically over the bumpy ground

Walking rhythmically over the bumpy ground
In a column, ants carry bread crumbs
Even the clouds are loathe to appear
On this stifling summer afternoon
Alone sits the lotus
Spreading the tranquility
Ripples ring outward over the water
The water lily pads tremble
Startling the drowsy crows in the trees
Splash! A frog jumps in the pond

(1985)
(translated by John Balcom)

GREAT HEAT[2]

Heat out of cold   Cold into heat
The city clamors   On a slowly cooling night
Under a solitary lamp   Longing like fire

---

[1]The ancient Chinese solar calendar is divided into 24 seasonal periods, each about 15.21 days in length. The names are: Beginning of Spring, The Rains, Waking of Insects, Vernal Equinox, Tomb Sweeping, Grain Rain, Beginning of Summer, Lesser Fullness of Grain, Grain in Ear, Summer Solstice, Lesser Heat, Great Heat, Beginning of Autumn, The Limit of Heat, White Dew, Autumn Equinox, Cold Dew, Hoarfrost, Beginning of Winter, Lesser Snow, Great Snow, Winter Solstice, Lesser Cold, and Great Cold. This and the next five poems are all selected from Xiang Yang's *The Four Seasons*, a collection of 24 poems for the 24 solar periods. "Lesser Fullness of Grain" begins on May 22.

[2]"Great Heat" begins on July 23.

Love buried carelessly	Pain enters the heart
Discarded by an oath	Already ice cold
Skyful of stars in the window	Sky full of stars
Glowing fully	Calls out
The sighs that summer	Your name and figure
Pass hotly	Before my eyes
In a stifling wind	A star falls

A star falls	In a stifling wind
Before my eyes	Pass hotly
Your name and figure	The sighs that summer
Calls out	Glowing fully
Sky full of stars	Skyful of stars in the window
Already ice cold	Discarded by an oath
Pain enters the heart	Love buried carelessly
Longing like fire	Under a solitary lamp
On a slowly cooling night	The city clamors
Cold into heat	Heat out of cold

(1985)
(translated by John Balcom)

WAKING OF INSECTS[3]

Last night the cold began its slow retreat
This morning bird song invades the forest
Scaled to match the light and shadow at dawn
The sunlight breaks through the window
To visit long-damp corners, silently
Warming shovels and plows. The north wind
Turns westward, surging
Clouds in the sky.
Hibernating insects prepare to emerge from the soil
I wander in the garden, following butterflies

Like last year, the plows are busy turning earth
Sweat and blood are worked into the new soil

---

[3]"Waking of Insects" begins on March 6.

Egrets perch lightly on the backs of buffalos,
earthworms wriggle
I plow and sow the fields
Of joy and sadness cultivated for generations
The distant green hills and nearby trees fill my eyes
It was cold last night, but the mountain stream is flowing
I plow this lovely land
Waiting for peach tree blossoms to echo
As thunder shakes down from the sky

(1986)
(translated by John Balcom)

HOARFROST[4]

The frost spreads from north to south
Along the shining black rails, an illusion
It drifts over cities, poor and remote places
Circles a railroad crossing
Then nestles on a shop sign at a little railway station,
Illumined by cars passing in the night
Snatches of "Buy My Dumplings" are heard
"Mending Broken Nets" is on the radio
Taiwan at the end of the eighties
Playing and singing songs of the early forties

That's the way homesickness is, up north
Crying for mom and pop in a karaoke bar
Beer cans and wine bottles lie scattered under the tables
Head of white foam rises and falls like frost on the table
So-called culture is the eastern replacing the western
Historic sites are just demolished walls
Folk customs ride a flowery float, and sightseeing
Is a young woman's thigh that everyone enjoys together
The middle class discusses the world and the future
Frost falls on the hair of those concerned about the world

(1986)
(translated by John Balcom)

---

[4]"Hoarfrost" begins on October 23.

LESSER SNOW[5]

After the red leaves have dropped, a light snow falls
Covering the Iowa hillsides in early winter
Like falling leaves, it drifts without letting up
Past the window of my temporary abode
It pauses to rest
In the swift wind, in a place
Not of my choosing, I
Heave a sigh as the other half of
The ashen sky watches
My home on the other side of the sea

Sometimes longing is like a light snow. Sometimes
It's more like the falling leaves that don't melt
But just slowly rot away
The fine snow on a morning in this foreign land
Can it be the bad dream from last night?
In which my late father
Came and stood before my window
And pointing to the snow falling all around
He said: "The snow is too cold, let's go
Home where the fallen leaves carpet the ground."

(1986)
(translated by John Balcom)

GREAT COLD[6]

By this time they should all be asleep
The lamp on the nightstand slowly goes out
The drawn curtains hang motionless
The streets are silent among the silent trees
The bridge pier is hidden beneath the spans
By this time they should all be asleep
The island curls up in a bedding of sea
The mainland lies covered on a desert pillow

---

[5]"Lesser Snow" begins on November 22.
[6]"Great Cold" begins on January 20.

Together Asia and America seek warmth
The North and South Poles exchange looks

By this time they should all be dreaming
The Earth quickly leaves its rails
Nebulae appear in space
Particles continue to war
Substances begin to merge
By this time they should all be asleep
Abandoned, I look up at the night sky
In a sea of stars that slithers like a giant snake
I cannot find the solar system of their dreams
Nor can I see the Earth where they sleep

(1986)
(translated by John Balcom)

焦桐

JIAO TONG

(1956–)

Jiao Tong (Chiao T'ung) is the pen name of Ye Zhenfu, who was born in Gaoxiong in southern Taiwan. He received a B.A. in drama and an M.A. in art from Chinese Culture University, and is pursuing a Ph.D. in comparative literature at Fu Jen Catholic University. He is currently associate editor of the literary supplement of *China Times* and an associate professor of Chinese literature at National Central University.

Jiao Tong started writing poetry in 1980 and has won a national prize. Best known for vivid portraits of human characters, he has published four books of poems to date. He also writes literary criticism, reportage, children's stories, and plays.

THE STORY OF HER LIFE

From the time her only close relative, A-Xiong, became a sailor
and drifted off to foreign places, she passed the next thirteen years
in a blur, and ended up beneath the neon bar signs of an ocean
port. In a narrow alley by the river, now thirty years old, she had
learned all the ways of the world, hawking the springtime of her
life in unlicensed buildings littered with cigarette butts and betel
juice. Thirteen years went by in a blur, as the clear river turned
murky and continued to flow into the sea.

That evening she discovered the naked customer on her bed was
none other than her long-lost older brother. Without stopping to
weep or put on clothes, she dashed out the door. In one instant she
gave her lifetime of love to the unfeeling water.

(1980)

(translated by Denis Mair)

OUT OF WORK

Constantly I dream of punching a time clock
From Wuchang Street a happy bus rounds the corner at West
    Gate District
Morning wind awakens the gleam of winter sun.

Every day I fill out forms and resumes,
I have combed the want ads over and over again,
The classified employment section thick with notices
That appears in the same spot each day
Jostling for space. The sun sets and rises,
Once my resumes have been mailed I fill out new ones.
Always a bundle of nerves, I stand in some office
Sounding off my background and age.

The sun rises and sets,
My heart full of wishes like a milkweed pod—
More distant than youthful dreams
Colder than poverty.

The pub closes for the night,
Alley cats lurk in the shadow of a building,

I kick an empty can from Wuchang to West Gate District:
The sun is down, streetlights are on,
From that glimmer at the edge of sky
There's no telling dusk from dawn.

(1987)
(translated by Denis Mair)

THE DEMON PLATOON LEADER

Yamaguchi Shintaro held the rank of second-class private and was assigned to the 124th Infantry Company. He was a fierce fighter, distinguished for the blazing intensity of his performance in battle. Everyone honored him with the title "Demon Platoon Leader," and he received an imperial medal of honor.

The Demon Platoon Leader survived a hundred battles. He was only wounded once, on the Siberian Front, when seven regiments lost a whole regiment's worth of fighting strength to syphilis. Thank heaven for penicillin: he escaped from the jaws of death and was sent to the Chinese battlefield.

From the time the Imperial Army landed at Hangzhou Cove until it took Nanjing, our intrepid platoon leader won the highest favor with bold exploits of raping four women each day.

The Demon Platoon Leader was a man of exceptional endowments. Each centiliter of his sperm contained 25,999 ferocious spermatozoa, with a volume per ejaculation of 20 milliliters. Each month he could produce seventeen gallons of highly corrosive sperm fluid. When the moon was full, his third testicle would appear, and his metal-hard penis would lengthen by 13 centimeters.

Patriotism smoldered in the heart of the Demon Platoon Leader: before each act of intercourse, he stood at attention and sang the national anthem.

(1993)
(translated by Denis Mair)

READING AT NIGHT

In this city under siege from all sides
The streets have all closed their eyes
A 60-watt bulb rouses itself while others sleep
To stand guard through the dark night
In this apartment where promises are locked out in the night

Moths invade in pairs
Two fallen moths land on a page
A comma and a period, keeping uncertain distance
Doing battle on the borderline of sleep

Out of fear of being mired deeper
In the clutches of sleep
I sit straight and turn these pages
Planning underground revolt against yesterday's conclusions

My future leaves its slumber once and for all
A story of some kind will break the siege and escape
Beginning and end fight an all-out battle in the alleys.
The shape of someone who has lost his footing
Mistakenly rushes into the minefield of reverie.

(1997)
(translated by Denis Mair)

MARTIAL LAW

The lock on the back door is seized up with rust
From not being opened for years
Narrow passageway locked as sternly as a snake's cage
Even though we hold the key tight
Latch that refuses to be moved by anything
Like a tongue about to speak, but thinking better of it
Open mouth entangled with nightmare murmurs
Open lips starving for language

(1997)
(translated by Denis Mair)

ERASER

A forgotten waltz steals back under my pillow
Abducting a half-finished dream
I remember a letter with no stamp
A postal transfer slip with no address
I rise from bed and crouch over an old desk
Sentences with object phrases hard to omit
Missing subordinate conjunctions
Blue-ink tears running down
Bashful dialect
Dwindling shape of a strawberry-colored dress
Hint of scent from black hair over the shoulder
All rubbed out by the eraser of dawn

(1998)
(translated by Denis Mair)

THE FREQUENCY I INFRINGE UPON

The frequency I infringe upon
Air-raid tunnel of the subconscious
Always against the law
Broadcasts distorted body image and odor
Sometimes receives a special short wave
In the manner of a ballroom dance
Rehearsal for love with no chance to happen.

Dragnet of sirens outside this air-raid tunnel
These days
Casualties of love are all too high
I try weaving unforgettable dialogue
To prove the leading man was at the scene.

My secret frequency is often low on voltage
It desperately needs an electric outlet.

(1998)
(translated by Denis Mair)

夏宇

XIA YU

(1956–)

Born in Taiwan but now dividing her time between Paris and Taipei, Xia Yu (Hsia Yü) is the author of four volumes of poetry. She first came to public attention in the mid-1980s with the appearance of *Memoranda* (1983), a self-published and self-designed collection of poems whose iconoclastic tone struck a deeply sympathetic chord in Taiwan's younger readers. Her other volumes, which she also designed and published herself, include *FRICTION.INDE-SCRIBABLE* (1995), a Dada-esque montage of found poems made from cut-up words and phrases from the poems in her second volume, *Ventriloquy* (1991); and her newest collection, *Salsa* (1999).

Xia Yu received a B.A. in film and drama from National Arts College and has worked in television and the theater. She now makes her living as a song lyricist and translator.

SWEET REVENGE

I'll take your shadow and add a little salt
Pickle it
Dry it in the wind

When I'm old
I'll wash it down with wine

(1980)
(translated by Andrea Lingenfelter)

HIBERNATION

It's only so that I can store up enough love
enough gentleness and cunning
just in case   it happens that
when I awaken I see you

It's only so that I can store up enough pride
enough solitude and indifference
just in case   it happens that
when I awaken you have gone

(1980)
(translated by Andrea Lingenfelter)

BRONZE

a little later it's peppermint
a little later still it's dusk

deep in a cave is buried a piece of bronze
to ward off
something
grown more corrupted with each day

(1981)
(translated by Andrea Lingenfelter)

POET'S DAY*

On Poet's Day
the one thing I don't want to do
is write poetry
My hair needs cutting
I need to put away my winter clothes
I want to work on writing a letter
and give some thought as to whether or not I really want to get
    married
Better yet, I could take a mid-day nap
The rush mat is cool like peppermint
Or should I have children?
The room has a particular odor
magnolias, apricots
L. Cohen
blends with his guitar:
"Your enemy is sleeping
But his woman is awake . . ."
He can help me finish eating these dumpling wrappers
and the whites of these salted duck eggs
He looks really good smoking a cigarette
He likes to tell jokes
But there have to be better reasons than those
Dear Ladies and Gentlemen
I shouldn't shed any more tears over it
The globe
is already 70 percent covered in seawater
Plus, the water in the kettle is boiling
First I'll brew a cup of tea
He phones:
"Hey, let's do something exciting!"
Soft
pleasing to the palate
easily digested
his lips

---

*Poet's Day is celebrated in Taiwan on the fifth day of the fifth month in the lunar calendar, the supposed day on which the great poet Qu Yuan (343?–278 B.C.) drowned himself.

the words he says
But the water is boiling
and first I have to brew a cup of tea
"To have red snapper from the Egyptian Nile
I'd rather be a woman in this life"
It's just a commercial
and besides I have to take a bath first
In short
poetry seems frivolous
and besides
it's kind of boring

(1982)
(translated by Andrea Lingenfelter)

PICNIC
— FOR MY FATHER

Father is having his beard shaved
The corners of his mouth have already darkened
I don't have the heart to remind him
He is already dead

Throughout the night we listen to Bach and keep vigil
His favorite Bach

We take him up to a high and windy place
Carrying out an arid, elaborate ritual
Give him a broad-brimmed hat, a juniper staff
Give ourselves clothing of hemp
Assemble in orderly ranks
Take him up to a picnic at a high and windy place

Take him up to a picnic in a high and rustic place
Kindle a bonfire, burning meager deliverance
I try to tell him, try to please him
"This really isn't the worst thing," "the return to immense
    solitude,
Utter annihilation," without worry of impediment
Without terror

He is docile and obedient too
He was ill too long, forcing himself to hang on

Like a battered old umbrella
Water dripping down
"Life is nothing but suffering."
I lie. I am twenty-four years old.
He should understand better than I, and yet
It's as if, fainter even than breathing,
I hear him say:
"I understand, but I'm afraid."

Faint, like eyelids
Fluttering shut. I speak of it
In aesthetic terms, this most mysterious portion of the universe
The one and only subject of poetry . . .

. . ."Now, do you remember how
when I was seven, I wanted you
to buy me a parachute?"

I was always straying off the subject
And then forgetting to come back
He waited, waited a long time
He said: "I'm afraid."
I can't go with him
My tactful explanation
He is lying down, never to speak again
He understands

In the past he didn't understand, the first time I
Refused, at thirteen
Because I was growing up fast and shy
Felt inadequate, fell farther and farther behind
We went to buy books.
An eccentric girl
Fond of art . . .

Everyone comes back
Holding a white handkerchief
Except him. He alone
Is left behind
Freshly shaven
Never to speak again

Carrying on a silent
Eternal picnic

(1982)
(translated by Andrea Lingenfelter)

THE SIMPLE FUTURE TENSE

When I'm a hundred years old,
I will squat in a corner in the dingy room
and write a weak, sentimental letter:
"I'm so destitute
and I keep gaining weight—
an eternal
pure contradiction!"

When I'm a hundred years old,
I will let the world climb into my lap
to do a perfect handstand,
even though we won't achieve better understanding
because of this.

I will still remember my funeral,
which will take place when I'm a hundred and one.
The world will be at the beginning of a new civilization
and tend to be conservative, untrusting.
I will hear someone say:
"She looks more honest now."
Dream is the shortest distance between two points,
dream is the truly smart one.
An aging surrealist,
I will fall asleep smiling.

But according to them, that is death.
My burial clothes will be too big, my casket too small,
the plot they give me will have too many ants . . .

All those men will come
whom I once loved,
some holding umbrellas,
others shedding tears.

(1983)
(translated by Michelle Yeh)

THE HIDDEN QUEEN AND HER INVISIBLE CITY

In her kingdom, one
outlandish map.
A kingdom composed of
fugitive bronze statues unfulfilled
deathbed wishes and promises uncovered traps
muddled clues and fingerprints being destroyed and
all of the lost eyeglasses and umbrellas, etc.
She's drawing dotted lines on the sly, an endlessly
expanding domain.
An exhaustively categorized museum of lost objects—what could
    be better?
What's more, in those moments before Fate and
History have given any sign,
she has drafted an autumn walking itinerary (destination unclear
but at every intersection a right turn)
has finished writing a light musical
fed the cat
written a letter
& tied a bow
in a heart that will never repent

(1985)
(translated by Andrea Lingenfelter)

PARABLE

On the day of my birthday I discovered an unfinished
parable that stopped at the end of the third paragraph but it was
    already clearly
a vague parable & in
the second paragraph I discovered that I didn't know what to do
    next
Such a clumsy parable it lingers every day
within three feet of the top of my head. He pulls his hat down
    straightens
his collar, crosses the street in the rain the crowds becoming
    aware of the crowds
not knowing what to do next   forty-two years old

On the eve of the lifting of the press ban a poem probes the
    question
of sensitive language. Is it really, really true that we can
brazenly use the word
"teapot"?

Exiting a movie house   two men who have used the same
    prostitute
in different rooms both of them
now with their women on their arms they trade
a meaningful glance

(1985)
(translated by Andrea Lingenfelter)

CHILDREN (1)

None of them speaks
on the revolving fire truck
full of worries from afar
Suddenly I want   at this moment
for all of them to die
& not grow up
& grow into identical postage stamps
so that in some indistinct night
someone will forcefully tear them off
giving them furry edges
all of them saw-toothed

(1985)
(translated by Andrea Lingenfelter)

CHILDREN (2)

In moonlight the color of wolves' fangs
the secret society made up of all of the lost children
At last all of them have pairs of roller skates
that they use to catch up to a world that's pressing them to grow
    up
They have a common grave
buried in it are clothes, shoes, and gloves too small for them
Spit out a mouthful of spit, let go the kite string

Mouths wide open, they often
laugh weirdly and abruptly
cut off fingers to make vows
numberless left ring fingers
thrown away in a pleasure garden by the seashore on a winter day
When short hair is ruffled by dawn breezes   they
might disdainfully tell you   everything   only because
an excursion they got permission to go on long ago was carelessly
    forgotten
on a weekday morning

The day they disappeared en masse was established
as an annual holiday
All of the children dress up as wild dogs and return
to the intersection where they were last seen   to stare wide eyed
at that home to which they can never return the excursion and
the insomnia before the excursion
the photo of a missing person on a milk carton
those 100 maxims used to make them grow up
into adulthood

(1985)
(translated by Andrea Lingenfelter)

YARMIDISO LANGUAGE FAMILY

(Walking on the margins of a strange language
like a wedding dress that had been tried on
suddenly disappearing on the eve
of the wedding)

Suddenly I'd like to use a language I don't understand at all
to express myself furthermore it's a profound expression and also
useful for any obscure and dangerous terminology for example
    there's
the Yarmidiso language family
They also use Yarmidisoese for editing newspapers compiling
children's textbooks publishing travel guidebooks making up
    crossword puzzles
etc., etc.
I must commit to spend ten years' time to understand how
to use Yarmidisoese to express affection, following the cellist

in the park home, each one using his or her mother tongue to
    teach the other
some common sayings and tongue-twisters
If you can steam my cold-steamed bean curd then steam my
cold steamed bean curd if you can't steam my cold steamed
bean curd then don't
oversteam my cold steamed bean curd—
Bean curd   the incorrigible bean curd
tied with a straw rope—
Spend another ten years' time learning how to debate   with
    precision
and without effort, insert all manner of unexpected terminology
like certain kinds of crustaceans
that can't conceal their claws
Spend yet another ten years and then be able to write poetry &
    when oleaginous
syllables press near my throat pass over the tip of my tongue
producing a pure sensory sensory sensory
joy   (discover the carnal love of words):
exploring searching   to use
every endearment   throw away the pen   smile
sigh   for the part of human nature that still hasn't been
penetrated by any language
even this beloved
this polished and refined
Yarmidisoese

(1985)
(translated by Andrea Lingenfelter)

EXCUSE

on the subway where the wooden benches have been rubbed
smooth and shiny by thousands of millions   of buttocks a woman
who just got off the train sits here writing in a diary occupying 1/5
of a seat she imagines I have no way to restrain myself from de-
scribing any "immediate circumstances" for example to describe
the woman now sitting in the subway where the wooden benches
have been rubbed smooth and shiny by thousands of millions   of
buttocks a woman who just got off the train sits here writing in a
diary occupying 1/5 of the seat she imagines

(1985)
(translated by Andrea Lingenfelter)

AFTERNOON TEA

after collective masturbation a row of them
sitting there reading the newspaper headlines each
evening spiders piss at the corners of their drooling mouths
    cockroaches
crawl over their copulating bodies laying eggs on naked
groins you know why we're headed for extinction?
I dreamed of a dinosaur with a scornful voice
interrogating me that's just what you're always talking about that
collective sense of failure

(1985)
(translated by Andrea Lingenfelter)

MEMORY

Forget   Two syllables
inside two lightly puffing cheeks
tongue tip pressed to palate   gently aspirated:
Forget. Plant some daylilies
Boil soup   Forget

Find a useful wall carve out a
useless hole construct a wooden frame & install
the glass soon winter snow will fall & I'll use
glass and snow to forget forget
you

The wind probably does it best
especially as a tornado   setting you down
on the floor of a phantasmagoric valley
You'll hear someone there
playing a piccolo   five holes plugged
with indecisive breath   The name of the tune is
"Memories"   scattered in the wind

Why not make up a new dance step? One step left
one step right three steps forward three steps back turn
around turn around turn around yeah the music suddenly
stops all of the shoes fly away all of the doors

bang shut all of the people
forget you

Come to a strange city carrying a jug
At first? It's nothing but simple
earthenware mixed-up clay
soft   heavy   compressed   kneaded
squeezed out   wholeheartedly
to make a jug   the size of the mouth
is the size of the empty space   How good it is
to make a jug so as to

forget you. Or perhaps take a stroll on the bridge
May one carry a picnic basket?
Walking along the edge of the steel of the will
hopping on one foot & step by step getting close
close to you and the sea & is it enough to use an entire sea?
Somersault three times in the air
and then fall
and then die

(1985)
(translated by Andrea Lingenfelter)

ODE ON A THING

Write on the body with a brush
A young body
carrying all of life's desires
and gradually ruined
As for the brush, it's really not a bad brush at all

Atheist and fatalist   world-weary but also
promiscuous   at this moment ever so peacefully
drinking almond tea
Surprisingly
there is still a little happiness

(1986)
(translated by Andrea Lingenfelter)

FAUVES

twenty-year-old breasts like two animals after prolonged slumber
awakening   showing the pink tips of their noses
exploring   yawning   looking around for something to eat
   just as before
they'll keep on growing up keep on
growing up   growing
up

(1987)
(translated by Andrea Lingenfelter)

MOZART IN E-FLAT MAJOR

I turn around.
Feel Monday's newly shaven cheeks lightly
brushing against my left shoulder

Most most beloved part
Most most important now

(1987)
(translated by Andrea Lingenfelter)

ENSEMBLE AGAINST THE WIND
— FOR F

Between sorrow and emptiness
I choose potpourri and lavender

Dreams strictly guard secrets between them
Between words it is the same

Baskets and wings lost on a beach
They will fly up on their own

Toward the depths of a summer day
Toward a light shining from the distance

What remains is our overstimulated senses
Having squeezed out from each other's bodies all
Of the season's remaining juices

It's as if we'd designated these the colors
Of happiness or of madness

Blended in various bottles
They cannot be labeled

You drill a pole into my head
At last I become your carousel horse

And then there are those enduringly patient umbrellas that still
    fly away in the end
After the rain they return wanting only to be a placid crowd of
    mushrooms

October, deeply buried in layers of cloud like memory
Before long we'll have our first snow

But I will return to my bright and sultry island
A crocus trembles and falls, 324,000,000 live and die

I hide my face in the bottom of a well
See in the abysslike sky another self

You only search thirteen unfastened buttons
For a garden full of Korean raspberry plants

There are times when I am definitely strange and far away
As if, untouched by a man, I had become pregnant with a
    fawnlike child

I find an excuse to break the glass
And escape to the most distant city

How, in a strange city, do I leave a sign
Love someone or buy a pair of shoes

Slowly I lost them
Quickly I finished off a poem
That rhymed like grasshoppers
Hopping and vanishing
In a clump of summer grass

Afterward I was left with nothing
Except for a bracelet
And a red mole between my eyebrows

Except for a piece of aluminum set inside the murky night
For a long time   I heard someone clearly saying
I love you

(1989)
(translated by Andrea Lingenfelter)

DANCING WITH MY BACK TO YOU

With my back to you, I walk on the island   wearing a morning
  glory
With my back to you, I stare at the kudzu vines cascading from
  the eaves
And poking through a bamboo fence
And comb coconut oil into my freshly washed hair
With my back to you, and a guilty conscience   walk away the
  beach far and
curved
With my back to you, I put on a brass ring
So in the night you'll be able to reproach me for one thing at a
  time, while
drinking   wine
Reproach me for hurriedly giving birth to my child
In a vast field of sunflowers with my back to you
For losing three buttons in the field of flowers
And gathering up all the sunflower seeds to pan-fry them
For oil
With my back to you, exiled, roaming joined a troupe of
  entertainers
Never again could I possibly become your impatient
Nervous wreck of a bride
With my back to you, I pay no attention to anyone not speaking
Reading an unfamiliar book
Rolling a cigarette
Drinking tea
You can still reproach me
This time when we part we can truly say it's forever
With my back to you, I weep

With my back to you, I break into wild fits of laughter
Carelessly taking another walk across
The Eternal Youth Bridge at the eastern harbor at Pingdong
Never again can we never again can we grow old together
With my back to you in the pouring rain
With my back to you, I dance with my back to you, profligate
With my back to you, I stand beneath a tree
Very happy for no reason
Only certain of it when I'm happy
You'll never again never again be able to reproach me
With my back to you with my back to you, I grieve
Grieving my joy

(1990)
(translated by Andrea Lingenfelter)

SPRING EVENING

facing   each other
            our bodies
        squeezed tight
a strange
        almost translucent
            hourglass

(1995)
(translated by Andrea Lingenfelter)

THE MERCURY THAT WE RAISED SO CAREFULLY

crossing
black ruined swings
seeping out from the borders
a drawn-out dance
pressing near the antechamber of the flesh
at six in the morning
a faint moon comes out

(1995)
(translated by Andrea Lingenfelter)

READING

on the tongue
a crab

(1995)
(translated by Andrea Lingenfelter)

POSTCARD

there's not much time
circumspect small town
not without mutual destruction
about to go far away
break the glass
fingernails are translucent

(1995)
(translated by Andrea Lingenfelter)

A DIFFICULT MORAL QUESTION

  still
kept in a fishbowl

(1995)
(translated by Andrea Lingenfelter)

FRICTION.INDESCRIBABLE

kitty	today	I heard
you call me	back	to a
mixed-up	baroque	
understanding	kitty	the problem
is my	forgetting	
is like a ghost	my	
crime is like	an opera	I
my lost	sleep	wilderness
excursions	the prob-	lem is
kitty my	revolving	
if it	were	meaningless
my weakness	is	

```
that      regret      I                      my
warm this             this
ambivalence           kitty
my    twinkling       my              punch
is just    its
most    beloved fish
```

(1995)
(translated by Andrea Lingenfelter)

THE RIPEST RANKEST JUICIEST SUMMER EVER

Summer sinks into the face of the clock in the eye of the cat
Sinks into chestnut-colored limbs

A 17-franc basket of peaches
Day four and already summer has run from ripe to rank

All spring long we dined as if we had all the time in the world
Followed with interest the color, light, and atmosphere

Observed the shadows of the grapevines advancing to this
Last evening of the postimpressionists

The dabs of light thicken on the hammock
Grow thin on the windblown curtain

Each stroke acquiring definition
As the last grape added bursts its skin

Must be August
Ripe for the Fauvists

Never again will mere light so delight us
And O how we weary of atmosphere

Our idle conversation spreads like vines in the arbor
In this, the ripest rankest juiciest summer ever

And O how we weary of style
Does style, after all, exist

So like the snow
Defiled at the merest touch

But even though the snow does not exist
The hammock is more manifest than ever

More than an April iris or an aperitif at six
Although compared to soccer broadcast live hardly anything exists

Our guest, an enthusiast of "Old Cathay," asserts that in these
   fallen days
Only armed revolution presents so many tragic implications

And then there is soccer
O how we dine as if we had all the time in the world

Smoked salmon, crab, and lobster
And will you look at the size of this oyster

If we could but find the proper outlet and the sympathies
To release our leftist tendencies

1906, Cezanne, caught in a storm, returns to his studio
Removes his hat and coat and collapses by the window

Taking stock of the table, its overturned basket of apples, he
   notices
The "appleness of the apples" and their shadows, the three skulls

The wardrobe, the pitcher, the crock
The half-opened drawer, the clock

It occurs to him proportion is hardly worth making a fuss about
He will not fret over whether the table is level or not

He closes his eyes and dies
His eyelids trace a line pointing straight to three o'clock

Still, there is something wanting in all this
Must be time for Matisse

(published 1999)
(translated by Steve Bradbury)

WRITTEN FOR OTHERS

I write a Chinese character in the palm of his hand
Making it as intricate as I can in the interest of
Arousing his interest I write it wrong so I can rub
It out and write it right from scratch stroke by seductive stroke
Drawing him into one pictographic raft after another
Until I let the air out of the raft and we sink
Into the lake until I say I love you
With neither root nor branch nor a nest to rest
I love you I love you and then I slow us down
Until we barely move at all until we come to hear
The very mesh of the gears upon our flesh
There is a cone of light that bares the fact that whoever
Invented motion pictures did so just so we could turn
Down the lights and learn to make love like this
In slow motion and in the slowest possible motion
I love you as we slowly
Dissolve into grains of light I love you
Until we then turn wafer thin
Without end O I love you
I love you
Until we come to be strangers to ourselves
So that others will come to imagine
They have seen through us

(published 1999)
(translated by Steve Bradbury)

PLAYERLESS PIANO
— FOR J.W.

Gone
Still I feel those fingers
On my flesh like the slow glissando
Of a playerless piano

A brief glance
Carries us to some unearthly
Shingle surging with clouds of stars

How did we complete
Those caresses
Our naked bodies glistening
Like two dolphins embracing like two glaciers
Slipping into a sea of fire

How did we ever come to converse like this
Thus rendering those accidental cities
We just so happened to be passing through
So precisely so consummately
Antipodal

We converse so we will know that to embrace is best
And we embrace so we can descend the stairs together
Saunter by a theater, casually buy our tickets
And enter to see a show so we will know
We are mightier than the silver screen

So we will know that among those many
Temporal planes we have time and again
Confirmed do coexist there is one which
Stands out clearer than the rest

(published 1999)
(translated by Steve Bradbury)

林彧

LIN YU

(1957-   )

Lin Yu (Lin Yü) is the pen name of Lin Yuxi, who was born in Deer Valley in Nantou County and is the younger brother of Xiang Yang. He graduated from World Journalism University and has worked as a journalist and editor for many years. Currently he is deputy chief editor of *China Times Weekly*.

To date Lin has published four books of poetry and two books of prose.

MY DREAM IS TAKING A TRIP
—SEEING A FRIEND OFF FOR HONG KONG

My dream is taking a trip
Leaving me at home alone

My dream said: I'm going far away
Where songs blossom in place of
Flowers; where flowers take the place of
Young girls' gazes; only young girls
Sitting at windows think of home
So, gently stand by your mailbox

Cautiously break each sunbeam
Into a bright zincograph
Carefully carve each inch of sea swell
Into a white dove's wing
And watch to your heart's content
Watch the grass grow, green shoots sprout
Cicadas chirr in empty courtyards
Dragonflies try to find a way out of your study

Boldly you write
Like a gardener, laboring and sweating
Sowing our faith, our hopes
And our love in lines
Pray frequently, calm and composed
That all people might leave this gloomy station
And with joy make their way to the bright bay

Later, my dream said: I'll be back soon
Very, very soon, to rest in your mailbox
When the snow comes
And I am a pure white letter, don't mistake me
For a snowflake from the sky, but remember
My stamp is a bright red peach petal

My dream is taking a trip, it says:
When I return, release the doves

Let their wings beat the frozen clouds
Until they ring

(1981)
(translated by John Balcom)

SPRING SINGS IN MY VEINS

Who lifts the rain's gauze skirt and enters the corridor of March?
Who hurls lightning from the jet-black forest? Who
Proofreads the land's manuscript, marked everywhere in red and
    green? Who
Who was it last night that trod softly on the blue tiles of my
heart? Who lifts the door of my lashes and
Stirs up waves on the pools of my eyes? He
Doesn't give me a glass of wine to drink, but makes me drunk all
    the same
Arbitrarily he demands I fly but without preparing
A pair of silver wings for me; in the sky now bright, now dark
He weeps and laughs, making my moods change
Like an umbrella now opened now closed
He likes to throw parties and send out invitations far and wide
On the sidewalk, in the park, in the square
On the shores of a slowly awakening stream
Under the cold moonlight, he slips into my veins
In my soon-to-brim blood, he rows a boat
Beats a drum, strums the rusty strings of my heart
Oh, an intruder named Spring
Spring sings in my veins

(1982)
(translated by John Balcom)

NAME CARDS

Some people are already snoring like thunder
Some people are still in the bar, others
Are kicking empty cans under the dim streetlights

People here. People there, here and
There, people are perhaps
Making their way up a narrow rickety staircase
with great effort

On a rainy night after a banquet, I
Organize the many different name cards
And softly intone those short poetic names

Suddenly, I forget their
Faces, voices, how they were dressed, and
The reason for exchanging name cards

Do they know who I am?
Here and there, I hear the sound
Of countless I's being torn

(1982)
(translated by John Balcom)

NUMBERS

In a heavy rain I crossed the street
Picked up the red receiver, but just stood there
I forgot the number, but I remembered his
Nickname, cough, and facial expression

I chose from among the ten basic numbers
Each one collided in my brain
Each number echoed the pitter-patter of the cold rain
Seven, my lucky number
Zero, the beginning and end of all problems
Eight, the number of reference letters for employment
They fell, each number held a memory
They fell in combinations
Like partners exchanged at a dance forming memories
A snatch of song, the price of a stereo
Date of birth, address, ID card number . . .
But I didn't have the phone number to call in for the day off

I dialed seven digits, I talked happily
A girl I didn't know laughed in the receiver
She didn't know my name, face, or identity
When she asked me where I lived, I'd forgotten

(1982)
(translated by John Balcom)

MR. D

He changes into his nightshirt, facing a bottle of wine
He lights a cigarette. The couple upstairs
Has already turned in; downstairs
The musician is tuning his cello

Who knows who is who, the stars move
The bottle's empty, knocked over
Bullfrogs croak on the outskirts of town
The musician is still tuning his instrument

He takes off his nightshirt, and walks out into the
moonlit lane
He kicks an empty can; it clangs
Hollowly, perhaps it contained fruit or
Caviar, once it was full and now it's

Empty. Everything's been eaten up
Only my nerves are still tightly strung
Everybody's full, only I am hungry
Hungry and squeezed into a can with others. He thinks.

(1982)
(translated by John Balcom)

THE IDIOT

Reading Dostoyevsky's
The Idiot, complacently
I take up my pen
To inscribe a poem

In the bookstore I pace
Before the crowded shelves, pretending
To be the most loyal of
Dostoyevsky's readers

Actually, I just want to see
My own book of poetry
Its pretty cover
And all those words laughing heartily

But, a row of
Idiots, idiots, idiot . . .
Only after a row of idiots, do I see
Myself standing shamefacedly at the far end of the shelves

(1982)
(translated by John Balcom)

CHAIR

Some have just left, others are slowly
Coming this way. Who among them
Will sit down? I'm a chair
I feel people's bodily warmth; I listen to
Their talk; I remember
Their looks; and I think
They too, all of them, must be
Chairs

I sit properly on a wooden bench
in the maple grove in the park
Could the person who just left be the
Girlfriend I broke up with last year?
Could someone I love or hate
Have sat here at another time?

They are not chairs, only I am
Empty, welcoming them and seeing them off
Waiting for them as they take turns coming and going
Yes, only I am a
Chair, enduring all
Shapes, weights, temperatures, and events

(1982)
(translated by John Balcom)

A BACHELOR'S DIARY

01:30 Dreamed I saw a warship carrying the stars away in the
       fog
03:30 A friend on the other side of the Earth trudged through
       the snow to mail a letter
05:30 Someone called; wrong number. He forgot to apologize
07:30 Tears on the rim of a milk glass; the bread moldy

09:30   A car accident occurred silently below the office
         building
11:30   The pencils and notebooks were all left in the deathly
         silent conference room
13:30   A plane flew low overhead; the Persian cat napped in
         the garden
15:30   The bank teller changed her hairstyle again
17:30   I guess the evening paper has no news about a drop in
         stock prices
19:30   Where to? After the bright neon lights was the hospital
21:30   The dull-witted pupil of the television
         A promiscuous chest exposed in the closet
         A beer can with an unsatisfied mouth
         A black receiver waiting for a voice in the ear
23:30   Binoculars; the lights in windows of the opposite
         building were going out, one by one
00:00   Rolled over on my wound; my wound cried it hurts
00:29   Rolled over on my wound; my mouth cried it hurts
00:59   Rolled over on my wound; my heart cried it hurts
01:30   Dreamed I saw a wooden ship glide silently across the
         cavernous black sky

(1984)
(translated by John Balcom)

劉克襄

LIU KEXIANG

(1957–)

Liu Kexiang (Liu K'o-hsiang) is from Taizhong County in central Taiwan. He received a B.A. in journalism from Chinese Culture University and currently works as an editor for *China Times*.

Liu started writing poetry in the 1970s. His political poems in the early 1980s were widely read on college campuses. Since then he has devoted himself to nature writing, which seeks to understand our living environment through "the changes of the four seasons and the activities of waterfowl." He has published three books of poetry and three collections of naturalist writings.

THE LOWER REACHES

Someone is walking along the banks of the lower reaches of the
   river
At first it is only reeds that sway behind his back

He squats down to survey the opposite bank
Noticing the woods where a circling river bird has alighted

Later on he appears on a sandbar
An egret flying in the dusk looks down

When he disappears into the woods, the egret follows the banks
Of the river's lower reaches—flying away beside the setting sun

(1978)
(translated by Andrea Lingenfelter)

POSTHUMOUS SONS

1890 . . .

1915, posthumous son, Remember-China Chen,
Who liked to speak in Chinese, died in the fighting at Tapani*

1951, posthumous son, Establish-Taiwan Chen,
Who liked to speak in Taiwanese, took his own life on a small
   island

1980, posthumous son, Unity Chen,
Who liked to speak in English, succumbed to illness in a foreign
   land

2010, posthumous son . . .

(1983)
(translated by Andrea Lingenfelter)

---

*Tapani is a place near Tainan in southwestern Taiwan where many were killed during a 1915 uprising against Japanese colonial authorities.

YOUNG REVOLUTIONARIES

All of the students from our village who went to the city to study
    teaching disappeared
That day, only Papa came back, panic-stricken
People say he was the only one to escape with his life. And if I
    remember it right
From that year on, he grew ever more doleful and joyless
Finally, he took a wife and fathered a son. Ignorant, I came into
    the world
When I grew up, my grandmother said I resembled him

In the late 1970s I started university
Perhaps it was determined by historical destiny
It was as if I'd encountered Marcuse before, and maybe I'd
    already known about
Socialism. That was an age of utter confusion
I got into underground publishing and distributed flyers
With my schoolmates. Many times I was warned by the
    authorities
I gave up the idea of studying abroad. Everything was telling us
We had no right to leave. Papa, who found it hard to
    comprehend
Repeatedly got into heated arguments with me

In the late 1980s, as if all had been reborn, or perhaps had come
    to an end
I married a woman
She . . . , I don't know how to describe her
Now I work for a transnational company
Own an apartment, we have
A son, I have saved up one million
So I can send him abroad to study someday

(1983)

(translated by Andrea Lingenfelter and Michelle Yeh)

HOPE

Someday there will be a spring
When our children and grandchildren may read
A front-page story like this:

The small water ducks are returning north from their winter
    migration
Cars passing by the Tamsui River
Are forbidden to honk their horns

(1984)
(translated by Andrea Lingenfelter)

TROPICAL RAIN FOREST

Took a tour to a small island between the Equator and the Tropic
of Cancer. Wet, humid green, ceaselessly fattening in the air. For
five days running, we pass through the rain forest. There is no snow
or prairie, nor hibernation, even in dreams. An ornithologist in our
group is here to look for a horned osprey particular to this place, a
species on the brink of extinction. Every evening as dusk descends,
we call out in imitation of this bird, but all we hear is our own
weak voices, sent out unanswered. The aboriginal guide says: with-
out sound, the forest will disappear. And I am once again too upset
to sleep; awake for the entire night, I press my cheek to the Earth,
spreading out my arms into a curve and holding it tight.

(1986)
(translated by Andrea Lingenfelter)

GOING HOME

Chirping of cicadas. Stilling of wind. A ceiling fan turned drowsily.
The cap of a fountain pen between his teeth, he stared out the
window at the afternoon, where I stood on tiptoe, my head showing,
my hand waving, before I happily ran inside. He lifted me onto his
lap, ruffled my hair, and smiled. Freshly wrapped in a page from a
monthly calendar was a book, and he wrote inside the cover my
name, *ex libris*, and the date, thirty-fifth year of the Showa Reign.*
A bird roosted on the rooftop, a blue river boulder *tung* bird that
had flown from Manchuria, with a body the color of vermilion-
glazed porcelain. Autumn is here, he said to himself, and he took
me by the hand to his office. We passed classroom after classroom
and cut across the playing field, making for our home in the teach-

---

*The thirty-fifth year of the Showa Reign corresponds to the year 1960.

ers' housing. I wonder what delicious foods Mama has cooked up, he said to himself; then suddenly he picked me up again and lifted me high over his head to ride on his shoulders.

(1986)

(translated by Andrea Lingenfelter)

THE STREET PERFORMER

The street performer's flute blows ever more shrill, and I bound up the stairs, frantically opening drawers. Is the monkey in the vest riding its unicycle? But the drawers are empty, there's nothing there, so I crawl under the bed. The sound of the flute is growing weaker, fainter; the little dog wearing a red scarf must have made its entrance already, a cap in its mouth! I've ransacked every corner— only my little sister's china piggy bank is left. All around it is very quiet; my heart alone is beating hard, sound of the flute! The piggy bank smashed, I gather up four or five coins and run downstairs. The entrance to the temple is deserted. They're gone! I rush through the streets, searching. Every alley is flooded with flute music, and monkeys and little dogs appear in every window. I hurry back home, climb up the water tank on the rooftop, and gaze out into the distance beyond the village. They have already climbed the steep slope and are walking across the span of the long bridge, about to enter another village. Hey, I shout at them hoarsely, waving with all of my might. The fifty-fifth year of the Republic, Raven day, winter.

(1986)

(translated by Andrea Lingenfelter)

DELTA IN THE OCEAN

In the next century, I will be like my father, with a terminal disease, a bent back (slightly hunched even in youth), raised blue veins coursing across bony arms, and facial muscles stretched tight over protruding cheekbones—those two cheeks, having borne the brunt of so many sorrows, grown hollow, leaving only the eyes, mournful in expression, yet still large and bright. One day, he abruptly left his home in the countryside and came north to see how his child was, and he sat as long as it took to have mid-day tea before he caught a train back south.

He was someone who rebelled against his times, his hands always thrust into his pants pockets, his eyes always watching the sky.

Delta in the ocean, island in the continent.
Please give me back the little station where only one train stops each day, the cobblestone road where a mother quail and her chicks cross softly in the early morning. My home is beside a not-too-distant graveyard, on the square in front of the temple, where ears of rice are spread out to dry in the sun. I splash in the shallows of the stream, humming a tune, and hear clomping on the bridge above: my father the grade-school teacher, holding a fishing pole, forever ambling by.

(1987)
(translated by Andrea Lingenfelter)

SHOWA GRASS*

While the fires of war burned, not yet out of high school, shouldering a gun taller than yourself, you went to the Malay Peninsula; throughout the journey, the sounds of death were your companions. Starting under a toxic equatorial sun, you threaded your way through sweltering rain forests; after you returned home, the pain of your wounds carried through to another, different campaign. By then you no longer had any way to restore yourself to yourself.

But there was one time when we cupped in our hands a shrike that had been nursed back to health, and went out to a grassy field to set it free; it shut its eyes and lay peacefully in the palm of your hand, not wanting to leave, and the seventeen-year-old you said: Go on, this isn't your home.

1951, Shuili, the railway terminus, *Eiketsu-san, otome no koigokoro o shirimasu yo?* Mr. Hero, don't you know the heart of a young girl in love? I have stood here and become a field of Showa grass left after the cane cutting; little red-orange flowers bloom year round, they are my eyes that droop after gazing toward the horizon. My twenty-fifth year also floats across the brook, the rice paddies, the

---

*Showa was the name given to the reign of the Japanese Emperor Hirohito. The era began in 1926 and ended in 1989 with the Emperor's death.

schoolhouse, until my feet come to rest at the foot of the wall of
your house, grown over with shriveled and waxen berries.

(1987)
(translated by Andrea Lingenfelter)

THE CENTRAL RANGE OF LITTLE BEAR PINOCHA

In the night, firelight deepens wrinkles
And eye sockets grow more sunken, hiding away
The glint of pupils denser than sorrow
You squat down on your sagging backpack
There's nothing left but roasted corn on the camp stove
The staple grain of this night and of a lifetime

Tomorrow morning, you'll thread your way through the forest full
    of pine needles like a water deer
Hearing the solemn soughing of hanging vines
Kano Tadao,* white-haired and middle-aged, traveled this way
He'd given up his soul to Taiwan when he was a child
Turning his back on the 1930s, he made seven solitary visits to
    Snow Mountain
You too want to strike out toward a ridge of no return
Leaving no descendents, planting nothing but your solitary, squat
    shadow
Letting your skull tumble down a slope of shattered stones

This is the region where camphor, juniper, and hemlock have
    disappeared in turn
Four hundred years without peace
All that remains is the quiet of a chilly plain
Teardrops fall from the tip of your nose
Right into a blazing, fiery dream
The life of a naturalist
Is lonely, so lonely

---

*Kano Tadao was a well-known Japanese ethnographer whose published work included books
on the aboriginal tribes of Taiwan.

Let star crows cry to waken death
Let stone tigers chew your flesh
Let winter nights bury your spirit

(1988)
(translated by Andrea Lingenfelter)

孫維民

SUN WEIMIN

(1959–   )

Born in Jiayi in southern Taiwan, Sun Weimin (Sun Wei-min) received a B.A. in Western languages and literatures from National Zhengzhi University and an M.A. in English from Fu Jen Catholic University. He now lives in Jiayi and teaches at Jingyi University while pursuing a Ph.D. at National Chenggong University.

Sun started writing poetry at the age of fifteen and has won numerous literary awards in Taiwan. A self-described "slow" writer, he published his first book of poems in 1991, followed by a second book in 1997. He also writes essays and literary criticism.

DELIRIOUS

A spider hangs from the ceiling, drops
and lands on my open book. "The jade tree's limbs
are made of coral, the pearl curtain, of hawksbill." It sneeringly is
    walking
as if filled with mute enmity, while I,
a large sick body, stand erect like a mountain.
There are gleams of spider thread before the evening window
like tiny cables tossing in the wind.
Behind me I hear others:
hundreds dropping straight down from the ceiling.
The tiny cables are swiftly rigged into a shining web,
blocking my retreat. Each spider
also seems to stand guard and sneer, as if
plotting against me, one large sick body,
plotting to hunt
and eat me.

(published 1990)
(translated by Mike O'Connor)

SPRING 1985

That year in the spring, I suddenly took sick,
an illness not particularly grave. Willow catkins
rose and fell in the wine of the air;
sparrows brushed lightly past damp, gleaming roof tiles.
I was still confined to the sick ward; every day
injections, drip IVs, and doctors
who discussed past and future bacteria.
In the end, I came to know my roommate well,
the history of his illness, and his family.
Blue-uniformed staff punctually brought the meals
and cursed, cleaning up the day's garbage—
every day, until I left the hospital.

Every day, before I left the hospital,
I passed through the evening corridors,
arriving at fir trees and the little rose garden,
where other patients and their relatives and friends

together sat on wrought-iron chairs. Sparrows
flew in the small rain of the setting sun and perched
in their own shadows. In the end,
I became familiar with even more bacteria,
past and future, as well as
present strains, realizing
that I myself, perhaps, was really not so sorrowful—
I suddenly took sick in the spring of that year.

(published 1993)
(translated by Mike O'Connor)

THE ENCOUNTER

A twist of fate, and he suddenly steps out of the evening southbound
express, walks through a scattering of commuters on the station
platform, and heads to the northbound local express. First he
climbs the steps to the number 5 car, with its weak fluorescent
lighting and breathing electric fans—a sound repeated in every car
he passes through. Then, after hesitating, he finally chooses to sit
in the number 7 car.

With his briefcase and bad dreams, he passes through a nearly
deserted section of the car, at which moment he sees me huddling
after work, exhausted, defeated; my hands like roots of late fall
*mangcao** on the illustrated *Classic of Mountains and Seas.***

(published 1993)
(translated by Mike O'Connor)

DREAM

He presses the handle of the water tank, then brushes his teeth
and washes his face.
A middle-aged man in the mirror studies him.
The famous theme of the string music returns, as his wife

---

*Mangcao, or *Miscanthus sinensis*, is a grass with long serrated leaves and tall plumes in fall.
**The Classic of Mountains and Seas (Shanhaijing)* is an ancient geographical work, possibly
of second–third centuries B.C., describing China and the neighboring lands. It contains much
ancient myth and folklore, and originally was accompanied by illustrations.

comes out of the kitchen and, with bowls and chopsticks, sets the
    natural wood table.
Flowers in a vase are quietly dying.
On pages two and three of the newspaper there are still
    unresolved political struggles,
the Middle East, sex scandals, and the puzzling case of scattered
    body parts.
8:37 A.M., she dutifully reminds him
to pick up his keys; he sits at the door tying his shoes.
As is customary, before leaving the house, he touches her left
    breast.

When he reaches the first intersection,
the light turns red. An old man in a sweatsuit looks around,
    passes through.
After the meeting I must find time to go to the bank, remember to
    be early for Friday morning's appointment, and be careful
    dealing with that beautiful boss in sheep's clothing,
he thinks. At this moment a white butterfly strikes his windshield.
He feels himself already perfectly awake.

But he is still dreaming.

(published 1994)
(translated by Mike O'Connor)

TRANSFER

Delayed by certain business and missing his usual evening local
express, he takes out a train schedule from his briefcase (so many
tiny numbers and place names squeezed into a narrow, precise
checkerboard pattern). Finally, he decides to go a different way —
north to a bigger station where, after a wait of seven minutes, he
can catch the Fuxing southbound.

He stands on the station platform in the thin, fast-fading light. Be-
cause his legs are stiff from the day and darkness is falling, he feels
now no need to speak or smile. With two minutes still before the
southbound's arrival, he suddenly realizes that there is no one in
the whole world who knows where he is, that some time ago he
broke connection with his usual commute and has gone so far as
to have no chance to make it home on time.

At his back, the first colors of night benevolently draw near, as if guarding an unbroken solitude, an unexpected freedom, glimmering like a star.

(published 1996)
(translated by Mike O'Connor)

GOING TO WORK

The train comes from another side of the world, again. Passengers, who each day choose the same seats, put down their briefcases and open newspapers that offer freshly cooked breakfasts of wars, elections, horoscopes, and the floating corpses of stocks, drifted here from afar.

At a large station, nursing-school students board the train; most do not talk of bacteria. "He kissed me here," she says. A man in the uniform of a dairy products processing plant opens his eyes and sees his nineteenth May streaming by the window.

In the end, why is the train running? A white-collar worker now and then senses he is moving without moving. But this commuter car must use electricity. For a short moment he has the temerity to be thinking this, before tuning again into the headset of his Walkman.

(published 1996)
(translated by Mike O'Connor)

LEAVING WORK

Every day the colors of dusk and the temperature are different, but the train is nearly always on time. The commuters, as is customary, sit in their own darkness, chests rising and falling. Some take out portable cassette players to isolate themselves from the gentle, grass-like swaying of the other passengers' heads.

It is said when life ends, it ends forever, but the retreating rumbling of the window view will inevitably return tomorrow. Besides, like morning, evening, autumn, and spring, it's always difficult to tell one pop song from another on the cassette. Ah, love—it lets the stars and moon fly through the heavens, makes a colored party balloon of the sun.

At a small station, boisterous students board the train, momentarily
disturbing the bourgeois passengers. It won't be long before enmity,
like a mutant strain of bacteria, breaks out again, harder to kill than
before. At present, wild birds have already homed to their nests, but
no need to worry—the train continues down the tracks.

(published 1996)
(translated by Mike O'Connor)

MOTORCYCLE

Late in the night not only that Yamaha is awake;
it skirts the rain puddle that the dusk left in the courtyard,
climbs up a dead banzai tree in the north,
discovering there is no exit. But doesn't stop—
In short, before two o'clock it arrives at the seventh-floor balcony
(in moonlight the gas tank shines like a god),
penetrates the hole in the window screen, sees
a cabinet, a uniform, a small clock, a newspaper
and can smell the odor of dreams and animal fat. In the bedroom
it continues to stick to a fated dotted line,
going fast, nearly 300 meters per hour,
passing through the right knee, pubic hair, a red scar . . .

When a hand crushes an ant at the corner of a mouth,
the engine suddenly loses noise in the desolate street.

(1998)
(translated by Mike O'Connor)

陳克華

CHEN KEHUA

(1961–)

Like Yang Mu, Chen Yizhi, and Chen Li, Chen Kehua (Ch'en K'o-hua) was born in the coastal city of Hualian. He trained as an opthamologist at National Taiwan Medical School and has practiced in that capacity since graduation. In recent years he has been a postdoctoral research fellow at Harvard Medical School.

Chen began writing poetry in 1976, while in high school, and published his first book of poems, *Whale Boy*, in 1981, followed by eight more. His recent poetry draws extensively on Buddhism, often underlining the conflict between body and soul. In 1997 he published a book titled *The Heart Sutra in Modern Verse*, which juxtaposes verses of the classic Buddhist text with twenty original modern poems.

A prolific and versatile writer, Chen has also written fiction, essays, plays, film criticism, and song lyrics.

CLOWN SPIRIT
—WATCHING MARCEL MARCEAU

little by little I no longer believe that
he's trying to please with his sadness—
the stage crowded with symbols
and allusions looks vast because
the swirling breeze of the imagination
gently triggers syllables in the brain

he says he's lonely

he writes poetry, juggling soft signs
that leave even less of a trace than words . . .
he binds himself
he is carving time
he plays a game of tug of war with himself, miserable child,
it seems as if too much probing
has made him a loner, off on his own and
immersed in a game he alone understands

then he's ripped to shreds
fought over by hordes of visible ghosts
he is tripped up by his own shadow
he smashes every mirror in the room
he tries to escape
he holds my hand, teaching me how to caress

there's no escape . . . . I agree
numerous silent thoughts
flash by in an instant—on stage
humanity is everywhere looking for a loophole
he insists on pointing it out without language
he shifts an enormous, invisible boulder on his own—

dribbling an innocent ball
he tells me that this is the planet on which we live
weary of Olympian tasks, he says he wants to take a break
and join the rest of humanity

(1983)
(translated by Simon Patton)

THIS LIFE

I see you so clearly walking toward me from my previous life
into my future
and into my future's future

the present is all I have. each time I wake
from dreamless sleep
I worry I've missed my chance,
my chance and you with it—

how I want to go back to that second of error
freeze-frame the image
and make time stop:
you forever getting up to go
and me forever reaching out my arms

(1985)
(translated by Simon Patton)

NO CHILDREN ARE BORN IN THIS INSTANT (FROM "IMAGINARY EXERCISES IN LOVE AND DEATH")

no children are born in this instant.
for so long in the infinite stillness not a single mystery has
    hatched—
deformed, remnant limbs droop from
a disorderly arrangement of vacant insect eggs.
I hear umbilical cords gather in darkness:
a snapping in two and falling

no desires are born in this instant.
I remain wide awake, torturing the flesh with
an extreme, wakeful tension like two adjacent internal organs
wearing away at each other fleshily day and night
and making my belly groan with obscure pain
right hand uncoordinates with left
wolf cries hide in my pupils, love
is sewn tightly into the muscles of my chest. no feelings of beauty
are born in this instant, the degeneration of an entire century
collects in the bags under my eyes

no voices are born in this instant.
those who once spoke
have packed up and left—
an inexplicable urgency closes in
I keep my mouth shut for this weakened, feebly pulsing world
should I burst out crying with tears of joy
for a silence so rare in the universe?
(there was originally no need for such tears)

and so there are no children born in this instant.
despair is like the extended description of thickened asphalt
the earth completely flat
breathing comes to a gradual halt in a place
far from the pillow. dark as a brick, night
shuts in and guards the already formed
you fill in the answers yourself
there are no questions in this instant

no questions are born in this instant

(1985)
(translated by Simon Patton)

— BALLPOINT PEN
(FROM "INTERIOR DESIGN")

even the dragonflies are dizzy, this sixth finger
signed obliquely to a paper surface
of pure white thought

turning and turning
like the blades of a helicopter unable to
take off, circling the thumb
but unable to raise intellect to the heights of spirit—
tired and irritable
and certain to roll off the table eventually

(1986)
(translated by Simon Patton)

BATHROOM
(FROM "INTERIOR DESIGN")

according to the list
in good order he takes off his tie, ring, dentures
glasses, credit cards
and condom. till he is completely
immersed in transparency

in front of the mirror he becomes
completely gentle
                world-caring
unable to debate or
have an erection.

(1986)
(translated by Michelle Yeh)

ON TV AFTER DINNER

on TV I watch a young father who
has taken out a mortgage on a house on a slope on some distant
    hills
mornings he wakes up smiling on slightly ruffled sheets, a dream
    of serenity
satisfaction in his eyes

I watch him exercising in the sunlight on that gently rippling
    lawn
his shoulder muscles supple, untensed; his breathing relaxed
he has just the right amount of epidermal fat on him. *Welcome,*
    he says. *Come*
and join us
his invitation is sincere
he flashes a set of sparkling white teeth

I watch another young father drive off in his car to
another far-off hillside
he has a very Chinese face, a very Taiwanese accent
a very Japanese work ethic

and very American consumer habits
he says: *Let me give you a word of good advice*
   This is the perfect choice for you —
although there aren't any houses on the hillside yet

on TV I see the smiling wife he has chosen
and his altogether too beautiful son
the three of them sitting down to
the recommended daily allowance of calories and balanced
      electrolytes:
I'll let you in on a little secret
the secret of true love
I lean forward in my seat
he tells me to wash with a certain brand of soap
and to use a new improved toilet paper
now on special

on TV I see a young father who looks a little like me
his hair is trimmed neatly at the back
he radiates confidence
Your shirt is a little creased, he warns me, *and the style is out of*
      fashion
You're a little hunched over, and your mood is negative.
There are flecks of white in your hair, and you have quite a bit of
      dandruff. on TV
I see
the me I should be, a lover of tidiness
smiling happily and standing in front of a house
I own

You don't still believe in those old ideals, do you? the man on TV
      asks me
in the forest of trees on the safety island
an occasional thin mercury streetlight shines
few cars travel the purplish asphalt road:
City, city. soon you'll have spread all the way up here . . .
he puffs on his cigarette nervously, a worried look in his eyes
unable to see the distance

on TV after dinner I see
(and finally remember) what that hillside used to look like
the long silvergrass and the patches of cinquefoil

in which a skinny brown kid from the neighborhood used to hide
leading his buffalo this way
he said: *Poverty killed off many of the finer qualities I once had.*
    . . .

yet prosperity has added such glorious miseries.
on the TV, I am convinced at this moment
that he has found true happiness—
this citizen of a subtropical island
who is also keen on physical fitness, public welfare, and culture
I feel a deep loathing and admiration for him
like I would for a brother who grabbed all the family advantages
    for himself

on the TV after dinner
from block after block of towering high-rise downtown apartments
a succession of young fathers hurries off to dispose
of the day's accumulated information and emotion
before tonight's garbage collection
inviolable, this city rhythm—*Good evening.*
Would you like to own your own home too?
inviolate, this adult destiny. every night
before the garbage truck shows up, all the young fathers rush out

to dispose of themselves

(1986)
(translated by Simon Patton)

MESSAGE BOARD AT A TRAIN STATION

A-Mei, A-Cao
I took the 11:37 southbound train first   the fact is I don't hate
    you
if the typhoon comes tomorrow
call me at (00) 7127#998*
father. my child, remember me
give birth to the baby first
Chen, don't wait for me
my home is not in TaipeiECHO: ECHO
what I owe you
I've already found a job

after a long, long time, essence
clashes with phenomenon   severely
may you   come home soon
three hens and Chinese broccoli
are all fine
yours most truly
will pay you back

(1992)
(translated by Michelle Yeh)

BUTTERFLY DREAM*

His love for me was arguably beyond ordinary friendship. . . .
  Without me, perhaps he would not have renounced the world
  and become a monk.

—Xia Mianzun on Master Hongyi

After all, I had to pass a life of utmost glory
before I could prove that all doctrines
are empty. I love your heart
I care for your form even more
such is our destiny. I am willing
to go through
a thousand, ten thousand
calamities, like a butterfly

losing its way in a tempest of blossoms
do I have to suffer like this each and every moment
cut off food, hair, thoughts
and must I cut off this mental flower of supreme beauty

---

*"Butterfly Dream" is based on the biography of the legendary Li Shutong (1880–1942). As a young man living in Shanghai, Li was a famous literatus—poet, calligrapher, engraver, and Beijing opera singer. He studied Western painting in Japan from 1905 to 1911, during which time he taught himself to play the piano and performed in the first modern Chinese drama staged by overseas Chinese students in 1907. After returning to China, he taught music and art at Zhejiang Teachers Academy, Hangzhou, until 1918 when, at the age of thirty-nine, he decided to become a Buddhist monk. Known as Master Hongyi, Li was highly respected as a great Vinaya teacher. Xia Mianzun (1886–1946), a colleague and one of Li's closest friends, was a writer well known for his essays.

so as to release myself
from the affliction of the tight chest and the dry tongue?

In the zenith of the sky a moon not quite full
like the branch I planted with my own hands, yet to bloom
a man of obsession, shallow in the understanding of the Way . . .
the butterfly bids spring blossoms farewell
it asks: how can you be so utterly unaware of your own beauty?

flowers live and die in their own way.
amid the living and dying of myriad blossoms
am I not just a man stealing a glimpse at their reflections in the
     water?
after all, a life is but a long good-bye
(may we be born and live together in peace and cultivate innate
     wisdom in another life)
so I leave behind love
so I leave behind obsession
so I leave behind sorrow
so I leave behind joy
so I

(1993)
(translated by Michelle Yeh)

SODOMY'S NECESSITY

waking from that dazzling night of the anus's first opening
we find that the back door was only unlatched, not locked
the womb and the large intestine are identical rooms
separated only by a warm wall

we dance amid desire's flowerings
limbs tenderly unfurling, feeling
that we are the start of a new breed
doomed in the face of the storm history is perhaps about to rain
     down on us
none of the unfortunate predictions uttered by the throat of
     Freud have ever come true

(we are the start of a new breed
exempt from poverty, sports injuries, AIDS)

allow us to bare our consciences and our anuses for your
    inspection
and under your illuminated magnifying glasses
you can examine how we writhe like members of the rat tribe
feeling ecstasy and agony
our body hair drenched in blood as if caught in a spill of dye —
    will we
have the good fortune to prove the necessity of sodomy in the
    years left to us?
the way things are going, we'll be on our way home before the
    back door's locked up
our bed lowered directly into the grave
the perverts having once again come to the end of their day of
    glorious deceit
no one knows what putrefying reasons lie concealed within the
    stitched-up wound
but at this point why don't we just bleed to death?

(whoever says he wants to go and corrupt morals is the first to
    leave the group
there where the flowers grow profusely he brandishes his halo
he at least will never prove sodomy's necessity . . .)

but the anus is only unlatched
misery constantly escapes from the crack under the door like
a light bulb blinking on and off throughout the night
as we embrace, embrace again, we refuse to believe that the ways
    of making love
have been exhausted
or that the pleasures of the flesh have been cast aside
but at this point why don't we just throw in our lot with the silent
    and healthy majority?
why don't we throw our lot in with the majority?
majorities are OK
sleep is OK
having sex is OK
not having sex is OK too
whether you tap it or push it open
the anus will always
remain unlatched . . .

(1995)
(translated by Simon Patton)

STILL

walking my twilight self through fallow fields I see
acres of withered sunflowers still tracking the western sun
with their proud heads

a lizard's tail shed on a ridge between fields
looks like a lithe snake in miniature
it doesn't stop wriggling
the whole time I watch

a kid from the village shows me a dead frog, long dead
he says: *Look! It's still moving* . . .
waving unconsciously, those webbed arms and feet
look like they'll go on for a long time to come

I walk on toward night's most perfect phase
reaching into the dark to my heart's content
the light of those stars still glows
but in that moment I realize they're long dead

I make my pause in the dusk of the daily round
and listen for death's performance still
head held high, I wave one hand
flapping it like the lizard's tail
and put on a show in the amber light of sunset . . .

I know that I'll still go on living, that we'll
go through the motions for a long time to come

(1996)
(translated by Simon Patton)

瓦歷斯 · 諾幹

WALIS NOKAN

(1961–   )

Walis Nokan, whose Chinese name is Wu Junjie, belongs to the Pai-Peinox group of the aboriginal Atayal tribe in Taiwan. He graduated from Taizhong Teachers College and teaches at Freedom Elementary School in his hometown, Heping Village, in central Taizhong County, which was devastated by the earth-quake on September 21, 1999.

   Walis Nokan started writing poetry at the age of sixteen; he has been editor of *Hunter Culture*, a journal dedicated to Taiwanese aboriginal culture, and is active at the Research Center for Taiwanese Aboriginal Humanities. He has published two books of poems. In addition to poetry, he writes essays, culture critiques, reportage, and fiction.

BACK TO THE TRIBE!

When he discovered that he was inch by inch disappearing,
Bihao, primary school teacher in the city, decided he must go
    back to the tribe.
That morning, Bihao got a call from the tribe
but eeh-eeh-ah-ah-ing, he no longer made sounds that Yaya
    understood.
Bihao's throat had become just like that of the lying dog,
disappearing on a quiet city morning!
Letting his tears stream into the receiver was all he could do
as if at the end of the line there were a priest receiving his
    confession.
When his people asked what he'd come back for—
Bihao managed to squeeze out a sickly sound: "To cure the pain
    in my throat."
But no one understood his A-me-ri-can.

When she discovered that she was inch by inch disappearing,
our Giwas, who sang in the city, decided she had to take her
    leave.
That night, Giwas turned on the fluorescent light in her room
and a deathly white hue covered the deep dark of her face.
Our healthy Giwas had become just like the child running down
    the mountain,
a face belonging to the Atayal inch by inch disappearing.
In the empty vastness of the city night
Giwas could no longer see her own face.
When her people asked what she'd come back to do—
Giwas, covering her white face with dark hands, said:
"To find my face back."

In "Back to the Tribe!" "Bihao" is an Atayal man's name. "Yaya" is a form of address for one's mother. As to "the lying dog": according to Atayal mythology, the dog was once able to speak but liked to lie to the Atayal people, driving them to cut its throat so that it could no longer speak words but only bark dog language. "A-me-ri-can" is a foreign language incomprehensible to the Atayal. "Giwas" is an Atayal woman's name. "Child running down the mountain": according to an Atayal legend, the Pingpu were a people who came down from the mountains in search of new arable land; because they played tricks to cheat those continuing to live in the mountains out of their rightful share, they were later the targets of ritual hunting. "Wadang" is an Atayal man's name, as is "Hajuong." "Yava" is a form of address for one's father, and "Yudas" for one's grandfather.

But in the tribe, who cares if your face is round or square?

When he discovered that he was inch by inch disappearing,
Wadang, strolling amid city jungle scaffolding, decided he must
    return to the tribe.
That day, oh! Not one cloud had the nerve to block the sun at
    high noon.
Our nimble Wadang in the glass of a skyscraper's windows
finally saw a tailless monkey lost in the city.
It was rocking back and forth, as if tied down in a huge
    mechanical trap—
at some point, the tribe's hunter had changed into a quadruped!
When his people asked what he'd come back to do—
Wadang flexed his pulsating muscles and said, excited:
"To go up the mountain and hunt!"
And what was the use of hunting, his people disdainfully asked:
"All prey now know about legislation on wildlife preservation!"

When he discovered that he was inch by inch disappearing,
Hajuong, our shift leader at McDonald's, decided he had to say
    good-bye to the city!
That day, before he left work, all the tired insects came back.
Our Hajuong received an epistle from across many mountains:
the orchard that Yava had tilled for over thirty years (this land, no
    less,
had become theirs through Yudas's lifelong struggle) had
    overnight
been stuck full of members of the tribe, just like the Japanese
    sun-flags.
In the blink of an eye (to be more exact, the offical date was
    December 3, 1994)
the orchard that had put him through middle school had been
    made state property.
In the reflection of glittering tiles produced by a capitalist
    empire, our Hajuong
at long last saw a pitiful fellow whose nationality had disappeared!
Didn't McDonald's pay him high wages? and his people asked
    him what he'd come back to do—
"To check carefully if the tribe is still here!"
For one who had not gone blind to say such things . . . his people
    said:
"This fellow—the city's driven him crazy! How sad!"

Like tired salmon covered with cuts and bruises, our people—
oh! all of our people in the city want to come back to the tribe!
Together they cut through the raging seas
weaving their way amid hidden reefs and shark attacks
straight toward the brook of young life.
No one knows what they will find,
but we are happy that our wandering people have finally come
    home!
Our wandering people have finally come home!

(published 1996)
(translated by Maghiel van Crevel)

ATAYAL (WAR, 1896–1930)

Atayal proverb: "ini ta vaii kai nkis ga, ijad atayal ba lai," or:
"If one does not know history, how can one know how to live?"

I. DAYBREAK (TAROKO, 1896)

Daylight rose from the Pacific Ocean: in the mornings our tribe
was awakened by the sun. Sunlight woke our people's footsteps,
sunlight woke the sleeping millet, and sunlight woke birds and
beasts in the forest.

Daylight rose from an ocean fleet: in the mornings our tribe was
awakened by cannon fire. Cannon fire alarmed our people's foot-
steps, cannon fire startled the harmless millet, and cannon fire scat-
tered birds and beasts in the forest.

II. MILLET (WULAI, 1899)

At the break of day, an ear of millet opened wide its eyes, and
in the faraway Taipei basin a national flag rose to the same height
as the sun, its flutter-and-flap accompanying cannonballs looking
for a target. Sometimes, when crossing over a mountain, the can-
nonballs would sow endless rows of fireflowers on the slopes, nitric
dust flying everywhere to soil the golden countryside.

Sometimes, the cannonballs would take to the skies even earlier
than the break of day and I could see them staring from wolfhound
eyes, barking and rattling their teeth. Then our people would
quickly squeeze us into their ears, trying to find the mountain tracks

that, three hundred years ago, had let them open up the border-lands—the only thing is that this time, they were fleeing in a panic.

III. Pillow Mountain (The Mountain in Front of Tak-ekan, 1902)

Modu grew millet on the slopes of Pillow Mountain, where Takekan Brook nourished the soil on Pillow Mountain: if he was not careful, the weeds would right away grow thicker and stronger than the millet. One morning in the ninth month, first a beelike bullet flew and slammed into the thriving beehive, and moments later war had swept away Modu's millet field.

Modu's millet did not know how to escape, but our people's bodies hid like leaves. From green shade, metal arrowheads poured like rain into the enemy's eyes. After the battle ended, the beehive that had moistened his wife's belly had turned into a pool of blood, and the millet field had become an unkept burial ground—but there was no one to hear Modu crying, because the sky had already grown dark.

IV. Salt (The Jiemeiyuan Incident, 1903)

One day, Father agreed to take us to look at the salt and at once our eyes were shining with a whitish light. In the sunshine, I knew that those were our salty tears.

One day, we went on a journey to Jiemeiyuan, on the banks of Muddy Brook, and those from Ganzhuowan Village of the Bunun people brought goods and drink. Behind them were some brightly flashing things, and I thought I knew that they were white grains of salt.

One day, Father and 130 of our people were lying down drunk at Jiemeiyuan, and brightly flashing blades chopped off their heads. That year, the dark Muddy Brook shone with a reddish light, and its water flowed on and would not return.

One day, I was leafing through *The Records of Governance of Barbarians*, and in the yellow glow of its yellowed pages found one sparkling, crystal-clear grain of salt after another—and then all of them flung themselves at my face, and once more made me see Yava and over a hundred of our people shed tears.

V. Guns (Luxuriance Mountain, 1910)

One gun had lost a lead bullet. The gun that had lost a lead bullet could no longer chase wild beasts in the forest, and the beasts in the forests no longer moistened the skins of their young. The gun, now full of sorrow, could only wait to grow rusty.

One hundred guns had lost their gunbarrels. The guns that had lost their gunbarrels could no longer chase the glory of the men in the tribe, and the men in the tribe no longer comforted the women's bellies. The guns, heartbroken, could only wait to grow old and die.

One thousand guns had lost their gunpowder. The guns that had lost their gunpowder could no longer chase the myths of Luxuriance Mountain, and the myths of Luxuriance Mountain were no longer told to the Monabo tribe. The guns, in their loneliness, could only wait to weep.

VI. Picturesque Rivers and Mountains (Beishiqun, 1912)

In winter, after the offerings to the ancestors' souls, the Japanese set up a huge painting canvas on the Mountain of Great Restraint. A black brush filled it with red colors, I saw them splash and sprinkle on our tribe at will. In winter, after the offerings to the ancestors' souls, all of the sky was filled with a splendid brilliance and in the distance, above the Mountain of the Giant Despot Peak, there rose a seven-colored rainbow bridge.

In winter, after the offerings to the ancestors' souls, the Japanese quietly wept for Kamiya Isaburô, assistant officer of the Military Police who had died in battle. Set off by the light of the moon, Yava's head was on the top left corner of the canvas; our people's legs were the grass on the prairie, their bodies were stones piled upon each other. It looked terribly like a torn-up painting, and I saw our people smile and set foot on the rainbow bridge.

VII. The Stele (Lidong Mountain, 1913)

On Lidong Mountain stood a pillar-shaped stele like a cannonball, on the stele stood Governor-General Sakuma Samata, and the insignia on the Governor-General's jacket illuminated the sky for those of the Qi'naji, the Malikuowan, and the Hehuan clans. This made the sky in its vastness break into cryptic laughter.

One day the stele walked down Lidong Mountain, past the tribe burned down by cannon fire, past the river that had swallowed the loom, past infants searching for their mothers' breasts. When the stele finally came to an open wasteland, it cleaned the tattoos off its body until it became a child of the earth.

VIII. The Arrow (Taroko, 1914)

The enemy's troops were advancing from Foggy Brook, and like a river surging the enemies flooded the countryside. No one saw a shapeless arrow slowly advancing.

The enemy's troops were advancing from Hehuan Mountain, and like autumn's fallen leaves the enemies covered the granaries. No one saw a colorless arrow slowly advancing.

The enemy's troops were advancing from Bazhalan, and like summer's wildfire burned our people. No one saw a scentless arrow slowly advancing.

When the enemy's commander-in-chief arrived to inspect Taroko Cliff, an arrow of History had just completed the task of entering and leaving the Governor-General's sweet shanks.

IX. Shadow Warriors (Vendetta Between the Malikuowan and the Jinnaji Clan, 1919–26)

We all know that the vendetta began with the deputy chieftain of Takejin Village mistaking the people of Wulai Village for monkeys and shooting them dead.

The people of Wulai Village mustered the Malikuowan clan and like a river flowed over the Takejin Brook. The people of Takejin Village mustered the Jinnaji clan and like wildfire engulfed the Malikuowan Brook. And after that, we all know the story that says "fire and water don't mix."

Only the Japanese police looked after the two clans. Seven years in succession, in the season of falling leaves, the Malikuowan and the Jinnaji each secretly received guns and ammunition. Both said that the Japanese police were benefactors of their clan, until starvation put an end to the vendetta.

X. Problems of Arithmetic (The Wushe Incident, 1930)

The Japanese rescued a child of Hege Village, and worked hard to teach the child how to count. One head ten heads a hundred heads—the child counted and silently spoke the names of our people: Walis . . . Mona . . . Bihao . . . Yopas . . . Suyan . . . until heaven was dim and earth was dark.

The Japanese rescued a child of Hege Village, and worked hard to teach the child how to count. Japan plus Hege Village equals obedience, Japan plus ten tribes equals loyalty, Japan plus a hundred tribes equals dedication . . . until our children became sons to the Japanese emperor, until all our children became conscript laborers on their Southern Expedition.

(1990s)
(translated by Maghiel van Crevel)

林燿德

LIN YAODE

(1962–96)

Lin's tragic early death in January 1996 silenced one of the most creative and dynamic literary voices in Taiwan of the 1980s and 1990s. Born in Taipei, Lin Yaode (Lin Yao-te) graduated from the Department of Law of Fu Jen Catholic University in 1985 and married the illustrator Chen Luxi in 1995.

Lin's writings, first published in 1978, encompass a wide range of literary genres—essay, short story, novel, literary criticism, drama, and, of course, poetry. He also received almost every major literary prize offered in Taiwan, was active in many poetry societies and journals, and was an important editor of literary journals and poetry series. His brief but extraordinary career has had a lasting impact on the development and study of contemporary poetry in Taiwan.

Poetry anchors Lin's works in the other genres, which tend to take lyricism as their mode of discourse, and certainly it is for his poetry that he is best remembered. Lin's poetic style ranges widely, yet there is at the core of all his writings an experimental, often difficult language that envelops a deeply conceptual, sometimes erotic-romantic, world. This is no better seen than in "The Red Chamber," included here.

THE TERMINAL

.............................I am
Lost in a sea of numbers
On the monitor
Row upon row of figures
   Come into focus and then drop off
Like a curtain falling on the world
In front of the terminal
My mind fragments into blips on the screen
Inside it
The circuitry is as obscure as a chamber of sacred texts

After working late, I make my way home along night-shrouded
    streets
With those programs harshly etched into my subconscious
There is now no erasing them
And I begin to wonder whether I am flesh and blood
Or a tangle of integrated circuits
After work, I
Become a terminal unplugged
A memory board without a power source
Data and figures
Collide and explode
   Endlessly
Like a collapsing galaxy

(1985)
(translated by Joseph R. Allen)

PREFATORY POEM
(FROM *A SILVER BOWL FULL OF SNOW*)

I
   Within the confines of the soul, all my elapsing gestures
           Transmigrate into a solid silver bowl
            Language brimming over like snow
Bathing the cosmos in light, the cosmos of light-years untold
That snow in the bowl, then,
Is language, is love
Is my fearless choosing. Absolute glory

Compressed
Into the eternity of that moment
  Gushing guile and disputation

II
The snowy gleam of silver
And snow's silver light
Gone in an instant
Faded from sight

When the snowy gleam of silver oxidizes into sulfur's raven stain
And when snow's silver light melts into the transparency of water
The raven stain folds into the jet-black focal length of the cosmos
  And transparency cleanses the feverish arch of the Milky Way
                                                    (1986)
                                (translated by Joseph R. Allen)

THE LIE OF A SPRING I TIGHTLY WIND

So I tell her
The lie of the spring I tightly wind
Every night
The same old line
Changing only in pitch
According to the season and the weather

Feelings are a cassette she crushes underfoot
And every night I listen to that scratchy song
To that broken tape
Snagged on the cusp of a crescent moon
And dragged slowly along
A darkened railway
Traveling toward the other unknown half of the earth

So I tell her
The lie of the spring I tightly wind
Every night
Always wondering
When the spring will
                    break

                                                    (1986)
                                (translated by Joseph R. Allen)

THE CONCEPT OF "NON"

A teacup, whole on the desk
A bamboo flute bored on the wall
And against the bureau a rimless tire

Startled awake in the early morning light
Faster than a flash, a swath of empty white, vast and wide
Smothers my thoughts with their wordy ant lines
A swath of empty white, vast and wide
From hub and aperture, from the cup's very void gushes forth
Something not found in records or in history books
The concept of "non"

More desolate than the cosmos itself
Nostalgia for time and space
A critique of the human race trapped in its own language
Quietly raises its eyes between the lines within the words

The concept of " ", hushed and hidden, so very cautious
Untouchable, beyond hearing, and out of sight
Soundless music, that neither matter nor desire
Can ever conquer
From hub and aperture, from the cup's very void slowly oozes.
   . . .

(1986)
(translated by Joseph R. Allen)

THE RED CHAMBER

Treading along the melancholia of those elegantly bound
   volumes
Their flyleaves frozen in a thin coat of snow
Splitting when touched, crumbling when raised up
Leaf after leaf of mist and clouds, yesterday was
The urn of a dream. Lifted from the earth
The clay seal breaks away bit by bit, and there falls
The memory of an eclipse.
The urn of a dream, a pottery void
The music of drumming tragedy
Cascading concentric patterns like spirals of a corridor

Night after night, obsession weaves its spider's web
Glistening with watery hues, forever
Denying dawn's rising light.
Lutelike necklines   finely woven wraps
    Emerald bracelets   and pale pink chemises
Along the walkways squeezed between one red chamber and
    another
Passing shoulder by shoulder.
It is you
Whom I encounter on the narrow path, asking about the brush of
    your hair
Against my cheek

In our shared palm we hold
Flower seeds of a different color
The rainbow's seven hues stream through the interlacings of our
    fingers
Scattering them, splashing their golden rays as they go
And I take you in my arms. Dark beads of dew
Surround our entwining limbs.
Swirling in the narrow, unending alleyways
Ancient tiles in a twirling
Vision make their escape.
And I take you in my arms; a fresh wind stirs.

A fresh wind stirs, forever slipping through
Our unfastened collars
Turning, turning, a back is glimpsed, and after that, one entrance
    hall
And then another
Passing on toward the vanishing courtyard.
A shared thought seeps over sculpted sashes
The chrysanthemum image stealing its way
Next door a lamp burns on the oil of orchids
Its vegetal essence scattering the charred fragrance aloft

Ultimately the classics are but
Voices in exile,
Always emerging from behind. Those
Oils of orchid melting within their orange blaze
And saying one more time: I love you.
The sediments of history quietly settle out

Embers with their anxious flickering light
Princes and kings, and their loyal men
Are reduced to a bevy of abandoned wives
Denied their faithful vows on gilded leaf.

The cast of the moon lifts the veils of darkness
And stars fall like rain, glittering with agitated rays
On distant tides, the ocean's horizon
Blossoms with its short-lived spring
Desire in that deserted Daguan Garden
Freezes their gestures in the depth of night
Ancient fossils buried in earthen layers.
The small path leads through flowerbeds
With their forever changing places
But the elegantly bound women never grow old
The twelve chosen beauties
Stand as tragic tombs cast in silver light
Under the skies of scuttling clouds.

A garden of peonies, fossils of petal upon petal
If you really love me
Then reach out with
Your slender fingers
And awaken, petal upon petal,
The spring of petal upon petal.

(1990)
(translated by Joseph R. Allen)

鴻鴻

HONG HONG

(1964–)

Yan Hongya, who writes under the pen name Hong Hong (Hung Hung), was born in Tainan and attended primary school in Taoyuan. After two years in the Philippines (1977–79), he returned to Taiwan to attend middle school. He started writing modern poetry while in junior high and studied modern dance and theater while in senior high. He majored in drama at National Arts Academy and after graduation worked as a journalist and editor. From 1993 to 1995 he served as chief editor of the revived *Modern Poetry Quarterly*; he founded a theater group called Secret Hunters in 1994. He has been active in Taiwan's avant-garde theater and film world as an actor, scriptwriter, and director.

Hong Hong has published three books of poetry, a volume of essays, a collection of short stories, and drama criticism.

ZOO CITY
(three selections)

1 *Lonely Elephant*

A bulky
enormous
blur,

the elephant,

passes through town
like a
fog,

gently touches
every single thing
(unbeknownst to us),
departs,
but leaves
its imprint on the walls;

disappears,
and we forget it.
Later, we find its carcass
atop the weather station
and realize it's been standing there all along,
waiting for its kind.

2 *Ravenous Pig*

After breaking out of the feedlot and bolting,
it lives for a spell off garbage piles,

then scurries in and out of hospitals
snatching up food.

On occasion, you can see it running through an
    intersection,
sleeping soundly in grade-school lavatories,
or sightseeing at the museum,
staring red-eyed,
drooling at the chin . . .
(we all feel taken aback)

But in the end it gets caught,
branded in red,
crushed and pulverized,
stuffed into cans
— its companions, the same —
and distributed to every supermarket in town.

At the dining table, we are eating minced meat —
a small wonder in life
disappears without trace.

3   *Night Dog*

Mercury vapor lamps shine on the broad avenue;
a dog
in the center of the intersection
hesitates.

No cars are passing;
what's it still waiting for?
The whole city some time ago
sank into the curse of death;
why won't you cross
to a safe place?

Are you giving thought
to the direction to go in,
or are you afraid
anytime that black car might come?

In the middle of the long night,
I also hesitate.

(1986)
(translated by Mike O'Connor)

A DROP OF JUICE FALLS

A drop of juice falls
on the poem that I'm reading;
I don't at once brush it away.
Slowly it spreads

on this scented, measured line of indelible feeling.
A drop of juice falls,
falls on a new poem by a poet far away
who, in youth, was exiled even farther
to labor as a boiler maker, coal miner, shop mechanic,
where he came to know the migratory birds, the grasses and
    leaves—and young girls existing only in dreams;
went to prison and then, in a political reversal, was assigned to
    warehousing,
    an insignificant position with nothing to do.
No one cares about any of this.
On a certain day in his forty-seventh year, a cherry tree bloomed
    outside his window.
He recalled a small alley from childhood, leading to that
sea deep in his heart; memory shining like sunlight
on the graffiti on the walls, so like a well-made poem, riding the
    wind,
flying over
the sea, landing on my desk.
I'm drinking the juice, but my heart's not in it,
waiting for summer to pass. One summer in childhood,
I stole my mother's bamboo bank, hit my older brother, and lied
    to my teacher.
When grown, I suddenly discovered I loved more than one girl,
    and so I began writing poetry.
After my older brother grew up, he taught me to flatten an
    aluminum can
after drinking from it, thereby decreasing the volume of the
    world's rubbish
and, in a way, saving humanity from its excesses.
In passing, I squeeze out one last drop of juice
and spill it on the poet's little alley. One drop of
juice, from who knows where—
remote South Africa or some other place? It was in an orchard
where it couldn't hear the demonstration outside, the racial
    clashes; also, no one cared
about this one dark fruit.
It didn't mind and kept growing;
didn't mind being squeezed and packaged;
didn't care one way or the other—

dripping.
Or, perhaps, it deeply desired to grow up;
felt pain when squeezed;
grieved as it dripped—
Either way, it's just poetic speculation,
which we can't rely on.
There is only its last fragrance,
color, brightness—
goose-down yellow—congealed on the poem.
When the hand lightly touches the glossy paper,
there is no way to feel the drop or the handwriting,
but when seen again, it
affirms the power of memory, full
fragrance, even to the extent of being sweet.
No one can mistake
it for a tear.

(1993)
(translated by Mike O'Connor)

WOMAN TRANSLATING

The dead woman in the garden
writes with intensity and speed—
a butterfly lifts up from the page.

Actually she is only translating—
work, like a spy's, requiring courage, secrecy, calm—
like the insubstantial God of Death who shadows form down to
     the very last detail.
The only prohibition: the prohibited cannot be translated.
To translate is to open.

The first room has antique furniture;
the second, pearls, jade, gold, silver, and crystal vessels;
the third is circular, surrounded by bronze mirrors;
the fourth has a saddle, chains, a hunting rifle, a leather whip . . .
She becomes momentarily dizzy,
drops the key.
Don't even mention the last forbidden room.

To translate in the garden
is better than standing on the deck of a boat approaching
    towering waves;
avoiding encounters with pirates, avoiding being thrown into
    cabins,
having to bear the sweat and tears in the bedding of the thousand
    women before.
It's better than going to the market,
having to hear gossip about the love affairs of other women's
    husbands;
better than going dancing at a dance hall—
those measuring gazes,
and not knowing which arrow is tipped with poison.
Better to translate than open the next room; better
than turning on the television
to see people of position talk with confidence and rehearsed
    smiles.
At least she knows she's already dead
and must take advantage of the time her husband is away
to quickly finish translating the book;
to leave something behind would be intolerable.

He has been standing in the shade of the trees watching her a
    long time,
watching love's last little remains—warm ashes—left on the
    paper.
Before she died, she was unable to discover
that he had many women.
Unable to make it to winter,
he split them into charcoal and stuck it in the stove, filling the
    room with fragrance.
He really wants to stick charcoal into her body,
make her burn.

But she is so composed,
her attention so focused,
she is perfectly oblivious to the day already darkening.
Yes, the book still has much to be done,
and translating requires such calm.

(1993)
(translated by Mike O'Connor)

NO WAR

No war sits in
my home's shaded hall;
no black cat crouches
at the turn of the stairs.

The dressing mirror breathes peacefully,
unfazed by the ant traversing it;
the books in the bookcase firmly bite their lower lips,
suffering book-eating worms to reach climax.

No dream was ever such a letdown.
Outside in my garden a beggar looks about.
No death was ever this depressing a departure,
unable to hear the sound of life.

On bamboo poles, clothes gradually lose their dampness;
in a distant place, a cigarette burns.
When fervent hope burns out, the real dark falls;
the soul's branches and leaves begin to shine.

At this moment I can sense you, always close at hand;
ah, darkness is life's best compensation.
But death can never permit any memories;
this time he brings the dawn.

(1993)
(translated by Mike O'Connor)

SUITCASE LOST AND FOUND

The suitcase lost and found
once stopped alone at
a place you have never been to,
in your evening in its morning.
Humidity caused it to awaken.
A critical remark was made to it
in an unfamiliar language—
a mysterious unforgettable encounter
like flying through a sea of clouds at night

and glimpsing from a window
a pair of bright eyes inside another airplane.

You happily have reclaimed the suitcase.
Open it everything's as before.
You take out a pair of socks, put them on take out a pen and
    write.
These possessions seem to you to be deep in thought,
but they really do not speak.
You suddenly realize,
perhaps you have never been friends and aren't master and
    servant;
you depend on them like an animal depends on food.
Toward you they still keep their silence
like a stain on your collar that can't be washed off,
to be endured a lifetime.

(1994)
(translated by Mike O'Connor)

SOMEONE I LOVED

After love,
the two sleep without stirring till dawn.
Words of love
are cast to the floor
along with a sleeveless jacket, crumpled tissue paper, a set of
    unfamiliar keys.
A glass of slowly cooling water reflects the bright, growing light;
a half-eaten scoop of ice cream
melts uniformly
on the dark-green rug;
its strong, sweet smell of milk continues seeping, seeping, seeping
    into
the lowest layers of the rug,
saturating each inch it passes through,
just like their tongues after love that began to turn bitter,
and there's no way to stop it.

In their dreams (whose dreams?),
in theirs, some people are dancing a duet out in the street,

going around in a large circle, slipping away toward someplace
    far,
tracing a perfect line
until out of sight.

(1995)
(translated by Mike O'Connor)

THINGS FREE OF ME

If I know a bowl of fruit, it can be a bowl that I love.
I love its transparency altering the shape of the fruit.
I love it placed on my table, even though this is a writing desk.
I love it holding fruit of every color, some fresh, some too long
    set out,
and whether I eat any or not.
Fruit combined looks exquisite or sublime.
The bowl bears it all in ignorance.
I love its ignorance.

If I know a watch, I can love this watch.
I love the long watchband, interrupted by the round watch face.
I love the watch lying gently face down on the table; hard then to
    imagine it dignified, secure on the wrist.
I love its three pinned hands, each turning at its own speed,
whether or not I perfectly understand these mechanical parts
    meshing together at its back.
It also doesn't understand how it divides my whole life.
The watch in ignorance still runs.
I love its ignorance.

If I know a dictionary, I can love it to distraction.
I love its fastidious ordered arrangement, every page full yet neat.
I love its giving names to everything of form or no form.
I love its wavy cover when shut and the naked line of its spine.
I love its having numberless keys with no need for keyholes and
    no need to open doors;
I don't even care what's behind the doors.

I love to read the multiple meanings of every unfamiliar word,
    thereby forgetting my own complexity.
I love its ignorance.

(1997)
(translated by Mike O'Connor)

許悔之

XU HUIZHI

(1966–   )

Xu Huizhi (Hsü Hui-chih) is the pen name of Xu Youji, who was born in Taoyuan in northern Taiwan and received a B.S. in chemical engineering from Taipei Institute of Technology. He has worked as editor for the *China Evening Express* and as chief editor of the literary supplement of *Liberty Times*. He is now Deputy Chief Editor of *Unitas*, a leading literary journal.

Xu started writing poetry in the 1980s, cofounded the poetry journal *Horizon* in 1984, and has published six books of poems in addition to prose. His work encompasses a broad range of themes and styles. From reflections on romantic love and existential angst in his early work, to political satire and realist nativism in the middle period, to metaphysical contemplation on the clash between body and soul and the hope of redemption through Buddhism in his recent writings, Xu powerfully articulates the central issues of our time. As he puts it, "Poetry is exquisite resistance." The object of resistance is not simply social injustice or political ideology; more important, it is attachment to the phenomenal world, which, according to Buddhism, is the cause of all suffering.

CORPOREAL FORM
— FOR AUNG SAN SUU KYI*

All through the night the familiar male body
Floats before my eyes
Only he can touch me
Touch the scars on my back
He has held me in his arms
I have borne and raised
His children
When I am sick he crouches
By the bed and kisses
My frail forehead

Frail Burma
Still mired
In my dream he stretches out both hands toward me
Trembling, then falling
I see British fleets sailing up
The upper Irrawaddy River in the dark
Eighteen-eighty-six, British India
Conquered the land of the Buddha
The colonizers brought farming technology
They thought that having fed our bodies
They would have fed our souls

Strikes and demonstrations
Brought us a new nation

---

*Aung San Suu Kyi, born on July 19, 1945, is the daughter of General Aung San, who led the Burmese against the British colonizers in the mid-1940s and was assassinated in 1947 before Burma achieved independence. At the age of fifteen, she accompanied her mother, Daw Khin Kyi, the Burmese ambassador to India and Nepal, to Delhi. After studying at Delhi University, she went to England and earned a B.A. in philosophy, political science, and economics from St. Hugh's College, Oxford University. She married Dr. Michael Aris at Oxford and had two sons. In 1988 she returned to Burma to lead the opposition party, the Nationalist League for Democracy, after the socialist leader Ne Win brutally suppressed prodemocratic uprisings. The NLD won over 80 percent of the votes in the national election in 1990, but the election results were annulled by the authorities. Aung San Suu Kyi was put under house arrest in July 1989. For her heroic, peaceful resistance in the face of oppression, she won the Nobel Peace Prize in 1991. After years of international intervention, she was released in July 1995, but there are still restrictions on her freedom. She continues to call for peaceful democratic reforms and free elections in Burma.

But new curses followed on its heels
The overbearing military regime
Arrested the president, closed down universities
And opened fire at the crowds . . .
—Were the Aung San family destined to die for this land?
Like my father, I had no choice but
To fight with this body in the name of love
My aging mother wrote me a letter
Saying she was sicker than Burma
This time I must push away the heavy fog of England
Abandon my husband and children, and return to my country
To taste the poisonous flowers and bitter fruit

Buddha of mercy
Gave me a pair of bare hands
To defy the army
Those who had fought alongside my father
Degenerated into heartless beasts
Ne Win issued the order
To annul the outcome of the elections
Those who betrayed the revolution
Surely betrayed the Buddha
In the crowd I heard them
Cry: Aung San! Aung San!
With a bashful smile
How I wanted to apologize
For my tardy return—

The young guards
Light up cigarettes
Outside my house
To fill their stomachs
Even if they cooked the stars in the sky
The Buddha would forgive them
Like forgiving an errant child
Now I shall choose hunger
In the endless cycle of transmigration
Only the Buddha can
Reap an abundant harvest of five grains
To fast, to go without food
To give oneself to the hungry tiger
The Buddha said, life does not end

With the first lamp or the second lamp
Where the sun doesn't shine
One vows never to lose compassion
And to be one of the hungry people

Before the silent Buddha
A perfectly contented soul
As if he is touching my
Shriveling body

(1991)
(translated by Michelle Yeh)

A FLEA ATTENDS THE BUDDHA'S SERMON

My Buddha, when you sit in your majestic pose
Like an ebbing sea, an immovable mountain
All I hear is cicadas' screech that fills my ears
Like a rolling tide it drowns out my call to you
I call you, my Buddha
I have followed you, attended your sermons for forty years
I've known for a long time that you have no Dharma to teach
And I have no Dharma to learn

You are the ferryboat carrying me across the river
Before the river is crossed, how can one burn the boat?
For forty years I've smelled your scent
Observed your form, watched Dharma grow like an abandoned
    infant
Yet you, my Buddha, you have become thinner and thinner
I can hear your bones collapsing in an instant

I too have my joy, but not the joy of Dharma
I am a flea, allowed to live in the folds of your robe
On your bosom

They still listen to your sermons
They either weep and grieve out of shame
Or rejoice at release from the corporeal form
I alone, I alone know
That you have nothing left to say

For the first time in forty years I will
Sadly but fearlessly
Bite you, and suck your blood
I will have the joy of Dharma, being the only one in this world
To have tasted your precious blood
I will have the sorrow of Dharma, having drunk
The last teardrop of the world

(1993)
(translated by Michelle Yeh)

MY COMPASSIONATE BUDDHA
—ANANDA'S* CONFESSION

My Buddha is like a wind, blowing out the flames of my love
My Buddha is like fire, illuminating the plague of my heart
My Buddha is like a mountain, setting free the wild hare of my
    body
My Buddha is like a forest, sheltering the birds of my greed
My Buddha knew that I would sleep with the Girl of Matanga**
    in my previous life
My Buddha consoled me, saying clarity grows out of filth and
    mud
My Buddha promised me that I would be the first to be freed in
    the next life
My Buddha touched me, caressed the top of my head
My Buddha is merciful, with supreme compassion
My Buddha, do not shed a tear for me

(1993)
(translated by Michelle Yeh)

BODY IN RUINS

While my head is still beautiful
Cut it off, carry it with your hand
Drum on it hard

---

*Ananda was the Buddha's favorite cousin. Popular among lay followers, especially women, Ananda reached sudden enlightenment after the Buddha passed away.
**Matanga is the name of a place, possibly a secluded forest fit for meditation.

I can't bear decomposing and gnawing maggots
My body in ruins is a sacred Dharma vessel
Now forgotten by the world.

(1993)
(translated by Michelle Yeh)

A BOWL OF RICE
— THE END OF AUNG SAN SUU KYI'S
HOUSE ARREST

This time when I leave the prison
The sun shines perfectly over the peninsula of Indochina
A rice bowl facing toward the ocean
I can feel my people and me
Like solid grains of rice
Rinsed and cleansed by seawater
In the sun's flames we use gun stocks for fuel
To cook slowly a bowl of rice
From the ten directions we've come
To the ten directions we shall give
Doves and tigers are welcome
Dragons and lambs are not to be turned away
A hungry baby bites down on the mother's nipple

I walk out of the prison
The guards who have watched me for years
Lower their heads in shame
When the land has turned into a grave for flowers and trees
And the sky into a cage for flying birds
There is nothing I can do
Except be a robust grain of rice
Refusing to go rancid and rot
What's more, I insist on smelling pure
Sprouting with difficulty, shooting up, and bearing fruit
Yes, in times of adversity
Life must still resemble rice-cooking
Requiring full concentration

Now I shall welcome the water
The Buddha extends his hands
To cleanse me, to cleanse us

I shall float in the water, to purify myself
Before the final, quiet fall
Awaiting fire

Awaiting fire
I feel my postmenopausal body
Grieving and rejoicing in cool autumn
I fetch water for rinsing
And cooking a bowl of rice
For the man-devouring hungry wolves
And the Buddhas of three worlds.

(1994)
(translated by Michelle Yeh)

SOON IT WILL BE COLD

Soon it will be cold
And the desire to make love
Maybe it will be empty like death when it's over
Yet it is and will be the only evidence

Soon it will be cold
And the fear of getting dressed
You will put on the clothes and leave
Soon it will be cold
Will-o'-the-wisps flicker in the ruins of the flesh

(1995)
(translated by Michelle Yeh)

PURPLE HARE

On the snow-covered prairie
Where a purple hare leaps
In the blink of an eye
Clovers grow everywhere

This winter
We scissor the cloth of the Milky Way
Garner the brightest star of Sirius
For a burial button
A hundred years from now

Ah purple hare purple hare
There goes a clever hare
Without a shred on

(1996)
(translated by Michelle Yeh)

THE IMPLORER

Implore your fingernails
Implore your hair
Implore your menstrual blood
Implore your nipples

Implore yellow rain from the heavens
Implore you to turn around when you leave
Implore the soul, if we have one

(1996)
(translated by Michelle Yeh)

NOTES ON THE CONTRIBUTORS

Joseph R. Allen, Professor of Chinese Literature at University of Minnesota, Twin Cities, writes on classical and modern Chinese poetry. His translations include *Forbidden Games and Video Poems: The Poetry of Yang Mu and Lo Ch'ing* and (with Zhang Jing) *Leaving China: The Later Poems of Gu Cheng (1989–1993)*.

Shiu-Pang Almberg received her B.A. in English from University of Hong Kong and her Ph.D. in Sinology from Stockholm University. A professor in the Department of Translation at Chinese University of Hong Kong, she is a prolific translator in three languages: Chinese, English, and Swedish. Her 1988 monograph on Chen Jingrong, with two hundred poems in English translation, is the most comprehensive study to date of the woman poet. She is compiling two bilingual glossaries for her prospective translation of Shen Congwen's monumental *Study of Ancient Chinese Costumes and Ornaments*.

John Balcom received his Ph.D. in Chinese and comparative literature from Washington University at St. Louis. Currently he is an assistant professor in the Graduate School of Translation and Interpretation at Monterey Institute of International Studies.

Steve Bradbury teaches at National Central University in Taiwan. His transla-
tions from the Chinese of Xia Yu are part of a book-length collection prepared
with the assistance of the poet. He has published translations from the Chinese
of Hong Hong and Yuan Qiongqiong, and from the Japanese of Kawabata
Yasunari and Kenzaburo Oe. He is currently working on a new translation (the
first in fixed rhyme and meter) of *The Prison Diary of Ho Chi Minh.*

Michael Day received his M.A. from the Department of East Asian Languages
and Literatures of University of British Columbia, Vancouver, Canada. A trans-
lator and critic of contemporary poetry from China, he teaches Chinese in
Prague.

Kirk A. Denton is Associate Professor of Modern Chinese Literature at Ohio
State University. He is the author of *The Problematic of Self in Modern Chinese
Literature: Hu Feng and Lu Ling* (1998) and the editor of the journal *Modern
Chinese Literature and Culture.*

Eugene Chen Eoyang teaches comparative literature at Indiana University,
Bloomington, and English at Lingnan University, Hong Kong. He has trans-
lated *Ai Qing: Selected Poems* (1982) and contributed to *Sunflower Splendor:
Three Thousand Years of Chinese Poetry* (1975) and *New Directions* (1982).
Among his publications on the theory of translation are a monograph, *The
Transparent Eye: Translation, Chinese Literature and Comparative Poetics*
(1993), and a coedited volume of essays, *Translating Chinese Literature* (1995).

Lloyd Haft is a poet, scholar, and translator in Chinese, Dutch, and English.
Born and educated in the United States, he is an associate professor of Chinese
at Leiden University, Holland. He is the author of *Pien Chih-lin: A Study in
Modern Chinese Poetry* (1983) and *The Chinese Sonnet: Meanings of a Form*
(2000) and the editor of *A Selective Guide to Chinese Literature 1900–1949,
Volume 3: The Poem* (1989).

Michel Hockx received his Ph.D. in Sinology from Leiden University. Cur-
rently he is Lecturer in Modern Chinese Literature and Language at the School
of Oriental and African Studies, London University. He is the author of *A Snowy
Morning: Eight Chinese Poets on the Road to Modernity* (1994) and the editor
of *The Literary Field of Twentieth-Century China* (1999).

Wendy Larson is Professor of Modern Chinese Literature at University of
Oregon. Her most recent book is *Women and Writing in Modern China* (1998).

Andrea Lingenfelter received her Ph.D. in Asian Languages and Literature from
University of Washington, Seattle, in 1998. Her dissertation is on Chinese

women poets from 1920 to the present. She has published translations of poetry by Zhai Yongming and Fu Tianlin, the novels *Farewell My Concubine* and *The Last Princess of Manchuria*, and film subtitles for *Temptress Moon*. Currently she is translating *Candy*, the first novel by the Shanghainese writer, Mian Mian.

Denis Mair is a poet and translator. He received his M.A. in Chinese literature from Ohio State University, has published many translations of Chinese prose and poetry, and is the Chinese Editor of *The Temple*, a multilingual journal of Pacific Rim poetry. Currently he lives in Los Angeles and does translation for Tienti Chiao, a religious organization in Taiwan.

N.G.D. Malmqvist is Professor Emeritus of Sinology at Stockholm University. He is a prolific translator of Chinese literature (classical, modern, and contemporary) and a member of the Swedish Academy.

Mike O'Connor, a native of the Pacific Northwest, is a poet and translator. His works of poetry include *The Rainshadow*, *The Basin: Life in a Chinese Province*, and *Only a Friend Can Know*. Translations include *The Tienanmen Square Poems*, *Setting Out* (a novel by the Taiwanese writer Tung Nien), and *The Clouds Should Know Me By Now: Buddhist Poet Monks of China*. The volume *When I Find You Again, It Will Be in Mountains: Selected Poems of Chia Tao* (779–843) was published in 2000.

Simon Patton is a Brisbane-based literary translator and scholar passionately interested in contemporary Chinese poetry. He currently holds a postdoctoral research fellowship at University of Queensland in Australia.

Jeanne Tai is a freelance translator and writer based in Cambridge, Massachusetts. She has published numerous translations of contemporary Chinese literature and is the coeditor of *Running Wild: New Chinese Writers* (1994).

Maghiel van Crevel received his Ph.D. in Sinology from Leiden University, where he is currently Assistant Professor of Chinese and Chair of the Chinese Department. He is the author of *Language Shattered: Contemporary Chinese Poetry and Duoduo* (1996) and numerous translations of contemporary Chinese poetry.

Jim Weldon holds a B.A. in Chinese from SOAS, London University. He is currently based in Hanyuan, Sichuan, where he works for the Development Organization of Rural Sichuan.

Michelle Yeh is Professor in the Department of East Asian Languages and Cultures, University of California, Davis. Her most recent publications are *Essays on Modern Chinese Poetry* (1998), *No Trace of the Gardener: Poems of Yang Mu* (1998) (cotranslated with Lawrence R. Smith), and *From the Margin: An Alternative Tradition of Modern Chinese Poetry* (2000).

Wai-lim Yip is a poet, translator, and scholar who publishes extensively in Chinese and English. He is a professor in the Department of Literature at University of California, San Diego. Among his numerous publications are: *Ezra Pound's Cathay* (1969), *Chinese Poetry: Major Modes and Genres* (1976), *Lyrics from Shelters: Modern Chinese Poetry, 1930–1950* (1992), and *Diffusion of Distances: Dialogues Between Chinese and Western Poetics* (1993).

Yu Guangzhong is a poet, essayist, translator, and scholar. He is Chair Professor and former Dean, College of Liberal Arts, at National Sun Yat-sen University in Gaoxiong, Taiwan.

Zhang Fenling received her B.A. in English from National Taiwan Normal University. She is a prolific literary critic and award-winning translator who often collaborates with her husband, the poet Chen Li. Zhang lives in Hualian and teaches English at Hualian Girls High School.

SELECT BIBLIOGRAPHY IN ENGLISH

INDIVIDUAL COLLECTIONS

Chang Shiang-hua. *Sleepless Green Green Grass and 68 Other Poems*. Trans. Stephen L. Smith. Hong Kong: Joint Publishing, 1986.

Chen Li. *Intimate Letters: Selected Poems of Chen Li*. Trans. Zhang Fenling. Taipei: Bookman Books, 1997.

Xia Yu (Hsia Yü). *Fusion Kitsch: Poems from the Chinese of Hsia Yü*. Trans. Steve Bradbury. Brookline, Mass.: Zephyr Press, 2001.

Xiang Yang. *My Cares*. Trans. John J.S. Balcom. Taipei: Independence Evening Post, 1985.

Jiao Tong. *A Passage to the City: Selected Poems of Jiao Tong*. Ed. Shuwei Ho, trans. Shuwei Ho and Raphael John Shulte. Taipei: Bookman Books, 1998.

Luo Fu (Lo Fu). *Death of a Stone Cell*. Trans. John Balcom. Monterey: Taoran Press, 1993.

Lomen and Jungtzu (Luo Men and Rongzi). *Sun and Moon Collection: Selected Poems of Lomen and Jungtzu*. Trans. Angela C.Y. Jung Palandri. Taipei: Mei Ya, 1968.

Xiang Yang (Hsiang Yang). *The Four Seasons*. Trans. John Balcom. Monterey: Taoran Press, 1993.

Yang Mu. *No Trace of the Gardener: Poems of Yang Mu*. Trans. Lawrence R. Smith and Michelle Yeh. New Haven: Yale University Press, 1998.

Yang Mu and Luo Qing (Lo Ch'ing). *The Forbidden Game and Video Poems: The*

Poetry of Yang Mu and Lo Ch'ing. Trans. Joseph R. Allen. Seattle: University of Washington Press, 1993.

ANTHOLOGIES

Cheung, Dominic, ed. & trans. *The Isle Full of Noises: Modern Chinese Poetry from Taiwan*. New York: Columbia University Press, 1986.

Ch'i, Pang-yuan, ed. & comp. *An Anthology of Contemporary Chinese Literature: Taiwan, 1949–1974*. 2 vols. Taipei: National Institute for Compilation and Translation, 1975.

Droogenbroodt, Germain, and Peter Stinson, eds. & trans. *China China: Contemporary Poetry from Taiwan, Republic of China*. Ninove, Belgium: Point Books, 1986.

Ing, Nancy, ed. & trans. *New Voices: Stories and Poems by Young Chinese Writers*. Taipei: Heritage Press, 1961.

————. *Summer Glory: A Collection of Contemporary Chinese Poetry*. San Francisco: Chinese Materials Center, 1982.

Lau, Joseph S.M., and Howard Goldblatt, eds. *Anthology of Modern Chinese Literature*. New York: Columbia University Press, 1995.

Palandri, Angela C.Y. Jung, with Robert J. Bertholf, ed. & trans. *Modern Verse from Taiwan*. Berkeley: University of California Press, 1972.

Rexroth, Kenneth, and Ling Chung, eds. & trans. *Women Poets of China*. New York: New Directions, 1972.

Yeh, Michelle, ed. & trans. *Anthology of Modern Chinese Poetry*. New Haven: Yale University Press, 1994.

Yip, Wai-lim, ed. & trans. *Modern Chinese Poetry: Twenty Poets from the Republic of China, 1955–1965*. Iowa City: University of Iowa Press, 1970.

Yu Kwang-chung, ed. & trans. *New Chinese Poetry*. Taipei: Heritage Press, 1960.

Other titles in the Modern Chinese Literature from Taiwan series

Now in paperback:

CHU T'ien-wen / *Notes of a Desolate Man*

A Taiwanese gay man reflects on his life, loves, and intellectual influences.

A *New York Times* Notable Book of the Year

A *Los Angeles Times* Best Book of the Year

"Superb. . . . A strong and perceptive voice now arises from Taiwan."
—*New York Times Book Review*

"By turns richly erotic, humorous, and devastatingly forlorn." —*The Seattle Times*

"[A] stylish meditation on marginalization, radicalization, and decay."
—*Los Angeles Times*

CHENG Ch'ing-wen / *Three-Legged Horse*

Twelve deceptively simple stories about Taiwan and its people by one of the island's most popular "nativist" writers

Winner of the Kiriyama Pacific Rim Book Prize

"A rare jewel." —*Pacific Rim Voices Book Review*

"Written in simple language yet rich with vivid details." —*New York Times Book Review*

"The finest examples of modern Chinese fiction I have come across in English."
—*South China Morning Post*

WANG Chen-ho / *Rose, Rose, I Love You*

A ribald satire of a Taiwanese village that loses all perspective and common sense at the prospect of fleecing a shipload of lusty and lonely American soldiers

"Delightfully irreverent." —*World Literature Today*

Cloth editions:

HSIAO Li-hung / *A Thousand Moons on a Thousand Rivers*

A prize-winning Taiwanese best-seller about love, betrayal, family life, and the power of tradition in small-town Taiwan

CHANG Ta-chun / *Wild Kids*

Two funny and tragic stories of youth from Taiwan's most famous and best-selling literary cult figure

"An addictive little literary treasure." —Mo Yan, author of *Red Sorghum* and *The Republic of* Wine